Nadja El Kassar

Towards a Theory of Epistemically Significant Perception

Ideen & Argumente

Herausgegeben von
Wilfried Hinsch und Lutz Wingert

Nadja El Kassar

Towards a Theory of Epistemically Significant Perception

How We Relate to the World

DE GRUYTER

ISBN 978-3-11-057827-0
e-ISBN (PDF) 978-3-11-044562-6
e-ISBN (EPUB) 978-3-11-044536-7
ISSN 1862-1147

Library of Congress Cataloging-in-Publication Data
A CIP catalog record for this book has been applied for at the Library of Congress.

Bibliografische Information der Deutschen Nationalbibliothek
Die Deutsche Nationalbibliothek verzeichnet diese Publikation in der Deutschen
Nationalbibliografie; detaillierte bibliografische Daten sind im Internet über
http://dnb.dnb.de abrufbar.

© 2015 Walter de Gruyter GmbH, Berlin/Boston
Dieser Band ist text- und seitenidentisch mit der 2015 erschienenen gebundenen
Ausgabe.
Umschlagsgestaltung: Martin Zech, Bremen
Umschlagskonzept: +malsy, Willich
Druck und Bindung: Hubert & Co. GmbH & Co. KG, Göttingen

♾ Gedruckt auf säurefreiem Papier
Printed in Germany

www.degruyter.com

To my parents, Riad and Silvia El Kassar

Acknowledgments

It is widely thought that being a philosopher means leading a lonely life. A life lived in solitude at one's desk or locked away in a library. I am grateful that my life as a philosopher differs greatly from this picture and that the process of working on this book has been as full of social interaction as it was. This book, which is the revised version of my PhD thesis, defended at the University of Potsdam in August 2013, did not come into existence at my desk only, but in innumerable conversations, and so I am indebted to many people for their contributions.

First and foremost, I would like to thank my supervisor, Logi Gunnarsson, who has been always willing to discuss every even so small thought of the dissertation and who has always encouraged me to stand by my position and defend it. I am also very grateful to Lutz Wingert, who has been a most interested, intellectually encouraging, challenging, and inspiring interlocutor.

I have had the good fortune to work on this book in many different places: Dortmund, Warwick, Berlin, Potsdam and Zürich. I would like to thank everyone who contributed to making these places stimulating environments for my work. I am particularly grateful to Quassim Cassam and the Philosophy Department at Warwick for being very welcoming and open for discussions during both my stays as a visiting PhD student in Fall 2009 and Spring 2011.

While working on this book I have profited immensely from many conversations, comments and discussions. In particular I wish to thank Daniel Alscher, Claus Beisbart, Jocelyn Benoist, Christine Bratu, Florian Braun, Bill Brewer, Jim Conant, Alex Davies, Naomi Eilan, Juan Camilo Espejo-Serna, Craig French, Johan Gersel, Andrea Giananti, Hannah Ginsborg, Stefanie Grüne, Johannes Haag, Martina Herrmann, Till Hoeppner, Andrea Kern, Felix Koch, Anna Kreysing, Ute Kruse-Ebeling, David Lauer, Hemdat Lerman, David Löwenstein, Guy Longworth, John McDowell, Esther Lea Neuhann, Alva Noë, Bernd Prien, Vanessa Rampton, Sebastian Rödl, Louise Röska-Hardy, Luz Christopher Seiberth, Norman Sieroka, Jussuf Thomas Spiegel, Charles Travis and Keith Wilson.

I have also benefited greatly from discussions of parts of this book at graduate conferences at Warwick, Essex and Essen, at the Congresses of the Deutsche Gesellschaft für Philosophie in Essen in 2008, and in Munich in 2011, at a workshop on Neo-Pragmatism in Münster in 2011, at the Congress of the Gesellschaft für Analytische Philosophie in Konstanz in 2012, and in Departmental Colloquiums at Potsdam, at Zürich, at Bern, and at Leipzig. I would like to thank the audiences for their feedback. Moreover, I am thankful to two anonymous reviewers for the series *Ideen & Argumente* for their valuable comments and suggestions. I also wish to thank Gertrud Grünkorn, Florian Ruppenstein and Johanna Wange for their assistance during the process of publishing this book.

Work on the thesis has been supported by the Studienstiftung des deutschen Volkes, and I wish to thank them for providing me with a PhD-scholarship that has genuinely combined financial and non-material support. I also wish to thank the Humanities Faculty of the Technical University of Dortmund for awarding me a scholarship for the first month of work on my thesis. I am particulary grateful to Lutz Wingert and the Chair for Philosophy II at the Swiss Federal Institute of Technology Zürich (ETH Zürich) for providing financial support for this publication.

My friends have always been very interested in what I am doing, in hearing what my thoughts are, and hearing about my progress. And even though most of them have not read one sentence of this book, they, too, contributed greatly to making work on this book as enjoyable as it was. I am thankful for their stimulation and support.

Finally, and most importantly, I wish to thank my parents and my siblings for being as great as they are, for being there with me – always and everywhere. I am incredibly grateful for the closeness that we share. And I will forever be grateful to my parents for teaching us the value of discussing black holes while having a pizza, and for loving us unconditionally.

Contents

Introduction

This book is concerned with the epistemic significance of perception. It wants to explain how it is that my seeing the colorful roof of the tower some few yards away can be a reason for my belief "I believe that the tower has a colorful roof." Or why I can say "I know that there is a cat on the mat because I see the cat on the mat." or "I believe that it is raining, because I hear the rain drops tapping on my window." In all of these cases my perceptual experience is cited as a reason for a belief. If a friend asks me, say, why I believe that there is a cat on the mat, I can answer this question by citing my perceptual experience of the cat on the mat, and – most importantly – my friend will accept my explanation, at least for standard situations.[1] So in this book I am concerned with explaining how this is possible. In other words, my aim is to explain how it is that perception can be epistemically significant. Which characteristics does perception have to have in order to be epistemically significant? The resultant view will be unified and balanced. It will not over-emphasize the nature of perceptual experience at the expense of epistemic significance nor vice versa. The theory simply explains how we relate to the world perceptually and this very explanation will elucidate how our perceptual experience makes us knowledgeable about the world.

The question that obviously has to be answered first is, what it means to say that perception is epistemically significant. First and foremost it means that perception, more precisely, any particular perceptual episode, plays an *epistemic role*: it can be cited as a reason for a belief, e.g. it can justify a belief or knowledge. Reasons are those entities that are used to justify a belief.[2] The easiest way to find reasons is to inspect answers to why-questions.[3] In my answer to my

---

1 Of course, there are cases in which my friend will not accept my answer, e.g. when she knows that I have been participating in an experiment that requires me to take a hallucinatory drug, but for now I will focus on standard cases in which there are no extraordinary circumstances that impede my perceptual experience and/or my judgment in some way.
2 I do not mean to suggest that reasons are only justificatory. Obviously reasons can have other roles too, e.g. they can be explanatory. But I will focus mainly on the justificatory role of reasons.
3 Note that the underlying assumption of this study might also be framed in terms of an internalist justification model, according to which the justification for the belief must be accessible to the believer and, e.g. is a mental state of the believer. But I do not want to use this terminology because it does not square with the set up of this book. Carving up the issue by using the distinction internalist vs. externalist would distract from one of the central topics, the nature of perceptual experience. Too much focus would be on the nature of justification, and the question of the nature of perceptual experience would be out of the limelight.

friend's why-question I told her that my perceptual experience is my reason, my justification for my belief by citing my perceiving the cat as a reason. Another formulation that I will use to express the epistemic significance of my perceptual experience is that of a "reason-relation": my perceptual experience of the cat on the mat stands in a reason-relation to my belief that there is a cat on the mat.

But the epistemic role of being a reason or a justification is not limited to those cases in which there is an explicit question for the grounds of my belief, and in which I give my perceptual experience as the reason for my belief. Even if my friend does not ask for my reasons for my belief, my perceiving the cat is the reason for my belief.[4] In other words, the epistemic role is not occasioned by a question for the reason for a belief. A perceptual experience does not become a reason by someone asking for it, it is a reason for the belief whether or not it is made explicit in a statement.[5]

In this introduction and in the book I will focus largely on the relation between perception and belief. But of course, the epistemic significance of perceptual experience also manifests itself in perceptual experience being apt to justify knowledge, and so the study also asks: how is it that perception can make a perceiver knowledgeable? Insofar as knowledge requires true belief – which is not to say that knowledge is exhausted by true belief – many of the considerations can be transferred to the case of knowledge. Whenever the claims and considerations that I make in the study cannot easily be transferred to knowledge, I will comment on this gap.

This remark and my examples will certainly have already made it clear that the perceptual experience that is the topic of this study is perceptual experience of rational beings, paradigmatically human beings. It will be perceptual experience of beings that are rational, that are capable of reasoning, and that can cite their perceptual experience as reasons for beliefs and knowledge. Perceptual ex-

---

4 Note that, of course, my belief could also be based on other reasons, e. g. my neighbor having told me that the cat is on the mat. But that was not the case in my example, and so this possibility is irrelevant.

5 Two questions about the relation between perceptual experience and belief must be distinguished. The question of how it is that perceptual experience is epistemically significant is not identical with the question of the causal role of perceptual experience in the formation of belief. This book examines the epistemic role of perceptual experience, not its causal role. This distinction comes with further important differentiations. Saying that perceptual experiences are epistemically significant does not automatically commit one to an inferentialist framework, i.e. one does not have to assume that the relation between a particular perceptual experience and a related belief have to be based on an inferential transition. These differentiations will figure in the background throughout the different chapters, but I will not discuss them head-on.

perience of non-rational beings will also be discussed in passing, but the main focus really lies on the perceptual experience of beings that can recognize reasons, cite reasons, and respond to reasons.

Let me add another important caveat about the subject of this study: the question "How is it that perception is epistemically significant?" is a propaedeutic question and so this study is a propaedeutic study.[6] I do not examine particular instances of perceptual experience and detail how they are reasons for belief, i.e. I will not go through an example for how a particular perceptual experience contributes to knowledge about the world. My proposal concerns the conditions for perceptual experience to be epistemically significant, and goes some way towards providing a theory of epistemically significant perception.

In these introductory considerations I present an overview of the different questions and answers that are involved in explaining the epistemic significance of perception and that I will discuss in the following chapters. It is, one might say, like the overture to an opera: all the protagonists and their themes and views are introduced, but in a slightly different arrangement and they are not yet fully developed. Yet they reappear throughout the opera – in this case, the book – and the audience will recognize them when they appear. I don't want to overstretch the overture-image, but there is another important analogy: an overture presents the themes of the different characters and situations, but without any explicit reference to the characters or the situations, it is only when the curtain rises and the singers appear on stage that one hears, sees and learns which theme belongs to whom. I will do something similar in this introduction: I will introduce the issues and the positions without yet linking them to any particular philosopher in order to focus on the topic of the epistemic significance of perception itself, rather than on the views of different philosophers. Only on the last pages will I start to connect the positions and themes with proponents.

I proceed in this introduction by answering two questions. First: which characteristics would allow perception to be epistemically significant? Second: do these characteristics match the nature of perception and of a particular perceptual experience? My overall aim in this book is to provide an account that does not privilege either of the constituents, i.e. epistemic significance or perception, but rather is unified and respects both. I take this to be the adequacy condition for any theory of epistemically significant perception. More on this later in the introduction.

---

6 I am indebted to Lutz Wingert who has brought out this observation in his examiner's report.

The *epistemic significance* of perceptual experience

Let me begin with the first question: Which characteristics would allow perceptual experience to be epistemically significant? The answer to this question can take two shapes. On the first, it says what it is about the content of perceptual experience (= perceptual content) that makes it epistemically significant. On the second, it points to other non-content related characteristics of perceptual experience that make it epistemically significant.

Note that in theories of perceptual experience the term *perceptual content* is notoriously ambiguous and can refer to different kinds of content. That is why I want to briefly introduce the different types of perceptual content that figure in those suggestions before I say more about the different potential explanations of the epistemic significance of perceptual experience.[7]

If perceptual content is understood as propositional content, then when I perceptually experience a blue table in front of me, I see *that there is a blue table*. The content of my perceptual experience has the same form as any other proposition *that p*. More about what is implied by such a claim soon; this is just to introduce this interpretation of perceptual content.

If perceptual content is understood as representational content, then one's perceptual experience consists in a representation. What is perceived is *represented as* being a certain way. In other words, if perceptual content is representational content, then "a subject's *perceptual experience* represents the world to be a certain way – the way the world *perceptually seems* to the subject – ..." (Byrne 2001, p. 201, emphasis in original). The content of perceptual experience is thus the representation of what the subject perceives in the world. E.g. when I see a blue table, the blue table is represented to me *as* a blue table. This representational content is correct or incorrect, e.g. my perceptual experience of the blue table is correct when I really see a blue table.

The view that perceptual content is representational content can be interpreted in two ways. Take the example of the blue table. The representational content *blue table* can be conceived to be non-conceptual content or conceptual content. If one takes representational content to be conceptual, then the perceptual content consists of concepts, e.g. I see the blue table *as a blue table*, and apply the concepts *blue* and *table*. This interpretation entails that for perceiving the blue table and having the conceptual content *blue table* the perceiver must possess the relevant conceptual capacities, i.e. in this case, the concepts *blue* and

---

7 The following considerations have benefitted greatly from observations that Lutz Wingert makes in his examiner's report.

table, and the capacity for classification. If one takes representational content to be non-conceptual, one holds that perceptual experience represents things as being a certain way without implying that perceptual experience must consist of concepts or that the perceiver must possess the requisite (or any) conceptual capacities. Sense-data or sensations are two possible suggestions for constituents of non-conceptual representational content.

Finally, perceptual content can also be understood as intuitional content, i. e. content which is the result of an inextricable cooperation of sensual intake and conceptual activity[8], involving the ability for demonstrative reference and the possession of concepts, e. g. *blue* and *table*. My conceptual capacities provide the form for the intuitional content *this-blue-table*. So when I see the blue table, I see *this-blue-table*. Such perceptual content is neither strictly conceptual, nor non-conceptual, nor representational, rather it is presentational: it makes the object of perception present to the being endowed with conceptual capacities.

So when one talks of "perceptual content" one can mean

(i)   propositional content

(ii) representational content

(iii) conceptual content

(iv) non-conceptual content

(v) intuitional content.

As I have said above, representational content and conceptual content, as well as representational content and non-conceptual content can be combined, and to some extent this possibility makes the distinction inextricably complicated and any neat presentation becomes almost impossible, but I hope that I will make it sufficiently clear when I talk about representational content in general, or about any of the mixed forms of representational content.[9]

---

8 In a Kantian terminology: of receptivity and spontaneity (Kant 1998, A50f./B74f.).

9 Part of the trouble certainly lies in the terms *representational content* and *representation* themselves. Various theories of perceptual experience that follow different aims and have different topics use these terms, and thereby invariably contribute to blurring the meaning of the expressions.

Hannah Fenichel Pitkin has provided an insightful examination of the concept *representation* for political philosophy, untangling the different understandings and on the way also presenting thought-provoking considerations of the concept *representation* in non-political contexts (Pitkin 1967). As far as I know there is no study of the different understandings in the philosophy of perception, but it would certainly be a worthy project that might help avoid problematic misunderstandings. Of course, it is very likely that my thoughts are also infected by those undetected mistakes and misunderstandings.

If one talks about perceptual content, one might also be talking about the phenomenal content of a particular perceptual experience. E.g. when I see the blue table, there is a what-it-feels-like character to my perceptual experience. Some say I have a blue-ish experience.[10] But this kind of content will be bracketed in most parts of my study. Of course, this decision goes together with the view that phenomenal content is not relevant for explaining the epistemic significance of perceptual experience. I will not argue for this view, but it is not uncommon for theories that examine the epistemic significance of perception to subscribe to this view, therefore I will just follow in this tradition and relegate readers to the debate about phenomenal content for more about this topic.[11]

With the introduction of different kinds of perceptual content completed, let us move to the different suggestions on how the epistemic significance of perceptual experience can be explained. I have said that the epistemic significance of perception can manifest itself by a perceptual experience being a reason for a belief. So the first place to look for characteristics that are required for perception being epistemically significant are other instances of reasons for a belief. The paradigmatic case of a reason for a belief is that of a belief being the reason for another belief.[12] A belief is a reason for a belief if it justifies the belief, or if it makes the belief rational. So the most obvious suggestion for a characteristic that perceptual experience must have to be epistemically significant is to say that perceptual experience must be like beliefs in order to be a reason for a belief.

What is it about beliefs that allows them to be reasons for belief? It is their propositional structure and their being tied into a rational structure.[13] E.g. my belief that today is Monday is justified by my beliefs that yesterday was Sunday,

---

One starting point for actually distinguishing different understandings of representational content in perceptual experience might be to examine the contexts in which this expression is introduced. E.g. most intentionalist theories introduce representational content into perceptual experience in order to account for cases of mis-perception. One might question whether a concept that is introduced in a situation of "epistemological crisis" (MacIntyre 1977) can be or should be transferred to a normal case. I am indebted here to Lutz Wingert who has put this point to me in conversation.

10 Cf. e.g. (Kriegel 2002).
11 E.g. (Tye 1995; Tye 2000), and more recently (Logue 2013; Logue 2014).
12 It is certainly no high-risk bet to claim that here every philosopher at once thinks of Donald Davidson's slogan: "Nothing can count as a reason for holding a belief except another belief" (Davidson 1992, p. 310).
13 I follow the orthodoxy and assume that beliefs have propositional content. I might be committed to denying that beliefs are dispositions, but cannot discuss this issue in this book. See e.g. (Schwitzgebel 2014) for more on the nature of beliefs.

and that Sunday is the day before Monday. Thus, my reasons for my belief that today is Monday are my beliefs that yesterday was Sunday and that Sunday is the day before Monday. There are inferential relations between the propositions *today is Monday* and *yesterday was Sunday* and these hold also when they are the contents of two beliefs of mine. And so the first explanation for how perceptual experience can be a reason for belief is that perceptual experience must have the same kind of content as beliefs in order to be epistemically significant: both perceptual experience and belief have propositional content. So when I see a blue table, on this conception, I see *that there is a blue table.* For reasons of conciseness I will refer to this as the Same-kind-of-content Suggestion.

I will call such a relation between perception and belief an internal relation, because the relation is based on, or rooted in, the structure of the content of the two correlates. I will not yet say more about objections against this proposal (such as, e. g. perception is not like belief, because it is belief-independent), but rather only list the suggestions that are logically possible and held by philosophers working on theories of perceptual experience.

Another interpretation of the internal relation between perceptual experience and belief suggests that perceptual experience and belief must have the same *type* of content for perception to be a reason for belief. I will refer to this second answer to the question of how perceptual experience can be epistemically significant as the Same-type-of-content Suggestion. Here the different understandings of "the content of perceptual experience" that I have introduced above become relevant. One possible answer starts by saying that perceptual content means "conceptual content", i. e. content which is constituted by concepts and which represents what is perceived as being a certain way.[14] E. g. when I perceive a table, the conceptual content of the perception would be *table*, or maybe also *this table*. I see *the table*.[15] Conceptual content and propositional content are of the same type, since propositional content is content that consists of concepts. Thus, according to this interpretation, perceptual experience can be a reason for belief, i. e. can be epistemically significant, because

---

14 Of course, trivially, one interpretation of the Same-type-of-content Suggestion could be to say that "perceptual content" means "propositional content". But since this possibility is already covered by the Same-kind-of-content Suggestion, and also more appropriately covered by this suggestion, I will not mention the Propositional-content Interpretation as a version of the Same-type-of-content Suggestion.

15 Note that this is one situation in which potential complications between conceptual content and representational content might appear. One might also call this content "representational conceptual content", but since the important feature of the content is that it is conceptual, I just refer to it as "conceptual content".

it has conceptual content just like the beliefs that it justifies. The reason-relation obtains between the conceptual contents.

Another possible interpretation of the internal explanation of the epistemic relation is that perceptual content means intuitional content, i.e. content that is the result of a shared involvement of sensual intake and conceptual capacities.[16] As I said above, on this interpretation of perceptual content the content of my perceptual experience of a blue table would be constituted by my sensory experience and my conceptual capacities. I see *this-table*. On this interpretation intuitional content and propositional content belong to the same type of content, namely conceptual content, i.e. content that involves conceptual capacities, and that is why perceptual experience and beliefs can be in a reason-relation, i.e. that is why perceptual experience can be epistemically significant.

Now, apart from these proposals that try to explain the reason-relation between perception and belief by reference to internal relations, there are also two groups of suggestions that do not build on an internal link between perceptual experience and belief. Rather, they refer to what – very broadly speaking – one might call external links. These are external links because they are not based on the structure of the content of the two correlates, perceptual experience and belief. They refer to an external element to explain the rational relation between perceptual experience and belief.[17] I will call these proposals External-link Suggestions. The first of these groups includes proposals that offer a story that explains how perceptual experience and belief can be in reason-relations. Since the reason-relation on these proposals is not established by reference to the content of the correlates, these suggestions are not linked to any particular claim about the structure of perceptual content nor, as a matter of fact, to perception having content at all. The content of perceptual experience can be non-conceptual representational content, i.e. it can be content that represents what is perceived as being a certain way, and that does not imply concept possession or conceptual activity in perceiving itself. Or the perceptual content can be a kind of intuitional content ('I see *this-table*.'), where the receptive, intuitional component is primary, rather than the conceptual component. But I will bracket this and other possible interpretations because it would make this overview unnecessarily complicated.

The external explanation for the reason-relation can take different forms, e.g. one can argue that perception and belief can be in a reason-relation, i.e.

---

16 Cf. (Sellars 1968). According to Sellars, intuitional content has the form *this-such*, e.g. *this-cube* (Sellars 1968, pp. 5, 9).

17 Of course, these theories standardly are externalist theories of justification (Pappas 2014).

are rationally related, because the perceptual system is the result of an evolutionary process in which it has been selected for this particular epistemic role.[18] Or, for example, another argument could observe more simply that perceptual experience and belief can stand in a reason-relation, because one can reflect upon the relation, i.e. one can question whether the perceptual experience really is a reason.[19]

Finally, the fourth suggestion severs any reason-relation between perceptual experience itself and belief. Perceptual experience is not strictly irrelevant to beliefs, but what does the justifying is not the perceptual experience itself, but thoughts and belief about the perceptual experience. There is no rational relation between perceptual experience itself and belief. I will call this the No-reason-relation Suggestion. To some extent this fourth suggestion is a radical version of the External-link Suggestion as the link between perceptual experience and belief is also external, but it is important to separate the proposals because there are important differences. The No-reason relation Suggestion does not attempt to establish a connection between perceptual experience and belief that qualifies as rational. The rational relations are between beliefs about the perceptual experience and other beliefs. The External-link Suggestions still want to have some rational role for perceptual experience.

The No-reason-relation Suggestion actually is independent of any claims about perceptual content. Perceptual content can be taken to be non-conceptual; but perceptual experience can also just be relational, i.e. consist in a bare perceptual relation between the perceiver and the object.[20] However, in current debates about the epistemic significance of perceptual experience the fourth suggestion almost exclusively goes together with the claim that perceptual experience does not have any content at all.

So broadly speaking, there are four groups of explanations for how perceptual experience can be epistemically significant, i.e. reasons for belief:

(i) the Same-kind-of-content Suggestion,

(ii) the Same-type-of-content Suggestion,

---

18 Peacocke is a defender of a version of this view, see e.g. (Peacocke 2004, p. 456). I will return to this argument in Section 2.2.
19 Again, Peacocke makes such a point, see e.g. (Peacocke 2001a, p. 255). I will also return to this argument in Section 2.2.
20 Donald Davidson's coherentist position according to which perceptual experience cannot justify beliefs, because only a belief can justify another belief, also belongs with this No-reason-relation Suggestion (Davidson 1992).

(iii) the External-link Suggestion,

(iv) the No-reason-relation Suggestion.

The nature of perceptual experience

Each of the above four suggestions provides an answer to the question "Which characteristics would allow perception to be epistemically significant?" giving necessary conditions and enabling conditions for the epistemic relation, but it does not suffice to look at these possible answers. If one only looked at epistemically significant states in general to find out how it is that perception is epistemically significant, one would run the risk of ignoring that the topic is epistemically significant *perception*. That is why, as I said, the adequacy condition for the theory developed in this study will be both appropriateness as a theory of perceptual experience and appropriateness as a theory of epistemic significance. I will therefore confront these four groups of suggestions with essential characteristics of perceptual experience and examine how the different answers fit for an account of perceptual experience.

There are a number of essential features of perception that constitute its character. Some are contested, e.g. phenomenal character (Does all perception have phenomenal character?). Others are more broadly accepted. One of those broadly accepted characteristics is that perceptual experience is receptive, i.e. that in perceptual experience the world impinges on the perceiver. Another one is that perceptual experience is of particulars, of objects in the world, and that it itself is particular, rather than general. When I see the cat on the mat I see the particular cat and not any generality. That means that my specific perceptual experience is inextricably set in the particular moment of perceiving the cat in these particular circumstances. In addition, perception is what one might call direct: we perceive the world directly, and not via an intermediary which tells us what the world is like.[21] Perceiving the world is not like looking at a photo and finding out about the scene pictured in the photo by examining the photo.

Particularity, receptivity and directness actually are interlocking characteristics. When I look outside the window, I see a large tower. What does it mean to say that my perceptual experience of the large tower is particular, receptive, and direct? Saying that my perceptual experience is particular means that it is a unique relation between the tower and myself. It is constituted by me perceiving that tower at this point in time from this spot. Such perception is receptive, since

---

21 Cf. e.g. (McDowell 1996) and (Putnam 1994, pp. 452 f.).

in order for me to perceive the tower I have to do nothing else than look at it. I am not constructing the tower in my perceiving it, I simply put to practice my visual capacities and thereby see the tower. Finally, my perceiving the tower is direct insofar as it involves no mediation by any non-perceptual content or by any inferences. This directness can also be framed in terms of immediacy.[22] In perceiving the tower I simply perceive the tower. I do not infer that the object that I see is a tower, I just see the tower. Any thought about the tower being a tower, any judgments, belief etc. come later. The fundamental level of perception thus is this: perceiving a particular object in the world, e. g. a tower or a tree or a river or a human being. Note that this perceptual experience is not in any way subjective, since in perceiving the tower I am related to the tower in the world. Perceiving the tower is being related to the tower in the world. I will say more about consequences of this description of perceptual experience later in this introduction.

Another central feature of our perceptual experience is that it is fine-grained, i. e. we perceive the details and nuances of the things that we see, and we can hear the cracking of an old sound recording and hear the song at the same time. The fine-grainedness is related to another crucial feature of perception: perception does not work like a camera, it does not provide the perceiver with snapshots of the world, but instead is process-like, continuous and flowing.[23] I can hear the background noises on Bruno Walter's Mahler-recordings because I do not just hear bits of the symphony that are then somehow put together. There is a continuous auditory experience of the symphony.[24] With this insight in mind one can also truly respect the fact that perception is multi-modal: it is not necessarily restricted to one sense-modality, instead several modalities working together make up perception. E. g. I would be surprised if a blue liquid turned out to taste like apple juice. And it is also a widely accepted fact that in listening to someone speaking my visual perception is also implicated.[25] Let me admit that unfortunately this book, too, like most other studies of perceptual experience, almost exclusively discusses cases of visual perceptual experi-

---

22 I do not take directness to be synonymous with givenness – e. g. Laurence Bonjour links directness, immediacy and givenness (Bonjour 2013). I think that givenness rather belongs with the receptivity of perception.

23 Cf. Noë's *Action in Perception* (Noë 2004).

24 Of course, there are many questions and issues related to auditory perception and especially auditory perception of a piece of music, but I will have to ignore these as they would lead my discussion into another field. For more see e. g. (O'Callaghan 2007; O'Callaghan 2014; Ledding-ton 2014).

25 Think e. g. of the McGurk effect (McGurk/MacDonald 1976). See also (O'Callaghan 2008; Shams & Kim 2010).

ence. But I try to improve on this problematic limitation at the end of the book by discussing whether the theory developed in this book manages to account for aural perception, more particularly for results from neurophysiological studies of aural perception.

Finally, a remark about the status of perception in human lives. Perception, very generally speaking, is a natural capacity that is not restricted to human beings. And perceptual experience is a natural going-on that is also not restricted to human beings. Animals also perceive the world. This simple observation is the basis of a number of controversial implications (e.g. Should one aim at one single theory of perception that covers both animals and human beings?), but I will postpone the discussion of these implications to later sections in the book. For now the fact that perceptual experience is a natural going-on will only be one of the characteristics of perception that I use to put the different interpretations of epistemic significance to a first test and to show which interpretations are compatible with the nature of perception, i.e. which interpretations are most likely to provide a unified account of epistemically significant perception.

Since these characteristics of perceptual experience are rather diverse – and the list is by no means complete – I will focus on the four characteristics that are arguably most central to perceptual experience: its particularity, its receptivity, its directness, and being embedded in human nature, i.e. its being natural. I will examine how these characteristics go together with the four groups of explanations of the possibility of epistemic significance. As you will see, the four characteristics will play different roles in developing a theory of epistemically significant perception. In particular, the naturalness of perception will come in at a later point than directness, particularity and receptivity.

I have said above that these characteristics are more broadly accepted than other characteristics of perceptual experience, but, of course, that does not mean that they are uncontested. Each of the characteristics can be interpreted in slightly different ways, e.g. directness does not have to be framed in terms of immediacy. Moreover, other authors might have chosen other characteristics to test this part of the adequacy condition, e.g. the fineness of grain could have figured more prominently. I take the four features listed above to be the central features of perceptual experience, but I cannot argue for this claim at this point and will have to leave readers with a promissory note: in the course of this book it will become clear why those are the most important characteristics of perceptual experience. I will also return to the adequacy condition in Chapters 7 and 8.

One more preliminary remark before I start bringing together the claims about the epistemic significance and the characteristics of perceptual experience: the following discussion will be broad stroke and I will have to ignore some of the details of the four suggestions for the explanation of the epistemic significance of perceptual experience, but those details will be spelt out and discussed in the nine chapters of this book. My aim here is only to present the dialectic, outline the argumentation space, and mark crucial benchmarks and crossroads that structure a theory of epistemically significant perceptual experience.

The epistemic significance of *perceptual experience*

So how do the four suggestions for explaining epistemically significant perception fare when faced with the essential characteristics of perception? The first suggesion, the Same-kind-of-content Suggestion, obviously has problems with the central characteristics of perception that I have discussed: on a standard interpretation, propositional content is constituted by concepts, it is inherently general, so it is unclear how perceptual experience that consists of propositional content can be particular. Moreover, there are worries about receptivity and directness. If one wants to say that perceptual experience is receptive and direct and that it has propositional content, one seems to be committed to saying that what the subject perceives are facts that are propositionally structured. This position comes at certain ontological costs and one might be reluctant to pay such a price. One consequence might be, for example, that one has to say that the world that the subject perceives is made up of facts, or of true propositions. In addition, it is doubtful whether it is even possible to say that perception that has propositional content is really direct, i.e. that in perceiving an object one has direct access to the object. Propositional content seems to slip between perceiver, perception and object and disallow directness. In other words, one seems to lose the very phenomenon "perceptual experience". There are also other important differences such as, e.g. that perceptual experience can present impossible states of affairs, whereas belief cannot do that, e.g. as in drawings by M.C. Escher or the waterfall illusion.[26] The Same-kind-of-content option seems appropriate for capturing the epistemic significance of perception, but inappropriate as an account of perception and perceptual experience.

For the second group of suggestions, the Same-type-of-content Suggestions, related and similar problems appear. In fact, there are grounds to suppose that the problems come with any internal account. The particularity and the directness of perception are problematic for the Conceptual-content Interpretation for the very same reasons as in the case of the Same-kind-of-content Suggestion: When concepts are part of the perceptual content, generality invariably tags

---

26 Cf. (Crane 1988a).

along, too, and that seems to clash with the particularity and directness of perceptual experience. And again representational content, too, slips between perceiver, perception and object, standing in the way of perceptual directness. Some people argue that it is necessary to assume that perception has representational content, because representations help us explain what the subject of an illusion or a hallucination perceives: she perceives the (mis)representation of the object.[27] But there seems to be one too many when perceptual experience includes perceiver, subject and representational content as it does on such representational theories, thereby disallowing particularity and directness.

The receptivity of perception might be less of a problem for the Conceptual-content Interpretation since one can emphasize that conceptual content is representational content and then offer an explanation of how the representational content of perceptual experience is the result of the impingement of the world on the subject's senses and how it therefore is purely receptive. However, the involvement of concepts in the perceptual content could also always turn out to be an obstacle to acknowledging the receptivity of perception. One would have to say how cognitive activity in the form of conceptual activity in perception is reconcilable with perceptual receptivity. Of course, many philosophers have undertaken this endeavor, but I will not mention any particular proposals, since in this Introduction it is not yet about proposals and solutions for such issues, I am just flagging positions and issues in order to arrive at the centerpieces of a theory of epistemically significant perception.[28] For now one sees that again one encounters serious tensions between the epistemic significance of perception and perception itself.

Whether the Intuitional-content Interpretation encounters the same tensions depends on various factors. Most notably it depends on how intuitional content is conceived and where the emphasis lies: is it with the sensational element of intuitional content or with the conceptual element? And how does the conceptual element of intuitional content manifest itself? If the conceptual activity is less explicit and strong than in the Same-kind-of-content Suggestion and the Conceptual-content Interpretation, there might be room for a happy marriage between epistemic significance and perception. For example, if the contribution of the conceptual element lies in the form of what is perceived, and the intuitional element provides the matter of perceptual experience, then one seems to be able

---

27 E. g. (Burge 2005).
28 I will return to the issue of whether the Conceptual-content Interpretation can accommodate the receptivity of perceptual experience throughout the book, e.g. in Sections 5.2 – 5.4 and Chapter 6.

to take particularity and receptivity into account.[29] As to directness, one will have to examine the nature of intuitional content, whether it slips between perceiver, perception and the object or whether perceptual experience just consists in intuitional content.

How do the External-link Suggestions fare? *Prima facie* it might seem that they will avoid the problems of the explanations that cite an internal link between perception and belief, e. g. they seem to be able to conceive of perceptual experience as receptive. But at second glance one sees that they, too, are likely to have a problem with the directness of perception: the non-conceptual content of perception might be seen to slide between perceiver, perception and object, because it, too, is taken to represent the world as being a certain way. And these problems also bring with them issues with accommodating the directness of perceptual experience. Again there seems to be one too many with non-conceptual representational content in the picture. If non-conceptual representational content consists of sense-data, then the 'one too many' is on the side of the object. Or on other interpretations in which the non-conceptual content is just the way the world is represented to the perceiver, the 'one too many' is on the perceptual side.

Intuitional content on the External-link Suggestion might be more appropriate for accommodating the directness of perception: the intuitional element might grasp just what it means to say that perception is direct. By acknowledging the role of sensation in perception (and perceptual experience), intuitional content seems to be able to have a place for the directness of perception, namely in the sensational component. As I have said above in my earlier remarks about intuitional content on the Internal-link Suggestions, one would have to examine the details of the involvement of concepts in intuitional content to rule out that the above issues of generality do not appear for this conception, but I will again postpone this discussion and instead point to some general issues for external-link views in general.

External-link options face a fundamental question that concerns their account of epistemic significance. One can doubt that the epistemic role of perception can be explained by a story about its evolution. Evolutionary accounts might offer a story of how the capacity for perception developed through natural selection, but it is not clear that their resources allow them to explain how perceptual experience came to play epistemic roles. For that they would have to explain how the very epistemic context has developed and it is not immediately

---

29 E. g. as in Schellenberg's Sellars reconstruction in (Schellenberg 2006) or also in Haag's interpretation in (Haag 2012).

clear that they could do that. An explanation according to which perception is a reason for belief because it can be reflected is also problematic, because it leaves the fundamental question unanswered: can we really rationally question the epistemic role of a particular perceptual experience that does not have conceptual content in the same way as we can question another belief? How is that even possible? Is such perceptual experience of the right form to be rationally criticized? It is questionable whether the External-link Suggestion really offers an explanation of the epistemic role of perception and whether it can do justice to the characteristics of perception.

The No-reason-relation Suggestion holds that perception and belief themselves are not epistemically related, but are only epistemically related by mediation, e.g. via the mediation of cognitive activity that latches on to what is perceived and links it to beliefs, i.e. perceptual experience becomes epistemically significant when it is coupled with something else, cognitive activity, and thus when it is not really 'pure' perceptual experience anymore. This conception will avoid issues with generality because it says that perceptual experience is particular, direct and receptive. But the crucial problem here lies in the epistemic significance of such perceptual experience: is such perceptual experience really epistemically significant? Perceptual experience is said to be epistemically independent, but at the same time possibly epistemically relevant for beliefs: it is unclear how on such a conception perceptual experience could be said to be a reason or a justifier, how it could be epistemically significant.[30]

The above examinations give us a broad picture of the predicament in which any theory of epistemically significant perceptual experience finds itself: epistemic significance and perceptual experience threaten to pull into different directions so that the theory and the very notion of epistemically significant perceptual experience itself are always in danger of disintegrating and vanishing. As I said above, my aim is to provide a unified account of epistemically significant perception, so it is no option to privilege one or the other element. Only such an approach can meet the adequacy condition that I have set up above: privileging either one of the two components would not do justice to the notion "epistemically significant perceptual experience" and one would again lose the very notion. So, my claim is that the two components cannot be fully understood without the other. One cannot understand perceptual experience without understanding the notion of epistemic significance, and one cannot understand epistemic significance without understanding the nature of perceptual experience.

---

30 Of course, that is Sellars's charge of the Myth of the Given (Sellars 1997). More about that later in Section 1.1.

This conceptual interdependence also becomes obvious if one realizes that the epistemic significance of perceptual experience is a special epistemic significance *qua* being perceptual, and that epistemically significant perceptual experience is special perceptual experience *qua* being epistemically significant.

This conceptual interdependence can also be found when one looks at another characteristic of perception: perception is a natural phenomenon. In other words, the capacity *perception* belongs to the nature of human beings and all other beings that are able to perceive. I have said that the naturalness is going to be an important characteristic, but so far in my discussion of the different suggestions it has not appeared. That is partly because of its peculiarly diverse role. On the one hand, it can lead one to aim for an account of epistemically significant perception that is just a modified version of an account of perception which holds for non-human animals and human beings. So one might be tempted to argue that one must first develop an account of perception in non-human animals and human beings, and then see how such perception can be epistemically significant in the case of human beings – and maybe other rational non-human beings. The External-link Suggestion might be one way such a theory could turn out, i.e. the evolutionary selection story might be what is needed to explain the epistemic significance of human perception that is otherwise essentially like non-human perception. On the other hand, one could hold that saying that perception is a natural phenomenon means that perception belongs to the nature of human beings and since human beings are rational beings, the theory of perception will have to take into account the role of perception in the lives of rational beings. I will not comment on this option here in the Introduction, but, again, it will be a theme that will be expanded in sections to follow.[31]

A third consequence of regarding perception as a natural phenomenon concerns issues of methodology: if perception is a natural phenomenon, it seems that natural sciences will have something significant to say about how perception works. In other words, one might decide to choose a naturalist approach to examining perception. The same decision can be made for epistemically significant perception: natural sciences seem to be able to help us in understanding how it is that perception is epistemically significant. This view is highly controversial as it might appear that the natural sciences that aim for finding laws and regularities in phenomena and processes cannot capture epistemic significance nor the epistemic significance of perception. The last chapter of this book will venture into this field of discussion to examine and discuss the relevance of em-

---

31 E.g. Section 2.1.

pirical findings from natural sciences for a unified theory of epistemically significant perception. I will suggest that even though empirical findings are most likely silent on the epistemic significance of perceptual experience they may be sensibly and carefully integrated into theories of perceptual experience that explain how perceptual experience is epistemically significant.

Finally, incorporating the idea of perception as a natural phenomenon is also very important for the overview of different explanations of how perceptual experience can play an epistemic role. The claim that perceptual experience has representational content has figured centrally in the explanations, and now with a naturalist approach in the picture one sees that there is another interpretation of representational content that one has to consider: representational content could mean content that consists in mental representations, i.e. in mental states that represent what is perceived. On this interpretation mental representations are conceived as "states of the nervous system that refer to entites in the world" (Carey 2009, p. 453). They are "instantiated in the brain" (Carey 2009, p. 457). The format of these instantiations is disputed, e.g. whether they are language-like or iconic (cf. Carey 2009, p. 457), but leaving such issues aside, one can note that this interpretation of representational content differs strongly from the previous suggestions because it conceives of representations as subpersonal, subdoxastic states. And this interpretation of representations as subpersonal states can also be used to explain the epistemic significance of perception.

On such an understanding of mental representational content, too, one could hold that the content is conceptual, but the claim would manifest a different understanding of concepts than in the previous views: concepts would be conceived as mental representations, rather than as constituents of propositions. They are mental symbols that refer to objects in the world, and are "instantiated in the brain" (Carey 2009, p. 457).[32] This suggestion will become relevant in the final chapter on the role of empirical science for conceptualism about perceptual experience, Chapter 9, and also in some of the detailed discussion of the exchanges between conceptualists and non-conceptualists, e.g. Section 2.7.

Note that this interpretation cuts across the internal-external-link distinction that I introduced above. It fits the internal link pattern, because on the interpretation concepts and beliefs are mental representations and that is what can be taken to explain the epistemic significance of perceptual experience. But it also fits the External-link pattern, because the reason-relation is not explained in terms of the particular contents of perceptual experience and belief. That is why rather than squeeze it into either pattern I will count it as a fifth suggestion.

---

32 Susan Carey makes this claim, see e.g. (Carey 2009, p. 453).

Now, for this option, too, one will have to examine whether it contains the features of perception that I have identified as central – particularity, directness, receptivity. One would have to say more about mental representations in order to determine whether it avoids the issue of particularity, or whether concepts conceived as mental representations aren't too general, either. At first glance directness and receptivity seem to be less problematic in this variety of representational content, as the mental representation might be just what perception is: maybe perceiving consists in a mental representation, in "states of the nervous system" (Carey 2009, p. 453). I will say more about these questions in Chapter 9. And of course, one will have to ask whether mental representations are what helps us explain how it is that perception is epistemically significant. E. g. a psychological approach might not really be concerned with the epistemic significance of perception, but only with explaining the psychology of perceptual experience, and thereby miss out on explaining the epistemic significance.[33]

Before I say more about the views that I develop in this book, let me return to the overture-metaphor once more. At this point it is time to lift the curtain and to reveal more of the stage and setting, just before the singers enter and the events unfold. In this introduction I have been weaving together two philosophical debates that are mainly led in separation: the first debate concerns the epistemic significance of perception, and the second debate concerns the content of perception. One might also capture them in terms of a debate about the epistemic role of perception and a debate about the structure of perceptual experience.

The debate about epistemic significance is led by conceptualists and non-conceptualists, with conceptualists claiming that the epistemic significance of perception requires perceptual experience to be conceptual and non-conceptualists claiming that non-conceptual perceptual experience, too, can be epistemically significant.[34] If one looks at the conceptualist position in more detail, one sees that there are at least two varieties of conceptualism. Conceptualism can be a claim about the content of perceptual experience, namely that it con-

---

33 Carey's approach is such a psychological approach, and even though she briefly mentions the relevance of epistemological questions, she herself does not discuss them (Carey 2009, pp. 489 ff.).

34 At this point I need to interject an important orthographical-terminological clarification: throughout the book I will use the hyphenated spelling to refer to the non-conceptualist position. Some non-conceptualists, e. g. Richard Heck (Heck 2001) and Christopher Peacocke (Peacocke 2001a), use the unhyphenated spelling, *nonconceptual*, but I find the hyphenated spelling clearer to mark the difference between the two views, especially the fact that non-conceptualists reject the conceptualist conception of perceptual experience. Moreover, the expression "nonconceptual" is a technical term in Charles Travis's theory that I will introduce in Chapter 5 and I will avoid confusions by using the hyphenated term for the non-conceptualist position.

sists of concepts. And it can be a claim about the conditions of perceptual experience, namely that it implicates the actualization of conceptual capacities.[35] The same two distinctions are possible for non-conceptualism. In this study I will eventually defend the conceptualist theory in the possessional sense.[36] On the possessional interpretation the conceptualist argues that the subject has to possess the concepts that characterize her perceptual experience in order to undergo that very perceptual experience (ibid). There is more to say about this interpretation, but at this point I just want to flag the distinction between the possessional and the compositional interpretation and return to it later.[37]

The debate about the structure of perceptual experience is led by relationists and non-relationists, with relationists claiming that perception fundamentally consists in a relation, and non-relationists claiming that perception is more than a relation, e. g. that it is contentful. I have already said that I am aiming for a unified account of epistemically significant perception and that I take epistemic significance and perceptual experience to be conceptually interdependent. This is also why I think that the two debates ultimately must not be dealt with separately and why this study brings them together. Of course, in a first step one needs to look at the two debates separately, but that is just setting the stage for the examination of the real issue – the epistemic significance of perception.

The claims that this book defends

Now the obvious question is: 'Which position is the one that I want to defend in this book?' A satisfactory theory of epistemically significant perception, I claim, must be a relationist conceptualist theory of perception. According to relational conceptualism, perceptual experience is a relation between the perceiving subject and an object of perceptual experience in which the perceiver actualizes her conceptual capacities. Perceiving an object in the world is being related to the object in the world. The relation is the product of the actualization of conceptual capacities in perceiving the object. E. g. when a subject sees a house, she sees it as something, e. g. as a house or as a building. Such a theory will satisfy the adequacy conditions: it will be able to explain how it is possible that perception is epistemically significant and it will also accommodate central features of

---

35 Thomas Crowther introduces this distinction in his (Crowther 2006, pp. 249–251).
36 Cf. (Crowther 2006, p. 251).
37 In Section 1.1.

perception, namely particularity, directness, receptivity and being part of human nature. It will reveal that epistemically significant perception essentially belongs to human nature.

In effect, the theory defended in this study will be a direct realist theory of the sources of knowledge: We directly perceive things in the external world and what we perceive allows us to make legitimate knowledge claims and endows us with reasons for belief and for knowledge. I directly perceive the cat on the mat and my perceiving the cat on the mat allows me to make the legitimate knowledge claim "There is a cat on the mat." It might seem that this theory is trivial and old hat. But it is not. Let me point out some advantages of the new theory put forward in this study to substantiate this claim.

This study offers answers to two epistemological problems. The epistemologist will understand how perceptual experiences can figure as reasons for belief and knowledge and she will see that an appropriate theory of the epistemic role of perception does not and must not require an extensive external 'machinery': perception and perceptual experiences themselves have all that it needs to play the epistemic role. There is no need for any vehicles or mediation for perception to be epistemically significant. All perceptual experience is epistemically significant *qua* perceptual experience by a rational being. A major advantage of the account is that it does not misconstrue perceptual experience. It takes account of the fact that perceptual experience itself is always a partial success: when one perceives something, one perceives something. Or to give a simple example: when I perceive a large tower, I perceive a large tower. Whether or not there really is a tower, or whether it is large or not does not matter to my perception of the large tower. I do perceive the large tower. Thereby I actualize my conceptual capacities, e.g. the concepts *large* and *tower*. Questions of correctness will only become relevant when I start reflecting about my perceptual experience, e.g. when the perceptual experience is brought into interaction with other perceptual intakes, e.g. from other sense modalities, or at other instances in time.

Some readers might be worried about the consequences of saying that perception is always a partial success, since I seem to be committed to saying something very bizarre: I seem to be committed to saying that there are no hallucinations nor illusions, since perception is always to some extent successful. But this worry stems from a misunderstanding of the claim that perception is partial success and from a feature of my conception that I have not yet acknowledged openly, namely its disjunctive nature. Let me briefly say something concerning this worry. Of course, I do not want to deny that there are hallucinations and illusions, it is just that the person who has a hallucinatory experience indeed perceives what it is that she perceives in the hallucinatory experience. But – and this is the disjunctivist move – this does not say anything constructive about the nature of veridical perceptual experience. The nature of the veridical and the non-veridical cases must be explained without assuming a common element shared by the two kinds of cases.[38] In a non-veridical perceptual experience I also perceive something, just like in the good case, but the explanations of the perceptual experiences are not parallel in the same way as is the impression of the perceptual experience. When I have a hallucination and I perceive a helicopter landing on the churchyard right in front of my office, I really do just that: I perceive a helicopter landing on the churchyard right in front of my office. My perceptual experience itself is neither wrong nor right, it is just what it is, namely my perceiving what I perceive. The claim is this: Perceptual experience always yields something, namely what the perceiver perceives. Questions of wrong and right only come in when the perceiver compares her perceptual intake to other perceptual intakes, or when she puts it to the test, or when she brings it together with additional information. E.g. when I remind myself that in the morning I took part in an experiment on some new pill and the researchers told me to watch out for strange incidents during the day, then seeing a helicopter land in front of the office might be such strange incident. But in the act of perceiving the helicopter landing this is irrelevant, I just perceive the landing helicopter.

Relational conceptualism and other theories of perceptual experience

Let me now briefly position relational conceptualism in the field of existing theories of perceptual experience by identifying some views of epistemically significant perception that the relational conceptualist theory opposes. Not all of those views will be discussed in the study, but I think it is helpful to see where relational conceptualism belongs in the bigger picture. Of course, trivially and most fundamentally, it rejects any skeptical view – including skepticism about our very access to the external world, i.e. the question whether we can ever have (perceptual) access to the external world, and skepticism about the epistemic power of perception, i.e. the question whether (fallible) perception can be a reason for belief. Relational conceptualism argues that not only can we have perceptual access to the world, but our perceptual experience also justifies our beliefs and knowledge claims.

In addition, it rejects a variety of representationalism that we can call a picture account of perception. According to such conceptions, perceptual experience produces a picture of the external world. There can be different versions

---

38 It is thus variety of "metaphysical disjunctivism" (Byrne/Logue 2008, p. 57).

of such a conception. E. g. perceptual experience can be taken to be like a mirror: perceiving the world is perceiving the objects and scenes in a mirror. Or in perceptual experience a representation of the world is created and that is the subject's perceptual experience. The representation corresponds to what is perceived in the external world, it is a likeness of what is perceived.[39] On my relational conceptualist theory perceptual experience is not a representation: it is direct and unmediated.

Another set of views that the relational conceptualist theory opposes are constructivist theories of perception. They hold that in perception the perceiver 'constructs' what it is that she perceives. Constructivism can come in different strengths: it can argue that the content of perception is constructed, or it can argue that what is perceived, the objects in the world, really are constructed by the perceiver. Relational conceptualism does not subscribe to any such claims, rather it is central that perceptual experience is of the mind-independent external world. Note that it is important to clearly distinguish relational conceptualism from constructivist views because it will seem that by saying that perception is in the first instance a success and not correct or incorrect the relational conceptualist assumes that what is perceived is constructed by the perceiver. Yet, here again I have to refer the reader to later sections of the study, to Chapters 7 and 8, there I will say more about how perceiving can be always partial success without being committed to a constructivist account of perception.

Finally, my relational conceptualism comes with a rejection of both strictly naturalist and anti-naturalist theories of perceptual experience and that is also an advantage of the theory.[40] I oppose philosophical theories that ignore empirical findings, but also those empirically-minded theories that ignore philosophical considerations. Instead I suggest how a philosophical theory of perceptual experience and empirical studies on perceptual experience can be brought together, co-existing and interacting. I will reach this conclusion by confronting the relational conceptualist theory with neuropsychological studies about aural perception (Chapter 9). This also allows me to indicate that and why the conceptualist theory also applies to aural perceptual experience and to make a step towards overcoming the fixation of theories of perceptual experience on visual experience.

Before I get to a brief overview of the chapters to come, let me finally say something about the selection of philosophers whose views will be discussed

---

39 Cf. (Pitkin 1969, p. 111).
40 I am indebted to Logi Gunnarsson for pointing out that relational conceptualism and both the naturalist and the anti-naturalist attitude are not necessarily connected.

in this study. In this Introduction I have approached the topic by asking the question of how it is that perception can be epistemically significant. I have considered the different suggestions one can offer for explaining epistemic significance *and* perception. Of course, one can also approach the issue from a different angle, namely by looking at the two debates which discuss perception and epistemically significant perception that I have mentioned above: the debate about conceptual capacities in perception and the debate about the content of perception. That is the approach that I have chosen for the rest of the book.

Before I say something about an alternative approach that I might have chosen, and that would have come with another list of names, let me finally put some names to the views that appear in those debates. The theories and claims of the following philosophers will be discussed in the book. John McDowell will figure most centrally as a proponent of the conceptualist theory. Other conceptualists whose work will be discussed are Alva Noë, Andrea Kern and Marcus Willaschek. Christopher Peacocke, Tyler Burge, Tim Crane, Richard Heck, Susan Hurley, M.G.F. Martin and others will appear as non-conceptualist critics of conceptualism. Wilfrid Sellars will also be mentioned because he has influenced McDowell's work, but he can be read either as a conceptualist or as a non-conceptualist and undercuts the distinction. Charles Travis and Bill Brewer will represent the relationist theory of perceptual experience. And to be precise they will also appear as non-conceptualist critics of conceptualism, but they will be relationalist non-conceptualist critics. More about these distinctions as the study unfolds.

Of course, I could have also looked at historic answers given in response to the issue of the epistemic significance of perception. Such an approach would mean looking at what Aristotle, Immanuel Kant, Georg Friedrich Wilhelm Hegel, David Hume, George Berkeley and others have said about the nature of perceptual experience and its role as reason for beliefs. Yet, this study is a contemporary, systematic examination of the issue of epistemically significant perception. As you have seen above in the list of philosophers that will be discussed, the proponents of the different positions – conceptualists, non-conceptualists, relationists and representationalists – will all be contemporaries of ours. Aristotle, Kant and Hegel will only figure indirectly in this study through philosophers who accept and develop their positions, most notably John McDowell, but also, e. g. Andrea Kern. Wilfrid Sellars is not a contemporary of ours, but he will still figure as a philosopher following in the steps of Kant. Hume's influence will even be weaker: His empiricist influence may be found in Bill Brewer and Charles Travis. But at the same time one has to be very careful with any such genealogical claims, since e. g. Travis would probably deny that his views are influenced by Hume's views. McDowell's case shows another respect in which claims about the influencing relations between philosophers are problematic:

McDowell does see himself as standing in the tradition of Kant and Hegel and as following up on central claims of theirs, but other Kantians and Hegelians explicitly criticize and reject his Kant and Hegel interpretations. I am well aware of the relevance of connections between philosophers of today and of earlier times, but since debates about their respective relations would be mainly distracting from examining the nature of epistemically significant perception, I have decided to stick to the contemporary authors and debates. Moreover, I think that these contemporary debates about perceptual experience and its epistemic significance deserve their own close examination for their own sake and without continuous historical backtracking.

Overview of the book

As I said, my aim in this study is to develop relational conceptualism as a theory of epistemically significant perceptual experience. This theory fulfills the adequacy condition that I have set up above: it explains how perceptual experience can be epistemically significant, and it does so without over-emphasizing either of the two elements. In order to finally get to relational conceptualism in Part III, several preparatory, intermediate and subsequent steps and discussions are necessary. They also constitute this book.

The book itself is divided into four parts that are each subdivided into chapters and sections. Chapters and sections are numbered in Arabian numerals. I will refer to sections by giving first the number of the chapter and then the number of the section in that chapter. So, e.g. 'Section 2.3' refers to Section 3 in Chapter 2.

Part I, "Conceptualism", concerns the classic debate between conceptualism and non-conceptualism sparked by McDowell's conceptualist theory in *Mind and World*. Chapter 1 introduces McDowell's conceptualism and traces developments in the formulation of conceptualism, including theories based on McDowell's conceptualism and McDowell's conceptualism itself. This chapter contains theories that belong to the Same-kind-of-content Suggestion and the Same-type-of-content Suggestion: McDowell's original *Mind and World* position fits with first suggestion. Other theories developed on the basis of *Mind and World*, e.g. the capacity approach to perception, or Bill Brewer's conceptualism fit with the second suggestion.

Chapter 2 then analyzes six arguments that non-conceptualism standardly puts forward against conceptualism. Non-conceptualist positions standardly belong with the External-link Suggestion. They argue that an external link allows perceptual experience to be a reason for belief. The chapter starts with the Argument from Animal Perception and examines why the argument does not bring the debate forward. In doing so it reveals a set of differences in motivation and assumptions that hinder a shared understanding. The Argument from Fineness of Grain and the Argument from Fallibility, too, are analyzed in a close reading since understanding the dialectic in the exchanges about these arguments proves particularly helpful for understanding the grounds of conceptualism. The sections on the Argument from Hyper-Intellectualization, the Argument from Concept Acquisition, and the Argument from Memory Experience are less detailed, but still contribute to understanding the dynamics of the debate. This large chapter ends with first conclusions about how non-conceptualist arguments do not stick with conceptualism.

Chapter 3 then ventures into recent changes of McDowell's conceptualism and starts discussing his "revised conceptualism" – as I will call this position. Revised conceptualism firmly belongs with the Same-type-of-content Suggestion – McDowell does not anymore defend the *Mind and World*-view that belongs with the Same-kind-of-content Suggestion.

Part II, "Relationism", then suspends this discussion by moving to another debate in which conceptualism is involved: the debate about content in perceptual experience. Recently, the classic debate between conceptualism and non-conceptualism has been overtaken, one may say, by a debate about whether perceptual experience has representational content or more generally content. The debate is mainly led by relationists and representationalists. The relationist view has also influenced the changes in McDowell's conceptualism and so I introduce two relationist theories by Bill Brewer and Charles Travis in order to further outline the context in which McDowell's conceptualism is currently developed. The relationist position would belong to the No-reason-relation Suggestion.

Chapters 4 and 5 present the relationist position by introducing two important relationist theories by Brewer and Travis. Travis's theory will be the principle relationist conception in this study. Chapter 6 argues that McDowell's revised conceptualism does not avoid the relationist objections brought forward by Travis – even though McDowell claims to be unimpressed and unconcerned by these objections. The relationist position is important for this study because it respects and accommodates the most important features of perceptual experience that I have outlined above, e.g. directness, particularity. It thus meets one half of the adequacy condition for theories of epistemically significant perceptual experience, namely being adequate to the nature of perceptual experience. But as I will argue, there is a problem with the other half, with explaining the epistemic significance of perceptual experience.

Part III, "Relational conceptualism", shows that relationism and conceptualism can be brought together into one theory and that the resulting theory meets the adequacy condition: it can explain how perceptual experience is epistemically significant. I will call this position "relational conceptualism". Chapter 7 develops the position, and Chapter 8 discusses arguments against it, including relationist and non-conceptualist arguments.

In the final part of the book, "Relational Conceptualism and Empirical Science", I will start confronting relational conceptualism with empirical, neuropsychological and psychological findings. The relation of empirical science to conceptualism is standardly contested, and I will argue against the common assumption that empirical science and conceptualism are incompatible. My argumentation is based on a discussion of empirical findings about aural perceptual experience that seem to contradict the conceptualist theory of perceptual experience. I will explain why the findings do not speak against conceptualism: some do not concern the traditional conceptualist theory, others are even grist to the conceptualist's mill. To substantiate this result I will further present psychological and developmental psychological findings that put forward or contain the claim that perceptual experience includes the actualization of conceptual capacities. This chapter transcends existing work on conceptualism in perceptual experience because it introduces two topics that have largely been overlooked: non-visual perceptual experience and empirical studies on perceptual experience. An outlook on further routes for relational conceptualism to examine and take concludes the book.

Reading recommendations

Let me end this introduction by some reading recommendations for readers that cannot read the full book, but are interested in certain of the topics discussed.

–   If you are interested in the classic debate between conceptualists and non-conceptualists from a conceptualist perspective, Chapter 1 and 2 are most relevant for you. As most encyclopedia entries are written by non-conceptualists, they contain non-conceptualist mis-readings of conceptualist replies and considerations. The two chapters of this book aim to clarify the conceptualist argumentation and thus avoid these mis-readings.
–   If you want to learn more about the development of McDowell's conceptualism, you might focus on Chapters 1, 3, and 6 and Section 2.8. For discussions of this revised conceptualism see in particular Chapters 3, 6, and also Chapter 9.
–   For an introduction to relationist theories and arguments, see Chapters 4 and 5.

- If you are already conceptualist enough and convinced that representational non-conceptualism à la Peacocke is wrong, you might want to start reading from Section 2.8.
- If you want to see a new approach to how conceptualism and empirical science can go together and complement each other, without one dominating the other, read Chapter 9.
- And if you want to take a 'short ride' through this book to relational conceptualism, you may focus on the following sections: Sections 1.1–1.3, 2.1, 2.8, Chapter 3, Section 4.1, Chapters 5, 6 and 7.

  Let me briefly say something about why these sections and chapters are part of the short ride. Sections 1.1–1.3, 2.1, 2.8 give the background of the conceptualist debate. Chapter 3 is important for understanding the development of traditional conceptualism and for understanding how relationism and conceptualism come to be connected in the current debate about perceptual experience. Section 4.1 provides a very short introduction into relationism. Chapter 5 details Charles Travis's relationist position and his criticism of representationalism and conceptualism. Chapter 6 is crucial because it contains a critique of McDowell's conceptualism and its attitude towards relationism and paves the way for relational conceptualism. Finally, Chapter 7 is indispensable on the short ride, because it introduces relational conceptualism.

But of course, if you are genuinely interested in the epistemic significance of perceptual experience, reading the whole book is the best bet for understanding what drives and feeds the proposal that is developed in this book.

Part I **Conceptualism**

1 Introducing Conceptualism

1.1 *Mind and World* – the Beginnings of Conceptualism as We Know It

I begin this book with a return to the origins of the current debates about conceptualism in perceptual experience: John McDowell's *Mind and World*. In this book-version of his 1991 *John Locke Lectures* in Oxford (McDowell 1996) McDowell develops a theory of experience as essentially conceptual. His basic claim is that experiences are "states or occurrences in which capacities that belong to spontaneity are in play in actualizations of receptivity" (McDowell 1996, p. 66). Conceptual capacities are actualized in a subject's perceptual experience of the world. This is the fundamental claim that is still at the basis of all conceptualist theories.

McDowell borrows Kant's terminology of receptivity and spontaneity to further explicate his conceptualist thesis: perceptual experience involves both receptivity, i.e. passive sensitivity to the world, and spontaneity, i.e. active exercise of self-conscious, rational capacities (Kant 1998, A50f./B74f.). Receptivity and spontaneity are inextricably involved in perceptual experience and so their roles in perception are not even "notionally separable" (McDowell 1996, p. 9). Saying that perceptual experience is conceptual entails that perception has conceptual content.

The starting point of McDowell's theory is the problem of how to conceive of the relation between minds and the world (cf. McDowell 1996, p. 3). This problem is intimately related to a number of further issues, like: 'What is the relation between experience and judgment?', 'What is the relation between judgment and the world?' or also 'Can thoughts bear on reality?' As we will see, in spite of later changes to his theory this cluster of questions is still at the centre of McDowell's project (see e.g. Conant 2012; McDowell 2008b; McDowell 2009a; McDowell 2009e; McDowell 2009g; McDowell 2009i; McDowell 2011b). I will now provide a brief overview over the six lectures of *Mind and World* as they are the grounding of McDowell's epistemological theory of perception. As we will continue to see throughout this book, *Mind and World* still is the primary place to find out where McDowell's heart lies in epistemology.

McDowell starts his examination into the relation between mind and world, as well as between thought and the world, by showing that the two positions standardly assumed in the debate, coherentism and foundationalism, are caught in a dilemmatic state.[41] Coherentists assume that experiences cannot count as reasons for holding a belief. Experiences are just causally linked to independent reality (McDowell 1996, p. 14). There is no rational constraint on experiences from the world and this means that our thoughts cannot be right or wrong about the world, and most importantly they cannot be thoughts of the world as it is. From this it also follows that our experiences cannot be justificatory reasons for our judgments (McDowell 1996, p. 14). Why is that so? A judgment j can only be justified by reasons $r_1, r_2, ..., r_n$ if j and $r_1, r_2, ..., r_n$ are of the same type, i.e. if they are all thinkables. Or as the most prominent coherentist, Donald Davidson, says, "Nothing can count as a reason for holding a belief except another belief" (Davidson 1992, p. 310).[42] If we say that a reason justifies a judgment, we also mean to say that the justificatory reason and the judgment stand in a rational relation to each other (McDowell 1996, p. 14). Unthinkables cannot enter in such a relation and thus they cannot serve as reasons for judgments. Since on the coherentist conception experiences are such unthinkables, they cannot serve as reasons for judgments (McDowell 1996, p. 14). Non-coherentists, including foundationalists, find this result unsatisfying, because it leaves our thought basically out of touch with the world. Moreover, our experiences cannot play a justifying role in judgments about the world.

Foundationalists do not accept this consequence, they want reality to impinge on experience and judgments. They hold that brute objects of experience, un-conceptualized "objects of pure ostension" (McDowell 1996, p. 66) just so can be reasons for judgments.[43] But they end up in an incoherent position, succumbing to what Wilfrid Sellars calls the *Myth of the Given*. Their foundationalist model fails, because for something to be a reason, it needs to stand in rational relations to other thoughts, e.g. judgments. A brute, un-conceptualized object, which is just pointed at, cannot be the ultimate foundation of judgments because this brute object is not a thinkable and thus cannot be taken up in judgment (McDowell 1996, pp. 8f.). Judgments are thinkables and as such they are conceptual (McDowell 1996, p. 6). Since they are results of the activity of spontaneity, they cannot be based on something un-conceptualized, i.e. something non-conceptual (McDowell 1996, p. 7). Thus, if we wanted to hold on to the thought that expe-

---

41 McDowell actually starts the examination with foundationalism and only then goes to coherentism. I take it that the order is irrelevant since McDowell in effect diagnoses an oscillation between the two positions. Note that in his summary of Lecture I (§8) McDowell also reverses the order.

42 This position is a variety of Suggestion 4 from the Introduction.

43 C.I. Lewis's *Mind and the World-Order* (Lewis 1929) contains one of the clearest example of a theory of justification that is a 'victim' of the Myth of the Given.

rience is fundamentally non-conceptual, we would again – as in the coherentist case – be left to accept that experience is outside the conceptual sphere and consequently cannot count as reasons for judgments.

Let me remind you of an important orthographical-terminological decision that I have briefly noted in the Introduction: throughout this book I will use the hyphenated spelling "non-conceptual" for all expressions that contain the term *non-conceptual*, e.g. "non-conceptualism", "non-conceptualist", or "non-conceptualists". Some non-conceptualists, e.g Richard Heck and Christopher Peacocke,[44] use the unhyphenated spelling to refer to their own position, but I find the hyphenated spelling clearer to mark the difference between the two views, especially the fact that non-conceptualists reject the conceptualist conception of perceptual experience.[45]

I will pause briefly to comment on the Myth of the Given. It is traditionally contested what exactly Sellars means by the *Myth of the Given* and whether there is anything like the Myth of the Given. The question of how to deal with the situation will continue to come up throughout this book. For now I want to say this much. According to Sellars, positions that fall prey to the Myth of the Given are inconsistent because they are caught up in incompatible demands: The foundation of empirical knowledge *that p* is to be epistemically independent, but at the same time it is supposed to epistemically ground *that p* (DeVries/Triplett 2000, pp. xxvi ff.; deVries 2011, par. 29). Non-propositional states clearly cannot fulfill those demands, because they are not part of any inferential relations that would be required for an epistemic grounding relation. Propositional states that are inferential are not epistemically independent and so they cannot be the foundation of empirical knowledge. Propositional states that are non-inferential are also not epistemically independent, because for a state to have an epistemic status other empirical knowledge has to be "presupposed" (deVries 2011, par. 29). That means that non-inferential propositional states also cannot be epistemically independent. All cognitive states are either propositional or non-propositional and thus there is no candidate state that can fulfill the givenness-demands.

In the light of this fundamental problem with foundationalism, the natural reaction seems to be to try and see whether coherentism does not after all provide an explanation for the relation. But McDowell predicts that one will continue to encounter the same problems as in the initial examination of coherentism and will ultimately be driven into a foundationalist position again, which we will

---

44 Cf. e.g. (Heck 2000; Heck 2007; Peacocke 2001a).
45 Moreover, as I have said in the Introduction, the expression "nonconceptual" is a technical term in Charles Travis's theory that I will introduce in Chapter 5 and I will avoid confusions by using the hyphenated term for the non-conceptualist position.

also find untenable and so we will be tempted to go back to coherentism *et ad infinitum*. We are going back and forth between a coherentist position and a foundationalist position (McDowell 1996, pp. 14, 24).

McDowell stops this oscillation – forever, as he takes it – by offering a third alternative: experiences are not just causally related to the external world (*pace* the coherentist) and they are not un-conceptualized (*pace* the foundationalist). They are impressions of the external world on our senses and those impressions are already shaped by conceptual capacities (McDowell 1996, pp. 9 f.). This means that those impressions are conceptual thinkables and thus those impressions are available for judgments to be based upon.

The central objection to this theory is the idealism objection (Lecture II. "The Unboundedness of the Conceptual"). How does this objection come up? McDowell holds that experience is openness to the world and that in experience we take in facts about the world, we take in *that things are thus and so* (McDowell 1996, p. 26). He thus considers the world to be inside the conceptual sphere. So, *that there is a desk lamp on the table* is the conceptual content of my experience and at the same time it is a perceivable fact in the world (McDowell 1996, pp. 27 f.). That seems to entail that the world is made up of facts, i.e. propositions, and thus is mind-dependent. It is those claims, which seem to commit McDowell to an idealistic position.[46]

McDowell rejects this objection by insisting that experience *is* of the mind-independent world. All that he wants to claim by saying that the world is inside the conceptual sphere is that there is no "ontological gap between" (McDowell 1996, p. 27) our thinking and independent reality, i.e. there is no "ontological gap between" (McDowell 1996, p. 27) what one can think of and what can be the case in the world: the external world is thinkable. He approvingly quotes Wittgenstein: "When we say, and *mean*, that such-and-such is the case, we – and our meaning – do not stop anywhere short of the fact; but we mean: *this – is – so*" (Wittgenstein 1953, §95, emphasis in original). According to McDowell, this insight basically is a truism and so any formulation of it will look suspicious. But such suspicions are unfounded. The idealistic objection is based on a fundamental mistake: saying that the external world is thinkable, as McDowell's conceptualism does, does not mean that the external world is constituted by our thoughts. Rather, the idea is that every aspect and feature of the external world can potentially be thought of that it is *per se* thinkable. The external world does not consist in thought. It is "outside thinking" (McDowell 1996, p. 28, emphasis omitted, N.E.), but still thinkable. If we examine a given justifi-

---

46 McDowell continues to be confronted with the idealism objection, cf. (Ayers 2004).

cation and we get to the fundamentum of the justification, we can be sure that this element consists in thinkable content that is provided by the joint activity of receptivity and spontaneity (McDowell 1996, pp. 28 f.). E.g. my justification for believing that there is a cup on my right is that I see that there is a cup on my right. This also means that strictly speaking perceptual experience not only has conceptual content, but also propositional content (McDowell 2009a, p. 258).[47]

These claims manifest the idea that the conceptual capacities that are operative in experience are integrated into spontaneity, i.e. into active and reflective thinking. The capacities are part of a rationally connected network (McDowell 1996, e.g. pp. 12, 29, 32). It is impossible to have a particular experience without relevant and related background knowledge and that is why it is impossible to understand the system of concepts, conceptual capacities and the external world from the outside (McDowell 1996, pp. 12, 34 f.). We need to be inside the system in order to understand it (McDowell 1996, pp. 34 f.). McDowell calls attempts at understanding the system from the outside "sideways-on view[s]" (McDowell 1996, p. 42) or "sideways-on picture[s]" (McDowell 1996, p. 35). Such views try to understand the facts in the world independently of thinking, of concepts and of conceptual capacities, but any such attempt is in vain, because the world as it is can only be understood from within the system of concepts, intuitions and the world. The conceptual sphere is "unbounded" (McDowell 1996, p. 83).[48] The conceptual cannot be circumscribed in boundaries with the world external to it: everything is conceptual (McDowell 1996, p. 44).[49]

---

47 This claim is later revised by McDowell (McDowell 2009a), and I will discuss this revision in later parts of the book, especially in Chapters 3 and 6.

48 As McDowell himself remarks, his talk of the unboundedness of the conceptual clearly fits with the rhetoric of Hegel's Absolute Idealism, which also claims that the conceptual is unbounded. Note however that this nod to Absolute Idealism does not mean that McDowell's position is after all an idealist position. As he has emphasized he does *not* say that the external world is made up of thoughts; it consists of thinkables, which can potentially figure in our thinking, but which are always under constraints of the external world, i.e. under constraint from outside thinking. McDowell's relation to Hegel is notoriously contested and controversial, cf. e.g. the exchange between Stephen Houlgate and McDowell in (Lindgaard 2008), or the exchange with Robert Pippin (Pippin 2002). McDowell himself famously writes in the *Mind and World* that the book should be read as a "prolegomenon to a reading of the *Phenomenology*" (McDowell 1996, p. ix). See also the beginning of his response to Richard J. Bernstein's essay in *Reading McDowell* (McDowell 2002). McDowell's his "Hegel and the Myth of the Given" (McDowell 2003) and his "Hegel's idealism as a radicalization of Kant" (McDowell 2009d) also further elaborate in how far he takes Hegel's position to be correct.

49 Bertram/Lauer/Liptow/Seel provide an interesting post-formalist interpretation of this claim. They argue that McDowell does not conceptualize the world, he does not bring concepts into the

Another large part of the objections that McDowell expects concern his claims about perception having conceptual content. Various theories of non-conceptual content contest his conception and McDowell discusses their objections in the third lecture ("Non-Conceptual Content"). In this lecture McDowell finally says more about "conceptual capacities". Those capacities need to be operative both in experience and in active thinking, i.e. in making judgments and deciding what to do, what to think etc. (McDowell 1996, pp. 46f.). As is already clear from McDowell's thoughts on the sideways-on view, conceptual capacities are inextricably entwined with concepts and are elements in a complex system whose elements are rationally linked (McDowell 1996, pp. 46f.). Together they constitute what McDowell calls a "view of the world" (McDowell 1996, p. 30, 37). Those elements are all open to critical reflection, a stance which is obligatory to the being that is in this system (e.g. McDowell 1996, p. 40).

McDowell's conception of conceptual capacities in perceptual experience contrasts with Gareth Evans's conception of an "informational system" (McDowell 1996, p. 48; Evans 1982, p. 122). This is the system of capacities that beings use when they take in information about the world via their senses, or by testimony and while keeping hold of information that they have acquired (McDowell 1996, pp. 48ff.). The intake of the informational system is non-conceptual; it is available both to beings with conceptual capacities and those beings without conceptual capacities. The only difference in the intakes of these differently equipped beings is that for beings that possess conceptual capacities the intake can be called "experience", while it is not an "experience" for beings without conceptual capacities (McDowell 1996, p. 49). In Evans's theory conceptual capacities only come into play after the experiential intake has been taken in. Obviously this does not fit McDowell's conception (Evans 1982, pp. 157ff.; McDowell 1996, pp. 46ff.).[50] Evans falls prey to the same mistake that McDowell has diagnosed for the foundationalist: the Myth of the Given (McDowell 1996, p. 51). For Evans, experiences are meant to work as reasons for judgments, but since they are not conceptually structured, they are not fit for taking up this role. This role would require them to entertain rational relations to other thoughts and to be open for critical scrutiny (McDowell 1996, p. 53).[51]

---

world, but *rather* brings the world into concepts (Bertram/Lauer/Liptow/Seel 2008, p. 277). I cannot discuss this interpretation here, but it certainly offers a fresh take on McDowell's theory.
50 This diagnosis constitutes a common stepping stone for other theories, e.g. for Charles Travis, see (McDowell 2008c). I will get back to it (e.g. Chapter 3).
51 We will see that Peacocke's non-conceptualist theory tries to explain how perception on a non-conceptualist account can meet these demands (Section 2.2).

From McDowell's point of view Evans's theory is thus inherently incoherent, but he still deems it helpful to consider Evans's motivation for arguing that experiential intake is non-conceptual. I will discuss non-conceptualist arguments such as Evans's in detail in Chapter 2 and so here I will only provide a quick overview. The first argument observes that the content of experience is very detailed, i.e. fine-grained. Since concepts cannot grasp all the fine details of experience, experience cannot be fully conceptual (McDowell 1996, p. 56). I will discuss this argument as the Argument from Fineness of Grain in Section 2.6. In response to the argument McDowell contends that for experience to be fully taken in conceptually in all its detail, the details do not have to be captured by concepts that are expressed by corresponding linguistic equivalents (McDowell 1996, p. 57). For colors to be fully conceptual they do not have to be expressible by special words, e.g. words like "red" or "green" for colors. Colors can be captured by recognitional capacities and in the presence of a suitable sample the color can be expressed linguistically (McDowell 1996, p. 57). E.g. we can use demonstrative phrases like '*that* x' to refer to a certain color in the presence of an object of that color. Note that the demonstrative phrase persists even in the absence of the specific object as long as it can be applied to thoughts based on memory (cf. McDowell 1996, pp. 58f.).

The second argument, the Argument from Belief-Independence, starts from the observation that perceptual experience is belief-independent, whilst judgments and reasons are belief-dependent. It then proceeds as follows: A belief is a disposition to make a judgment and thus involves operations of conceptual capacities (McDowell 1996, p. 60). So if one claims that experience and conceptual capacities are inextricably connected and coeval, then this will entail that experiences, too, are dispositions to make judgments (McDowell 1996, pp. 60f.). Such a conception would marginalize the experiential element in experience: "In a picture in which all there is behind the judgement is a disposition to make it, the experience itself goes missing" (McDowell 1996, p. 61).[52] McDowell agrees with this insight, but denies that it affects his own conception, because, first, his own conception does not include the idea of experience as a disposition for judgment and, second, conceptual capacities and experiences are not connected in this indirect way, but rather conceptual capacities are already active in experience (McDowell 1996, p. 62). Any move from experience to a judgment thus is not based on a mere disposition, but rather firmly based on the fact

---

[52] Of course, such a theory would flounce the adequacy condition that I have set up in the Introduction.

that *that thing is thus*, i.e. it is firmly based on facts about the world (McDowell 1996, p. 62).

The third argument observes that human beings and non-rational animals share the capacity of perception and capacity of memory (McDowell 1996, p. 63). But animals cannot entertain conceptual content, thus in order to accommodate the shared capacity of perception we have to say that the perceptual content for animals and human beings is non-conceptual. The only difference between them is that human beings process this intake by using their conceptual capacities (McDowell 1996, pp. 63f.). I will discuss this Argument from Animal Perception extensively in Section 2.1 since it will help us understand better the debate between non-conceptualists and conceptualists. A conception which conceives of human and animal perception as sharing a common core is highly unfavorable to McDowell as it presents another version of the Myth of the Given (McDowell 1996, p. 64). He strongly rejects this so-called "highest common factor conception" (McDowell 1996, p. 113)[53] and instead argues in favor of what one might call a disjunctivist conception.[54] Both animals and human beings have perceptual sensitivity to features of their environment, but they have very different types of sensitivity: human sensitivity is inextricably linked to the faculty of spontaneity, i.e. to conceptual capacities and concepts of understanding whilst animal sensitivity is not. This alternative conception leads to a basic and intuitive problem: how can human beings be natural beings when their sensitivity, a feature of their naturalness, is "permeate[d]" (McDowell 1996, p. 65) by what is supposed to distinguish them from other animals, namely their spontaneity, their understanding (McDowell 1996, p. 65)?

McDowell aims to explain why people are reluctant to embrace a position like his – a position on which receptivity and spontaneity are coeval in human perceptual experience – and oftentimes even overlook it. Eventually he wants to lead the way out of this unfounded hesitancy and away from this "blind spot" (McDowell 1996, pp. 61, 69).

If one makes the reasoning behind the hesitancy and the blind spot explicit, one will find that it has the following outline:

---

53 For more on the highest common factor conception see (McDowell 1998a). I will also touch upon this conception in Section 1.3.

54 Note that this is not the disjunctivism that McDowell is famous for (e.g. Haddock/Macpherson 2008b). I will get to this feature of his epistemological theory at the end of this section and in Sections 1.3, 2.7.

(1) Non-rational animals[55] are natural beings.

(1') The life and essence of non-rational animals is entirely contained in nature.

(1") The sensory interactions of non-rational animals with their environment are "natural goings-on" (McDowell 1996, p. 70).

(2) We are like non-rational animals because we are also perceptually sensitive to our environment.

(2') Sentience is a feature of non-rational animals' lives and it is a feature of our human animal lives.

(3) The sentience of non-rational animals is one way in which their animal being, their purely natural being, actualizes itself. (McDowell 1996, p. 70)

(4) Our human sentience is an aspect of animal life, so it is also one way in which our natural being actualizes itself.

(5) If (1) to (4) are correct, then our experience cannot be conceptually structured and permeated by spontaneity and rationality, since it is unclear how something natural, viz. our human sentience, can be structured by spontaneity, which allows us to think actively and independently.

For McDowell's conception to be correct this argumentation must be false. And of course, this is what McDowell tries to show. McDowell argues that this argumentation is based on a common, but false conception of nature. It regards nature as coextensive with the "realm of law" (McDowell 1996, p. xv), the realm which is made intelligible by the natural sciences only (McDowell 1996, p. 71). This nature is "disenchanted" (McDowell 1996, p. 70). Life in the logical space of reasons cannot be made intelligible by natural sciences, it can only be made intelligible by reference to criteria of rationality or to norms (McDowell 1996, pp. 71 f.).[56] McDowell thinks that if we take this diagnosis seriously, we have to aim at a "re-enchantment of nature" (McDowell 1996, p. 74). This is no re-enchantment which leads us back to supernaturalistic, "pre-scientific" (McDowell 1996, p. 72) times, but a re-enchantment which allows for rationality and responsiveness to meaning to be integrated into nature (McDowell 1996, pp. 77 f.).

---

55 In *Mind and World* McDowell calls non-rational animals "dumb animals" (e.g. McDowell 1996, p. 69). I have exchanged this tendentious terminology for the expression "non-rational animals".

56 For a description of 'life' in the space of reasons see (Wingert 2012).

In *Mind and World* McDowell's position concerning the realm of law and nature is very strict: he clearly separates the realm of law and the space of reasons. For example, non-rational animals are taken to be subject to "biological imperatives" (McDowell 1996, p. 117) and so it appears that their behaviour can be fully explained by natural laws. But since then he has dropped this separation. In his response to a paper by Mischa Gubeljic, Simone Link, Patrick Müller and Gunther Osburg (Gubeljic/Link/Müller/Osburg 2000) McDowell admits that this conception is too rigid. The life and behaviour of non-human animals cannot be fully explained in terms of natural laws (McDowell 2000).[57] This amendment is also in line with a claim that McDowell makes in a later response to Robert Brandom: If one claims that the behaviour of non-human animals can be fully explained by natural laws, then one basically claims that animals are like inanimate artifacts and this certainly cannot be right (McDowell 2009f, pp. 286f.).

In further developing his own conception McDowell argues against other attempts at trying to explicate the relation between rationality (i.e. spontaneity) and nature: Bald naturalism follows a strictly reductionist route and tries to conceive of rationality, which includes conceptual capacities, only in scientific terms (McDowell 1996, p. 73). Davidson's coherentist approach proceeds yet differently: He holds that rationality and spontaneity belong both into the space of reasons *and* the realm of law (McDowell 1996, pp. 74f.). In other words, they are *sui generis*, because they cannot be reduced only to scientific terms, *pace* bald naturalism. But at the same time they can still be examined in a scientific investigation. They can be scientifically investigated, because the constituents of *sui generis* rationality and spontaneity can and do stand in causal relations (McDowell 1996, pp. 74ff.).

According to McDowell, both approaches are wrong, instead we should follow a "naturalism of second nature" (McDowell 1996, p. 91). The key idea is to regard spontaneity as *second nature* to human beings. McDowell's prime example for human second nature is Aristotle's *phronesis* (McDowell 1996, pp. 79ff.).[58] The *phronimos* has the ability to immediately see what is required, what is right in a given situation. This ability is acquired over time in a process that is natural to human beings (McDowell 1996, p. 84). Any changes to it will be undertaken from within *phronesis*, just like on the Neurathian boat, which is overhauled while at sea (McDowell 1996, p. 81).[59] Human second nature in general is devel-

---

57 This amendment allows for another response to criticism about McDowell's conception of second nature and *Bildung*. See my (El Kassar 2008).

58 Note that this is but one example of human second nature. Note also that animals, too, have second natures. See below for more on this topic.

59 Cf. (Neurath 1932/33).

oped in the ordinary process of upbringing; McDowell calls this process by the German word *Bildung* (McDowell 1996, p. 84). Note that human second nature in general consists of much more than *phronesis* (McDowell 1996, p. 84).[60] In being brought up we human beings acquire conceptual capacities. Rationality and the ability to understand rational demands become second nature to us. A human being is thus essentially a rational animal. Our rationality is in our nature (McDowell 1996, p. 85). Note that McDowell later – in response to criticism (McDowell 2000) – clarifies that the acquisition of a second nature is not restricted to human beings. Non-human animals can acquire second nature in training: "It can be second nature to a dog to roll over, say, on the command 'Roll over.'" (McDowell 2000, p. 98). That however does not mean that for non-rational animals the process of developing their second nature is the process of *Bildung* as in the case of human beings. On McDowell's conception non-rational animals would not be able acquire the very same second nature as rational human beings (e.g. McDowell 1996, p. 84).

All important elements of McDowell's conceptualist theory are now in the picture. Lectures V and VI can be regarded as applications and extensions of these elements. Lecture V ("Action, Meaning and the Self") has a particularly broad scope: it starts with a review of McDowell's arguments in favour of the Kantian credo "Thoughts without content are empty, intuitions without concepts are blind" (McDowell 1996, p. 89), then goes on to generalize McDowell's previous claims and finally offers a critique of Kant's conception of the self.[61] It becomes clear that McDowell's ideas on experience are part of a larger picture and that his claims can be extended to other fields that also include actualizations of active natural powers. Amongst those are bodily movements: Intentional bodily movements are actualizations of our active human nature and are as such permeated by our conceptual capacities (McDowell 1996, p. 90). The Kantian credo can be modified to fit bodily movements: "Intentions without overt activity are idle, and movements of limbs without concepts are mere happenings, not expressions of agency" (McDowell 1996, p. 90). Intentionality is in the bodily movements and not in some internal hideaway.[62] Let me briefly note that since the

---

60 At first look it seems easy to give examples for other elements of second nature, e.g. inferencing abilities, linguistic abilities. But at second glance one realizes that the list of examples can quickly become trivial, e.g. do playing, fighting, calculating belong to second nature, too?
61 I will not go into the details of this critique. Note also that McDowell has changed his views on Kant's theory, see e.g. (McDowell 2009j).
62 McDowell has continued to develop these considerations. See e.g. (McDowell 2010b; McDowell 2011a).

present book is an examination of perceptual experience, I will not follow up, nor comment on a possible extension of conceptualism to action.

The second topic in this lecture is a rejection of a certain way of bridging the supposed gap between nature and norm. This way of bridging the gap claims that meaning is constituted in social processes. McDowell rejects this strategy because it would mean that *how things are* cannot be independent from social processes of determination (McDowell 1996, pp. 92ff.). He makes a general claim on how to approach dualisms, like the one between nature and norm: one should not try to bridge the gap by using material from one of the sides, because this would mean that one *accepts* the dualism. Instead the dualism itself should be abandoned (McDowell 1996, pp. 94f.).[63] Note that this will also be McDowell's strategy in responding to skepticism (see Section 2.7).

The last lecture ("Rational and Other Animals") delves into the matter of human beings as rational animals and their differences to non-rational animals. Before he gets to this topic McDowell considers whether the possibility of illusion has any effects on his conception and he concludes that his position remains unaffected by the fallibility of experience. McDowell defends a *disjunctivism* that allows him to say that fallibility does not make the idea of openness to facts and reality unintelligible. Fallibility does not present an argument in favour of a highest common factor conception of experience, according to which veridical and illusory perception share a common core and the only difference between them is that veridical perception accords with reality (McDowell 1996, p. 113). The skeptic wants to say that a subject can never have knowledge of the state of affairs in the world, because perceptual experience is fallible (McDowell 1996, p. 112). McDowell holds that the fallibility of perception is not as significant as the skeptic makes it seem to be. In arguing for this claim McDowell's "aim is not to answer sceptical questions, but to begin to see how it might be intellectually respectable to ignore them, to treat them as unreal, in the way that common senses has always wanted to" (McDowell 1996, p. 113). One does not even need to consider the questions of the skeptic about illusions since the skeptic's objection makes it impossible to understand how we can even have empirical content (McDowell 1996, p. 112). McDowell takes up and elaborates on these considerations in his later debates with Tyler Burge and Crispin Wright (McDowell 2008b; McDowell 2010a; McDowell 2011b); James Conant, Andrea Kern and Sebastian Rödl have helped pursue this project (Conant 2012; Kern

---

63 Here McDowell relies heavily on his interpretation of Wittgenstein's quietism (cf. McDowell 1996, p. 93). But his assumptions and the quietist position itself are highly controversial as the quietist rejects any attempts at a constructive theory of how the bridge between nature and norm can be built. For such criticism see (Quante 2000) and (Wright 2002b).

2006; Rödl 2007). I will go back to this response and discuss it in detail in Section 2.7 as the Argument from Fallibility. This analysis will bring out further central elements in McDowell's theory.

One issue that McDowell still has to discuss at the end of *Mind and World* is how to conceive of the outer and inner experience of non-rational animals. If it is spontaneity and conceptual capacities which bring the world and the self into view, then for non-rational animals outer and inner experiences of objective reality are impossible. So the question is whether McDowell's theory entails the claim that mere animals are not sentient (McDowell 1996, p. 114). McDowell avoids this conclusion by taking up the terminology of *world* and *environment* from Hans-Georg Gadamer (Gadamer 1990, pp. 447 ff.; Gadamer 2004, pp. 440 ff.). The idea is that animals live in an environment in which they are exposed to biological imperatives which they simply follow. Their environment is a succession of opportunities and problems, to which they merely react (McDowell 1996, p. 115 ff.). Human beings, on the other hand, live in a world and that means that they can take stances on something that they encounter in the world. They can make decisions and are in what Gadamer calls "free-distanced orientation" (McDowell 1996, p. 116; Gadamer 1990, p. 448; Gadamer 2004, p. 442). Yet, living in an environment does not rule out sensitivity, it just includes sensitivity that is different from human sensitivity (McDowell 1996, pp. 118 f.). McDowell also gives the following explanation as to why his theory does not include non-rational animals: they are not helpful in his project of understanding how there can be thought about the world. He does not want to reject scientific studies on animal perception etc., they are just irrelevant to his project (McDowell 1996, p. 121). I will return to this explanation in discussing the Argument from Animal Perception.

In fact, McDowell even suggests that mere animals can be regarded as having something like "proto-subjectivity" (McDowell 1996, p. 119). However, this still does not mean that they can have inner experiences or outer experiences like rational animals, because such experiences are impossible for them as they do not have conceptual capacities (McDowell 1996, p. 121). Any other view than this would mean that we retain a highest common factor conception of subjectivity (McDowell 1996, p. 113), in which, e. g. perceiving like a bat is factorized into having some non-conceptual content plus the bat's special mode of orientation to the world (cf. Nagel 1974). Being a bat is radically different from being a rational animal and thus cannot be factorized in this simplistic way. McDowell adds that on this conception we do not need an evolutionary story, or any such explanation of how rational animals came to possess spontaneity and conceptual capacities (McDowell 1996, p. 123). The reference to *Bildung*, the natural process of maturation in a human being's life, is enough and any more detailed story is in danger of turning into a form of bald naturalism. We may, however, talk about the role of language in the initiation into the space of reasons (McDowell 1996, p. 125). Language is "a repository of tradition, a store of historically accumulated wisdom about what is a reason for what" (McDowell 1996, p. 126) and thus learning a language is the initiation into the space of reasons. Nonetheless this is not an appeal to "conservatism" (McDowell 1996, p. 186), since changes to reasons and rational relations can always be made, but the initiation into the space of reasons forms the basis for those changes.[64] In order to be able to make those changes, one has to live in the space of reasons (McDowell 1996, p. 126). As human beings we are always able, and to a certain degree even required, to improve our understanding (McDowell 1996, p. 126).

These are the tenets and claims of *Mind and World* and to a large degree they still hold for McDowell's conceptualism today, i.e. in 2015. Most of McDowell's papers on perception and epistemology after *Mind and World* provide elaborations on claims from *Mind and World* rather than full-fledged changes. I will not yet discuss the most recent crucial changes to McDowell's conceptualism, e.g. in (McDowell 2009a), since they are mainly irrelevant for the non-conceptualist objections that will be reviewed. Most of the non-conceptualist arguments even cannot concern the changes because they were published earlier. Only towards the end of Part I will I briefly introduce "Avoiding the Myth of the Given" (McDowell 2009a). In what follows I will first comment on the term "conceptualism" and then mark out details of McDowell's understanding of conceptual capacities. I will end this introduction into conceptualism by focusing on McDowell's disjunctivism and the related capacity conception of perception.

There is some ambiguity in the term "conceptualism" that Richard Heck and Thomas Crowther mark out in two separate articles. The claim that perceptual experience is conceptual can be understood as a compositional claim or as a possession claim – that is how Crowther puts the distinction. On the compositional version the question is "Is p composed of concepts?" (Crowther 2006, p. 249) and on the possessional version the question is: If S is to undergo an experience with the content p, does she have to possess the concepts that characterize p? (cf. Crowther 2006, p. 251). In other words, according to the "compositional sense", the distinction between conceptual and non-conceptual content concerns the "composition of the truth-evaluable contents of perceptual experience" (Crowther 2006, p. 250, emphasis deleted, N.E.). A content p is standardly taken to be composed of concepts iff p is built up only from Fregean senses. On the "Possessional Sense" the distinction between conceptual content and non-

---

64 For criticism of this argument see (Ginsborg 2006c) and Section 2.4.

conceptual content concerns the issue of whether there is a connection between the content of a subject's perceptual experience and the subject possessing certain concepts (cf. Crowther 2006, p. 251). Does S have to possess the concepts that characterize p in order for her to undergo an experience with the content p? What is at issue here is not the nature of the constituents of the truth-evaluable content, but what it is for a subject to be related to a truth-evaluable content in perceptual experience and whether a subject has to be capable of a certain way of thinking to be in a relation to a truth-evaluable content.

Heck distinguishes between the content view and the state view of conceptualism – and of non-conceptualism (Heck 2000, p. 485). The content view is a claim about the content of perceptual states and cognitive states. The content view-conceptualist holds that perceptual and cognitive states have the same content, the content view-non-conceptualist holds that perceptual experience has "nonconceptually constituted content" (Heck 2000, p. 485) and beliefs have "conceptually constituted content" (Heck 2000, p. 485). Note that Heck uses the unhyphenated spelling of non-conceptual to refer to the non-conceptualist position. But, as I said above, I will stick to the hyphenated spelling in my own writing, and, of course, will leave quotations from Heck unchanged. The same will apply for Peacocke's claims – he, too, uses the unhyphenated spelling (e. g. Peacocke 2001a), and I will leave quotations from his writing unchanged.

Now, Heck distinguishes the content view from the "state view" on which the conceptualist claims that the subject must possess conceptual capacities in order to be in the perceptual state. Perceptual experience and beliefs are different states that might well consist in the same content, but differ as regards their concept-(in)dependence. State view non-conceptualism holds that perceptual experience and belief are different in so far as the former is "concept-independent" while the latter "concept-dependent" (Heck 2000, p. 485). Heck's distinction has been widely taken up as a way of distinguishing forms of (non-) conceptualism (see e. g. Byrne 2003; Bermúdez 2009). I take Crowther's distinction to be more plausible from the viewpoint of a conceptualist, e. g. Heck formulates the different views mainly in terms of non-conceptualism. But not much hangs on this detail and so I will not further discuss the distinctions, nor the question of whether Crowther and Heck make the same distinction.[65] Let me just say that the conceptualism that I will develop and defend in this study will make a possessional claim.

---

65 Crowther in fact regards Heck's distinction as unconvincing (Crowther 2006, pp. 272–275).

1.2 Details of Conceptual Capacities in Perception

An important question that is open at this point is what McDowell takes himself to say when he claims that conceptual capacities are actualized in perceptual experience.[66] What do conceptual capacities do in perceptual experience? McDowell's article "Conceptual Capacities in Perception" (McDowell 2009b) contains – as the title suggests – more detailed explanations of the nature of conceptual capacities and their relation to rationality. Experience can rationally ground judgment because it has the same type of content as judgments. In other words, "[t]he content of intuitions is of the same general kind as the contents of judgments" (McDowell 2009b, p. 127).[67] The links between experience and perceptual beliefs consist in an "explanatory nexus that depends on ... workings of rationality" (McDowell 2009b, p. 128). But what does *rationality* here mean? McDowell explicates rationality as "responsiveness to reasons as such" (McDowell 2009b, p. 130). "Responsiveness to reasons as such" (McDowell 2009b, p. 130) needs to be distinguished from mere responsiveness to reasons. An individual that possesses responsiveness to reasons as such has the capacity to step back from an inclination to act or judge and consider whether she should be so inclined. In contrast to that, an individual that is responsive to reasons *simpliciter* reacts only in a way which is determined by its nature.[68]

Obviously the main context in which one encounters responsiveness to reasons as such is in reasoning. In engaging in an act of reasoning a subject shows itself to be responsive to reasons as such. Its reasoning is not determined by or dependent on any actual stimulus or any contextual determinants. McDowell emphasizes that rationality is a capacity that is operative even if it is not actively exercised. A rational individual does not have to step back continuously and always actively consider her reasons for an action; all that matters is that she can step back.[69] The rationality of an agent can be seen in her ability to answer questions about why she did do what she just did, e. g. we can ask her why she turned

---

66 For another examination of the role of conceptual capacities on McDowell's theory see (Pippin 2013).
67 Note that the claim is ambiguous on whether the content of perceptual experience is propositional or not. I will discuss what exactly it amounts to in the section on McDowell's "Avoiding the Myth of the Given" (McDowell 2009a), Chapters 3 and 6.
68 More on McDowell's conception of responsiveness to reasons further down in this section and in Section 2.2.
69 For the same observation outside the context of the philosophy of perception, and instead in the context of reason and rationality see (Raz 2013, pp. 86 f.).

right at a signpost (McDowell 2009b, p. 129). But McDowell also reminds us of
the special character of the rationality of such responses:

> What shows that [a rational subject, N.E.] goes to the right in rational response to the way
> the signpost points might be just that she can afterwards answer the question why she went
> to the right – a request for her reason for doing that – by saying 'There was a signpost
> pointing to the right.' She need not have adverted to that reason and decided on that
> basis to go to the right. (McDowell 2009b, p. 129)

A being which is merely responsive to reasons, e. g. a gnu that runs away because
it smells a lion, cannot be said to possess concepts that might be used in char-
acterizing the reasons. Of course, an animal fleeing from a predator acts for a
reason, and it can discriminate between dangerous situations and undangerous
situations, but it cannot be said to possess a concept like *danger*, because it does
not have "the ability to take dangerousness into account in reasoning" (McDowell 2009b, p. 130). So the difference between a rational individual and a non-rational individual basically comes down to the rational individual being able to
include the things she perceives in a given situation in acts of reasoning, say,
what to believe and what to do (McDowell 2009b, p. 130).

The subject's rationality, her responsiveness to reasons as such, "consists"
(McDowell 2009f, p. 287) in conceptual capacities. As we have seen, in *Mind
and World* McDowell explains that conceptual capacities are acquired by learning a language (McDowell 1996, p. 126). In later writings he adds that conceptual
capacities are acquired "by being initiated into a social practice" (McDowell
2009f, p. 287). For a subject that has acquired conceptual capacities

> [they] are at work not just in reasoning but, in general, in responding to reasons as such,
> whether or not it takes the form of explicitly drawing conclusions from reasons in forming
> beliefs or in acting. (McDowell 2009b, pp. 130 f.)

This conception does not entail that relations between perceptual belief and experience, e. g. an entitlement relation, must be conceived of and explained in
terms of inference (McDowell 2009b, p. 131). Instead it is a transcendental argument that ultimately makes us see that perceptual experience rationally entitles
a subject to a belief:

> The belief is intelligible in terms of a rational entitlement to it supplied by the experience.
> And since having the experience constitutes a rational entitlement to belief whether or not
> one acquires the belief it entitles one to, that same rationality must be at work in one's hav-
> ing the experience at all, even if one does not acquire the belief it entitles one to. ... [I]f our
> notion of an experience is to be capable of playing the role it plays when we explain per-
> ceptually based beliefs as manifestations of rationality, we must understand having such

an experience – being in possession of such an entitlement – as itself, already, an actualization of the conceptual capacities that would be exercised by someone who explicitly adopted a belief with that content. (McDowell 2009b, pp. 131 f.)

So McDowell's argumentation here basically comes down to this: rationality is responsiveness to reasons as such and rational subjects who are responsive to reasons as such have to possess conceptual capacities. For conceptual capacities to play this role particular acts of reasoning do not have to be explicit acts of drawing conclusions or inferences: rationality is a capacity that can but does not have to be exercised. The potential for exercising it is enough for allowing rationality its crucial role in the relation between perceptual experience and judgment.

Let me add a brief remark about one of McDowell's responses to critics who argue that non-human animals also possess conceptual capacities. In his response McDowell says that "[t]he connection between conceptual capacities and rationality is a *stipulation*" (McDowell 2009b, p. 132, my emphasis, N.E.). One might also have a different conception of conceptual capacities and on this different conception non-human animals might be found to possess concepts like *danger*, but that is simply not McDowell's conception of conceptual capacities.

McDowell surely means well with this remark on the stipulation, but I think that it is ultimately unhelpful since it takes away attention from the transcendental argument and the larger project of his theory. If the main thing to say about the connection between conceptual capacities and rationality as responsiveness to reasons as such was that it is a mere stipulation, it would not be clear why other contesting positions like the non-conceptualist position should be rejected. As we have seen, McDowell's restriction of conceptual capacities to rationality and responsiveness to reasons as such actually has a better rationale. Within the transcendental project we have to conceive of conceptual capacities as rational capacities for responsiveness to reasons as such. McDowell's talk of a stipulation makes it seem as if his conception is not something that can be argued for since it ultimately rests on a stipulation that might be arbitrary. But really that is not McDowell's argument: the connection between conceptual capacities and rationality really is a substantial claim; it is something that can be (and is) argued for and that is not just stipulated.

I will return to the issue of different understandings of *conceptual capacities* in Section 2 of Chapter 2 when I will collect different notions of concepts, conceptual capacities and rationality. We will also continue to find that the transcendental argument for conceptualism is the strongest argument for McDowell's theory (e.g. Section 2.7).

1.3 Conceptualist Disjunctivism and the Capacity Approach to Perception

In the *Mind and World*-terminology McDowell's conceptualist theory is a theory of perception as "openness to reality" (McDowell 1996, p. 26). This construction obviously invites skeptical objections: Experiences can be misleading, see e.g. the Müller-Lyer-illusion that McDowell himself refers to. Moreover, we are mostly unable to distinguish veridical and illusory experience. The two lines of the Müller-Lyer-illusion look like two lines that really differ in lengths. These observations combine to a version the Argument from Illusion:

(1) In the case of veridical perceptual experience of p, the perceiver's perceptual experience warrants her knowledge about p.

(2) In the case of illusory perceptual experience of p the perceiver's perceptual experience does not warrant her knowledge about p.

(3) To the perceiver veridical perceptual experience of p and illusory perceptual experience of p are phenomenologically indistinguishable.

(4) The perceiver's perceptual experience of p in the veridical case cannot warrant her knowledge about p.

This version of the argument is also sometimes referred to as a "sceptical argument from error" (Brewer 1999, p. 230).[70] In the light of these undeniable facts about the epistemic role of our perceptual experience the critic comes to two conclusions. First, *pace* the conceptualist, perception cannot be "openness to reality" (McDowell 1996, p. 26). Second, if veridical and non-veridical perception are not distinguishable, then veridical perception cannot be a truly reliable justification for a true belief. Its justification would always be defeasible. McDowell's theory of perception as openness to reality comes, so we might say, too late: before he can say anything about perception as openness to reality he needs to deal with the fallibility of perceptual experience.

In response to this objection McDowell unfolds his disjunctivist theory of perceptual experience. These considerations will return when I discuss McDowell's reply to the Argument from Fallibility, but I still already need to introduce them here, in order to detail McDowell's disjunctivism. McDowell argues that the move from fallibility of perceptual experience to the defeasibility of percep-

---

70 For this version of the argument see e.g. (Burge 2005, p. 56). In its original version the Argument from Illusion is an argument against the claim that perception is of material objects (cf. Ayer 1969; Crane 2014).

tion as justification is wrong. The Argument from Illusion does not provide any ground for a Highest Common Factor conception of perceptual justification as is suggested by the above objection. The indistinguishability of veridical and illusory experience and the fallibility of perceptual experience do not entail nor warrant the claim that veridical perception is not openness to the world. McDowell is a disjunctivist whose theory fits the following description:

> [A] state in which it looks to S as if p is *either* a state of S's seeing that p, and thereby being put in a position to know that p, and so acquiring an indefeasible reason for believing that p, *or* a state in which it merely looks to S as if p, in which S acquires no such reason, and so is not put in any such position. (Haddock/Macpherson 2008b, p. 7)

Note that McDowell's disjunctivism is an *epistemological disjunctivism*. He is not so much concerned with the nature of veridical, illusory and hallucinatory experiences – as is phenomenal disjunctivism – but rather with the role of perceptual experience as epistemic grounds of beliefs. Phenomenal disjunctivism argues that veridical, illusory and hallucinatory experience have fundamentally different phenomenal character, e. g. (Martin 2002; Martin 2004). The third type of disjunctivism – Byrne and Logue talk of "metaphysical disjunctivism" (Byrne/Logue 2008, p. 57)[71] – goes back to J.M. Hinton who argues that veridical, illusory and hallucinatory experience do not share a common element (Hinton 1967): "[T]here is no kind of (reasonably specific) mental state or event common to the good case and the bad cases" (Byrne/Logue 2008, p. 68). Metaphysical disjunctivism is concerned with the nature of veridical, illusory and hallucinatory perceptual experience.[72]

There is debate about whether McDowell's epistemological disjunctivism entails metaphysical disjunctivism or not (cf. Byrne/Logue 2008; Haddock/Macpherson 2008b; Soteriou 2014), but I will not enter into this discussion.[73] For

---

71 Haddock and Macpherson call it "disjunctivism about the nature of experience" (Haddock/Macpherson 2008b, p. 1).

72 Dorsch puts the claim of the position as follows: "[m]etaphysical disjunctivism about perceptual experiences claims that some of these inner experiences (i. e., perceptions) are constituted by objects in the outer world, while others (i.e., hallucinations) are not" (Dorsch 2011, p. 306).

73 Let me just briefly refer to an interpretation of McDowell put forward by Bertram/Lauer/Liptow/Seel. They seem to read McDowell as a metaphysical disjunctivist who argues that veridical perceptual experience is constituted by the perceived object in the world (Bertram/Lauer/Liptow/Seel 2008). On their interpretation McDowell's rejection of the skeptic's objection is justified by the constitution of the conceptual content of perceptual experience: "[t]he question of a fit or a reference of language to the world really does not come up anymore because the conceptual

this book what I take to be undisputed is that McDowell endorses an epistemological disjunctivism since this feature of his conception of perception remains central throughout his work.[74] It manifests itself clearly in his most recent remarks on perception as a capacity for knowledge (McDowell 2010a; McDowell 2011b).[75]

In these recent papers McDowell puts less emphasis on the idea of conceptual capacities being actualized in perceptual experience. This idea is now included in talk of perception as a capacity for knowledge: perception is not just a receptive state in which the perceiver has access to the world by perceiving the world, she is also made knowledgeable about the world. By perceiving the world she is exercising a perceptual capacity which puts her in the position to have knowledge about the world. McDowell explains: "a perceptual state in which some feature of the environment is present to one is an act of a rational capacity for knowledge, a capacity in whose exercises one knows things and knows how one knows them" (McDowell 2011b, p. 44). The claim that conceptual capacities are actualized in perceptual experience is part and parcel of the claim

---

content of the thoughts and expressions of a person only just constitutes itself through her being in a world and it is thus *per se* 'world-containing'". ["Die Frage nach dem Passen oder dem Bezug von Sprache auf Welt stellt sich dann in Wirklichkeit nicht mehr, weil der begriffliche Gehalt der Gedanken und Äußerungen einer Person sich durch deren Sein in einer Welt allererst konstituiert und darum *per se* "welthaltig" ist."] (Bertram/Lauer/Liptow/Seel 2008, p. 276, my translation, and footnote omitted, N.E.).

74 Bill Brewer develops a conceptualist theory of perceptual experience that suggests a similar disjunctivist move as the one construed by Bertram et al.; he too, takes perceptual content to be world-involving and most importantly for this section he shows us how metaphysical and epistemological disjunctivism could be brought together on a conceptualist theory developed from McDowell's conceptualism. On Brewer's theory that is clearly most strongly influenced by McDowell's conceptualism (Brewer 1999, p. 149, fn.1) perception has "perceptual demonstrative contents" (Brewer 1999, p. 231) and he rejects the "argument from error" (Brewer 1999, p. 230) by claiming that when a subject has experience with perceptual demonstrative contents she recognizes that in these contents the world is made "epistemically accessible" to her (Brewer 1999, p. 231). Clearly such disjunctivism is epistemological disjunctivism, but it starts from a theory of the nature of perceptual experience and in that also fits into the category *metaphysical disjunctivism*. Brewer explains that "... when [a person] is right about the world, as he necessarily is if the content in question is of the perceptual demonstrative form which he takes it to be (given the world-dependent view of such contents) he automatically recognizes the content in question as providing the reason for his endorsing this content in belief which it thereby does indeed provide" (Brewer 1999, pp. 231f.).

75 Talk of perception as a capacity for knowledge also figures in McDowell's "Perceptual Experience: Both relational and contentful" (McDowell 2013), but since the paper is part of McDowell's argumentation against relationist theories of perceptual experience, I will bracket it in this section, and include it later when I discuss McDowell's reaction to relationism.

that perception is a capacity for knowledge since the perceptual capacity for knowledge is a rational, self-conscious capacity. This internal connection makes it possible that in perceiving the world and acquiring observational knowledge the subject knows that she has this knowledge based on her perceptual experience. Eliza knows that there is a lighthouse because she sees it. And she knows that she knows about the lighthouse being there by seeing it.

For want of a better name I will call this formulation of the conceptualist position in terms of capacities the 'capacity approach to perception', or short the 'capacity approach' or the 'capacity conception'. Now, one difference between McDowell's original conceptualism and the capacity approach is that the latter puts more emphasis on the epistemic role of perception: veridical perceptual experience provides conclusive warrant for empirical knowledge (McDowell 2011b, p. 52). McDowell follows Sellars in holding that such knowledge is a standing in the space of reasons and thus must be the act of a rational being with linguistic skills (cf. McDowell 2011b, pp. 9 ff., 14). There is an unfortunate gap in McDowell's works on the capacity approach, since McDowell does not say why he has shifted to talk about perception being a capacity for knowledge, but I think we can fill this gap by turning to other authors who also apply and defend a capacity approach to perception to find out more about why it might be good to defend a capacity approach to perception as a capacity. Andrea Kern and Sebastian Rödl are the most intuitive candidates for this: Rödl develops a complex disjunctive conception of perception as a self-conscious capacity for receptive knowledge (e. g. Rödl 2010) and Kern defines perception as 'a rational, sensory capacity to know'[76] (Kern 2013, p. 394). Both theories will appear in the responses to the non-conceptualist Argument from Fallibility. Here I will focus on what they have to say about perception as a capacity and since Kern is most explicit about the advantages of the capacity approach, I will restrict myself to her remarks.

According to Kern, the claim that perception is a capacity for knowledge is most appropriate for capturing perception because it includes the two sides of perception: it has perception be both receptive and rational (Kern 2006, p. 301). That is how perception in rational beings such as human beings is: perception can be independent of beliefs – i. e. be merely receptive – and it can be essentially linked to beliefs – i. e. be rational.

Note that perception and knowledge are inextricably connected in Kern's theory: the capacity conception does not just cover perceptual experience, but also knowledge. Both perceptual experience and knowledge are *epistemic ca-*

---

[76] Kern's expression in German: "vernünftige, sinnliche Erkenntnisfähigkeit" (Kern 2013, p. 394)

pacities.[77] Strictly speaking, Kern's capacity approach is about epistemic capacities in general, and not just about perceptual experience, but I think that this detail can be ignored here.

The obvious question to ask is why we should think of perception as a receptive rational capacity for knowledge. Kern gives two related arguments that are reminiscent of McDowell's arguments against the skeptic and in favor of disjunctivism (see above). Her first argument holds that we can only make sense of the idea of empirical knowledge, i. e. of knowledge of the world, if we conceive of knowledge as a receptive, rational capacity (cf. Kern 2006, p. 184). Her second argument points out that if we conceive of knowledge as a receptive, rational capacity we can deal with the skeptic's objections that all conceptions of knowledge face: Agrippa's Trilemma (Kern 2006, pp. 55ff.) and the Aporia of Knowledge (Kern 2006, pp. 99ff.). The capacity conception of perceptual knowledge manages to reconcile the facticity of knowledge and the fallibility of knowledge that the Aporia of Knowledge seems to leave irreconcilable.

Single state views of knowledge, i. e. views according to which knowledge consists in the description of a single act rather than in an exercise of a capacity (Kern 2007, p. 245), cannot deal with the Aporia of Knowledge. Their fundamental mistake is that they subscribe to the idea of world-independent reasons: they take it that having a reason *per se* must be independent from the facts in the world since true and false beliefs have the same mental basis.[78] Kern calls this 'the dogma of the world-independent basis'[79] (Kern 2006, p. 145) or also the 'independence-condition for reasons for belief'[80] (Kern 2013, p. 375). According to her, a notion of reasons that tries to incorporate the independence-condition makes it impossible to understand how there can be empirical knowledge. Kern's argument runs as follows:

(1) Judgments and beliefs are spontaneous acts, i. e. they have normative, self-conscious explanations. A belief is a case of a subject affirming a conceptual content based on reasons. Answers to the question "Why do you believe that…?" offer reasons for the truth of the belief (Kern 2006, p. 150).

---

77 Cf. (Kern 2007; Kern 2011).

78 Tyler Burge makes this assumption (e. g. Burge 2005, pp. 22 f.) and this claim will thus be crucial for his Argument from Fallibility, Section 2.7.

79 Kern's German formulation is "das Dogma der weltunabhängigen Grundlage" (Kern 2006, p. 145).

80 Kern's German formulation is "Unabhängigkeits-Bedingung für Gründe für Überzeugungen" (Kern 2013, p. 375).

(2) Empirical beliefs and judgments have objective content, i.e. their truth depends on the way things are in the world. If a belief is based on reasons (as of 1), and if it is to have objective content, then the reasons for the truth of the belief must be mental states that contain and account for the world-dependence of the reason. Such reasons are receptive reasons that are the result of the world affecting the subject[81] (Kern 2006, p. 150).

(3) Views who assume that reasons for belief must be world-independent[82] also emphasize that good cases and bad cases are indiscriminable to the rational subject and so the subject cannot have receptive reasons that support the objective content of the belief (Kern 2006, p. 150).

(4) Views who assume that reasons for belief must be world-independent cannot explain how there can be receptive reasons. But empirical beliefs are based on receptive reasons (see 2) (Kern 2006, p. 152).

(5) It follows from (1) to (4) that theories which assume that reasons for belief are world-independent cannot explain how there can be empirical beliefs. They do not manage to introduce the very states whose truth they are doubting (Kern 2006, p. 152).

Kern concludes that we need to make room for receptive reasons, for world-dependent reasons, if we are to make sense of the notion of empirical beliefs in the first place.[83] But even more than that, we need to make room for the notion of knowledge as a rational capacity, because it allows us to make sense of world-dependent reasons.

What is so special about rational capacities? Rational capacities are general and time-less, i.e. they are not particular states or acts at a particular time (Kern 2006, pp. 188 f.). And yet they are intrinsically related to acts that actualize the capacity and such acts are particular acts at a particular time. The being that possesses a rational capacity possesses a general capacity that can be actualized at particular moments in time. The acts that actualize the capacity only have their identity because of the very capacity. That is the first central trait of rational capacities: Rational capacities thus are constitutive unities, i.e. they are consti-

---

81 It is here that we see that Kern's work is a further development of McDowell's thoughts on perceptual experience.

82 According to Kern, both internalists such as J. L. Austin, but also externalists such as Fred Dretske and externalist inferentialists fall under this category.

83 This, too, is already clear in *Mind and World:* "empirical content as such (even as possessed by mere presentiments) is intelligible only in a context that allows us to make sense of direct rational constraint on minds from the world itself" (McDowell 1996, p. 112, fn.2).

tuted by acts that actualize the capacity but that have their particular identity only because of the capacity (e.g. Kern 2006, pp. 194 ff.). That also means that if we identify an act as being an actualization of a rational capacity, we are at the same time manifesting an understanding of the self-same capacity (Kern 2006, p. 205).[84]

What is special about perception as a rational capacity? It is a receptive rational capacity and the act that actualizes the capacity is a sensory act which is causally dependent on the fact in the world that is the conceptual content of the empirical judgment (Kern 2006, pp. 153 f.). That is why perception and knowledge can go together. Eliza believes that her friends are sitting on the bench. The truth of her belief depends on the world and so Eliza's reasons for her belief are sensory acts. It is in line with McDowell's conception of perception that Kern claims that the sensory acts have the same conceptual content as the empirical judgments based on them. The difference between the judgment and the sensory acts lies in the causality of the sensory acts: a sense act is a causally imposed conceptual idea ["kausal aufgenötige begriffliche Vorstellung", (Kern 2006, p. 154)]. The fact in the world is both the conceptual content of the sensory

---

84 Kern suggests that we can understand this particular relation better if we examine a difference between rational capacities and habits. The acts that belong to a particular habit – like drinking coffee in the morning – are intelligible independently from the habit, the acts that belong to a rational capacity are not (Kern 2006, pp. 199 f.). This feature also figures in the second trait of rational capacities. They are normative, i.e. identifying an act as an actualization of a capacity carries with it a measure for the exercise of the capacities (Kern 2006, pp. 213 f., 251). If we say that Eliza is swimming, we automatically gain the standards for deciding whether Eliza is exercising the capacity successfully or unsuccessfully. The third feature again is closely connected to the first two features: rational capacities explain the acts that actualize them (Kern 2006, pp. 220 f., 252). Eliza making a frog kick with her legs in the water is explained by her actualizing her rational capacity 'swimming'.

But note that since rational capacities are general, they always subsume the successful *and* the unsuccessful case. Kern refers back to Aristotle who holds that every capacity contains its actualization and its opposite (Kern 2006, pp. 218 ff.; Aristoteles 2009, IX.2, 1046b4 – 7). The difference between the successful and the unsuccessful consists in a decision undertaken by the subject who has the rational capacities (Kern 2006, p. 224). The subject decides about the right thing to do in the given circumstances. A subject that possesses rational capacities also possesses *logos*, i.e. the capacity to think, understand and judge. In actualizing a rational capacity she actualizes her *logos*-capacity – clearly a rational capacity – and does what is the thing to do given the circumstances and given the standards of the capacity. In other words, she makes a decision. A rational capacity thus is characterized by such an act of decision and the content that consists in doing what is appropriate to actualizing the rational capacity. The intimate connection between possession of a rational capacity and possession of *logos* is also central for capacities being explanatory – remember, that is the third feature of rational capacities.

act and the cause of the sensory act (Kern 2006, p. 154). That means that Eliza can only perceive that her friends are on the bench if things are indeed the way she takes them to be based on her sensory act. And in addition, it also means that Eliza's reason for her belief, her sensory act, is a world-dependent, truth-guaranteeing reason, because it only obtains if things are as Eliza perceives them, i.e. if Eliza's belief is true (cf. Kern 2006, pp. 175 f.). Here we are in well-known McDowellian waters: First, since the claims present an application of McDowell's disjunctivism and second, because Eliza's sensory act has an irreducible factive meaning.

The causality in perception is a special causality: it is an irreducibly normative causality. According to Kern, we need the notion of irreducibly normative causality (Kern 2006, p. 272) in order to make sense of the necessary truth of knowledge based on perception. Knowledge based on perception is necessarily true, because it only obtains if the subject possesses the rational capacity for knowledge. Knowledge based on perception is not simply true because the world is really as the judgment says. It is necessarily true, because the subject will only come to the judgment, it will only have knowledge, if things being as they are in the world has causally imposed ["*kausal aufgenötigt*" (Kern 2006, p. 154)] the act on the subject that possesses rational capacities. The causally imposed act still has a normative character, because its identity is determined by the rational capacity 'knowledge' of which it is an actualization and as such it automatically carries with it its own explanation and the norms that it is subject to. It is explained by being an actualization of the capacity for knowledge and the norm that the act is subject to is 'truth'. Such a normative act can justify a judgment (Kern 2006, p. 159).

At this point we are already far into McDowell's works on conceptualism that follows through with the epistemic role of perceptual experience and includes it in the very account of perception. One can sum up this conceptualism that McDowell, Kern and Rödl subscribe to as follows: perception is a capacity for acquiring knowledge that combines receptive capacities and conceptual capacities. This capacity approach will return in the discussion of the Argument from Fallibility. But before I can start with presenting the non-conceptualist arguments against conceptualism, I will once more take a step back to a time closer to *Mind and World* and look at two other conceptualist theories that were also developed from McDowell's early conceptualist considerations.

1.4 Two Developments of Conceptualism: Conceptual Content as Perceptual Demonstrative Content and as Enacted Content

Bill Brewer and Alva Noë have developed two conceptualist theories on the basis of McDowell's conceptualism from the times of *Mind and World*. This section will take one short look and a slightly longer look at the two theories. These theories need to be introduced even though they themselves will not figure all the way through this study, because Brewer and Noë have given what I take to be important replies to standard non-conceptualist arguments and, for Noë's theory in particular, one needs some background to be able to present these replies.

There are two particular reasons why I will be – and I take it, may be – brief with Brewer's theory as presented in his *Perception and Reason* (Brewer 1999). First, Brewer has abandoned large parts of this conceptualist theory and has developed the relationist Object View of perceptual experience (Brewer 2011) that I will discuss in Part II of this book. Second, Brewer's responses to non-conceptualist criticism can largely be understood without too many details of his own account and solely on the basis of McDowell's conceptualism.

Now, Brewer argues that perceptual experiences are reasons for empirical belief and knowledge: It is "an undeniable datum that perception is a basic source of knowledge about the mind-independent, spatial world" (Brewer 1999, p. 18). The claim consists in at least two more fundamental claims: first, a claim about the basicness of perception for knowledge ("perception is a basic source") and second, a claim about the relation between perception and empirical beliefs ("perception is a basic source of knowledge about the mind-independent, spatial world"). Perceptual experience is a reason for belief and knowledge because it provides the perceiving and thinking subject with "experiential demonstrative contents" (Brewer 1999, p. xvi). Such demonstrative contents include reference to the mind-independent objects in the world and therefore ensure that the empirical beliefs are really about the objects in the world. The demonstrative contents are a subject's reasons for empirical belief only if the subject possesses the concepts and conceptual capacities required for utilizing the content in a conclusion, i. e. a conclusion from perceptual experience as reasons to the empirical belief.

I cannot be similarly quick with Noë's account since some might be surprised to hear me call it a conceptualist theory and I therefore need to explain this label. In addition, Noë departs from McDowell's notion of conceptual capacities and thus I need to say more to introduce the theory. Noë's *Action in Perception* (Noë 2004) argues that "perceiving is a way of acting" (Noë 2004, p. 1). Perceptual experience is contentful because we exercise our sensorimotor skills in perceptual experience and those sensorimotor skills are basic conceptual capacities. Perception thus is conceptual.

Noë's enactive approach to perception[85] starts from rejecting the widespread conception of perception as a snapshot, in which the perceiver takes in all there is to the scene in front of her in just one instance. The eye is not like a camera and "vision is [not] a quasi-photographic process" (Noë 2004, p. 35). The following example illustrates that clearly: if you see a telephone on the desk in front of you, then you do not grasp the telephone and its surrounding in one instance and thus perceive it. You do not "open your eyes and … are given experiences that represent the scene – picture-like – in sharp focus and uniform detail from the center out to the periphery" (Noë 2004, p. 35). That model would have your visual capacities work like a camera. But really, you do not visually perceive all the sides of the telephone in the blink of an eye, instead you complement what you see by further knowledge. This further knowledge is sensorimotor knowledge. It consists in knowledge of two types of movements: (1) movements you could make in relation to the object which would change your perception of the object, and (2) movements and changes the objects itself could undergo, which would again change your perception of the object (Noë 2004, pp. 64 f., 168 f.). This sensorimotor knowledge is a necessary condition for experience having content (Noë 2004, p. 131).[86] Sensorimotor knowledge of the way 'how things appear to the subject' is going to change as the subject moves or as the object moves determines how things are, i.e. it constitutes the factual content of experience (Noë 2004, pp. 168 f.). On Noë's approach perceptual content is "two-dimensional" (Noë 2004, p. 168); it is both factual and perspectival, i.e. it consists in factual content and perspectival content. 'How things appear to the subject' constitutes the second dimension, "perspectival content" (Noë 2004, p. 168). On Noë's approach "[p]erception thus is world-directed and self-directed" (Noë 2004, p. 168).

Noë's description of how we perceive a telephone reveals more about the enactive approach. As I have noted, Noë emphasizes that we do not and cannot perceive all sides and aspects of the telephone in looking at it; we must also add our sensorimotor knowledge of what we would we see, say, if we moved closer to the telephone or if we took it in our hands. The telephone in all its detail "is only present *virtually*" (Noë 2004, p. 50, emphasis in original). The details are not all there, but they are all readily accessible for me, e.g. when I move towards

---

85 Noë also calls it *actionism* (Noë 2010).

86 Note that Noë in effect here offers a transcendental argument (Noë 2004, p. 183). I will get back to this observation.

the telephone. I am related to the unseen parts of the telephone by "patterns of sensorimotor contingency" (Noë 2004, p. 63), by moves I could make to see these unseen parts. This observation generalizes: "[t]he world is present to me now [i.e. when I perceive it, N.E.], not as represented, but as accessible" (Noë 2004, p. 192). That also means that perceptual experience is always amodal, i.e. even though I actually do not perceive the whole telephone, say, because parts of it are hidden by a piece of cloth, my perceptual experience is as of the whole, un-occluded telephone (cf. Noë 2004, pp. 61 f.).

As Noë himself says, his theory of perception is a conceptualist theory of perception: perception is conceptual. At first sight this categorization might seem surprising, and some will certainly question whether enactivism can really be in line with McDowell's conceptualism. Let me briefly introduce Noë's explanation of why his theory is a conceptualist theory. The key move behind this claim is that sensorimotor skills are taken to be conceptual or proto-conceptual skills (Noë 2004, p. 183). A perceiving subject possesses sensorimotor concepts. Sensorimotor concepts are basic, i.e. they are the basis for our concept-using practices, and it is those concepts which enable our contentful perceptual experience. But why are sensorimotor skills conceptual? To answer this question Noë refers back to Wittgenstein's insight that "understanding is akin to an ability" (Noë 2004, p. 199): Wittgenstein's thought leads Noë to the idea that concepts are practical skills and some practical skills are "simple concepts" (Noë 2004, p. 199).

Noë further develops his conception by discussing common arguments against the claim that experience is conceptually structured: the "Argument from Animals and Infants" (Noë 2004, p. 184), the Argument from the Belief-Independence of perception and the Argument from Fineness of Grain. I will not present his responses in this section, but postpone them to the chapter on non-conceptualist arguments and conceptualist responses (Sections 2.1, 2.6). One objection, though, concerns Noë's approach in particular and should therefore be addressed now. A non-conceptualist might try to stage the following argument:

(1) Some concepts are based on simpler concepts and we must understand those simpler concepts in order to understand those larger concepts, i.e. concepts stand to each other in asymmetrical relations.

(2) Understanding and applying those simpler concepts does not depend on the thinker's possession of other concepts. Simpler concepts are simply applied when they apply and the perceiver who applies them has such a grasp of the concepts that she knows when to apply them. The application of the simple concepts only requires the perceiver's

grasp of them. One example for those concepts might be observational concepts.

(3) Such simpler concepts are not based on conceptual content, but on non-conceptual content.

Noë rejects this conclusion as wrong: simple concepts are not based on non-conceptual content, but on exercises of sensorimotor skills. The principles of "sensorimotor contingency" (Noë 2004, p. 206) constitute the possession of simple concepts, e.g. observational concepts. In our experience of, say, a tomato, we base our experience on the presence of the tomato and at the same time we go beyond the mere presence of the tomato: the sensory presence of the tomato, our sensorimotor skills and our understanding constitute the perceptual experience of the tomato. Remember, on the enactive approach perception is virtual and the content of perception and experience are not presented "as represented, but as accessible" (Noë 2004, p. 192). Perception does not consist in a "content-bearing" (Noë 2004, p. 2) "internal representation of the world" (Noë 2004, p. 2) in the brain. That obviously entails that the boundaries between thinking of an object and experiencing an object are not that strict. Moreover, our relation to the world thought and our relation to the world via experience only differ in degree, since our ability to experience the world is the basis for our ability to think about the world; they both share the common basis: sensorimotor understanding.[87]

It probably seems most natural to follow up on this introduction of conceptualist theories by a chapter on non-conceptualist theories, but I will not do that

---

[87] Noë discusses further objections that are particular to the enactive approach in later articles and thereby aims to clarify the enactive approach (e.g. Noë 2008). Here I will only refer to one intuitive objection from these different objections. This objection simply notes that the enactive approach overemphasizes the role of movement for perception. It is wrong to hold that perception requires movement (e.g. Campbell 2008). But Noë explains that this interpretation of the enactive approach is mistaken, since enactivism does not hold that perception requires movement. Perception requires sensorimotor knowledge, i.e. knowledge of the sensory effects of movement, but the possession or exercise of such knowledge does not require movement. Of course, it might be the case that actual movement is required for the development of sensorimotor knowledge, but enactivism does not have to take a stand on this issue, this is a matter of empirical investigation. According to the enactive approach, perception is active, but not in the sense that it requires one to move. One must only understand the relevance of movement to action, and what would happen if one were to move. Perception is intrinsically movement-sensitive, but it does not require actual movement. Of course, that would be counter-intuitive since paralyzed people can see. Note also that we can see flashes of light in small units of time in which movements would be impossible. Perception thus could not require actual movement.

since non-conceptualist theories mainly are theories that reject conceptualism and so I find it better to present non-conceptualism by introducing and discussing its arguments and, I might add already, by showing how and why its arguments are mistaken.

2 Examining Non-Conceptualist Arguments against Conceptualism

I believe that the debate between conceptualism and non-conceptualism has reached a level of argumentative saturation. Participants continue to propound the same arguments, but do not achieve any substantial success. I will thus begin this section with an analysis of a prominent argument, the Argument from Animal Perception, to see what is wrong in the debate between conceptualism and non-conceptualism. The analysis will unearth parameters that will be useful for looking at the other non-conceptualist arguments and the conceptualist responses. I will look at six non-conceptualist arguments in total:

1. The Argument from Animal Perception

2. The Argument from Hyper-Intellectualization

3. The Argument from Concept Acquisition

4. The Argument from Memory Experience

5. The Argument from Fineness of Grain

6. The Argument from Fallibility

In the course of the chapter I will also reserve space to include an overview over central notions of concepts and conceptual capacities in play in the debates.

2.1 A Close Reading Analysis of a Standard Non-Conceptualist Argument: the Argument from Animal Perception

The original shape of the Argument from Animal Perception

The so-called *Argument from Animal Perception* is fairly simple and intuitive: non-rational animals do not have the sort of conceptual capacities that human beings have, but they surely do perceive the world. The representational content of animal experience is simply non-conceptual. So if both human beings and animals are sensitive to the world, then it must be obviously wrong to say that human perception is exclusively conceptual and requires the actualization of conceptual capacities. Human perception must be at least partly non-conceptual (cf. Bermúdez/Cahen 2015; Collins 1998; Hurley 2001; Peacocke 2001a). So the non-conceptualist account of perception is the correct account of perception.[88]

Note that strictly speaking the Argument from Animal Perception is a subcategory of an Argument from Animal and Infant Perception since similar questions and worries apply to the experience of human infants who do not yet possess concepts. The Argument from Infant Perception observes that pre-linguistic, pre-conceptual human infants share representational content with adult human beings; therefore concept possession and linguistic capacities cannot be constitutive for adult human perception. This parallel is emphasized by Josefa Toribio. In her article on non-conceptual content she subsumes these two arguments under the label "Continuity Argument" (Toribio 2007, p. 454): the Argument from Infant Perception and the Argument from Animal Perception both accuse the conceptual theory of wrongfully ignoring the continuity between animals and human beings, and infants and adult human beings. But I have separated the arguments because there is an important difference between them. The Argument from Infant Perception has a broader scope than the Argument from Animal Perception since it also concerns another non-conceptualist argument that I will call the Argument from Concept Acquisition: how does the conceptualist explain processes of concept acquisition in infants? I will say more about this aspect of infant perception in the discussion of that very Argument from Concept Acquisition and only mention it in the present section when necessary.[89] This section is going to focus on the Argument from Animal Perception, because the argument has relevance for the general debate. My analysis of the exchange about the argument will provide insights with which we can approach and assess other non-conceptualist arguments.

In his replies to the Argument from Animal Perception McDowell has made it clear that he does not want to say that non-rational animals are not sensitive to their environment. Animals are sensitive to their environment. He takes what Christopher Peacocke has called the "hard line" on animal perception (Peacocke 2001a, p. 260) because he wants to solve a "transcendental mystery" (McDowell

---

[88] From (Sieroka 2015) one can construe an interesting version of the Argument from Animal Perception. Sieroka points out that a large part of neurophysiological findings about the "human cognitive apparatus [is] drawn from animal studies" (Sieroka 2015, p. 95) and so we basically *have to* assume that there is a line of development from non-human animals to human animals. The premise 'perceptual experience in non-human animals and in human beings is in an important way similar/the same' as held in the Argument from Animal Perception would thus be supported by neurophysiological practice. But neither of the defenders of the Argument from Animal Perception puts forward this consideration.

[89] Considerations concerning concept acquisition will also return in Section 2.4 and Chapter 9.

1998d, pp. 411 f.), namely the question of "How can there be such an act as making up one's mind about how things are in the world?" (McDowell 1998d, p. 410) The transcendental mystery is almost inextricably connected to the question of how experience can justify judgment. If you want to answer those questions, it does not make sense to try to find answers in animal perception, since animals cannot "make up [their] minds about how things are in the world" (McDowell 1998d, p. 410).[90]

This reply has been regarded with suspicion, because it embraces the following unintuitive consequence: the visual experience of animals and human beings cannot contain the same representational content (Peacocke 2001a). *A fortiori* non-rational animals cannot have beliefs. According to Peacocke, the main reason for saying that perception cannot be fully conceptual but instead has to include non-conceptual content is that human beings and animals do share a common element in the representational content of experience. So clearly, Peacocke's and McDowell's intuitions are contradictory. Peacocke explains his intuition as follows:

> In my view the most fundamental reason – the one on which other reasons must rely if the conceptualist presses hard – lies in the need to describe correctly the overlap between human perception and that of some of the nonlinguistic animals. While being reluctant to attribute concepts to the lower animals, many of us would also want to insist that the property of (say) representing a flat brown surface as being at a certain distance from one can be common to the perceptions of humans and of lower animals. The overlap of content is not just a matter of analogy, of mere quasi-subjectivity in the animal case. It is literally the same representational property that the two experiences possess, even if the human experience also has richer representational contents in addition. If the lower animals do not have states with conceptual content, but some of their perceptual states have contents in common with human perceptions, it follows that some perceptual representational content is nonconceptual. (Peacocke 2001a, pp. 613 f.)

Before we look at the conceptualist responses to these considerations in more detail, I want to introduce two objections by Michael Ayers against Brewer's and McDowell's conceptualist conception. I have not introduced Brewer's full theory and here we see that we really do not need the details of Brewer's conception. Ayers's objections in effect concern McDowell's theory and Brewer's conceptualist theory.[91] Ayers attacks both Brewer's and McDowell's conceptualist

---

90 For a discussion of the role of the transcendental questions in McDowell's conception see (Conant 2012). I will also examine this issue extensively in Section 2.7.
91 The separate treatment of the two theories might also be due to Ayers's criticism being split into two articles: one a response to Brewer (Ayers 2002) and another an investigation of McDowell's and Davidson's theories (Ayers 2004).

theory for misconceiving the relation between human and animal perceptual experience.[92] Against Brewer's conceptualism he objects that the conception does not fit with "how we ordinarily and naturally think of the experience and mentality of animals and infants" (Ayers 2002, p. 6). It is simply unclear why it should be impossible for the content of a human experience to be available to a dog. This objection clearly parallels Peacocke's et al. objection outlined above and it is also clearly applicable to McDowell's theory, too.[93]

Ayers's criticism of McDowell's conceptualism complements his arguments against Brewer's conception. First, he emphasizes that McDowell is wrong to deny that animals also do have world-views. In fact, Ayers accuses McDowell of defending an "eerily Cartesian view of animals" (Ayers 2004, p. 261), even though he sees that McDowell rejects taking any such view (Ayers 2004, p. 261).[94] The second objection argues that McDowell's exclusion of animal per-

---

92 Ayers offers extensive criticism of McDowell's conception, e. g. he accuses McDowell of developing an idealist position. I will only focus on the Argument from Animal Perception, for his other arguments see (Ayers 2004).

93 Ayers's second objection goes further than the standard objection and provides an alternative taxonomy of knowledge. On Ayers's construal, the conceptualist thinks that human perception is conceptual because "knowing how we know is not, in the case of perceptual knowledge, a matter of knowing our reasons for a conclusion, but a matter of being aware of how we stand in cognitive relation to reality. And that is given ... in the character and content of perception itself" (Ayers 2002, p. 17). A dog cannot reason, cannot possess knowledge and so it seems fitting to think – as the conceptualist does – that it cannot have the same kind of perceptual experience as a reasoning human being. But Ayers suggests that maybe we need to distinguish two types of knowledge. *Primary knowledge* is awareness of objects "as objects of perception spatio-causally related to us" (Ayers 2002, p. 15). This type of knowledge includes awareness of the warrant ("credentials", Ayers 2002, p. 15) of knowledge. Secondary knowledge refers to the case of "know[ing] something without knowing how one knows it" (Ayers 2002, p. 15). Animals could possess the second type of knowledge and so we could argue that animals have perceptual awareness, e. g. of their own physical presence, because they have a "point of view" (Ayers 2002, p. 16).

94 The matter is apparently very delicate as one can see in McDowell's response to Ayers's criticism that McDowell's conception contains an "eerily Cartesian view of animals" (Ayers 2004, p. 261). McDowell responds to this criticism in a long footnote that is vehement and angry and deserves being quoted fully:

"Michael Ayers, in 'Sense Experience, Concepts, and Content. Objections to Davidson and McDowell', says (p. 239) that I am equivocal about perceptual awareness on the part of non-rational animals. (He spells out this claim at p. 261. There he says my thinking tends in the direction of a Cartesian view of 'animals', though – the other side of my supposedly equivocal stance – my exposition is 'larded with disclaimers') This reflects his finding it obvious that what perceptual awareness is for rational animals cannot be different in kind from what it is for non-rational animals. The result is that when I deny that non-rational animals have, in the way of perceptual awareness, what we have, he cannot hear that except as implying that they do not have

ception and infant perception is based on a wrong conception of the connections between perceptual experience, concept possession and self-consciousness. On Ayers's construal McDowell thinks that "awareness of oneself as a material thing and awareness of an objective world are mutually dependent" (Ayers 2004, p. 259) and that human perceptual experience therefore includes possessing the concept of a person and self-consciousness. This claim is just part and parcel of arguing that perceptual experience is conceptual and automatically makes animal and infant perception non-conceptual. According to McDowell, animals – at most – possess proto-subjectivity. Ayers criticizes this view because McDowell "underestimates the cognitive capacities of some animals" (Ayers 2004, p. 259) and also clearly begs the question (Ayers 2004, p. 259) in basing his theory on this close connection between perceptual experience, concept possession and self-consciousness. He simply ignores the fact that animals and infants do have sensory states with intentional content, too.[95]

Conceptualist replies to the Argument from Animal Perception

Brewer agrees with McDowell's general reply to the Argument from Animal Perception: referring to animal perception does not show that the conceptualist claim is wrong. Animals, too, are sensitive to their environment, but this sensitivity is different from the human case (Brewer 1999, p. 177). Brewer's claim can be captured in the following phrase by McDowell: "we have what mere animals have, but we have it in a special [thoroughly conceptual, N.E.] form" (McDowell 1996, p. 64). But Brewer is also aware that this reply is going to give rise to the Argument from Infant Perception: human infants do not have the same conceptual capacities as adult humans, but they obviously have perceptual experiences. Now, if animals and adult human beings do not share a common form of non-conceptual experiential content, but in fact have two different forms of perceptual sensitivity, how can the conceptualist explain the development of human infants to adult humans? At this point the Argument from Animal Perception becomes the Argument from Animal and Infant Perception: "how [does] perceptual

---

perceptual awareness at all. This is an example of the bad effects of bringing one's own sense of what is obvious to reading someone else. It can make for being unable to hear what someone is saying. And it is especially bad practice when, as in this case, the target of the reading is precisely questioning the sense of what is obvious that controls the reading. Ayers's suggestion that my thinking tends towards a Cartesian denial of consciousness to non-rational animals is groundless." (McDowell 2009b, p. 134; pages in McDowell's quotation refer to Ayers 2004).
95 Cf. also (Ayers 2002, p. 16).

sensitivity of the one form develop smoothly into perceptual sensitivity of the other, thoroughly conceptual, form?" (Brewer 1999, p. 177).

Brewer points out that this question[96] – "how [does] perceptual sensitivity of the one form develop smoothly into perceptual sensitivity of the other, thoroughly conceptual, form?" (Brewer 1999, p. 177) – is problematic both for conceptualists and non-conceptualists, because both have to tell a story about how conceptual capacities develop in beings without conceptual capacities. Conceptualists *and* non-conceptualists have to explain how human infants without conceptual capacities develop into adult human beings with conceptual capacities. At the same time, conceptualists and non-conceptualists also face different problems. There are two linkages in adult human perceptual experience: first, the relation to perceptual experience of animals and infants and, second, the relation to conceptually structured thought about the world, e. g. as in beliefs. The non-conceptualist can account for the first connection, because animals, infants and adult human beings have non-conceptual perceptual content. But her problem is that she cannot account for the second connection: how can non-conceptual perceptual content and conceptual thought be connected? The conceptualist, on the other hand, can account for the second connection, but she cannot easily account for the first connection.

McDowell explains the first connection only handwavingly by noting that there is a "substantial continuity" (McDowell 2009b, p. 133) between human beings and animals, but remaining tight-lipped about the details of this continuity; it seems to consist in responsiveness to reasons that both human beings and animals are capable of (McDowell 2009b, p. 133). Since this handwaving response leaves too many questions open, I will suggest another way for dealing with this challenge in the review of the Argument from Concept Acquisition. What I want to highlight at this point is that both conceptualists and non-conceptualists face a challenge in dealing with the linkages of adult human perceptual experience, and it is not *per se* clear whether either of them fails or succeeds in accounting for the connection. Brewer's response gives us first indication for concluding that the Argument from Animal and Infant Perception does not and cannot tell against the conceptualist claim. I will follow up on this topic at the end of this section.

Marcus Willaschek provides a very concise response to the Argument from Animal Perception and deserves to be outlined, because it differs from McDow-

---

96 As I said above Toribio subsumes the two arguments under the name Continuity Argument (Toribio 2007) and when one looks at Brewer's remarks in response to the Argument from Animal and Infant Perception, one sees why one might bring the two argument branches together.

ell's and Brewer's responses and yet is very similar in spirit. He argues that the argument is circular: it simply presupposes that beings with conceptual capacities and beings that do not possess conceptual capacities have the same experiential content without offering any further argument for that. Non-conceptualists might argue that animals and human beings share the same experiential content because they have the same (or at least similar) sense organs. But this reply is circular, too: non-conceptualists do not show that same (or similar) sense organs lead to same experiential content.[97] Moreover, the conceptualist argues in favor of just the opposite claim, namely that perceptual experiences of conceptually endowed beings do depend on sense organs and concept possession and so non-conceptualists cannot just say that having similar organs means having the same kind of perceptual content (Willaschek 2003, p. 268). I will get back to Willaschek's reaction to non-conceptualism when discussing conceptualist responses to the Argument from the Fineness of Grain (Section 2.6). And he will also figure in the development of relational conceptualism.

Finally, one more conceptualist answer needs to be added: Alva Noë's enactivist reaction. Noë's response to the Argument from Animal Perception is very interesting, because it is rather surprising and slightly uncommon for a conceptualist: he replies that animals and infants do not lack conceptual and inferential capacities. The use of concepts by adult human beings fulfills the generality constraint, and in the same way the use of concepts by non-human animals is general, too (Noë 2004, p. 185). One can see that, e. g. in a monkey being able to see a fellow monkey as "of high status" (Noë 2004, p. 201) and to recognize other monkeys as of higher status. Animals are subject to what Noë calls "holism and normativity" (Noë 2004, p. 201), since their responses to their environment are "constrained by intentions and primitive practical rationality" (Noë 2004, p. 201). Such behaviour also implies and allows for concept possession.

Note that this response depends on a different, the enactivist, conception of concepts and so Noë explains that critics of conceptualist conceptions overlook this option because they have an unsuitable understanding of concepts (Noë 2004, pp. 185 ff.). They think that (a) in order for a subject to possess a concept, the subject must "know the criteria that govern (and justify) its application" (Noë 2004, p. 185, brackets in original, N.E.), and that (b) the subject only uses concepts in "explicit, deliberative judgment" (Noë 2004, p. 187). But Noë explains

---

97 Note that the version of the Argument from Animal Perception that I have constructed from (Sieroka 2015) in footnote 88 may be taken to offer the argument that Willaschek is looking for. The Argument from Animal Perception is well-founded, because large parts of neurophysiological findings about the "human cognitive apparatus are drawn from animal studies" (Sieroka 2015, p. 95).

that assumption (a) is only part of the story: at the base of our concept practices there are conceptual skills which are situation-dependent and context-bound (Noë 2004, p. 186). Those underlying conceptual skills are the conceptual skills that adult human beings share with animals and infants, e.g. the very basic sensorimotor skills required for perception on the enactive account (Noë 2004, pp. 183 f., 186). A non-conceptualist might feel tempted to interject that this move means that the conceptualist after all thinks that concepts are applied on non-conceptual grounds, because Noë's conceptualism admits that we do not apply a concept like *red* on the basis of criteria. But Noë clarifies his response and explains that the idea is not that concepts are not applied on the basis of criteria, but rather that they are not applied on the basis of grounds at all (Noë 2004, pp. 185 f.).[98]

Assumption (b) is only part of the story, too. Concepts are not restricted to appearing in "deliberative judgment" (Noë 2004, p. 187), but rather they can also figure as background conditions on the possession of further skills (Noë 2004, p. 187). As an example Noë points out that we can see that a monkey possesses the concept "*kin-group member*" (Noë 2004, p. 187) in the specific treatment of his relatives, even though it never engages in "explicit deliberative judgment" (Noë 2004, p. 187). The application of concepts in deliberative judgment is simply not the only way that concepts can figure in thought and reasoning.

At the end of this brief overview of the Argument from Animal Perception and three conceptualist responses to it, the next natural question is this: why doesn't the argument convince anyone to change their position? Why does the argument not help in improving the exchange between conceptualists and non-conceptualists? Is there something wrong with the argument? I want to suggest that the problem lies much deeper and that we should examine what happens when conceptualists and non-conceptualists discuss the Argument from Animal Perception. It will be helpful to put the conceptualist-non-conceptualist debate into a broader context and to go beyond the non-ending argument-exchange. In transcending the exchange I will not provide a solution to it, but we will see more clearly what it is really about.

Why the Argument from Animal Perception fails

The Argument from Animal Perception is routinely and standardly put forward against conceptualism despite the various conceptualist responses. How can

---

98 For more on the basis of conceptual capacities in Noë's enactivism see Section 1.4.

we explain this deadlock? Apparently the Argument from Animal Perception is inefficient as it does not convince conceptualists. But the conceptualist responses to the Argument are also inefficient as they do not make critics of conceptualism drop the argument. What is the problem? I want to suggest that if we look at the exchange between McDowell and Peacocke, the problems can be made particularly clear.

Peacocke argues that non-conceptual perceptual experience of the subject S can rationally justify her beliefs because the subject S is "entitled to take her experience at face value" (Peacocke 2001a, p. 254). The entitlement is based on a naturalist explanation of instance-individuated perception. On Peacocke's theory concepts are abstract entities that are individuated by possession conditions which necessarily include non-conceptual content (Peacocke 2009). The possession conditions of concepts can ensure that a judgment which includes the concepts is correct. McDowell on the other hand argues that only conceptual content can rationally justify a subject's beliefs. In perceiving the world the subject obtains fully conceptual perceptual experience of the world and at no point does non-conceptual content enter the picture. These two conceptions of concepts and concept possession clearly do not square. I will say more about the details of Peacocke's conception and the different notions of concepts later (Section 2.2).

As might be expected, the differences also extend to the notion of conceptual capacities. As we know, according to McDowell, possession of conceptual capacities is implied by being a rational subject. A rational subject is one that is capable of responsiveness to reasons as such and responsiveness to reasons as such requires conceptual capacities: "I use the idea of conceptual capacities in a way that is governed by this stipulation: conceptual capacities in the relevant sense belong essentially to their possessor's rationality in the sense I am working with, responsiveness to reasons as such" (McDowell 2009b, pp. 129 f.). Non-rational animals are responsive to reasons, but not responsive to reasons as such, because they cannot "step back" and reflect on their reasons. Responsiveness to reasons as such is "coeval with command of a language" (McDowell 2009b, p. 135) and so beings with conceptual capacities must be beings who are speakers (McDowell 1996, pp. 115 ff., 125 f.; McDowell 2009b, p. 135). This does not hold for non-rational animals and so they do not possess conceptual capacities as McDowell understands them. The major distinction between non-rational animals and rational human beings is found in their different ways of responding to reasons and this fundamental difference carries over to a fundamental difference in the way perceiving works in non-rational animals and rational human beings (non-conceptual versus conceptual). But as I have noted above, McDowell thinks that there is a "substantial continuity" (McDowell 2009b, p. 133, fn. 5) that underlies this fundamental difference. McDowell leaves open what this continuity might consist in, but the candidates are clear: experience as sensitivity to the environment and responsiveness to reasons.

Peacocke does not state explicitly what he takes conceptual capacities to be, but I take it that he thinks that only beings that possess concepts and that can be in conceptual states, i. e. states with conceptual content, can possess conceptual capacities (see e. g. Peacocke 1998, p. 386). Conceptual content here needs to be understood as content constituted by concepts. Peacocke cannot follow McDowell's terminological move and conceive of conceptual capacities as implicated by rationality understood as responsiveness to reasons as such since he starts his project from a theory of concepts and then works his way up to conceptual capacities and rationality. McDowell on the other hand starts from explaining how empirical content is possible for rational beings.[99] On Peacocke's theory rationality enters the picture through another door: Peacocke talks of a "rationality profile" (Peacocke 2009, p. 442) of concepts. Such a rationality profile contains the non-inferential transitions that the concept allows for. We might say that for Peacocke the rationality is in the concepts, whereas for McDowell concepts are in rationality.[100]

A less demanding notion of concept possession and the term "concept" could try to conceive of concepts as perceptual capacities, e. g. the capacity for perceptual discrimination. So here a concept could be something like a way of experiencing. But such a less demanding notion threatens turn out to be trivial. I will expand on this issue in the next section (Section 2.2). The important insight for this study is that the discrepancy extends wider than the debate about the Argument from Animal Perception: it is in the basic terms of the debate.

And, finally, Peacocke and McDowell do not share the same notion of "entitlement". McDowell locates entitlement in self-determining rationality (McDowell 2009b, p. 132, fn.4). Peacocke's conception of "entitlement" on the other hand can be captured by what Tyler Burge calls "warrant" (cf. Harman 2006). Epistemic warrant, according to Burge, has an internalist variety, *justification*, and an externalist variety, *entitlement* (Burge 2003, p. 504). Justification is based on reasons, and the subject who is justified in holding a given belief must have concep-

---

99 McDowell conceives of rationality as self-determining rationality, i. e. a rational agent who is responsive to reasons as such is capable of determining her actions and belief by herself.

100 Note that on Peacocke's conception a subject's rationality needs to be understood as embedded rationality. Peacocke explains that "in respecting the norms of embedded rationality the thinker is also respecting those [norms] that are made available precisely because he is embedded in his world in a certain way, or is in states which are individuated by the ways they are embedded when the thinker is properly connected to the world" (Peacocke 2005, p. 178). Clearly, responsiveness to reasons as such is not merely embedded rationality.

tual access to those reasons and thus to the justification. Entitlement on the other hand does not presuppose that the warrant is conceptually accessible to the subject and the "warranting features include relations between the individual and an environment" (Burge 2003, p. 505). McDowell clearly would not accept an externalist form of warrant as set out by Burge. For him, warrant must be conceptually accessible in order to be warrant at all, that is just the point of the conceptualist position. As a non-conceptualist Peacocke obviously would not and could not follow McDowell in this. In the context of the Argument from Animal Perception we can mark out that on the Peacocke-Burge notion animals can have warranted beliefs about the world, and on the McDowell notion they cannot.

If one looks at these differences between McDowell's conceptualist approach and Peacocke's non-conceptualist approach to the relation between experience and judgment, it is far from surprising that in their disputes they have not reached consensus. "Conceptual capacities", "entitlement" and "rationality" are central terms in the debate about conceptualism in perception, and if those central terms are not understood in the same way, real consensus is highly unlikely. The same holds for other players in the debate, like Martin, Crane, Burge, Brewer, Noë, and so I want to suggest that the same basic problem explains the inefficiency of other arguments in the debate between conceptualism and non-conceptualism. Hardly ever do the arguments exchanged in the debate acknowledge the two issues that are the heart of the dispute. I have just touched upon the first issue: the two sides do not use the same terminology and, most importantly, do not put their different terminologies into relation.[101] The next section will come back to these different conceptions of *concept* and *conceptual capacities* and provide an overview of different views held by the theories that are relevant to this book.

The second issue concerns the plain fact that the two parties do not share the same goals and thus they do not share the same underlying background assumption. Peacocke's premier aim is to account for the fact that humans and non-linguistic animals share certain perceptual contents (Peacocke 2001b, pp. 613f.). McDowell's premier aim is to answer the transcendental question "How can there be such an act as making up one's mind about how things are in the world?" (McDowell 1998d, p. 410) These aims are so different that it is hardly surprising that the views clash. For example, if Peacocke were to say

---

101 Hannah Ginsborg's "Empirical Concepts and the Content of Experience" (Ginsborg 2006b) is a rare exception. She is one of the few to remark on the differences in understanding; e.g. she identifies more demanding and less demanding notions of the term "concept" (Ginsborg 2006b, pp. 355f.).

that under the assumption of a more lenient conception of "warrant" and "entitlement" it might after all be helpful to look at animal perception for answering the transcendental question, the issue would still not be solved: McDowell could not allow for the relaxed notion of warrant or entitlement, partly because his notion of "making up one's mind about how things are in the world" (McDowell 1998d, p. 410). constitutively contains the capacity for and the exercise of critical reflection. In order to argue that animals are relevant for McDowell's endeavor Peacocke would have to show that animals can critically reflect the content of their perceptual experience and their perceptual beliefs; he would have to show that they are responsive to reasons as such.[102]

One might object at this point that these results do not extend beyond the debate between Peacocke and McDowell and cannot help us in the debate between non-conceptualists and conceptualists in general. It is probably not such much contested and does not need further argumentative support to say that Peacocke's theory is a paradigmatic non-conceptualist theory of perceptual experience. As we will see, many non-conceptualists refer to features of Peacocke's theory in explications of their own theories (cf. e.g. Bermúdez 2009, pp. 462f.; Heck 2000, p. 511; Toribio 2007, pp. 447f.)

But for conceptualism things might be not so simple, e.g. Noë's conception is so fundamentally different from McDowell's that our observations do not apply to his theory. Noë says that animals possess the same basic concepts as we do – McDowell would not agree to that. Moreover, Noë includes psychological studies in his theory, whilst McDowell rejects their relevance for really understanding perceptual experience (e.g. McDowell 2011b, p. 56). Yet, this objection is too quick and does not barr the way to applying the findings to the debate between conceptualists and non-conceptualists in general. We have seen that Noë's response to the Argument from Animal Perception radically departs from McDowell's and Brewer's standard responses, but Noë includes a central element from McDowell's conceptualism in his story: the transcendental argument. He explains that we can only make sense of perceptual experience as presenting the world if perceptual experience is conceptual (Noë 2004, p. 183). That is a fundamental, if not the most fundamental argument of McDowell's conceptualist

---

102 Behind this failed attempt at reconciliation we find another fundamental underlying difference between McDowell and Peacocke: Peacocke takes a naturalist approach towards perceptual experience (cf. e.g. Peacocke 2005), whereas McDowell rejects any such approach outrightly (cf. e.g. McDowell 2010a; McDowell 2011b). Naturalist approaches in this context aim to explain perceptual experience by help of empirical sciences like psychology. More precisely, empirical sciences are taken to explain how perceptual experience must be understood. The naturalist-anti-naturalist difference will also be relevant at the end of this study, in Chapter 9.

theory. Moreover, his attitude towards the inclusion of empirical science findings is not one-dimensional, he is not a naturalist conceptualist, e.g. he is skeptical about naturalistic theories of perception and also colors (see e.g. Noë 2004, Chapter 4). One may thus extend the insights about the Peacocke-McDowell debate to other conceptualist theories. The above brief analysis of the debate between Peacocke and McDowell reveals that the state of the debate is unsatisfying: the use of terminology is very disparate and so continued incongruities seem likely. In this presentation and discussion of non-conceptualist arguments against conceptualism and the conceptualist responses *we* have to be aware of those differences.[103] In the following section I will therefore pause for more general remarks regarding the following parameters:

(1) Concepts and Conceptual Capacities
Which understanding of "concepts" and "conceptual capacities" is employed in the theories?

(2) Rational relations
What do the theories say about the relation between experience and judgment and knowledge, respectively? Is the relation rational? How do the theories conceive of "rationality"? Which understanding do they have of terms like "justification", "entitlement", "warrant"?

(3) Argumentative aims
What do the theories aim for? What do they want to show?
Throughout this next section, and in fact, throughout the whole study, differences in the argumentative aims of the theories and approaches will become apparent. The questions of what the trajectory is on which the theory of perception is developed and what goal the theories have will be made explicit.

A complete overview would also have to include

(4) Normativity
How do the theories conceive of normativity? Where does normativity come from? Do the theories argue in favor of naturalistic approaches or non-reductionist approaches? Is normativity intrinsic to particular phenomena, e.g. meaning?

These questions are highly relevant for the study, but they require a thorough examination that cannot be provided here. I will thus not discuss them in detail.

---

103 See also (El Kassar 2011).

2.2 Excursus: Remarks about Concepts, Conceptual Capacities, and Rationality

When talking about concepts in philosophy several authors come to mind, e.g. Eric Margolis, Stephen Laurence, and Jerry Fodor. Yet I will not include the considerations of these authors into this chapter, as they approach the issue of concepts from a very different angle than the authors discussing the issue of conceptualism vs. non-conceptualism in perceptual experience. Their taxonomies would introduce considerations that are partly distracting in the present exchange and so I will stay with authors who are involved in the discussions about conceptualism and non-conceptualism, e.g. Alex Byrne, Christopher Peacocke, Richard Heck, John McDowell. McDowell and Peacocke will figure most prominently since what one might call the classic debate about conceptualism and non-conceptualism is still strongly connected to their views and exchanges. And since the aim of this chapter and its different sections is to analyze and understand this debate it is best to focus on their works.[104]

Let me start this overview with the most important terms: *concepts* and *conceptual capacities*. Christopher Peacocke (Peacocke 2009) and Alex Byrne (Byrne 2005) provide a helpful distinction of three notions of *concept* that are in use in the debate about concepts: (1) concepts as abstract objects, (2) concepts as mental representations, (3) concepts as "grammatical fictions" (Peacocke 2009, p. 440).[105] The standard theory that conceives of concepts as abstract objects is Fregean in nature: concepts are Fregean senses. Concepts understood as Fregean senses are neither mental nor physical. Concepts understood as mental representations, on the other hand, are something that is literally in the head, perhaps a semantically interpreted word in a language of thought. They are "particulars located in time and space" (Peacocke 2009, p. 440) A being only possesses the concept *horse* if this mental representation is part of her cognitive machinery (Byrne 2005, p. 231). According to the third understanding, also called the Pleonastic sense, someone possesses the concept *F* iff she believes that ...F... (Byrne 2005, p. 232). Or as Peacocke puts it:

> We may, on this view, legitimately rewrite 'John believes elephants can swim' as 'John stands in the belief-relation to the Thought elephants can swim.' We can equally rewrite

---

104 So for more general theories of concepts, see e.g. (Fodor 1998; Margolis/Laurence 1999; Margolis/Laurence 2014).
105 Alex Byrne actually talks of the Psychological sense, the Fregean sense, and the Pleonastic sense (Byrne 2005, pp. 231 f.). But it is clear that the expressions refer to the same three understandings of *concept* as in Peacocke's distinction.

it as 'John believes the Thought consisting of the concept *elephants* in predicational combination with the complex concept *can swim*.' But, on this view, there is no more to concepts than is legitimized by the underlying true sentences that legitimize talk of concepts.
(Peacocke 2009, p. 440)

Someone who believes that Seabiscuit is a horse possesses the concept *horse*
(Byrne's example). Note that one might regard apparent reference to "the concept *horse*" as a mere *façon de parler*. Byrne notes that the semantic value of
the predicate "is a horse" can serve as the concept *horse*. On the latter understanding of *concept* it is "uncontroversial" (Byrne 2005, p. 232) that there are
concepts and that people possess concepts. Only the first two understandings
of *concept* are controversial. And one may add: the first two senses of *concept*
are most relevant in the debate about conceptualism (cf. Introduction to this
book). The third understanding may thus be ignored in the present context.

Byrne also notes that most definitions in the debate subscribe to the Fregean
sense of *concept* (e. g. McDowell, Evans) and therefore link concepts to the capacity of judgment and inferential capacities: the paradigmatic place in which
we find concepts is in judgments and beliefs.[106] Several interrelations between
concepts and other notions are implicit in this connection between concepts
and inferential capacities: concepts and the Generality Constraint; concepts
and rationality; concepts and language; concepts and conceptual content; concepts and conceptual capacities. Let me say a few things about these connections, each of which would deserve their own examination – and have, of course,
received it in other studies.

Concepts are widely agreed to be subject to the Generality Constraint.[107] See
e. g. Richard Heck's conception of concept possession: grasping a concept "is to
have a cognitive ability – the ability to think of a thing as a horse – an ability
whose possession partially explains one's ability to entertain various beliefs
about horses" (Heck 2007, p. 124). Possessing a concept in effect is more than
just being able to have a belief containing that concept. It also extends to the
ability to entertain other beliefs that contain the particular concept. We use linguistic expressions like 'to recognize something *as* something' or 'to see something *as* something' in order to express conceptual activity. Clearly, if propositions are constituted by concepts, then sentences like 'Eliza believes that the
window is open.' also qualify as a linguistic expression of concept possession.

---

106 Cf. also (Toribio 2007, pp. 448 f.).
107 Charles Travis rejects this assumption, see (Travis 2008), but we will ignore his pragmatist
conception for now.

There is hardly any doubt that beliefs and judgments are constituted by concepts – beliefs and judgments have conceptual content. Agreement about the fact that cognitive states like beliefs are composed of concepts still allows for disagreement about whether those concepts are also required for perceptual experience, i.e. disagreement about the constitutional nature of perceptual states. For example, in his above remarks on concept possession Heck is in general agreement with authors like McDowell, Evans, Willaschek, et al. about the fact that judgments and beliefs, i.e. cognitive states, are composed of conceptual content, but Heck argues that it is still an open question whether perceptual states are conceptual or not. More importantly for Heck's position: he thinks that this question is an open empirical question. Heck's conception is an example for a naturalist non-conceptualist position: according to him, perceptual states are non-conceptual and we have to examine them empirically.

Even though – as I mentioned above in passing – McDowell and Peacocke can be taken to disagree about whether a theory of perceptual experience has to be naturalist or not, I will not further discuss differences between naturalist empirical approaches to concepts and non-naturalist empirical approaches to concepts, since that would lead us to a further debate about methodology. I will however get back to the issue of the relation between conceptualism and empirical studies in the final chapter (Chapter 9), and I will suggest that these areas are compatible.

Let me briefly note that Heck's rejection of the conceptualist approach is not based on his naturalist convictions. Heck prominently puts forward a version of the Argument from Fineness of Grain against conceptualism (see Section 2.6) and argues that even though both cognitive states and perceptual states are compositional, they are composed from different elements and have different structures. Perceptual states are not made up by concepts; their content is non-conceptual. Heck thus defends what, as I have said above, he calls the non-conceptualist "content view" (Heck 2000, p. 485): perceptual states and cognitive states have different contents: non-conceptual versus conceptual content. Perceptual experience has "nonconceptually constituted content" and beliefs have "conceptually constituted content" (Heck 2000, p. 485).

Concepts, language and rationality

It is difficult to clearly distinguish the different elements that are central to understanding the notion *concept*. E.g. when one wants to discuss the conditions of concept possession one cannot separate that from the question of how concepts and language are related. So before I get to say more about concept possession, let me briefly pause for some remarks about concepts and language. If concepts constitute beliefs and judgments, it seems necessary to say that concept possession requires linguistic capacities. Davidson famously argues that having beliefs, possessing concepts and natural language skills necessary go together (Davidson 1975). A definition of concepts that takes the connection between language skills and concepts seriously can be found in Willaschek's work: he suggests that concepts must be understood in analogy to predicates. He explains that the role of concepts in judgments (and other propositional attitudes) is the same as the role of predicates in assertoric statements.[108] If one possesses a concept *F*, one knows what it means to say that something is *F* and one knows what things that are *F* have in common (Willaschek 2003, pp. 266 f.). But such views of concepts as being related to language skills are also criticized, e. g. for not capturing the possibility of concept possession in animals, e. g. (Bartels/Newen 2007).[109]

Remember that McDowell does not just link concepts and language skills, but also rationality (cf. McDowell 1996, pp. 125 f.; McDowell 2009b; McDowell 2009g, pp. 43, 92, 111).

> [I]t is by being initiated into one's first language that one comes to have a conception of reasons at all. It is not that prelinguistic human beings are already responsive to reasons (in a strong sense: to reasons as the reasons they are)," and that when they learn to speak they acquire a means to give expression to exercises of that supposedly antecedent capacity. The topography of the space of reasons is encapsulated in the content of concepts. (McDowell 2009k, p. 168)

It is also in line with this view that McDowell puts forward a circular account of concept possession. An externalist, naturalist, sideways-on view, such as e. g. Peacocke's theory of concepts, must be rejected because it cannot explain how perception itself can yield reasons for belief (cf. McDowell 1996, p. 168). In order to explain how rational relations can obtain between perception and judgment one needs to maintain a circular conception of concepts and concept pos-

---

108 Note the parallel to Sellars: he conceives of conceptual activity as analogous to overt linguistic acts (McDowell 2009i, p. 11).

109 Wanting to be able to say that non-rational animals can possess concepts leads the enactivist conceptualist Noë to give up on the tight connection between concepts and language skills. According to him, sensorimotor capacities are conceptual: sensorimotor capacities ("practical skills", Noë 2004, p. 199) are "simple concepts" (Noë 2004, p. 199). To some extent they are just like Fregean concepts, because for them concept holism and normativity of concepts holds (Noë 2004, p. 201). But they are also unlike Fregean concepts, because they are "situation-dependent and context-bound" (Noë 2004, p. 186). This alternative conception allows him to hold that non-human animals also possess conceptual capacities, in pretty much the same way as human adults (see Section 2.1).

session (McDowell 1996, pp. 166 ff.). An appropriate account of concept possession must be situated in the space of reasons and already presupposes that the subject has a standing in the space of reasons. The circularity can be justified by referring to McDowell's aim of explaining a thinker's thoughts and beliefs. He is not interested in providing an account that is compatible with neurophysiological conditions of concept possession. Concepts and beliefs are not be "[identified] as something that one thinks when ... where what follows 'when' is a condition external to possession of the concept" (McDowell 1996, p. 168) since such definitions lose the content of the thinker's thought.

Other than that McDowell does not say much more about concept possession. Instead he reverts to talking about conceptual capacities and he can do that because of the above interconnection between concepts, or conceptual capacities, and rationality. Possession of conceptual capacities is manifest in a subject's "responsiveness to reasons as such" (McDowell 2009b, p. 130). A subject who is responsive to reasons as such is able to step back from her own thoughts and actions and reflect her reasoning.

McDowell makes two central statements about the relation between reasoning abilities and conceptual capacities. His remarks in *Mind and World* suggest that possessing conceptual capacities just *is* being open to reasons: if a human being acquires conceptual capacities, that is just a part of its acquisition of a human second nature, i.e. being a creature that gives and understands reasons. At the same time "having one's eyes opened to reasons at large" (McDowell 1996, p. 84), too, is a way of acquiring human second nature. From these two sentences one may conclude that on McDowell's conception the possession of conceptual capacities goes hand in hand with "having one's eyes opened to reasons at large" (McDowell 1996, p. 84).[110] These remarks also reveal that on McDowell's conceptualist theory concepts, conceptual capacities and rationality, or: rational capacities are inextricably connected. We have also seen this in the previous sections on McDowell's capacity approach (Section 1.4).

---

110 McDowell's explanation of second nature can also be taken to support our interpretation. He explains that the acquisition of second nature consists in the "general phenomenon: initiation into conceptual capacities which include responsiveness to other rational demands besides those of ethics" (McDowell 1996, p. 84). Cf. also (Ginsborg 2006c, pp. 81 f.).

Concept Possession

But how do McDowell's remarks relate to other theories of concept possession more generally? And how do other participants in the debate about conceptualism understand the relation between conceptual capacities and concepts?

Thomas Crowther provides a helpful distinction between three understandings of concept possession which allows one to contextualize McDowell's claims:

(1) Concept possession as discriminatory ability: to possess the concept F is to have the ability to recognize Fs and to discriminate Fs from non-Fs.

(2) Concept possession as linguistic ability: to possess the concept F is to possess the ability to use the linguistic term F on the right occasion in the right way.[111]

(3) Concept possession as inferential ability: to possess the concept F is to possess a range of different judgmental and inferential abilities, e.g. Eliza who possesses the concept F must be disposed to judge 'That is F.' when she is presented with an F. The sensitivity to analytic or rational relations involved in the possession of these abilities cannot be brutely causal as in the "hardwired recognitional capacities" (Crowther 2006, p. 248) which animals and pre-linguistic infants use to distinguish Fs from non-Fs in their environment. But note that this does not imply that these inferential abilities are necessarily verbal.

Since McDowell puts his theory about concept possession in terms of conceptual capacities the theory falls between type 2 (concept possession as linguistic ability) and type 3 (concept possession as inferential ability). Clearly, McDowell (and the conceptualist Brewer) is not interested in the first understanding – Toribio calls it the "minimalist" view of concept possession (Toribio 2007).[112] According to McDowell, concept possession is more than a discriminatory ability, it consists in possession of inferential abilities and on certain interpretations also in the

---

111 This understanding clearly is in the Wittgensteinian and Fregean tradition.

112 Toribio offers a distinction of understandings of "concept possession" that is similar to Crowther's taxonomy. She adds that the first "minimalist" understanding (concept possession as discriminatory ability) is not philosophically interesting. It is only on the second and third understanding that we find a philosophically interesting debate. This debate – inter alia – revolves around the "challenge ... to show that a creature need not be a full-blooded reasoner in order to count as a full-blooded representer" (Toribio 2007, p. 449). Note that Hannah Ginsborg's views on discriminatory capacities and their relations to primitive normativity (e.g. Ginsborg 2006a) undercut Toribio's assessment to a certain degree.

possession of linguistic abilities. We can also see such an interpretation in Brewer's definition of perceptual conceptual states: they are "mental state[s] with *conceptual content ...* [that is, their] content is the content of a possible *judgment by the subject*" (Brewer 2005, p. 217, emphasis in original).

As I have said, McDowell opposes externalist theories of concepts and concept possession. Peacocke's theory is one of the most paradigmatic theories of concepts in the debate between conceptualists and non-conceptualists. Peacocke actually undercuts Crowther's distinction as for him concept possession means possessing a discriminatory ability and the ability to "reflectively recognis[e] something to be an *X*" (Toribio 2007, p. 449).[113] Peacocke thinks that the possession conditions of concepts can ensure that the judgment which contains the concepts is true. This conception of concepts and concept possession is highly elaborate and complex and therefore requires more explanatory space than the previous conceptions. Furthermore, Peacocke's conception also deserves more explanatory space since many non-conceptualists refer to his conception of concepts as a promising way of explaining how there could be a rational, justificatory relation between non-conceptual perceptual content and conceptual cognitive states (cf. Bermúdez 2009, pp. 462f.; Heck 2000, p. 511; Toribio 2007, pp. 447f.). But since detailing and discussing the theory extensively would take us off track from examining the exchange between non-conceptualists and conceptualists I will introduce it only fairly briefly.

A theory of concept possession

Peacocke's fundamental assumption regarding concepts is that a theory of concepts is always a theory of concept possession. This is what he calls the "Principle of Dependence" (Peacocke 1992, p. 5): a possession condition of a given concept says what it is to possess a given concept and at the same time individuates the concept (Peacocke 1992, p. 6).

An example of what such a possession condition could look like is given for the concept *red:*

The concept *red* is that concept *C* to possess which a thinker must meet these conditions:

---

113 Note that I do not take that to defeat Crowther's distinction, rather it is a sign that there might not be just one way of carving up the field of theories of concept possession. Taxonomies that are set in the field of linguistics, for example, would certainly come up with a different result.

1. He must be disposed to believe a content that consists of a singular perceptual-demonstrative mode of presentation m in predicational combination with C when the perceptual experience that makes m available presents its object in a red' – region of the subject's visual field and does so in conditions he takes to be normal, and when in addition he takes his perceptual mechanisms to be working properly. The thinker must also be disposed to form the belief for the reason that the object is so presented.
2. The thinker must be disposed to believe a content consisting of any singular mode of presentation k not meeting all the conditions on m in (1) when he takes its object to have the primary quality ground (if any) of the disposition of objects to cause experiences of the sort mentioned in (1). (Peacocke 1992, pp. 7 f.)

The first part of the possession condition is an observational possession condition, the second part is a non-observational possession condition. Wayne A. Davis explains the relevance of the non-observational possession condition. It is needed to account for situations, such as this: "even if I am not perceiving a car, I am disposed to believe that it is red if I believe that it has the reflectance properties that cause it to look red to people" (Davis 2005, p. 294).

If, as I said above, judgments are made up of concepts, then the content of the judgments depends on the references of its conceptual constituents. Referential relations therefore are not external to judgment and belief, but implicated in the nature of judgment and belief, in judgment and belief being made up of concepts. Peacocke postulates what he calls "The Identification": possessing a concept or grasp of a concept "is knowing what it is for something to be [the] semantic value" (Peacocke 1992, p. 23) of the concept. On Peacocke's account the reference of a concept is what makes correct the "belief-forming practices" (Peacocke 1992, p. 26) in which the concept figures. At the same time, since the belief-forming practices also appear in the possession conditions of concepts, the belief-forming practices themselves also individuate the concepts. On such an account truth and reference are inextricably involved in the concepts we possess.[114]

Now, if possessing a concept is knowing what it is for something to be the semantic value of a concept, every concept has to have a "determination theory" (Peacocke 1992, p. 17), i.e. an account of how the semantic value of a concept is fixed. So Eliza who possesses the concept *red* is in a position to know what it is for the thought (e. g. *The book is red.*) to be true. Having a determination theory

---

114 See also (Peacocke 2009).

involves: (1) knowing what it is for an object to fall under *red*, (2) knowing what it is for an object to be the referent of *book*, and (3) grasping the "significance of predicational combination" (Peacocke 1992, p. 44).

Consider the following example: Eliza is in a book store, she is standing in front of a shelf and she sees a red book. She thinks 'I want to look at this book.' This thought is controlled by perceptual information which Eliza has acquired in her perceiving the book in a particular way. The perceptual demonstratives and the other concepts which appear in Eliza's thought are individuated by two special types of non-conceptual representational content: *scenario content* and *protopropositional content*. They cannot be individuated by conceptual content because that would lead to a circular conception, so we need at least one type of non-conceptual content. On Peacocke's theory we must aim at a non-circular account of possession conditions of concepts in order to make sure that the concepts are individuated by their possession conditions (cf. Peacocke 1992, pp. 12, 89).

According to Peacocke, scenario content is the most basic type of non-conceptual representational content, which is presupposed by all other types of representational content. This basic type is a *spatial* type: it is "individuated by specifying which ways of filling out the space around the perceiver are consistent with the representational content's being correct" (Peacocke 1992, p. 61).

We have to take two steps in fully specifying an instance of those types: first, we fix an origin and axes. The second step is specifying a set of ways of filling out the space around the origin, or also just one way of filling out the space around the origin (Peacocke 1992, pp. 62f.). Let us look at the two steps in more detail. Peacocke calls a spatial type developed in these two steps, i.e. such a "way of locating surfaces, features, and the rest in relation to such a labelled origin and family of axes" (Peacocke 1992, p. 64), a *scenario*. If you take the scenario to the real world as it is at the moment of the perceiver perceiving, i.e. if you take the origin and the labelled axes to the real world, the world around the perceiver is what Peacocke calls the *scene*. The correctness of the content of experience is determined by the scene falling "under the way of locating surfaces and the rest that constitutes the scenario" (Peacocke 1992, p. 64). In other words, what is correct or incorrect is an instantiation of the spatial type in the real world. The content is not assessed relatively to an object, but outright assessed (Peacocke 1992, p. 64). For perceptual experience this outright-assessable content is what Peacocke calls a *positioned scenario*. The positioned scenario consists of three elements:

– the scenario,
– an assignment of real directions and places in the world to the labelled axes and origins of the scenario,
– an assigned time at which the perceptual experience occurs.

The positioned scenario is the representational content itself; it yields "the objective content of an experience" (Peacocke 1992, p. 67). There is no further mental representation of the content involved as an intermediary etc.[115]

From Peacocke's perspective there are several advantages to a theory that acknowledges scenario content and understands the objective content of experience as a positioned scenario. First, scenarios offer a noncircular way to ground conceptual content on some level of non-conceptual content. Scenarios are not built up from concepts. In determining the scenarios we make use of a conceptual apparatus, but the elaborateness or sophistication of this conceptual apparatus is independent of any actual concept possession on the subject's part. So we might be able to use scenarios to build up a hierarchy of concepts which is not circular. Second, and in addition to this advantage for a theory of conceptual content, scenario content is also advantageous because it can accommodate a central characteristic that the content of perceptual experience is supposed to have: the scenario can also include the fine-grained content of experience. As we will see in Section 6 of this chapter it is a classic worry of non-conceptualist theories that the fine-grained content of experience cannot be fully captured by the concepts which the perceiving subject possesses (The Argument from Fineness of Grain). The advantage of the scenario account is that it can use concepts to describe a scenario, but is not committed to having concepts as components of the representational content of the experience. It also does not have to say that the experiencing subject has to possess the concepts used for describing the scenario. On the scenario account the scenario is not identical with the various ways of picking out the scenario, which make use of concepts. The content of experience does not contain any concepts involved in picking out the scenario. It only

---

115 Let us take Peacocke's original example (Peacocke 1992, p. 62) in a slightly modified version and try to understand what happens in the two steps of specifying a scenario content. Suppose, we have an origin O_1 given by the property of being the centre of the chest of the human body. The axes are labelled as A_1 'direction back/front with respect to the centre', A_2 'direction left/right with respect to the centre', and A_3 'direction up/down with respect to the centre'. Imagine Tom and Eliza who are in front of Buckingham Palace. Tom looks straight ahead at Buckingham Palace, Eliza also looks at Buckingham Palace, but with her body turned toward a point on the right. Both Tom and Eliza fit with the above spatial type as circumscribed by the origin O_1 and the axes, A_1, A_2, and A_3, i.e. the origin and the axes are labelled in the same way for the two. If we confront this scenario with the real world, what we get are two positioned scenarios, one for Tom, one for Eliza. Both will have different correctness conditions because they are different instantiations of the spatial type.

consists in a part of the scenario, namely the spatial type, *not* any descriptions of the type.[116]

In spite of these advantages, Peacocke himself notes that scenario content is not enough to individuate perceptual concepts. One can illustrate the problem with the following case: Tom perceives a square and a regular diamond. How does the theory explain the difference between Tom's perceptual experience of the square and of the regular diamond? How could Tom distinguish between the two related concepts, *square* and *regular diamond?* Here, scenarios are not enough, because scenario content does not offer a way to explain how and when Tom perceives something as a square and not as a regular diamond (and *vice versa*). We need an additional element for that distinction that connects the mastery of a concept to non-conceptual content. Peacocke does so by introducing a second layer of non-conceptual representational content: protopropositional content.

Protopropositions consist of one individual (or individuals) and a property or relation, so if a representational content contains a protoproposition with the elements individual I and property p, part of the representational content will be that the individual I has the property p. Protopropositions are truth-apt. Peacocke calls them proto-*propositions,* and not proto-thoughts because they "contain objects, properties and relations, rather than concepts thereof" (Peacocke 1992, p. 77). And they are *proto*-propositions because they are not determined by some conceptual content that the experience, in which they appear, possesses (cf. Peacocke 1992, p. 77). Protopropositions can contain properties or relations like *square* or *parallel to* and those "properties and relations can be represented as holding of places, lines, or regions in the positioned scenarios or of objects perceived as located in such places" (Peacocke 1992, p. 77). Note that, again, since protopropositions do not include concepts of properties and relations, but the properties and relations themselves, the inclusion of protopropositions in individuating conceptual content does not make the account circular.

In the above case of the difference between perceiving something as *square* or as *a regular diamond* the additional level protopropositional content is helpful, because with this extra level one can say that perceiving the object as *square*

---

116 The scenario account can also accommodate two further characteristics of the content of perceptual experience. The content of perceptual experience is "analogue" (Peacocke 1992, p. 68), i.e. it is specific and determinate. The content of perceptual experience is also "unit-free" (Peacocke 1992, p. 68), i.e. it is not given in any particular measure. Finally, the scenario account also allows for amodal contents of experience, because it allows for an interaction between different sense modalities like visual and tactile experience in a particular content (Peacocke 1992, p. 69).

and perceiving the object as *a regular diamond* have two different protopropositional contents, but share the same positioned scenario content (Peacocke 1992, p. 78). So we do not have to revert to talk of perceiving different symmetries in explaining the difference between perceiving something as *square* or as *a regular diamond*.[117]

Concepts and conceptual capacities

What does Peacocke say about the relation between concepts and conceptual capacities? Just like McDowell, he seems to think that conceptual capacities are at least partly constituted by possession of concepts. But unlike McDowell he says more about how conceptual capacities and concepts are linked: he links the term to the holding of the Generality Constraint. See his definition of the Generality Constraint:

> Generality Constraint   If a thinker can entertain the thought *Fa* and also possesses the singular mode of presentation *b*, which refers to something in the range of objects of which the concept *F* is true or false, then the thinker has the conceptual capacity for propositional attitudes containing the content *Fb*. (Peacocke 1992, p. 42)

Possessing a "conceptual capacity for attitudes with the content *Fb*" (Peacocke 1992, p. 42), according to Peacocke, is more than possession of the concepts that make up the content *Fb* and it is also more than the ability to entertain a thought that *Fb*. Rather, it entails that "the thinker is in a position to know what it is for the thought *Fb* to be true" (Peacocke 1992, p. 43). Peacocke argues that a subject that possesses a concept, i.e. the possession conditions for the concept are fulfilled and the subject is able to determine the semantic value of the concept, also fulfills the Generality Constraint. I take it that we can understand this claim to imply that the possession of conceptual capacities also in-

---

117 Protopropositional content also occurs in memory, recognition, and the construction of a cognitive map of a subject's world and plays an important role in facilitating those processes. If the experience of thinker Tom includes protopropositional contents, then Tom does not have to remember the "highly detailed scenario contents, with their specifications for each point" (Peacocke 1992, p. 78), because he only has to "remember the salient properties and relations in which the object and its parts were perceived to stand" (Peacocke 1992, p. 78). In the case of recognition, rich protopropositional contents help with recognizing objects when Tom sees them from a different angle, or distance than in previous encounters. The protopropositional contents are also much simpler than scenario contents and thus can be included in Tom's cognitive map of the world more easily.

cludes possession of capacities for understanding implications and drawing conclusions, in other words, rational capacities. This again fits with what McDowell says since, according to him, exercises of conceptual capacities put one in the space of concepts (cf. McDowell 1996, p. 7). Relations like probabilification and implication hold between those exercises (McDowell 1996, p. 7). Command of this complex network of conceptual capacities, concepts and relations is what justifies moves from perceptual experience to beliefs.

Both Peacocke and McDowell do not explicitly state that conceptual capacities *are* rational capacities, but their respective argumentations certainly do support the claim that conceptual capacities include rational capacities. Remember, e.g. McDowell saying that "conceptual capacities ... belong essentially to their possessor's rationality in the sense I am working with, responsiveness to reasons as such" (McDowell 2009b, p. 129). This may well be understood to also justify my interpretation. Therefore, in this book I will understand conceptual capacities as also implying rational capacities.

Concepts and rational relations

One more spotlight is important in this cursory examination of the notions of concepts and conceptual capacities in the traditional debate about conceptualism. As I have said, McDowell argues that perceptual experience can only make beliefs and judgments rational if it is taken to imply the actualization of conceptual capacities. At the different stages of his theory that means that perceptual experience has propositional content, or that it is has conceptual content. He rejects Peacocke's models of concept possession and the relation between perception, belief and judgment, because Peacocke cannot make sense of rational relations between perception, belief and judgment. McDowell claims that on Peacocke's theory perceptual experience cannot constitute reasons for belief – in spite of Peacocke insisting that it can (e.g. Peacocke 1992, p. 80) – and therefore it is inadequate to McDowell and conceptualism at large. Since McDowell's criticism from *Mind and World*, however, Peacocke has elaborated on how on his conception, too, perception can constitute reasons for belief and how there can be rational relations between perception and belief. I will very briefly offer some details of his views so I can add why McDowell (and the conceptualist Brewer) would still reject them.

For Peacocke there is a basic connection between semantic value, possession conditions, correctness, and rationality: the key idea is that if the correctness conditions of the non-conceptual content that constitutes the possession conditions of the particular concept, say, *square,* are fulfilled, the object really is square.

> If the thinker's perceptual systems are functioning properly so that the non-conceptual representation content of his experience is correct, then when such experiences occur, the object thought about will really be square. (Peacocke 1992, p. 80)

According to Peacocke, these connections are rational because the non-conceptual content which appears in the possession condition of the concepts employed in the judgment has a "correctness condition that concerns the world" (Peacocke 1992, p. 80). There is no need to refer to any additional empirical information about the property of being square. As I have said above, rationality for Peacocke is in the concepts, rather than concepts being constitutive of rationality. According to Peacocke, a transition from non-conceptual content to conceptual content is rational if the subject S is entitled to take her experience "at face value" (Peacocke 2001a, p. 254), and if the observational concept involved is such that the subject must "be willing to judge it" (Peacocke 2001a, p. 254) if faced with a particular non-conceptual content. Peacocke's task for philosophy is to explain why transitions like the transition from non-conceptual content to conceptual content are "good" transitions. What does "good transition" mean? I take it that for Peacocke it means the following:

(a) A transition from non-conceptual content to conceptual content is a good transition if it is rational to take perceptual experience at face value (Peacocke 2004; Peacocke 2005).

(b) A transition from non-conceptual content to conceptual content is a good transition if the non-conceptual content of a perceptual experience makes the conceptual content of an appropriately related judgment correct (Peacocke 2001a; Peacocke 2005).

(c) A good transition is a transition that is open for rational scrutiny (Peacocke 2001a).

Peacocke's first explication (a) starts with the claim that perceptual experience is complex, more specifically, relationally complex. This complexity can be seen for example in perceptual experience being instance-individuated.[118] Instance-indi-

---

118 The second type of relational complexity that perceptual experience exhibits is its being part in developing a layout of the world and history of the world. It can be found in the relation between perceptual experience, i.e. its spatial representations and temporal contents, and what we might call the subject's view of the world. Perceptual experience forms and is formed by the

viduated perceptions are the most basic level of representational content. Peacocke continues: "What makes these perceptions [i.e. instance-individuated perceptions, N.E.] have the content they do is the fact that when the subject is properly related to the world, the holding of these contents causally explains the subject's experience as of their holding" (Peacocke 2004, p. 447).

In order to explain the complex phenomenon 'perceptual experience', according to Peacocke, we have to refer to the process of natural selection. The perceptual system has developed through natural selection and it goes hand in hand with the perceptual system having developed through natural selection that it will mainly represent correctly (Peacocke 2004, p. 456).[119] A perceptual system that has developed through natural selection cannot be generally incorrect or inaccurate, because otherwise it would not have 'survived' through this process. So the best explanation for perceptual experience at once also explains why subjects are entitled to take their experience at face value: their perceptual system simply is one that represents mainly correctly and accurately (Peacocke 2004, p. 456).

Note that this natural selection story only holds for instance-individuated perception, e.g. perceptual experience of shapes. Non-instance-individuated perception is perception of objects such as computers or soldiers (Peacocke's examples). The latter perception does not require for the subject to be perceptually related to a soldier (Peacocke 2004, p. 457; Peacocke 2005, p. 89). Peacocke explains that we are still entitled to take representational contents that are not instance-individuated at face value, because there is *informational entitlement* to take such contents at face value. Informational entitlement is an additional source of perceptual entitlement. The source for instance-individuated contents is basic perceptual entitlement, as discussed above. Informational entitlement consists of background information or informational states that make a certain judgment reasonable. This information can be found in memory, testimony,

---

"subject's conception of the spatial layout of the world around him ... [and] the subject's conception of his history, and the history of the world around him" (Peacocke 2004, p. 456).

119 Peacocke thinks that complexity should be explained by the "Complexity Reduction Principle" (Peacocke 2004, p. 454; Peacocke 2005, p. 83). The principle reads as follows: "Other things equal, good explanations of complex phenomena explain the more complex in terms of the less complex; they reduce complexity" (Peacocke 2004, p. 454; Peacocke 2005, p. 83). It goes together with the following addition: "It is more probable that a complex phenomenon has a complexity-reducing explanation than that it has no explanation, or that it has one that does not reduce complexity" (Peacocke 2004, p. 454; Peacocke 2005, p. 83). I cannot discuss this principle here as it would lead the argumentation into a different direction. For a more thorough examination of the Complexity Reduction Principle see e.g. (Wedgwood 2007) and (Madison 2011).

and knowledge (Peacocke 2005, p. 102). A third source of perceptual entitlement is "sequentially corroborative perceptual entitlement" (Peacocke 2004, p. 466): a sequence of experiences can give a thinker additional entitlement to take its later members at face value, because those later experiences fit with the earlier experiences. "... [T]he later members are as one would expect them to be if indeed the contents of the earlier members of the sequence are veridical" (Peacocke 2004, p. 466).

Peacocke's second explication (b) for why non-conceptual content can make the conceptual content of an appropriately related judgment rational is firmly based on the idea that the correctness condition of a particular non-conceptual content "ensures" (Peacocke 2001a, p. 254) the correctness condition of the conceptual content. It basically extends the above remarks about the powers of non-conceptual content to guarantee the correctness of the concept application. Remember, Peacocke grounds concept possession and conceptual content in non-conceptual content, more specifically scenario content and protopropositional content. If an experience is correct, i.e. if the scenario content is correct and the protopropositional content is true, then the perceiving subject cannot but be entitled to judge that p and "be willing to judge" (Peacocke 2001a, p. 254) that p. As we have seen, the possession condition of a concept specifically contains reference to the world, i.e. to the scene, so if a subject possesses a concept and all the possession conditions are met, then she is at once entitled to move from the non-conceptual content of her experience to conceptual content as in a perceptual judgment. In other words, the correctness of a particular non-conceptual content "is a priori sufficient for something to fall under the concept *square*" (Peacocke 2005, p. 60) because the non-conceptual content features in the possession condition of the very concept.

Let me try to illustrate this with an example: Eliza sees a book. If Eliza possesses the concept *book*, then the non-conceptual way in which things are given in a certain condition *A* implies that she is required to make the judgment '*This is a book*' which also contains the concept *book*. W. A. Davis offers a helpful paraphrase of the connection between perception and judgment: Eliza possesses the concept *book* if she is "willing (disposed, prepared) to judge *This is a book* in [condition] *A*, [i.e. broadly speaking when she sees a book]" (after Davis 2005, p. 311, my additions in square brackets, N.E.) and so it must be rationally mandatory for Eliza to judge '*This is a book*' if she is in condition *A*. Eliza is "rationally required to judge *This is a book*, and therefore is justified in believing it" (after Davis 2005, p. 311). This is how the fact that the correctness conditions of the non-conceptual content of a perceptual experience are fulfilled ensures that the correctness conditions of the conceptual content of a perceptual judgment are fulfilled.

Peacocke's third explication (c) of why the transition between non-conceptual content and conceptual content is a good transition marks the fact that such transition is always open to rational scrutiny. Rational scrutiny of the transition between non-conceptual and conceptual content is always possible for a subject, because she can always ask something like "Is something's looking *that way* [as in the experience she just has, N.E.] a reason for judging that it's square?" (Peacocke 2001a, p. 255). *That way* here not only contains the way in which the object is perceived, way *W*, but also the mode of presentation of the experience, i.e. the way the object is given for subject S, Eliza. This way W_S, e.g. W_{Eliza}, includes the spatial bodily relation between the object and the perceiving subject. Thus with the demonstrative concept *that way* one can refer conceptually to the non-conceptual content and thereby include it in an act of rational scrutinization. "*[T]hat way*" provides for conceptual reference, without requiring the referent to be conceptual.

It would certainly be worth examining these considerations in favor of rational relations between non-conceptual content and conceptual content, but again a closer analysis would distract from the bigger project of a unified theory of perceptual experience that takes in insights from conceptualism and relationism. Moreover, it is clear that in spite of the high degree of elaborateness in Peacocke's explications McDowell would not accept this kind of conception as an appropriate rendition of rational relations between perceptual experience and judgment. For McDowell, Peacocke's model still is externalist in a problematic way: the argumentative weight still lies on particular external elements and thus the model is still a sideways-on conception. McDowell would be able to just repeat his previous criticism. The account "falls short of establishing what Peacocke needs: namely, that non-conceptual content attributable to experiences can intelligibly constitute *a subject's reasons for* believing something" (McDowell 1996, p. 163, emphasis in original). One might say: Peacocke only explains how perceptual experience is an enabling condition for judgments being based on perception. It does not explain how it yields reasons (cf. McDowell 1996, p. 163). And I think that McDowell is right in saying that rational relations cannot be explained from without the space of reasons, purely naturalistically. I will say more about this throughout and return to the issue in particular in Chapters 7 and 9.

Before finishing this section let me add that Peacocke's model of rational relations between perception and judgment and rational transitions from perception to judgment is also in line with Tyler Burge's anti-individualist, externalist conception of justification (Burge 2003). According to Burge, perceptual experience can entitle a subject to a certain perceptual judgment even though the subject does not possess all the concepts required for understanding the rational relation. I will touch upon Burge's conception in the next section, so here I will only note the following: according to Burge, Eliza is warranted in believing that there is a tree whether or not she possesses the concept *tree*. She simply possesses an "epistemically externalist entitlement" (Burge 2003, p. 504). If she possesses all conceptual capacities required for explaining why she is justified in believing that there is a tree, she possesses an "epistemically internalist entitlement" (Burge 2003, p. 504). Burge and Peacocke are satisfied with "epistemically externalist entitlement", but McDowell clearly is not. In the assessment of the debate about the Argument from Animal Perception I have already pointed out that McDowell and Burge disagree about whether *entitlement* and *warrant* are to be restricted to a technical understanding. Their disagreement is yet again an indication of the deep-reaching divergence in the understanding of fundamental terms of the debate.

I will discuss Burge's criticism of McDowell's conceptualism in the next section and also in Section 2.7. Burge regards a theory of rational relations between perception and belief that does not accord with his and Peacocke's theory as hyper-intellectualized (Burge 2003). From Burge's viewpoint McDowell's conceptualism is guilty of just that mistake. The Argument from Hyper-Intellectualization is a common argument that will be in focus in the next section and so after these more general remarks on the notions of *concepts* and *conceptual capacities* and *rationality* in play in the non-conceptualist-conceptualist debate I thus return to the collection of argumentative exchanges between non-conceptualists and conceptualists. Throughout the collection and in fact throughout the whole book one should keep in mind the fundamental differences in project and in definition that have become apparent in the last sections.

2.3 Reviewing the Argument from Hyper-Intellectualization

What may be called the *Argument from Hyper-Intellectualization* in fact comes in at least two varieties. One version claims that the epistemological project which underlies Brewer's and McDowell's conceptualist theories, namely the examination of the epistemological role of perception, is privileged unduly. Susan Hurley is one of the proponents of this variety of the Argument from Hyper-Intellectualization. Hurley argues that Brewer is wrong in thinking that in order to explain how we can refer to particulars we need to understand the role of perception (Hurley 2001). Clearly the argument can be extended to include McDowell's conception, too, and so I will formulate Hurley's objection so that it concerns both Brewer, McDowell and conceptualism more generally.

According to Hurley, conceptualist accounts are too narrow because they miss that referring to particulars does not just depend on perception, it also depends on motor intentions and actions (Hurley 2001, p. 424). They prioritize the epistemological project and as a consequence they prioritize the epistemological side of the mind and downgrade the practical side of the mind (Hurley 2001, pp. 424 f.). "Reasons" as understood by Brewer and McDowell are almost exclusively reasons for belief. Reasons for action are only considered in parenthesis (Hurley 2001, p. 424). Hurley rejects this approach as wrong by pointing out that reasons for belief and reasons for action are not identical. Beings can act for reasons, i. e. they can act intentionally, even if they do not possess conceptual abilities. In fact the capacities involved in acting for reasons are not conceptual capacities because they are neither context-independent nor decompositional (Hurley 2001, p. 426).[120] According to Hurley, the conceptualist is wrong to focus on the epistemological project when she wants to understand and explain the human mind since beings without conceptual capacities can have reasons for action that are reasons for these beings, too: they still have their own points of view, their own perspectives, and that is all that is required for a being to have reasons for its actions (Hurley 2001, p. 426).[121] Reasons for actions are prior to reasons for belief (Hurley 2001, p. 425).

Brewer responds to Hurley's objections by criticizing her terms and assumptions. It is not wrong to favor epistemological concerns since perception is in fact more fundamental for intentions than action. Every subject needs to perceive the world in order to be able to form intentions in the first place (Brewer 2001, p. 454). In addition, Hurley's notion of conceptual capacities is too strong. According to Brewer, context-dependent capacities are still conceptual, because they figure in premises or conclusions of inferences and thus cannot but be conceptual. He explains that "[c]onceptual activity is perfectly consistent with merely bounded, imperfect and context-bound rationality" (Brewer 2001, p. 454). Brewer also remarks that on Hurley's conception acting for a reason is just "acting in the context of a complex set of dispositions to mainly appropriate action in suitably related circumstances" (Brewer 2001, p. 455). This conception by itself does not and cannot explain how reasons are reasonable to the subject herself. Possessing a point of view is not enough for having one's own reasons. Hurley's

---

120 Note that McDowell would certainly reject this construal outright. See McDowell 2010b, especially pp. 431 f.

121 Hurley herself does not say so, but we can extend her conclusion as follows: if this claim is correct, then human beings who have a point of view *and* conceptual capacities are not just thinking creatures who happen to act and move in the world. Rather, they are acting *and* thinking creatures.

criticism simply does not get to the gist of the conceptualist argumentation (Brewer 2001, p. 456).

The second version of the Argument from Hyper-Intellectualization is more concerned with human perceptual experience or human epistemic life at large. Tyler Burge is the most vocal proponent of this objection from hyper-intellectualization (Burge 2003, pp. 503 f., 528 f.). According to Burge, on the conceptualist conception experience threatens to be a kind of judgment. Concepts are predicates of possible judgment, and so perceptual experience cannot be conceptual, because perceptual experience is judgment-independent and thus non-conceptual. An account of perceptual experience which does not see that is hyper-intellectualized because it implies that human beings are in full control of their cognitive lives.[122] Their cognitive capacities require having language, self-consciousness, ability to understand reasons etc. Knowledge and warrant in the case of human beings need to be understood in terms of fulfilling an epistemic duty or an epistemic responsibility. Perceptual knowledge would thus involve steps of inferencing and explicit reasoning.

On this conceptualist account – according to Burge – we thus face four problematic consequences. First, perceptual knowledge turns out to be based on inferences; second, conceptualism presupposes a high conceptual sophistication of the perceiver. This presupposition implies, third, a distancing of human cognitive abilities from their human animal roots. And finally, conceptualism also comes hand in hand with a chauvinist attitude towards animals according to which animals do not have beliefs about the world and maybe even lack "genuine perceptual systems" (Burge 2003, p. 503). In more recent articles, Burge has extended his criticism to include disjunctivist conceptions more generally (cf. Burge 2005). His primary focus however still lies on McDowell's conceptualist conception of perceptual experience and of perceptual knowledge (Burge 2003; Burge 2011a) and I am also going to focus on this part of his critiques.

McDowell's responses to Burge relate both to his criticism of the conception of perceptual experience and the conception of perceptual knowledge. The arguments in defense of the conception of perceptual knowledge will be discussed in Section 2.7 when discussing the Argument from Fallibility. McDowell rejects Burge's second worry (high sophistication presupposed in human beings) by pointing out that a conceptualist notion of perceptual experience would only in-

---

122 Note that it is not unlikely that someone who puts forward the Argument from Hyper-Intellectualization also supports the Argument from Animal and Infant Perception, but the arguments do not have to go together. The Argument from Hyper-Intellectualization can also start from human perceptual experience and criticize the conceptualist theory because it does not do justice to perceptual experience.

volve hyper-intellectualization if one assumes a dualism of intellect and senses. On a unified model of intellect and the senses, as proposed by McDowell, there is neither excessive conceptual sophistication nor hyper-intellectualization (McDowell 2009b, p. 137, fn. 11). On this unified model the first worry also turns out unsubstantiated since it does not contain an inferential step, nor any explicit reasoning in deriving belief or even knowledge from perceptual experience (cf. McDowell 2010a, p. 247).

McDowell deflects Burge's charge of a chauvinist attitude towards animals (fourth objection) by pointing out that his claims about perceptual experience and knowledge do not entail any claims about non-human animals not having perceptual experience. Perceptual experience by human animals and by non-human animals are two types of actualizations of one genus, capacity for perceptual experience (McDowell 2011b, pp. 19 ff.).[123] In human beings actualizations of this capacity, i. e. perceptual experiences, are naturally informed by the conceptual (and rational) capacities that human beings possess *qua* being human beings. It is in the nature of their perceptual experience to be informed by conceptual capacities.

More particularly, it is in the nature of human beings to have such perceptual experience (cf. McDowell 2009a, pp. 271 f.). This claim allows McDowell to issue a surprising rejoinder against Burge's worry that conceptualists separate human beings from their animal nature: it is Burge's conception that separates human beings from their animal nature, because Burge disregards that human nature is that of being a reasoning creature.[124] McDowell's conception is free of any such charge because it acknowledges the special nature of human beings, which is that of rational beings.[125]

---

123 Of course, we have seen this move in the conceptualist reply to the Argument from Animal Perception.

124 Dreyfus's claim that McDowell succumbs to the Myth of the Mental is met with a similar response. McDowell argues that Dreyfus falls prey to the Myth of the Disembodied Intellect. For details see (McDowell 2007a; McDowell 2007b; McDowell 2009m; Schear 2013).

125 Let me briefly point out that Noë, too, discusses an over-intellectualization charge, brought forward by Hubert Dreyfus. Dreyfus argues that we do not need to know how we get into contact with the world in order to be in contact with the world. Rather, we are "skillful[ly] coping" (Noë 2004, p. 66) with the world and that does not involve any knowledge about our contact with the world. Noë tries to eleviate Dreyfus's worry by pointing out that knowledge about our contact with the world on his conception is merely "implicit, practical understanding that [the subject is] coupled to the world in such a way that movements produce sensory change" (Noë 2004, p. 66). We might put the response crudely: knowledge how we are in contact with the world is not propositional knowledge but *practical knowledge* and so there is no need to worry about an over-intellectualization. Again, clearly, Noë's response is innovative, but departs

McDowell and Burge's disagreement about the nature of perceptual knowledge also reveals the underlying disagreement about the role of empirical science for understanding perceptual experience. As we noted above, Burge is one of the proponents of a naturalist approach to perceptual experience and is thus bound to disagree with McDowell's non-naturalist approach. The issue of empirical science in theories of perceptual experience will return prominently at the end of this study.

2.4 Reviewing the Argument from Concept Acquisition

The name *Argument from Concept Acquisition* brings together at least two different, yet closely related qualms about the conceptualist approach. First, worries about how concepts are acquired on the conceptualist approach. These worries concern both the acquisition of first concepts *and* the acquisition of concepts by and large. Second, worries about the conceptualist theory being circular.

One of Michael Ayers's objections against McDowell is an example for the standard form that the first worry usually takes.[126] Ayers rejects McDowell's claim that conceptually informed thought is required for experience to have content by making the following observation:[127]

> In general, experience comes before concepts, and it is because we experience the world as we do that we are in a position to acquire the concepts appropriate to any account of things in the world, or of that experience. (Ayers 2004, p. 255)

Peacocke basically makes the same objection as Ayers, but his objection about concept acquisition also extends to the second worry, the circularity of the conceptualist account. Peacocke argues that conceptualists cannot offer a satisfying account of the acquisition of observational concepts. He discusses the example of the acquisition of the concept *pyramid:* in learning an observational concept

---

from McDowell's conceptualist account. One could say more about the relation between Noë's response and McDowell's theory, but this intra-conceptualist analysis would lead us too far away from the conceptualist-non-conceptualist debate.

126 For another version of the argument see (Forman 2008).

127 Ayers thinks that McDowell's talk of conceptual content means that the world is "quasi-linguistic" (Ayers 2004, p. 249) and that acquisition of conceptual content is identical to exercises of one's language capacities ("linguistic conceptualism", Ayers 2002, p. 6). McDowell explicitly denies this reconstruction of conceptualism in his response to Ayers criticism (McDowell 2009b) and so I will ignore it and restrict Ayers's criticism to the issue of the acquisition of conceptual capacities.

the subject must be faced with an instance that (a) allows her to rationally apply the concept, (b) entitles her to apply the concept and (c) does not already include the concept *pyramid*, i.e. that does not lead to a circularity. Peacocke's non-conceptualist position meets all three requirements, because it can say that a subject can perceive something as being pyramid-shaped without already having to possess the concept *pyramid*. The content of such an experience would simply be non-conceptual content. Of course, the subject would still be able to acquire the concept *pyramid* from this experience: the non-conceptual content is thus that judgments which involve the concept are rationally sensitive to it. Note that this rational sensitivity as construed by Peacocke is not a case of inference, since it does not include conceptual contents and inferential relations can only hold between conceptual contents.

I have already mentioned McDowell's response to such objections above: Non-circular approaches are simply inadequate to capture the nature of concepts, especially observational concepts. Accounts of the acquisition of observational concepts cannot but be circular – if they were not, they would stand outside of the space of reasons and would not capture the phenomena that occur in the space of reasons (cf. McDowell 1996, pp. 166 ff.). In a similar fashion, Brewer, too, questions why accounts for concept acquisition should have to be non-circular. Like McDowell, he, too, holds that non-circular accounts for concept acquisition are impossible: empirical content is always partly determined by its reason-giving relations with perceptual experience and so it will always contain concepts and not allow for a non-circular account (cf. Brewer 1999, p. 181).

Another objection that falls under the first type of the Argument from Concept Acquisition tries to take the conceptualist position to an extreme conclusion: conceptualists are taken to hold that concepts and conceptual capacities are innate. Adina Roskies and Hannah Ginsborg each develop versions of this argument.

Roskies starts from the claim that learning a concept consists in "forming a stable association between a mental representation and some perceptual quality or range of qualities" (Roskies 2010, p. 115).[128] This process must also involve the subject becoming aware of the concept, since she will be able to actively use the concept in thought. Roskies suggests that the conceptualist might try to explain the awareness of the subject by holding that the content of the newly acquired concept consists in other concepts. But she quickly rejects that notion by arguing

---

128 I will ignore any issues related to the question whether Roskies and McDowell and Brewer even share the same notion of concepts, e.g. on Byrne's and Peacocke's distinction that I have introduced in Section 2.2.

that it does not make sense to suppose that concepts are compositional (Roskies 2010, p. 116). The only alternative for the conceptualist is to claim that observational concepts are innate. Compared to such a result, Roskies thinks that non-conceptualist theories are much more "plausible" (Roskies 2010, p. 116).[129]

Obviously McDowell and other conceptualists would not accept Roskies's argument. Let us focus on what one could respond on McDowell's theory. One could say that innateness is not the only option for conceptualism. McDowell offers an alternative: human beings acquire concepts by being initiated into a language community. This acquisition is part of the larger process of developing a second nature – the process of *Bildung*. Language learning opens the way into the space of reasons, because in learning a language a subject learns rational connections (cf. McDowell 1996, p. 126, but also Ginsborg 2006c, pp. 81f.). If one emphasizes the community aspect of being initiated into a language community, one also gets McDowell's second claim about acquisition of conceptual capacities: conceptual capacities are acquired "by being initiated into a social practice" (McDowell 2009f, p. 287). The conceptualist thus does not have to say that conceptual capacities are innate, but instead can refer to their being acquired by learning a language and "being initiated into a social practice" (McDowell 2009f, p. 287). In addition, we might put forward another argument against Roskies's conclusion that is McDowellian in spirit: concepts do form a network of concepts and so there is no one single starting point for the acquisition of concepts. It is more like a gradual process in which there is no one single stage in which we move from 'no-concepts' to 'concepts'.[130] Given the network-like nature of concepts we might maintain that a non-circular approach would not capture the nature of concept acquisition.[131]

Hannah Ginsborg, however, tries to construct another innateness objection from the second McDowellian response that I have just introduced. She suggests that emphasizing the role of language learning for concept acquisition and acquisition of rational connections still requires that a subject sees an object *as* green if it is to acquire the concept *green* from confrontation with that object. For otherwise we could not explain why the subject does not acquire the concept *grue* rather than *green*. Ginsborg suggests that McDowell might argue against

---

129 For an extended version of the "learning argument" see (Roskies 2008).

130 Cf. "The topography of the space of reasons is encapsulated in the content of concepts. And one does not acquire first one concept, then a second, and so forth. There must be several concepts if there are any. In Wittgenstein's image: 'Light dawns gradually over the whole' (On Certainty §141)" (McDowell 2009k, p. 168).

131 For empirical support for the connection between conceptual development and language, see (Carey 2009; Carey 2011a). I will introduce Carey's considerations in Section 9.2.

these claims by saying that learning the concept *green* simply actualizes an innate potentiality for possessing the concept *green* (Ginsborg 2006c, p. 83). But she thinks that this reaction conflicts with McDowell's insistence that there is a standing obligation to critically reflect one's concepts and one's concept use. If concept acquisition was only the actualization of an innate potential, then one could not reflect and change one's concepts.

Yet Ginsborg admits that there is an easy response for McDowell. He could say that concepts could be criticized using other concepts from the network of concepts (Ginsborg 2006c, p. 84). But that easy response prompts another objection: Such a model of concepts and concept acquisition would be coherentist and it would not explain how children can acquire empirical concepts (Ginsborg 2006c, pp. 86 f.). Again Ginsborg is well aware what McDowell would respond to this objection; he would reject the coherentism-objection because it is based on a sideways-on view (Ginsborg 2006c, pp. 87 f.). Such a view is fundamentally wrong: we can only raise questions about concept acquisition in those contexts in which concept possession is presupposed (Section 1.1; McDowell 1996, pp. 35 f.). Ginsborg's coherentism-objection presupposes that the conceptual is *not* unbounded, that there is something outside the conceptual, and that children who do not yet possess concepts are taken to live in this space. Since McDowell shows that the conceptual is unbounded this objection, too, fails.

Ginsborg rejects this response, but note that her rejection is not based on the response itself, but rather based on a problem with the context in which McDowell's claims occur. McDowell thinks that his remarks on the nature of concepts and conceptual capacities are part of his corrections of Sellars's interpretation of Kant (McDowell 2009e; McDowell 2009g; McDowell 2009i). But Ginsborg shows that McDowell's Kant interpretation does not concern the same question as Sellars's Kant interpretation. Sellars's question is "Why does the perceiver *conceptually represent* a red (blue, etc.) rectangular (circular, etc.) object in the presence of an object having these qualities?" (Sellars 1968, p. 18, emphasis in original). McDowell's question is that of the possibility of objective purport. His response might be acceptable for that question, but it certainly is not acceptable for Sellars's question. Ginsborg concludes that Sellars's question results in the following obstacle for McDowell's language learning-response:

A child cannot acquire the relevant conceptual capacities, even with training in the use of language, unless there is something given to her in sensation which she can recognize as correlating with the use of the words she is learning, and which thus serves as a cue or guide to the appropriate use of those words. (Ginsborg 2006c, p. 89)

But there are two reasons why Ginsborg's argument is not successful. As Ginsborg rightly notes McDowell and Sellars approach different questions and McDowell's question which asks for objective purport is more fundamental than Sellars's. Thus we may conjecture that Sellars's question is secondary and really does not concern McDowell's project. In other words, Sellars's question does not make sense without presupposing that McDowell's question has been answered.[132] Moreover, Ginsborg's argument is still based on the assumption that we can give a straightforward, non-circular account of the acquisition of conceptual capacities that has different stages which are clearly demarcated and that there is something like a starting point for when children really possess conceptual capacities. As I said above it is not clear why we need such a non-circular account, let alone whether it is feasible.

One can summarize the responses to the Argument from Concept Acquisition as follows: Regarding worries about how concepts are acquired on the conceptualist account, conceptualists can give a story of acquisition. The story might be circular, but as McDowell and Brewer show any acceptable account of concept possession and thus any account of concept acquisition will have to be circular. This finding leads to a crucial, general criticial question about the argument and the responses: Is the identification of circularity ever a decisive argument against a conceptualist theory? Here one can adapt Brewer's remarks on causal explanations and constitutive explanations (Brewer 2005, p. 222) and distinguish two kinds of circularity, *causal* circularity and *constitutive* circularity. Causal circularity would be a circularity in causal dependences; constitutive circularity would, e.g. find a constitutive property both in the explanans and the explanandum.[133] In the present case that would mean that concepts figure both in the perceptual experience itself and in the conceptual capacities that are acquired from perceptual experience. Causal circularity would be problematic, while constitutive circularity can be justified, e.g. if one examines a transcendental question, as do McDowell, Brewer and other conceptualists.[134] A transcendental approach would be more likely to face the circularity charge than naturalist theories, but its circularity is likely to be constitutive circularity rather than causal circu-

---

132 This response applies the insights of Conant's diagnosis of the skeptical theories. I will introduce the diagnosis in Section 2.7.

133 For explanations of causal explanation and constitutive explanation see (Kuorikoski 2008).

134 E.g. Kern (2006) and Rödl (2010).

larity. Again, we need to link back the theories' claims about, in this case, circularity to their overall aim and context in order to judge the case.[135]

2.5 Reviewing the Argument from Memory Experience

The *Argument from Memory Experience* is most prominently articulated by Mike Martin in his article "Perception, Concepts, and Memory" (Martin 1992). The idea of his argument is to show that perception is not like belief – as Martin thinks one would have to suppose on a conceptualist conception – by looking at the relation between perception, belief and memory.[136]

Martin starts from the uncontroversial observation that perceptions give rise to belief and to memory. If one says that a content is conceptual, that means that it has "a significant structure" (Martin 1992, p. 746) which is determined by the abilities of the thinker who has the belief. So, accordingly the conceptualist – as Martin construes him – has to hold that if "it appears to [a subject] as if *p* [, then the subject] possesses those concepts necessary for believing that *p*" (Martin 1992, p. 747). More importantly, "experience is conceptual in the way that belief is, if [this conceptualist claim] holds for all propositions *p* such that it can appear to one as if *p*" (Martin 1992, p. 747).

I will introduce the following example in order to bring the relation between perception and memory into focus.[137] It is perfectly normal that in a given situation a subject fails to notice an object in a scene that she perceives, e. g. I go into the office of a colleague, talk to her for a while. I might not have noticed the new book on the table and so I will be unable to form the belief that there is a new book on my colleague's table. There are two possible conclusions to draw from this example:

(a) I have experienced the book, even if I did not notice it and am unable to form a belief about it ("belief-independent view of experience", Martin 1992, p. 749).

---

135 For an account of non-vicious circularity in a theory of personal identity see (Gunnarsson 2010, pp. 43 ff.). Gunnarsson argues that two concepts explaining each other is a case of non-vicious circularity if each concept can be partly understood without the other concept.

136 Charles Travis also puts forward an argument against McDowell that may be conceived as an Argument from Memory Experience; I will call it the Argument from New Concepts for Past Experience. But since this argument is issued in another context, namely the context of the debate between Travis's relationist conception and McDowell's conceptualist representationalist conception, I will not discuss it here but later in Section 5.4.

137 For Martin's original example, see (Martin 1992, pp. 749 f.).

(b) I have not experienced the book, because I am unable to form a belief about the book ("belief-impinging view of experience", Martin 1992, p. 753).

Martin wants to offer "mental and experiential evidence" (Martin 1992, p. 749) for the *belief-independent view of experience*. According to this view, experience is that which can be noticed, but is not necessarily actually noticed (cf. Martin 1992, p. 749).

The idea is this: in memory experience, a subject can recall a certain experience and this recalling is generally independent of the subject's beliefs at the time of the original experience, so experience cannot be conceptual. The link between experience and memory experience is no coincidence: for example, memories "inherit whatever authority they have from being the traces of past perceptions of how things were" (Martin 1992, p. 752). And memory experience can also change a subject's beliefs, e. g. if I think back to me talking to my colleague I may form the belief that there was a new book on her table. So "[m]emory experience can ... be a source of evidence about how things were experienced independently of what the subject then believed" (Martin 1992, p. 753). Of course, memory is defeasible, but still the point holds that the belief-independent view gives a good explanation of the connection between experience and memory.

The belief-independent view entails the rejection of what Martin regards as the conceptualist claim, namely that "the content of one's experience must be constrained by what concepts one then has" (Martin 1992, p. 753). It becomes clear that one should reject conceptualism if one realizes that the content of memory experience "can be determined independently of which concepts the subject had at the time of perceiving" (Martin 1992, p. 754). Of course, later improvements of one's conceptual capacities change one's memories, but that does not show that the perceptual experience itself is restricted by concepts.

Martin introduces the following example to make the case against conceptualism:

> Suppose Mary is a keen board-games player, and often plays a game involving unusual dice. Once such game involves the use of a twelve-faced die [a dodecahedron, N.E.] and an eight-faced die. ... Mary does not have the concept of the dodecahedron. Although she discerns a difference between the twelve-faced die and the eight-faced one in the context of the game, the difference she focuses on concerns color spots and shape; both dice are just many-shaped to her. As things stand, she would treat any many-shaped die as being of the same type as the dodecahedral one if it had the same number of color spots on its faces, and would not take any other object that was dodecahedral to have anything significantly in common with the dodecahedral die other than being many-shaped, a quality it would also share with the octahedral one. Hence she employs no concept that

picks out all and only dodecahedra: here we have an example of someone who fails to have a concept that she might otherwise apply to observed shapes.

There is no difficulty in supposing that Mary can acquire the concept of a dodecahedron, nor that in acquiring the concept she can come to apply it to objects of a distinctive visual appearance: a regular dodecahedron has twelve faces each with five sides. Now imagine that Mary has acquired the concept but not yet gone back to playing her game. She happens to think back to the last time she played the game and recalls her best move, which involved throwing one of the dice. She suddenly realizes that the die she then threw was in fact a dodecahedron.[138] (Martin 1992, pp. 754f., footnote added, N.E.)

Martin argues that the "judgment that [Mary] threw a twelve-faced die" (Martin 1992, p. 756) can be taken to be appropriate to her past experience, even though Mary did *not* possess the concept at the time of the experience. Saying that perceptual experience is conceptual thus in effect contains not more than an "arbitrary restriction on the way things can be experienced" (Martin 1992, p. 756).

Martin considers an explanation that a conceptualist might give in response to his example and observation.[139] The conceptualist could offer the following justification for such a restriction: experience can only present the world as being a certain way if the experiencing subject can *understand* what that way is. If a subject S has a perceptual experience with content C rather than content D, then there must be a difference between C and D that S must be able to grasp. The difference must lie in something which the subject can "appreciate as being the case" (Martin 1992, p. 756). Being able to "appreciate [something, N.E.] as being the case" (Martin 1992, p. 756) entails that the subject must possess the requisite concepts for such appreciation and so experience must be conceptual. But Martin objects that this explanation presupposes that the subject must be aware of the difference between C and D at the moment of having the perceptual experience with the content C. It is not clear why this has to be the case or, why on a non-conceptualist model the subject should be unable to perceive that difference.

In response the conceptualist can still insist that recognizing the difference between two experiences at least requires the possession of recognitional capacities for recognizing the relevant differences. If she did not possess the relevant recognitional capacities, then the subject could not perceive the difference, because she could not perceive the relevant features which constitute the difference. But Martin rejects this argument because it presupposes that experience

---

138 Note that this element will figure in Travis's Argument from New Concepts for Past Experience.

139 The response is based on a conceptualist theory that Peacocke once held (Peacocke 1983).

must include noticing, i.e. that the belief-impinging view is correct. In addition, it confuses experience as making a recognitional capacity available and experience as making the exercise of a recognitional capacity possible (Martin 1992, p. 757). If experience without noticing is possible, as the memory-example suggests, then no conceptual capacities, including recognitional capacities, are required for perceptual experience. Moreover, the conceptualist argument would also entail accepting that Mary might be unable to make out differences in, say, hue if she did not possess the particular color concepts. This seems to be counterintuitive: we can distinguish two color hues, say, crimson and scarlet, even though we do not possess the two color concepts.

Martin regards the fine-grainedness of experience, which I will discuss in the next section, as additional indication for the claim that conceptualism is wrong: a subject will never have all recognitional capacities for all the ways that experiences can differ. Conceptualists usually try to circumvent this problem by saying that the experiencing subject can refer to the different features and elements in experience by demonstrative concepts or "demonstrative thought" (Martin 1992, p. 759). But this response fails because it does not show that the recognitional capacity is at work during experience, rather than only after the experience. What the non-conceptualist disputes is not that a subject can acquire concepts based on experience, but rather that concepts are necessary to *have* a particular experience. And so Martin sums up: concepts and cognition are only relevant for "how one reacts to the world" (Martin 1992, p. 761) and for one's means-end-rationalizations etc. "Perception and experience [however, N.E.] ... are a matter of the world making itself apparent to us" (Martin 1992, p. 761) and not a matter of a subject's abilities in thinking about and reasoning with the perceptual and experiential content. Martin's argument is taken to show that "[w]hat can be perceptually apparent to a perceiver is not limited solely to what she can reason about" (Martin 1992, p. 759). He eventually concludes: "one cannot satisfactorily account for how things appear to a perceiver solely in terms of conceptual content, that content that figures in one's reasoning" (Martin 1992, p. 763).

It is interesting to note that none of the philosophers involved in the conceptualism-non-conceptualism debate really responds to the Argument from Memory. James Genone is a rare exception (Genone 2006). Genone offers two possible conceptualist responses to these two arguments: The conceptualist could argue that the simple concepts that Mary originally applied to her experience of the die are concepts that constitute the concept *dodecahedra* and thereby explain the relation between the sophisticated concept *dodecahedra* and simpler recognitional capacities (Genone 2006, pp. 97 f.). She could also insist that Mary did possess and actualize demonstrative concepts in her perceptual experience of the twelve-faced die (Genone 2006, p. 98).

I do not think that these responses would satisfy Martin, as they still leave his main problem unanswered: if Mary applies a newly acquired concept in her memory of her perceptual experience, the conceptualist will have to grant that the same concept can also be applied to her actual perceptual experience that took place at t_{-1}.[140] In fact we might even be forced to confront a radical interpretation of Martin's argument that seems to worsen the case for conceptualism: Martin might be taken to suggest that even though Mary does not possess any concepts at all, she could still have the particular experience that she has and she could still remember her past experience. After having acquired the appropriate concepts she could simply apply those to her past experience.

Here we have reached what looks like another dead-end in the debate between conceptualists and non-conceptualists. The only possible conceptualist response seems to consist in rejecting the example as incoherent; she does not understand how Mary could have her particular experience without possessing concepts and conceptual capacities. But I think that the radical interpretation of Martin's argument does turn out helpful if we keep in view the insights from the overview of conceptions and aims of conceptualists and non-conceptualists (Section 2.2). At the end of the section I wanted to keep in mind the differences in aims of conceptualist and non-conceptualist theories and so here we have to mark out the following difference: Martin's argumentation is largely phenomenological, but all conceptualist theories that we have discussed so far are firmly based *on transcendental considerations*.[141] *That* is why Martin's radical example is not coherent to the eyes of the conceptualist: there could be no perceptual experience of the world in the first place if we did not explain how perceptual experience can have empirical content. And so in his objection Martin uses a notion that he cannot avail himself of. We can also put the point in terms of the following image: The Argument from Memory Experience starts too far down the stream that is called *Empirical content* and does not see that conceptualism really is concerned the source of the stream. Martin does not understand the motives of conceptualism: conceptualism is not interested in a theory of perceptual experience, but in a theory of epistemically significant empirical content.

I think that we can also further question certain assumptions that underlie Martin's criticism. First, it is not at all clear why a conceptualist has to assume

---

140 "The concept of a dodecahedron is still applicable to how she remembers things as being, and so to how things appeared before she had the concept" (Martin 1992, pp. 754f.).
141 Noë's case is interesting because he argues phenomenologically (Noë 2004, p. 33) *and* transcendentally (Noë 2004, p. 187).

that the same concepts have to be actualized in perceptual experience and in the memory of the perceptual experience.[142] I will say more about this point in the development of relational conceptualism (Chapter 7). Moreover, Martin's suggestion that on a conceptualist theory Mary could not see a central element that is to be found in the perceived scene if she did not possess the relevant concept presupposes what I will call *completeness* of concepts in perception. He seems to presuppose that all possible concepts that can be applied to the scene have to be applied and included in perception and also that concept application cannot be corrected upon new knowledge. It is not clear why a conceptualist has to accept these two presuppositions. I will come back to these two conditions in Section 7.3; there I will argue that conceptualism does not have to subscribe to the Completeness Requirement nor to the Correctness Requirement.

2.6 A Close Reading Analysis of the Argument from Fineness of Grain

The Argument from Fineness of Grain

In this section I will offer a close reading of the Argument from Fineness of Grain since understanding the conceptualist answers to the Argument will provide important material for developing relational conceptualism. The basic idea guiding the so-called *Argument from Fineness of Grain* is that experience is so fine-grained that concepts, which are in their very nature general, can never capture all the grains of the experience.[143] This seems quite obvious. Look, for instance,

---

142 Martin's implicit assumption seems to be something like the equivalent of the *Dependency Thesis* which he puts forward in his criticism of intentionalism, i.e. views that argue that perceptual experience has intentional, representational content. The Dependency Thesis concerns the nature of visualizing and it claims that "[t]o imagine sensorily a φ is to imagine experiencing a φ" (Martin 2002, p. 404). In other words, if I imagine an apple, then I imagine how the apple would look. There are thus two components in the visualizing: the object of visualizing and the object of vision. So if I visualize an apple, then I visualize the apple as it would look if I would perceive it veridically. In a similar way memory of perceptual experience is apparently supposed to be composed by two components: the object of memory and the actual state of perceptual experience. This claim is certainly contestable. For criticism of Martin's Dependency Thesis, see e.g. (Burge 2005).

143 The *Argument from Fineness of Grain* is also sometimes construed as an Argument from the *Richness of Experience*, cf. (Bermúdez 2009, p. 460). I will not consider this difference here as I take these arguments to be conceptually related and thus the argumentation would only have to

at our color experience: we can discriminate much more color shades than we have color concepts. In the light of these considerations perceptual experience cannot be fully conceptual[144] (Evans 1982, Peacocke 1992, Peacocke 2001a, Heck 2000, Heck 2007).

The standard response of conceptualists is to say that conceptualism can after all acknowledge the fine-grainedness of experience namely with the help of demonstrative concepts. We do not have color concepts for all the color shades that we can perceive, but we can grasp them with demonstrative concepts like *that shade* when referring to the color of a shirt. These demonstrative concepts are perceptual demonstrative concepts which are made available by a particular experience.

This response has again been attacked in a number of ways. Richard Heck says that demonstrative concepts cannot be part of the content of experience, because that precludes any substantive claims about how the referent of the concept should be fixed (Heck 2000, pp. 493 f.). On McDowell's conception the referent of a demonstrative color concept is supposed to be fixed by a sample of the color in the world, so the demonstrative concept *that color* would have to refer to the color that a particular object really has. According to Heck, however, this conception cannot deal with cases of misperception (Heck 2000, p. 494). If the perceiving subject Eliza perceives the color of the scarf as green, when in fact it is blue, a judgment in which her demonstrative concept appears would be wrong. Heck's example is this: Consider a subject who says "*That* part of my desk is *that* color" (Heck 2000, p. 494), but she misperceives the color of the desk. In this case the content of the judgment and the content of her experience would not be identical, because the experience would not represent the desk as being *that color*$_{veridical}$ but as *that color*$_{misperceived}$. So Heck concludes that conceptualist demonstrative concepts are not apt for capturing the content of experience.

The problem of conceptualism here lies in the reference-fixation for demonstrative concepts: if conceptualists want to say that the reference of a demonstrative concept is fixed by samples in the world, then they cannot deal with cases of misperception. If they want to say that the reference of a demonstrative concept is fixed by the content of experience, then they run into a circularity objection: the reference of a demonstrative concept cannot be fixed by the content of expe-

---

be modified slightly to fit an *Argument from Richness of Experience*. For an account that separates the two arguments see (Lauer 2014).

144 Actually two observations lie behind this apparent incongruence between concepts and perception. First, experience is too fine-grained for concepts to capture all the grains. Second, concepts are too general to capture the grains of experience.

rience, because the self-same concepts are supposed to figure at the level of experiential content.

It looks as if this is a heavy blow for the conceptualist position. José L. Bermúdez (Bermúdez/Cahen 2015) further adds to the problems for conceptualists: their demonstrative-concepts-move is only a *response* to the Argument from Fineness of Grain and so even if the move turns out successful, conceptualists will not have shown that the conceptualist theory itself is correct. Much more is needed to substantiate the conceptualist theory itself. So even if the Argument from Fineness of Grain is rejected by means of demonstrative concepts, one must not forget that their inclusion in the theory is only a by-product of a response to an objection.

Peacocke has also brought forward a version of the Argument from the Fineness of Grain: he tries to show that demonstrative concepts are too fine for capturing the particular degree of fine-grainedness of a particular experience (Peacocke 1998, pp. 381f.; Peacocke 2001b, pp. 609f.). One can illustrate his point with the following situation: Eliza and Tom both perceive a scarlet scarf. Tom possesses the concept *scarlet*, Eliza does not possess the concept *scarlet*. Now the idea is this: even if Eliza does not possess the concept *scarlet*, the representational content of her experience and Tom's experience will still have common elements, because both perceive the same finely-sliced shade. These shared elements cannot be captured by demonstrative concepts, conceived as supplemented demonstrative concepts, i.e. demonstrative concepts that contain general concepts, because there can be a number of very different supplemented demonstrative concepts in the content of one experience. The supplemented demonstrative concepts slice too thinly: they offer a number of concepts that might capture the experiential content, but they do not capture this one common element in Tom's and Eliza's experience (Peacocke 1998, p. 382; Peacocke 2001b, pp. 609f.).

Peacocke originally introduces his objection by pointing out that McDowell's solution leads to "overascription" (Peacocke 1998, p. 382). McDowell is already wrong in thinking that the phenomenology of experience can be captured by demonstrative concepts included in the experience, because demonstrative concepts slice too finely.[145] An experience of a shade of red that includes demonstrative concepts might well include demonstrative concepts like "that shade", "that red" or "that scarlet". Very different conceptual contents would thus figure in a given representational content of a certain experience and why should any of the

---

[145] Note that this conclusion is the exact opposite of Sean Kelly's criticism of demonstrative concepts. Cf. (Kelly 2001a; Kelly 2001b).

demonstrative conceptual contents be favored for capturing the fine-grained content? To say that the content of perception is fully conceptual therefore implies overascription (Peacocke 1998, p. 382). In other words, to ascribe concepts to the content of experience is to equip the content of perception with too many concepts. McDowell could not reply that we should simply pick the most specific demonstrative concept in the repertoire, because that would mean that for two persons the experience of one object would differ at the finest-grained level. According to Peacocke, the whole conception is wrong; the correct view sees that one single shape makes various demonstrative concepts available to different people. Again, demonstrative concepts cannot capture this common fine-grained experiential content made available by the shape perceived (Peacocke 2001b, p. 610). This fine-grained content could be captured by unsupplemented, i.e. non-conceptual, demonstratives:

> For each fine-grained property, relation or magnitude given in perception, the anti-conceptualist should hold that there is some nonconceptual way in which it is given. An unsupplemented perceptual-demonstrative 'that' made available to a thinker because he perceives something in a given nonconceptual way. (Peacocke 2001b, p. 610)

It is clear that the different versions of the Argument from Fineness of Grain put pressure on the conceptualist position. So what are conceptualist responses to the non-conceptualist observations?

Conceptualist responses to the Argument from Fineness of Grain

The Argument from Fineness of Grain voices a very widespread concern about conceptualism and so all conceptualists introduced until now offer responses to the Argument. As I have said, the standard move of conceptualists, including McDowell and Brewer, is to introduce demonstrative concepts into perceptual content. But as we have also seen, this response is far from convincing. Marcus Willaschek has tried to avoid these problems and we will look at his response later. But before that let's look at McDowell's, Brewer's and Noë's responses to the Argument.

McDowell's response to the repeated criticism is to continue to refer to demonstrative concepts in perceptual experience.

> [T]his picture of an ordinary conceptual repertoire, as too coarse-grained to capture all the content of experience, ignores the fact that we can credit even ordinary subjects of experience with conceptual capacities that are exactly as fine-grained as necessary, because they are expressible with the help of demonstratives. Demonstratives used in the relevant way

make how things figure in experience itself, with all its fineness of grain, partly constitutive of the expressive resources of the language. (McDowell 1998d, p. 414)

In response to Peacocke's objection that demonstrative content slices too finely McDowell amends the formulations that he has been using in *Mind and World*: instead of talking of an object having *that color* he suggests that we should talk of an object being colored *thus*. Eliza and Tom might perceive the scarlet scarf differently, but this difference is captured by saying that they both perceive it as being colored *thus*. In their experience different conceptual capacities are actualized even though they are both expressed by the term 'colored *thus*'. 'Colored *thus*' is constituted by the linguistic expression and by the shade itself (cf. McDowell 1998d, p. 415) and further formulations can be carved out from this basic thought. This amendment is also a response to Heck's problem of misperception – even though McDowell does not actually put it as a response to Heck – since 'colored *thus*' allows for the subject to mis-perceive the color of the desk.

Brewer offers a similar solution to Heck's problem of misperception and this solution is really offered as a response to Heck: Brewer refers back to Evans's idea that successful demonstrative reference to an object depends on the subject's ability to "keep track of the object in question over time" (Brewer 2005, p. 223) and adapting her attitudes to any possible changes that might occur. If the subject was unable to do that, her demonstrative judgments could turn out wrong. In the same vein, there are tracking conditions on the successful demonstrative reference to a color shade of an object in the subject's view. Mistakes are possible on this account and in those case the subject simply does not possess the relevant demonstrative color concept.[146]

---

146 Brewer furthermore responds to other objections against demonstrative concepts by Heck and Peacocke. Remember that Heck appeals to the intuition that the experience of a color sample explains the possession of demonstrative concepts, and so the content of experience could not contain the relevant demonstrative concepts. To this Brewer replies that we need to distinguish between causal explanation and constitutive explanation: experience does explain the possession of demonstrative concepts, not in a causal way – as Heck assumes – but in a constitutive way. The demonstrative color-shade concept is a *constituent* of the experience of the color-shade (Brewer 2005, p. 222).

Regarding the objection from the problem of reference fixation Brewer replies that this is not the only possible "account of what fixes the semantic value of demonstrative concepts" (Brewer 2005, p. 222). Instead the conceptualist could offer the following alternative. *That (x) shade* "is a concept of the fine grained color of [(x)] in virtue of the fact that the subject's attitudes towards contents containing it are suitably sensitive *that color itself*, where this sensitivity in large part depends upon his normal neurophysiological perceptual processing" (Brewer 2005, p. 222).

In his response to Peacocke's observations concerning the success of demonstrative refer-

Noë's enactivist response to the Argument from Fineness of Grain

Noë again provides conceptualist responses to the Argument from Fineness of Grain that differ from McDowell and Brewer. Yet his responses deserve proper attention since they allow for promising developments of the conceptualist account. Noë agrees with the non-conceptualist observation that, for example, we do not have concepts of all shades in the same way that we have concepts of hue categories, but he argues that this fact does not harm conceptualist claims like 'One can "embrace shades of colour within one's conceptual thinking" (McDowell 1996, p. 56).' There are several reasons for that.

First, the Argument from Fineness of Grain is based on the tacit assumption that conceptualists think that every perceiver possesses something like a "perceptual lexicon" (Noë 2004, p. 191), which allows the perceiver to possess concepts of all perceptible features. But conceptualists would not subscribe to such a strong assumption. They would also not hold that a perceiver has names for every perceptible feature. Noë shows that such an assumption would be wrong by referring to the case of visual experience of a face: the perceiver does not have conceptual knowledge of every perceptible feature of the face, but she can still grasp those qualities in thought (e.g. a smile), because those features can simply be thought of as features a face might have.

Second, and more fundamentally, Noë rejects the very idea of richness and the 'wealth' of perceptual experience. He points out that perceptual experience does not represent a scene in far more detail "than any characterization I could hope to formulate" (Heck 2000, p. 490). Phenomena like change blindness[147] and inattentional blindness[148] show that the basic conception of perception employed in the Argument from the Fineness of Grain is mistaken: "the world is present to me now not as represented but as accessible" (Noë 2004, p. 192).

---

ence Brewer again insists on the possibility of successful demonstrative reference. Peacocke offers an alternative account of how demonstrative references can be sure to refer to the object. According to him, we need to combine the non-conceptual *way* in which the relevant shade is presented in experience and the bare demonstrative element "that", to ensure that the demonstrative concept does not fail to refer (see Peacocke 2001b, p. 610). Brewer rejects this proposal and stresses that the demonstrative reference is successful because it is made up of the demonstrative element and the subject's attention towards the shade which is a neurophysiologically enabled relation.

147 Change blindness refers to cases in which a subject does not see changes to the scene that she perceives.

148 Inattentional blindness refers to cases in which a subject does not see changes to the scene that she perceives because her attention is distracted.

The non-conceptualist critic might want to insist that if the perceiver does not have names for the content of her perception, then she does not have descriptive or conceptual resources to capture the qualities that we can perceive. Noë however replies that the conception of experience of the non-conceptualist critic is still wrong: As we have seen above (Section 1.4), Noë holds that visual content is virtual all the way out and that means that things are given indeterminately and also not in the blink of an eye (Noë 2004, p. 193). The perceiver's inability to characterize what she sees determinately does not show that the perceiver lacks the relevant concepts, but only that experience is really indeterminate.

Let us look again at color experiences to understand Noë's point. As I have said Noë admits that it is true that we do not have a unique name for every shade of color, but he does not think that this tells against conceptualism. Since colors are part of a structurally uniform system, we can conceptualize any shade via "color-concept-formulae" (Noë 2004, p. 194), e.g. *dark red*. This does not just hold for colors, but also extends more generally: Conceptual capacities "can be extended … formulaically to every novel perceptual quality that we encounter" (Noë 2004, p. 195). So in a way there are no entirely new experiences, because no experience requires utterly new conceptual devices to conceptualize it. Noë further illustrates this feature of concepts in perception by outlining an analogy to numbers in mathematics: there are infinitely many natural numbers; we do not have concepts for every single one of them, but we have the formula to extend our existing concepts to every possible natural number. Our grasp of concepts is just that formulaic. We have the conceptual means to capture any shade in color space (Noë 2004, pp. 195 f.).

The issue of re-identifiability of concepts seems to cause some problems, since for perceptual demonstrative concepts it is possible that one is only in possession of a concept in the presence of an instance of that concept and thus one would be unable to re-identify it. But Noë insists that even in those cases one still did have a concept in the presence of the instance. He compares color shade concepts to computational problems: in nondeterministic polynomial problems one can go through the problem once one has a correct answer, but there is no general algorithmic solution for it (Noë 2004, pp. 197 f.). Something similar holds for color shades: in the presence of their correct instances, they obviously apply, but without the correct instances one cannot know whether they apply. This is simply part of the nature of those special concepts: they are not used without the sample. But this characteristic does not tell against the conceptuality of perception (Noë 2004, pp. 197 f.).

The idea of "color-concept-formulae" and the extendability of concepts indeed is very attractive – and I will make use of it later – but it also raises questions about how these formulae and extensions are generated. In particular, it might bring the Argument from Hyper-Intellectualization back into focus: Noë's notion of concept-formulae seems to be a clear case of over-intellectualization, especially for the Burgean version of the Argument from Hyper-Intellectualization. But the question about the generation of the formulae and extensions and the Argument from Hyper-Intellectualization can both be answered by one response. The key notion on Noë's conception are sensorimotor skills. They "are the basis of our possession of the sort of recognitional capacities we draw on when we, as McDowell suggested, deploy perceptual demonstrative concepts to *make sense* of perceptual qualities" (Noë 2004, p. 199, emphasis in original). Our grasp of sensorimotor regularities and rules allows us to understand how aspects like color, shape etc. are going to vary if certain conditions like the position of the perceiver or the lighting conditions change. Having a grip on those changes and variations is "our grasp of what it is for something to be *presented* as cubical, or spherical" (Noë 2004, p. 198, emphasis in original), so our sensorimotor skills are necessary for us to "embrace perceptual qualities in thought" (Noë 2004, p. 199) and that means that they are conceptual.[149]

Because concepts are based on the fact that features and aspects of objects and properties are systematic, they and the recognitional capacities which are founded on them do appear in all types of experiences, even in novel experiences. In other words, sensorimotor skills and sensorimotor concepts constitute the possession of observational concepts.[150]

This response to the Argument from Hyper-Intellectualization thus reminds the critic of Noë's special take on the relation between sensorimotor skills and concepts. Conceptual capacities are based on sensorimotor skills that do not presuppose explicit understanding or a high level of intellect. I will return to Noë's responses to the Argument from Fineness of Grain since they help see space for developing and further explicating the conceptualist account of perceptual experience. At the same time I will try to not subscribe to Noë's emphasis on sensorimotor skills. But before I get to this endeavor I will look at Willaschek's response to the Argument from Fineness of Grain.

---

149 I will later separate the idea of color-concept-formulae from sensorimotor skills and use it to develop the conceptualist response to the Argument from Fineness of Grain (Section 2.6).
150 Note that some of the sensorimotor skills might well be subpersonal, but still they are conceptual, because their attribution is governed by considerations involving the holism and normativity that is natural to the space of the conceptual (cf. Noë 2004, p. 201).

Willaschek's response to the Argument from Fineness of Grain: the phenomenal component in perceptual experience

Marcus Willaschek's discussion of the Argument from the Fineness of Grain deserves attention, because Willaschek's theory is an interesting hybrid: Willaschek does not want to defend a non-conceptualist position, but he also does not think McDowell's response to the Argument from the Fineness of Grain is successful. Put crudely, he wants to establish a position between Peacocke and McDowell.

Peacocke thinks that the content of perception is *autonomous* intentional content, i.e. it is intentional content that does not presuppose concept possession. Willaschek is a conceptualist who thinks that the content of perception is not autonomous. "No perceptual experience, at least for adult human beings, without concepts"[151] (Willaschek 2003, p. 266). But Willaschek also does not want to be like McDowell – at least the McDowell of *Mind and World*[152]: He does not want to have to talk about demonstrative concepts. He takes the conception to be wrong-headed, because demonstrative concepts are not a type of concept, but rather a hybrid – they are general, because they are concepts, but they also contain something unique, because they contain a demonstrative reference (Willaschek 2003, p. 274).[153] As we have said, McDowell refers to demonstrative concepts in reply to the Argument from Fineness of Grain, but Willaschek thinks that McDowell's answer backfires. Willaschek's point is this: the non-conceptualist can interpret McDowell's reply to fit her own agenda. McDowell admits that we need demonstrative references to fully describe our perceptual intake and, according to the non-conceptualist, this clearly shows that the content of perception cannot be fully grasped by concepts, i.e. it shows that perception is indeed non-conceptual.

According to Willaschek, McDowell cannot avoid this conclusion since he ignores that there is a special quality to experiencing the object of perception that can only be referred to by demonstrative reference. We cannot refer to it in any other way because the quality does not exist independently from experience. This quality, a phenomenal quality, cannot be expressed in a general description: we have to accept that experience has a phenomenal component that is integral to the content of experience. This phenomenal component requires de-

---

151 "Keine Wahrnehmung, jedenfalls bei erwachsenen Menschen, ohne Begriffe" (Willaschek 2003, p. 266). All translations of Willaschek's text are mine.
152 Of course, there is no mention of "Avoiding the Myth of the Given", because Willaschek's book was published before the latter.
153 Cf. also (Kelly 2001a). Kelly holds that demonstrative concepts are like chimeras because they have a singular term as a body and a general concept as a head.

monstrative reference. Note that this does not mean that experience has non-conceptual content.

Willaschek argues that he can avoid the non-conceptualist consequence by offering a theory which avoids McDowell's mistakes and the mistakes of Peacocke's theory: the content of perception is not fully conceptual, but it is also not non-conceptual: it is phenomenal and conceptual (Willaschek 2003, p. 275). "Perceptual experiences are conceptually articulated phenomenal experiences"[154] (Willaschek 2003, p. 278).

This new theory by Willaschek retains three elements from McDowell's theory. First, there is no perception without concepts. Remember from Section 2.2 that Willaschek conceives of concepts as analogues to predicates: the role of concepts in judgments, beliefs and other propositional attitudes is analogous to the role of predicates in declarative sentences. Possessing a concept F means that one is able to see that a is F, i.e. one knows what it is for something to fall under F and one knows what those things that fall under F have in common (cf. Willaschek 2003, p. 267). In a footnote he adds:

> To me the crucial difference between human and animal in this respect seems to lie in the fact that the exercise of conceptual capacities – in the more narrow sense in which only humans possess them – is bound up with participation in a norm-governed practice of giving and taking reasons and justifications. Our perceptual experiences accordingly therefore are different from those of non-conceptual beings, because it is essential to the contents of our experience that they can serve as justifications of beliefs.[155] (Willaschek 2003, p. 280)

The second commonality between McDowell and Williaschek is in line with this description of the role of conceptual capacities in human perceptual experience: experience and justification are essentially linked. Willaschek explains: "Beliefs grounded in perceptual experience normally depend *causally* on reality in such a way that they do justice to the *normative* demand of epistemic correctness"[156] (Willaschek 2003, p. 264, emphasis in original).

---

154 "Wahrnehmungen sind begrifflich artikulierte phänomenale Erfahrungen" (Willaschek 2003, p. 278).

155 "Der entscheidende Unterschied zwischen Mensch und Tier scheint mir in dieser Hinsicht darin zu liegen, daß die Ausübung begrifflicher Fähigkeiten im engeren Sinn, wie nur Menschen sie haben, an die Teilnahme an einer normgeleiteten Praxis des Gebens und Nehmens von Gründen und Rechtfertigungen gebunden ist. Unsere Wahrnehmungen unterscheiden sich von denen begriffsloser Wesen demnach deshalb, weil es für die Inhalte unserer Wahrnehmung wesentlich ist, zur Begründung von Überzeugungen dienen zu können" (Willaschek 2003, p. 280).

156 "Auf Wahrnehmung beruhende Überzeugungen [hängen] normalerweise von der Wirklichkeit genauso *kausal* [ab], dass sie dem *normativen* Anspruch epistemischer Richtigkeit genügen" (Willaschek 2003, p. 264).

Perceptual judgments are subject to "epistemic correctness". "Epistemic correctness" is made up of two standards: (a) justification, i.e. a practice that can only be understood from within the community of people who give and understand justifications, (b) material truth, i.e. referring to (mind-)independent truth (Willaschek 2003, p. 263). Third, experience is passive and that means that the involvement of concepts is passive. The 'perceptual exercise' of a concept is not open to our rational control, because perceiving that the stick is bent is phenomenal experience and thus it is a passive process (Willaschek 2003, p. 278).[157]

Concepts are required for grasping phenomenal qualities, i.e. qualities that objects have if they evoke a certain phenomenal experience. Again: the whole process is passive, but still conceptual. The conceptual capacities involved in seeing that the stick is bent are not deliberately exercised. The passive reaction is part of a phenomenal experience, namely that the stick looks bent. The content of experience thus is conceptual and phenomenal.

Willaschek's theory might avoid McDowell's problem with the non-conceptualist Fineness of Grain argument, but it has its own problems. Let me briefly note two objections: First, Willaschek does not offer an answer to what we are to think of the connection between the conceptual and the phenomenal elements in perception – he just moves the problem to another stage: in *Mind and World* we want to know what the connection and the cooperation between receptivity and spontaneity looks like and in Willaschek's theory we want to know what the cooperation between conceptual and phenomenal is. Willaschek basically only introduces a third level, the *phenomenal*.

Second, Willaschek's examples, e.g. seeing the stick in the water to be bent, do not fit with the examples of the Fineness of Grain argument. The Fineness of Grain examples are about cases in which the subject does not possess the concepts required for the perceptual intake, but all of Willaschek's examples are cases in which the content is linguistically and conceptually expressible – without having to use demonstrative concepts. Maybe the difference between the ex-

---

157 "Die phänomenale Verwendung von Begriffen besteht dagegen in ihrer passiven, unserer unmittelbaren rationalen Verantwortung entzogenen Inanspruchnahme in der begrifflichen Artikulation des phänomenalen Aspekts der Wahrnehmung. Jemand, der den Begriff geknickt beherrscht, nimmt einen geraden Stab, der ins Wasser gehalten wird, als geknickt wahr. Seine begriffliche Fähigkeit, etwas als geknickt zu erkennen, kommt dabei ohne sein Zutun zur Anwendung. Wird der Stab nicht ins Wasser gehalten, gilt dasselbe für die Fähigkeit, gerade Gegenstände zu erkennen. Ausgelöst wird diese passive Reaktion aber als Teil einer phänomenalen Erfahrung – nämlich der, daß etwas geknickt (oder gerade) aussieht" (Willaschek 2003, p. 278).

amples is unintentional, but nevertheless one should note that Willaschek's examples are not helpful for responding to the Argument from Fineness of Grain.[158]

The problems in Willaschek's conception cannot be discussed further here[159], and his claims will still be relevant for us, because he, too, shares a conceptualist claim that will feature centrally in the relational conceptualist theory developed in this book. As I have said, Willaschek holds that there is no perceiving without concepts, and this crucial conceptualist claim is a fundamental tenet of the relational conceptualist position (Section 7.3).

---

158 Another problem concerns Willaschek's idea of the phenomenal aspect. It is not clear why the phenomenal aspect is not in a problematic way non-conceptual. Is it because non-conceptual means 'You don't have to possess concepts in order to have the particular sensory intake?' The real problem behind this question is that Willaschek does not explain what he means by 'phenomenal use of concepts in perception' (Willaschek 2003, p. 278) and how we are to conceive of passive experience. In fact, one may think that he cannot explain what he means by that because his claim that perception is conceptual only comes down to saying that perception requires concept possession and this type of conceptuality claim is not enough for explaining the passivity of experience. Talk of concept possession itself generally lays emphasis on the active side of concept possession, e. g. as in concept application in judgments. It is unclear where the passive element comes in. In addition, the only traces of an explanation of the passivity of concept application in Willaschek's theory actually lead to Peacocke's theory of concepts. See again:

"The perceptual application of the concept *bent* (in the perceptual experience that the stick *looks* bent) is withdrawn from our immediate control because the perceptual experience that something looks bent is a phenomenal experience [Erfahrung] and insofar a passive process. If the way that something looks ... is in this way conceptually 'articulated', the concepts are also *passively* in use. Since this form of concept application specifies how its environment perceptually *appears* to a perceiving subject, one can (in contrast to *doxastic* concept application in beliefs) speak of a *phenomenal* use of concepts in perceptual experience" (Willaschek 2003, pp. 277f., emphasis in original).

The difference to Peacocke is that Willaschek does not think that the content of perception is autonomous, but note that it is far from clear whether this difference really obtains or whether Willaschek only says that it holds. Willaschek thinks that the conceptual component is evoked by the phenomenal experience (Willaschek 2003, p. 278) and Peacocke holds that the correctness condition of a particular non-conceptual content "ensures" (Peacocke 2001a, p. 254) the correctness condition of the conceptual content. Remember, Peacocke grounds concepts and thus conceptual content in non-conceptual content, including especially scenario content and protopropositional content. The correctness of a particular non-conceptual content, i. e. scenario content and protopropositonal content, "is a priori sufficient for something to fall under the concept *square*" (Peacocke 2005, p. 60) because the non-conceptual content features in the possession condition of the very concept. Willaschek's reference to the phenomenal element of perception and the idea that this phenomenal element is what brings about the involvement of conceptual capacities in experiences brings him very close to Peacocke and is likely to entail problematic consequences.

159 For further criticism of Willaschek's conception, see (Kern 2006, p. 256, fn. 87).

Insights for conceptualism from the Argument from Fineness of Grain

As I said above, I think that Noë's response to the Argument from Fineness of Grain contains important insights for conceptualism in general. But in order to cash out this relevance most clearly I want to bracket Noë's enactivism. I do not think that taking in Noë's conceptualist insights requires accepting enactivism. For example, agreeing with Noë that the very conception of experience as representing the world in its fine-grainedness is wrong does not require us to subscribe to enactivism. All that it means is that experiential content does not contain all the different grains that a particular act of experience might be found to have (cf. Noë 2004, pp. 191 f.). If one is cycling past a field of flowers, one's experience is not going to contain the number of flowers on the field or all the different colors that the flowers have or a presentation of the hoverfly that is sitting on one of the flowers, etc. One can put the point generally: Experience in its very nature is incomplete and not exhaustive. A particular instance of experiencing does not contain all the different features or elements or grains of the particular experience explicitly. It is not subject to what I will call the Completeness Requirement (Section 7.3). Behind this insight there are two different, yet related observations. The observation that experience is not exhaustive is partly based on the plain fact that we do not take in everything in experience in the blink of an eye. And the observation that experience is incomplete furthermore notes that experience also includes content[160] which is *associated* with the original experiential content.

I will say more about the notion of associated 'content' and the incompleteness of perceptual experience below. But first I want to note that this conception also fits with McDowell's amended position as presented in "Avoiding the Myth of the Given" (McDowell 2009a).[161] I will introduce and discuss the details of this position in Chapters 3 and 6, but for the present concerns the following claims by McDowell are relevant: McDowell holds that if I have a bird in view, "my experience makes the bird visually *present* to me" (McDowell 2009a, p. 259, emphasis in original). I can know that this bird is a cardinal. This knowledge is non-infer-

---

160 One has to be careful with talking of *content* of perceptual experience. Here it is just a façon de parler. See later, e. g. Chapter 7. Thanks to Matt Soteriou who has suggested this possibility in conversation – without endorsing it as correct.

161 Note at the same time that my talk of "associated" differs slightly from McDowell's use of the term: McDowell talks about concepts and the conceptual capacities associated with them. When I talk of associations between conceptual capacities I want to capture the fact that different conceptual capacities and different concepts can be associated. McDowell does make similar claims, but he does not use the expression "associated" for it.

ential knowledge, since I can immediately recognize that the bird is a cardinal, without any acts of inference. Still, those concepts that appear in the knowledge do not have be part of the content of the experience. McDowell explains: "[the] content whose figuring in [perceptual] knowledge is owed to the recognitional capacity need not be part of the content of the experience itself" (McDowell 2009a, p. 259). The person who possesses the recognitional capacity can recognize different pieces of content in a form such as the form *animal*. Among those are different modes of space occupancy, like "shape, size, position, movement or its absence" (McDowell 2009a, p. 261) and "postures such as perching and modes of locomotion such as hopping or flying" (McDowell 2009a, p. 261). So recognizing the form of the intuition entails different additional features which originally were not part of the intuition, like *cardinal* or *animal* in the cardinal-case.

McDowell's remarks are sketchy, and I will discuss the position in greater detail later, but at this point I still already want to offer the following interpretation of what happens when I see the bird. Note that this interpretation goes beyond McDowell's conception. A bird is an animal, so my perception is unified by the form *bird*. This intuitional unity implies something like a 'diffusion-chain'. The intuitional content diffuses through contents and concepts related through the unifying form. This is also how we might spell out the above notion of *associated content*. The elements of this diffusion chain can be made explicit, but they do not have to be made explicit, they can remain implicit. What are the elements of this diffusion-chain? They are other concepts and contents related to the unifying form. If we follow McDowell's remarks from "Avoiding the Myth of the Given", that minimally includes common and proper sensibles relating to the perceived object (McDowell 2009a, p. 260). I would like to add, and thereby go beyond McDowell, that the relations are composed by memories of previous experiences, by locations on cognitive maps, as well as by formulae, and most importantly by language. As McDowell explains in "Avoiding the Myth of the Given", intuitional content can be brought to the level of discursive content by "carv[ing] it out" (McDowell 2009a, p. 263) with the help of linguistic expressions, i.e. by using existing linguistic expressions or coining new linguistic terms. Note that these claims presuppose that saying that perceptual experience is conceptual does not mean that we have "words for every aspect of the content of our experience" (McDowell 2009m, p. 320). McDowell continues, "[n]o aspect is unnameable, but that does not require us to pretend to make sense of an ideal position in which we have a name for every aspect, let alone be in such a position" (McDowell 2009m, p. 320).

My idea of using *formulae* goes back to Noë's notion of the color-concept-formula: colors are part of a structurally uniform system, we can conceptualize any shape via "color-concept-formulae" (Noë 2004, p. 194). As we have seen, according to Noë, this does not just hold for colors, but also extends more generally: conceptual capacities "can be extended ... formulaically to every novel perceptual quality that we encounter" (Noë 2004, p. 195).[162] We possess myriads of other formulae, e.g. house-formula, weather-formula etc. Those formulae do not just consist of concepts, but also of conceptions, i.e. systems of beliefs.[163] Speaking in terms of the picture of the diffusion-chain, I want to suggest that the diffusion-chain basically makes available implicit and non-inferential knowledge by perceiving. Calling the chain a diffusion-chain emphasizes the non-inferentiality of the knowledge. Something like an osmotic chain would be the equivalent to inferential knowledge.

This sort of conception also allows for the presence of broad concepts in perception: If Eliza sees a person with a friendly face, the content of her experience can be expressed by something like 'She has a friendly face.' That might be all that Eliza sees at the moment. She does not have to be able to say *what* it is about the face that makes her see it as a friendly face. If she further investigates her experience, she might be able to say that the person is smiling and that this why she sees her as having a friendly face. Saying that perceptual experience is conceptual does not commit one to saying that all the different facets of particular perceptual experience that one might be able to perceive if one looks at the experienced scene in more detail, is captured fully in some singular perceptual experience of the perceiving subject. Experience simply is not like a painting in a museum that does not change and that a subject can look at unhurriedly to carefully take in all the detail.

At this point the following objection might come up: This conception of concepts is too weak: those concepts do not even satisfy the generality constraint. Someone who might make this objection is Richard Heck: to say that beliefs have conceptual content is to say that the content of beliefs can be decomposed or has a "constituent structure" (McLaughlin/Cohen 2007, p. xv).[164] Possessing a concept thus is more than just being able to have a belief containing that con-

---

162 One can say more generally that conceptual capacities come in bundles (cf. McDowell 1996, p. 31). It is impossible for a single conceptual capacity to exist independently from other conceptual capacities (cf. e.g. McDowell 1996; McDowell 2009b). This observation holds both for their acquisition and their actualization. When describing the acquisition of conceptual capacities we cannot single out one capacity which marks off the beginning; and when describing which conceptual capacities are actualized, say, in thinking a thought *p* we cannot mark out a precise collection of conceptual capacities.

163 The helpful addition made by (Davis 2005) can be applied here.

164 Note that Heck does not in fact make this objection; he does not even talk about intuitional content, because McDowell's introduction of this terminology only comes later.

cept. Contents of beliefs are significantly structured and so the generality constraint is automatically incorporated. So, a state has conceptual content if certain generalizations hold for the state, and if the holding of the generalizations can be explained in terms of the structural features of the state. To say that perceptual content is non-conceptual thus means that relations that typically exist between beliefs and that are constitutive of their being beliefs do not hold for perceptual content. Mixing concepts and unifying forms, as I have just suggested, would result in a new understanding of concepts, which are not genuine concepts anymore. The intuitional content of perceiving a bird and the conceptual content of the judgment "This is a cardinal." are not structured in the same way. "The bird is a cardinal." can be decomposed into *a is F, a, F, b is F, a is G* etc., so *a* and *F* can be recombined. How should the same things hold for the intuitional content? Can such intuitional content be decomposed and can it be generalized and can the structural features of this content explain why the generalizations are possible?

Heck thinks that this is not possible for perceptual content and he would probably also say that this is not possible for intuitional content: there is no one single proposition that can represent intuitional content of a perceptual experience, because perception is not articulated in the same way as structured propositions. In addition, perceptual experience includes expectations about how the experience will change as the subject moves, changes her position etc. Those expectations are rational and thus require us to say more about the relation between perceptual contents. Intuitional contents understood as structured propositions, which they will have to be according to Heck, if they are conceptual contents, do not help us in explaining those relations. In fact they cannot help us, because the relations between perceptual contents are also 'local'.[165]

Yet throughout this possible objection it does not become clear why we need the extreme version of the Generality Constraint. For example, Noë has argued that the possibility of re-identification might be strongly context-dependent (Noë 2004, p. 197). It is not clear why *locality* should be an unsurmountable problem. And Travis, for example, has even argued that the Generality Constraint does not hold (Travis 2008). Travis claims that concepts, i.e. generalities, are occasion-sensitive and so concepts cannot be generalized without attending to the

---

165 Heck likens the case of perceptual content to cognitive maps: "relations on cognitive maps should be *local* in the sense that objects are located on such maps only (or at least primarily) relative to nearby objects and not relative to all the objects the map represents" (Heck 2007, p. 128, emphasis in original). Since relations between perceptual contents are 'local' they will defy any attempts at generalizing them and *a fortiori* they will not satisfy the generality constraint.

surrounding in which they appear. This rejection is part and parcel of Travis's anti-representationalist objections against non-conceptual representational theories of perceptual experience which I will approach in Chapter 5. Note also that it is not clear why, as the objection presupposes, concept application in perceptual experience should automatically deliver propositional content. Relational conceptualism will build strongly on this insight.

Before moving to the final non-conceptualist argument, the Argument from Fallibility, let us stop to look at what one learns from the Argument from the Fineness of Grain: One sees that there is not what I will call a *Completeness Requirement* nor a *Correctness Requirement* on the conceptual repertoire actualized in a particular perceptual experience (Section 7.3). Conceptualists do not have to hold that all concepts that could be actualized *are* indeed actualized in a particular perceptual experience. Concepts and conceptual capacities are flexible and so is their actualization. This condition will also be central in the relational conceptualist theory developed in this book.

2.7 A Close Reading Analysis of the Argument from Fallibility

The continuing debate about the Argument from Fallibility

The Argument from Fallibility comes from the debate between Tyler Burge and John McDowell about which theory of perception is correct. It is not commonly cited as a non-conceptualist argument against the conceptualist theory of perception, but I think it belongs in the context of arguments against conceptualism, since it is brought forward as an argument against McDowell's conceptualist theory from a non-conceptualist, namely Tyler Burge. Understanding McDowell's response will take us back to the capacity version of conceptualism (Section 1.3) and it will allow me to emphasize the transcendental character of conceptualism. I will start the section by giving the Argument from Fallibility and the claims against which it argues. Note that Burge does not call the argument the *Argument from Fallibility*, but the name captures the gist of this argument and Burge's argument fits the description of the Argument from Fallibility. Then I will give McDowell's response to the Argument from Fallibility. In order to explicate why McDowell takes his response to work I will introduce remarks on skepticism and the nature of capacities from Jim Conant, Andrea Kern and Sebastian Rödl. They will draw attention to the commitments and tenets of conceptualism.

The Argument from Fallibility criticizes the epistemological role that conceptualism gives to perception. Since the capacity-version of conceptualism is how McDowell currently phrases the particular epistemic role of perception his reply will be in terms of perception as a capacity for knowledge. Let me remind you of the views of the capacity-theory. It starts with Sellars's claim that language-using beings live in the space of reasons and that for those beings knowledge is a position in the space of reasons (McDowell 2011b, p. 10). If Eliza, a being who lives in the space of reasons, knows *p*, then she can state what it is that she believes. If Eliza knows this because she has looked outside her window, then her knowing that the sun is shining is a case of observational knowledge that she has obtained through her perceptual capacities. Since Eliza is a self-conscious, rational being she can state not only that her belief that the sun is shining is knowledge, but also *how* the fact that the belief is rationally grounded makes for its status as knowledge. That, however, does not mean that Eliza's observational knowledge is inferential knowledge and it is here that the debate between McDowell and Tyler Burge sets in. I have looked at parts of their debate in the section on the Argument from Hyper-Intellectualization, but one cannot but note that their debate has expanded in content and cannot be satisfactorily dealt with only in terms of the Argument from Hyper-Intellectualization.[166]

Of course, in Burge's work the Argument from Fallibility is accompanied by other arguments, e. g. the Argument from Hyper-Intellectualization. I will not say anything about this argument because I have already discussed it, but before I get to the Argument from Fallibility, I will briefly mention another related objection that is worth looking at. In this other objection Burge notes that McDowell's conception of knowledge after all does entail that observational knowledge is inferential knowledge. McDowell rejects this objection rather quickly. He starts by pointing out that he follows Sellars in holding that observational knowledge requires the knowing subject to be reliable in acquiring observational knowledge and to have knowledge of her own reliability (McDowell 2011b, pp. 11 f., 44 f.).[167] Such reliability and the knowledge of the reliability can figure in inferential knowledge, but does not have to do that. This comes out clearest if we compare 'proper' inferential knowledge and observational knowledge. Eliza's knowledge that the sun is shining could also be based on her seeing reflections of light on her sofa and her inferring from this that the sun is shining. Her knowledge which is based on her looking outside the window and seeing the sun does not include an inference like this and it is still warranted knowledge that is rationally grounded.

---

166 At the moment the exchange stretches over three published papers by each (Burge 2003; Burge 2005; Burge 2011a) and (McDowell 2010a; McDowell 2011b; McDowell 2013b).
167 Note that McDowell's reliability claim here does not mean that his position is like Brandom's. For McDowell's distancing from Brandom's "reliable differential responsive dispositions" (Brandom 1994, p. 119) see e. g. (McDowell 1998d) or (McDowell 2009f, pp. 286 f.).

So let us move to Burge's second objection, to what I want to call the "Argument from Fallibility". As I have said, the Argument from Fallibility does not strictly attack the conceptualist claims of McDowell's theory of perception, rather it criticizes the epistemological framework of conceptualism; more particularly it attacks the truth-guaranteeing role that perception is supposed to have for knowledge. Burge argues that – as McDowell puts it – "the warrant a perceptual state provides for a belief cannot guarantee the truth of a belief that it warrants" (McDowell 2011b, p. 28). A subject can cite her perceptual experience as a warrant for her belief, but her perceptual experience can always turn out to be false and so in this case the perceptual warrant for the belief would not really guarantee the truth of the belief (Burge 2005, p. 56). Let me illustrate this observation by the following example:[168] Eliza sees her friends on a bench in the park; she stops to tie her shoe laces, then looks at her friends again and wants to cross the lawn to talk to them. Unbeknownst to Eliza, while she was tying her shoe laces, her friends have been replaced by duplicates. Now, according to Burge, Eliza's perceptual state is the same when she sees her friends and when she sees the duplicate-friends, since the proximal stimulations are indiscriminable to Eliza (Burge 2005, p. 27). In the first instance, pre-tying-shoe-laces, Eliza's belief that her friends are on the bench is true; in the second instance, post-tying-shoe-laces, it will appear to Eliza that her belief that her friends are on the bench is true, too (Burge 2005, p. 26). But as we know, her belief is *not* true. Burge's generalizing move is that all cases of perceptual experience are open to a challenge like this and so "perceptual states as such can provide only inconclusive warrant for beliefs" (McDowell 2011b, p. 30). So in a nutshell: the Argument from Fallibility starts from the fact that perceptual experience is fallible – it can always fail to present the world as it is – and that most of the time the perceiving subject cannot make out which of her perceptual experiences are veridical and which are not. From this the defender of this argument concludes that perceptual experience cannot offer conclusive warrant for belief, let alone for knowledge. The parallels to the Argument from Illusion (see Section 1.3) are obvious and to some extent McDowell uses the same disjunctivist strategy against both. I will say more about this below.

Before we start looking at McDowell's responses to Burge, I want to note that the gist of McDowell's arguments can already be found in his *Mind and World* when he rejects the objection that the possibility of misleading experience means that perceptual experience cannot be openness to the world (McDowell

---

168 For Burge's example see (Burge 2005, p. 26).

1996, pp. 111 f.). His responses to Burge's criticism can basically all be put under the slogan that he gives out in *Mind and World:*

> The aim here is not to answer sceptical questions [i.e. in the present case, Burge's objections, N.E.], but to begin to see how it might be intellectually respectable to ignore them, to treat them as unreal, in the way that common sense has always wanted to. ... Traditional epistemology cannot be vindicated by the sheer possibility of asking, 'How do you know that what you are enjoying is a genuine glimpse of the world?' ... If someone insists on asking that, on some particular occasion, an appropriate response might start like this: 'I know why you think that question is peculiarly pressing, but it is not.' If the question still stands, nothing particularly philosophical is called for in answering it. (McDowell 1996, p. 113)

Fortunately, McDowell's direct response to Burge is more detailed than these scarce remarks in *Mind and World*, so there is more material to look at in this section. It is still helpful to keep the above agenda in mind and remember that this is the basic structure of McDowell's argumentation.[169]

McDowell's response to the second objection is rather brief, but there is a large, unarticulated argumentative backdrop and I will work on carving out this backdrop by putting McDowell's dealings with skepticism and the capacity approach in the center of attention. As I have said, the Argument from Fallibility (Burge's second objection) in effect states the conclusion of the Argument from Illusion: a perceiving subject can neither distinguish the perceptual state caused by a real object from the perceptual state caused by a duplicate of that object, nor from the perceptual state caused by some appropriate brain stimulation in the absence of the object. That means that a perceiver can never know whether the perceptual states on which she bases her observational knowledge are of the good type, or any of the other two types (duplicate or "referential illusory case" (Burge 2005, p. 26), e.g. as in appropriate brain stimulation). Consequently, the perceiver can never take her own perceptual states to offer indefeasible warrant for the belief that she bases on it. In his reply to Burge McDowell again brings up Sellars's idea that perceptual knowledge consists in positions in the space of reasons. This conception of knowledge, he claims, rules out Burge's claim that perceptual states cannot guarantee the truth of perceptual beliefs. If Eliza knows

---

169 It is also very interesting to note that McDowell himself does not ever point out to Burge that he has basically made all those points in *Mind and World* already. He only refers to them in an article that discusses Crispin Wright's criticism of McDowell's treatment of the sceptic (McDowell 2008b, p. 386, fn.9; McDowell 2009c, p. 237, fn.16). I will discuss this article in the course of this section in order to spell out McDowell's "transcendental argument" (McDowell 2008b, p. 380).

that the sun is shining, and if her knowing this is conceived as her possessing a standing in the space of reasons, and if this standing is based on an actualization of her capacity for knowledge, then her knowing that the sun is shining is simply incompatible with that belief being wrong. McDowell insists:

> When all goes well in the operation of a perceptual capacity of a sort that belongs to its possessor's rationality, a perceiver enjoys a perceptual state in which some feature of her environment is *there* for her, perceptually *present* to her rationally self-conscious awareness. (McDowell 2011b, pp. 30 f., emphasis in original)

And when all goes well the subject really is entitled to say that she has knowledge of p. In a response to Robert Brandom McDowell makes it clear that the possession of knowledge, the possession of a standing in the space of reasons is inextricably connected to the subject being entitled to the possession of this knowledge (McDowell 2009 f). He explains that the space of reasons could also be called "the space of entitlements" (McDowell 2009 f, p. 284) and reminds us that in his theory "entitlement and truth do not come apart" (McDowell 2009 f, p. 281). That leads him to reject the conclusions that Burge draws from the fallibility of perceptual experience. Of course, perceptual experience is fallible, but that does not mean that it cannot ever provide a subject with conclusive warrant for knowledge. It is just part and parcel of perception being a *capacity* for knowledge that it is fallible. Any capacity is fallible, because it can always be exercised inadequately, but that mere possibility does not mean that the subject exercising the capacity does not possess it at all. In other words, the fallibility of the perceptual capacity for knowledge must be treated like the fallibility in any other capacity. McDowell refers to an analogy between the capacity for empirical knowledge and the "capacity to sink eight-foot putts" (McDowell 2011b, p. 39) to support his claims: A golfer who has the "capacity to sink eight-foot putts" (McDowell 2011b, p. 39) does not always successfully sink an eight-foot putt, but still we would not say that she lacks the "capacity to sink eight-foot putts" (McDowell 2011b, p. 39). Burge's argumentation – and the Argument from Illusion – however, suggest just that for the case of perception as a capacity for knowledge. They would say about the golfer that she does not possess the "capacity to sink eight-foot putts" (McDowell 2011b, p. 39) because she is not guaranteed to sink every eight-foot putt.

Let us stop here and take a step back to look at McDowell's reaction to the Argument from Fallibility so far. McDowell holds that we are allowed to exclude and ignore the Argument's worries about the relation between perception and knowledge. Why is that? First, his reaction clearly traces back to his disjunctivism: veridical and illusory or hallucinatory perception are introspectively indistinguishable, but from this it does not follow that perception is neutral as to whether it is veridical or non-veridical. Put bluntly and slightly trivially: Veridical perception is veridical and non-veridical perception is non-veridical.

Second, the disjunctivist framework also explains what McDowell says about the relevance of fallibility of perceptual experiences. McDowell insists that unsuccessful cases of exercising one's perceptual capacity for knowledge, as with Eliza when she sees the duplicate-friends in the park, do not affect the successful cases of exercising one's perceptual capacity for knowledge. Even if one emphasizes that Eliza cannot discriminate the successful case and the unsuccessful case, that still does not entail that there are no successful cases of exercising her perceptual capacity for knowledge at all. Burge, however, wants to conclude just that; he basically argues that given that Eliza cannot rule out the unsuccessful case we are not allowed to claim that the successful case ever obtains.

McDowell further tries to block Burge's conclusions by introducing two kinds of fallibility. Burge's cases of doubt are different from cases in which one is indeed justified in doubting one's capacity for knowledge. Eliza would be justified in questioning her perception as a capacity for knowledge if she was a participant in an experiment which includes the possibility that her friends are secretly replaced duplicates, and if she knew about this feature of the experiment. In those circumstances Eliza could not exercise her capacity for knowledge. There would be a "determinate possibility" (McDowell 2011b, p. 52) for a false belief formed on the basis of her perceptual experience that Eliza cannot rule out and so in the experiment she cannot be said to actualize her capacity for knowledge. Yet McDowell argues that Burge's objection does not concern any "determinate possibility" (McDowell 2011b, p. 52) of failure, but only the sheer possibility of failure and so it does not warrant any suspension of the capacity for knowledge as manifested by perceptual experience.

From the perspective of the Argument from Fallibility this response is certainly not satisfying and in his lecture McDowell discusses a possible gap that a defender of the Argument from Fallibility might still think to discern. She might think that the gap in McDowell's argumentation is this: McDowell's argumentation cannot ensure that the subject knows that her exercise of the capacity for knowledge is successful. Since the good case and the bad case are indiscriminable the subject can never know that her experience is an instance of the good case and so she cannot have empirical knowledge. But McDowell insists that this is no problem on his conception. It is worth looking at his whole statement on this issue because the response reveals two important facets: first, McDowell's observation about the capacity for self-knowledge and second, a crucial omittance in his argumentation for this observation.

In response to this, we need to emphasize the connection between reason and self-consciousness. A rational perceptual capacity is a capacity not only to know certain kinds of thing [sic] about the environment, but, on an occasion, on which one knows something of the relevant kind through the exercise of the capacity in question, *to know that that is how one knows it.* The capacity– of course fallible – to know, on certain occasions, that one's experience is revealing to one that things are a certain way, which is a bit of self-knowledge, is just an aspect of the capacity – of course fallible– to know through experience, on those occasions, that things are that way. It is a single capacity, self-consciously possessed and exercised. A bit of rational perceptual knowledge includes knowledge that it is through perception that one know whatever it is that one knows about the environment. And we need to avoid that bad inference from the fallibility of the capacity, not only in connection with its guise as a capacity for knowledge about one's environment, but also in connection with its guise as a capacity for self-knowledge. ...

Defective exercises of a perceptual capacity can be indiscriminable from non-defective exercises. It is a mistake to infer that even on an occasion on which the capacity is working perfectly, the current exercise of it is, for all one knows, defective. (McDowell 2011b, pp. 41 f., emphasis in original)

These remarks are entirely in line with what I have said above about the capacity version of conceptualism (Section 1.3). McDowell observes that perception as a capacity for knowledge is a self-conscious capacity: Eliza knows that she knows that the sun is shining by having seen the sun through her window. Eliza knows how she knows, but, since this knowledge is based on a capacity, it, too, is fallible. Just imagine that unbeknownst to Eliza, her sitting room has been relocated to a TV studio and she did not see the sun, but a well-made fake sun. But even though Eliza cannot discriminate her successful 'knowing that she knows that the sun is shining from looking outside the window' and the unsuccessful 'knowing that she knows that the sun is shining from looking outside the window, but she is in a TV studio and the sun is not real', there is no reason to be suspicious about her capacity (itself) to *know how she knows that p.* Fallibility is just in the nature of a capacity.

McDowell's argument might be intuitively appealing to some, but it certainly is not to Burge (cf. his responses in Burge 2011a) and even on a charitable reading there are some gaps in McDowell's overall argumentation. He is tight-lipped regarding the question of why acknowledging the fallibility of the perceptual capacity does not preclude accepting that the capacity is successful in the good case: he only refers to the golfing-analogy and discusses the psychological experiment-cases. But he does not offer further arguments for the claim that the perceptual capacity for knowledge is a self-conscious capacity or for the claim that the perceptual capacity for knowledge is the same as the capacity to know how one knows. Note also that it is far from clear that the golfing-analogy really is successful. The analogy helps to illustrate the general idea, but is the capacity to sink eight-foot putts really like the capacity for knowledge by perception? Of course, the exercise of both capacities depends on 'the world' playing its part, i.e. no disturbing wind gusts and no manipulation of the objects of perception, but that might not be enough for such an analogy.[170]

And finally, it is still open why Burge's questions – and that means the Argument from Fallibility – may even be ignored rather than answered. In order to answer this question I will take a detour and focus on Cartesian vs. Kantian skepticism, first, and then on self-conscious capacities. In the next paragraphs I will introduce the distinction between Cartesian and Kantian skepticism that James Conant has highlighted. Understanding that and how this distinction applies to the debate between McDowell and Burge and the Argument from Fallibility will make it clear why McDowell takes it that he can ignore Burge's questions.

Ignoring the Argument from Fallibility I: McDowell as a Kantian skeptic

In his "Two Varieties of Skepticism" (2012) Conant claims that there are two varieties of skepticism to be found in philosophy: *Cartesian skepticism* and *Kantian skepticism*.[171]. The Cartesian skeptic about perceptual experience is interested in the question whether what she is experiences is real (Conant 2012, p. 5). The Kantian skeptic about perceptual experience is interested in the conditions for her experiencing something in the world (Conant 2012, p. 5). Here already it is clear to which sides Burge and McDowell belong: Burge addresses Cartesian skepticism and McDowell addresses Kantian skepticism. Conant actually offers five examples from different fields of philosophy in which Cartesian skepticism

---

170 Moreover, there seems to be another difference between the two capacities: the capacity to sink eight-foot putts is acquired by learning and it is no capacity that lies in the nature of human beings, whereas the perceptual capacity for knowledge is second natural to human beings. If we follow McDowell's story on the acquisition of conceptual capacities being second nature and just an actualization of one's human potential (cf. e.g. McDowell 1996, p. 126, and also Ginsborg 2006c, p. 83) we might thus detect another crucial difference that might harm the analogy.
171 Conant explicitly acknowledges that the terms might be tendentious and could be problematic in the eyes of a historian of philosophy, e.g. regarding the question whether what Conant labels Cartesian skepticism can be found in writings that predate the writings of Descartes. Conant emphasizes that no such questions are to be answered by his distinction. He also adds that the distinction between Cartesian and Kantian skepticism is not meant to entail that Kant was not interested in Cartesian skepticism: "I am not making an historical claim about which problems are (and are not) discussed in the writings of Descartes or Kant. Rather I am making a philosophical claim about a congruence to be found in the shape of the problems themselves, regardless of whose writings they appear in" (Conant 2012, p. 7, footnote deleted, N.E.).

and Kantian skepticism are found. He argues that "Cartesian skepticism" and "Kantian skepticism" do not just concern skepticism about perceptual experience.[172] But here, since the topic is perceptual experience, I will focus on his analysis of the two varieties of skepticism in perception. Conant sums up the difference between the two skepticisms in three catchy pairs:

(i)   The Cartesian skeptic is interested in the actuality of her perception; the Kantian skeptic is interested in the possibility of her perception (Conant 2012, p. 5).

(ii) The Cartesian skeptic asks about what she perceives as *being* so; the Kantian skeptic asks about what she perceives as being *so* (Conant 2012, p. 5).

(iii) And finally, the Cartesian skeptic is interested in questions of truth; the Kantian skeptic is interested in the objective validity of judgment, which Conant calls "objective purport" (Conant 2012, p. 6).

Before I go into any further detail regarding the nature of the two skepticisms, let me briefly emphasize what the use of Conant's distinction is for the above debates. Conant himself argues that the distinction allows four insights for philosophy, three of which apply to the present exchange between McDowell and Burge about the Argument from Fallibility. First, we can see that the same philosophical terminology has different meanings depending on the skeptical question that is at the heart of the philosophical theory. Second, it reveals philosophers' misunderstandings of each other's writings. And, third, it helps understand the source and nature of skepticism. Those insights will be central for us in understanding what is really going on in the debates about perception as a capacity for knowledge and what McDowell and Burge disagree about.[173]

The central perceptual case of the Cartesian skeptic concerns the question of how the perceiving subject can know that things are as they seem to her in her perceptual experience. The skeptic wants to find that special element which ensures that her perception is veridical. She is faced with a gap between the inner world and the outer world that she wants to bridge. The central perceptual case of the Kantian skeptic, on the other hand, concerns the question of how the per-

---

172 The other examples center around questions of other minds, language, intentional action and art.

173 The fourth insight makes out instances in which philosophers did not see that their colleagues were not trying to solve the particular paradox that they were taking them to solve, e.g. Hilary Putnam takes McDowell to discuss the Cartesian paradox, when in fact he is discussing the Kantian paradox (Conant 2012, pp. 53 ff.).

ceiving subject can "so much as *present* things as being a certain way" (Conant 2012, p. 14, emphasis in original). The Kantian skeptic wants to know how the world can be revealed through her senses. The gap that she faces is between "sensory blindness", which is merely causal, and "sensory consciousness", which reveals the world being a certain way (Conant 2012, p. 14).

Conant finds nine features that are distinctive of the Cartesian problematic and also nine features that are distinctive of the Kantian problematic. The Cartesian skeptic starts with a concrete example that is a best case of knowledge. Her example is concerned with a particular person at a particular time and place in which the viewing conditions are optimal. The object involved in the example is an unexceptional, average object and so the claim made in the example is exemplary of a class of claims [Element 1]. Starting from this best case of knowledge the Cartesian skeptic sets forth the possibility of doubting the particular claim, e. g. because of the possibility of the perceiver unknowingly being victim to an illusion [Element 2]. Given the possibility of doubt the subject cannot gain knowledge from her perception in this particular case. Since the starting claim is exemplary for a class of claims the problems generalize to all knowledge [Element 3]. The possibility of doubt leads to general doubts in our practice of acquiring knowledge. Our practice is "unmasked" (Conant 2012, p. 27) in a "discovery" (Conant 2012, p. 25) [Element 4]. The perceiving subject that follows the route of the Cartesian skeptic is disappointed in knowledge: she thought that she was able to attain knowledge, but it turns out to be impossible [Element 5]. She is disappointed because something that is possible is not actual [Element 6]. The perceiving subject has encountered a limit to her capacities; there is something that she wants to be able to do, but cannot do [Element 7]. Her inability consists in an inability to bridge a "Cartesian gap", e. g. the gap between inner world and outer world [Element 8]. Cartesian skepticism, however, is an instable position because it cannot be actualized in practice: the perceiving subject has to live her life as if she can bridge (and has bridged) the Cartesian gap [Element 9].

The Kantian skeptic starts from examples which contain abstract objects. She is concerned with objects *überhaupt*. Her examples are not concrete and do not contain any "specification of epistemic standing" (Conant 2012, p. 31) [Element 1]. The Kantian question asks how the senses can offer the subject awareness of the world and also how thoughts can be about the world. The Kantian skeptic finds that it is neither possible to answer these questions nor to avoid them. She thus finds herself in a *boggle* (Conant 2012, p. 32) [Element 2]. The inability to answer these questions leads to a paradox: the subject cannot make sense of her experiencing a particular [Element 3] and she is left with finding her own cognitive capacities a "mystery" (Conant 2012, p. 33) [Element 4].

Faced with this outlook the subject falls into despair[174] [Element 5]. More precisely, the despair arises when the subject finds that something that she takes to be actual is not possible [Element 6]. The space of possibility collapses as there is nothing to do [Element 7]. The Kantian gap, e. g. between "sensory blindness" and "sensory consciousness" (Conant 2012, p. 35), leads to the loss of possibilities. But note that the gap is so basic that in order to *see* the gap, the subject already has to have bridged it [Element 8]. Without having bridged the gap the worry of the Kantian skeptic cannot even be understood and so it can neither be actualized theoretically nor practically [Element 9].

As I said, I want to suggest that Conant's distinction between Cartesian skepticism and Kantian skepticism can help understand the controversies in the debate between Burge and McDowell. One adjustment needs to be made in order to make this application more evident. Conant does not talk of the Argument from Illusion nor of the Argument from Fallibility, but only of the "Cartesian skeptic", yet it should be clear that a large number of the nine features of the Cartesian problem can also be found in the Argument from Illusion and the Argument from Fallibility.[175] In other words, one can regard the Argument from Fallibility and the Argument from Illusion as arguments of the Cartesian skeptic. Admittedly not all features of Cartesian skepticism are fulfilled by the Argument from Fallibility, e. g. there is no talk of disappointment, but these differences are not important, since I do not mean to argue that Burge deals with Cartesian skeptic, or that McDowell deals with Kantian skeptics.[176] Rather, the distinction is meant to reveal the underlying motivations of McDowell's and Burge's projects and that is only possible if one sets their project in the framework proposed by Conant. Thus the crucial insight for the McDowell-Burge debate about the Argument from Fallibility is this: Burge's observations and arguments are shaped by the concerns of the Cartesian skeptic; McDowell's arguments and replies are shaped by the concern of the Kantian skeptic. This difference already becomes obvious in their different topics: Burge is clearly worried about the difference between "experiencing something and *actually* experiencing it" (Conant 2012, p. 4, emphasis in

---

174 There is no disappointment, because disappointment presupposes that the subject has a view of what she aims for (Conant 2012, p. 33).

175 See for example Chapter 1 of Alfred J. Ayer's *The Foundations of Empirical Knowledge* (Ayer 1969).

176 Burge is not a Cartesian skeptic, but his conception is a response to Cartesian skepticism. In the same way, McDowell is not a Kantian skeptic, but his conception is a response to Kantian skepticism. Burge raises doubts about a particular "best case of knowledge" (Conant 2012, p. 25); McDowell asks how our senses can be of the world and how our thoughts can be about the world.

original) and he is interested in the truth of a claim or of perception. McDowell on the other hand is clearly fundamentally interested in the conditions of the possibility of experiencing something. He is worried about how perception and judgment can have "objective purport" (Conant 2012, p. 6).

In this frame of the debate it is most relevant to look at the philosophical insights that Conant gains from the distinction. Conant shows that the same philosophical vocabulary has different meanings depending on the skeptic context in which they appear. For the present debate this becomes especially clear for the very notion of *fallibility:* Burge conceives of fallibility as a threat to perception and knowledge. McDowell conceives of fallibility as logically included in perception and knowledge. It is in the nature of perception and knowledge to be fallible, no threat is radiated by it. The sentence 'Perception is fallible.' has very different implications for Burge than for McDowell. With this in mind one will be more careful in discussing their exchange. If one sorts Burge's observations with the Cartesian problematic and McDowell's observations with the Kantian problematic, one will also be clearer about the forces that drive their thoughts (cf. Conant's third insight, Conant 2012, pp. 42f.).

Conant importantly notes that McDowell applies what he calls the *Kantian way with skepticism* (Conant 2012, p. 42) and this explanation gets us to the final steps of seeing why McDowell thinks that Burge's objections and the Argument from Fallibility can be ignored. The Kantian way with skepticism regards the Cartesian problem as a special case of a more general problem, the Kantian problem: the Kantian skeptic questions the possibility of experience of the world, the Cartesian skeptic only questions the actuality of her experience of the world. The best way to respond to a Cartesian skeptic is to first think through her implicit assumptions, i.e. the *possibility* of experience of the world, and confront her with an even more fundamental skepticism, which questions her implicit assumptions and shows that her own position is incoherent. Then, if one has dissolved the more fundamental skepticism, i.e. Kantian skepticism, one will have also done away with Cartesian skepticism. Clearly this is McDowell's strategy in responding to Burge and this answers the question why McDowell thinks that one can ignore Burge's questions: he gives Burge his – McDowell's – answer to the Kantian skeptical problem and holds that in having solved this problem, he has also solved the Cartesian problem. The Cartesian skeptical problem is the "initial guise" (Conant 2012, p. 44) of the Kantian skeptical problem.[177]

---

177 Conant offers a description of the Kantian strategy that we can also read as a succinct summary of McDowell's strategy: "[The] Cartesian skeptical paradox can be shown to be merely a special case of a more general worry, ..., [and] once this is shown, Cartesianism will be robbed

It is here that we can start to understand what McDowell's strategy against the skeptic as put forward in *Mind and World* implies. Look again at the passage that I have quoted above.

> The aim here is not to answer sceptical questions [i. e. Burge's objections, N.E.], but to begin to see how it might be intellectually respectable to ignore them, to treat them as unreal, in the way that common sense has always wanted to. ... Traditional epistemology cannot be vindicated by the sheer possibility of asking, 'How do you know that what you are enjoying is a genuine glimpse of the world?' ... If someone insists on asking that, on some particular occasion, an appropriate response might start like this: 'I know why you think that question is peculiarly pressing, but it is not.' If the question still stands, nothing particularly philosophical is called for in answering it. (McDowell 1996, p. 113)

McDowell thinks that it is "intellectually respectable to ignore" (McDowell 1996, p. 113) skeptical questions, such as Burge's skeptical questions, because Burge's skeptical questions are at most secondary, if not superfluous next to the Kantian skeptical question.

But Conant's distinction also shows us why it is not easy for Burge to understand McDowell's response and what could be missing from McDowell's response to Burge. In other words, we might take a suggestion from Conant on what could help Burge understand McDowell's solution and the feat that it has achieved. Burge has to see that his Cartesian worry is a version of the Kantian worry. Conant would also have some advice for how McDowell could help Burge understand his position. McDowell's Kantian way with skepticism would have to be supplemented by the "Wittgensteinian way with skepticism" (Conant 2012, p. 63). On the Wittgensteinian way with skepticism the skeptic is taken back to her own strategy so she can see where she went wrong and why her steps were wrong (Conant 2012, p. 64). This way of dealing with the skeptic is "a supplementation of the Kantian way" (Conant 2012, p. 63) that McDowell omits. He does not show Burge where he went wrong and why his steps were wrong. Burge still needs to be brought "back to the place where he started, where he already is and never left, but in such a way that he is able to recognize it for the first time" (Conant 2012, p. 63).

So we have now seen that at the basis of McDowell's rejection of the Argument from Fallibility and Burge's objection lies the particular transcendental framework of McDowell's theory of perception. It is within this framework that the objections can be rejected. But there is another set of claims that McDowell

---

of all its force and will wither away of its own accord without requiring any additional form of specialized treatment" (Conant 2012, p. 69).

makes in response to Burge's objection and that cannot be explained by these explications about the general framework. They concern McDowell's claim that

> [a] rational perceptual capacity is a capacity not only to know certain kinds of thing [sic] about the environment, but, on an occasion, on which one knows something of the relevant kind through the exercise of the capacity in question, *to know that that is how one knows it.* ... It is a single capacity, self-consciously possessed and exercised. A bit of rational perceptual knowledge includes knowledge that it is through perception that one know whatever it is that one knows about the environment. (McDowell 2011b, pp. 41 f., emphasis in original)

In order to understand why McDowell takes perceptual knowledge to be coeval with knowledge that one knows by perception one needs to understand what it means to say that perceptual experience is a rational capacity. In other words, one needs to understand what sorts of arguments underwrite the capacity conception of perception. In what follows I want to refer to two arguments that Andrea Kern develops in her capacity conception of perception. She spells out transcendental and epistemological arguments that McDowell's conception appears to build on. In reconstructing the arguments one can further understand why on a conceptualist capacity conception Burge *cannot* claim that perceptual states can only offer inconclusive warrants for perceptual beliefs (McDowell 2011b, p. 32). Rödl offers related arguments, but for reasons of conciseness and because explicating his arguments would require more theoretical background than in the case of Kern, I will focus on her argumentation. Moreover, the function of the transcendental and epistemological arguments becomes very clear in Kern's argumentation. I will only refer to Rödl's arguments towards the end of this section, and indicate similar arguments in footnotes.

Ignoring the Argument from Fallibility II: Logico-transcendental and capacity-based arguments for perception as a capacity for knowledge

As I have said above, Kern's theory is also a conceptualist theory and her arguments and claims clearly build on McDowell's theory of perception.[178] She would not be able to hold these particular views without McDowell's theory, but as regards the argumentation for perception as a capacity for knowledge and responding to criticism of the Burgean type, she offers a more complete argumen-

---

178 The same holds for Rödl. E.g. he writes, "It would be apt to describe our objective in this chapter as that of articulating the account of self-consciousness and spontaneous knowledge contained in McDowell's epistemological writings." (Rödl 2007, p. 147, fn. 11)

tation.[179] Thus, citing her theory in order to explain McDowell's theory is rather more like transplanting an organ that has been built from the receiver's tissue than like transplanting an organ from an independent donor.

As I have said in Section 1.3, Kern explains that perception is 'a rational, sensory capacity to know' (Kern 2013, p. 394).[180] It is manifest in an act that consists in a nexus between the subject and a fact. E. g. Eliza knows that there is a book on the shelf, because she sees the book. Perception has its particular identity, i.e. being the reason (ground) for a belief, because it actualizes the unity 'knowledge'[181] (Kern 2006, p. 16). The unity 'knowledge' can also be rephrased as '*rational* capacity for knowledge' (Kern 2006, p. 16, emphasis in original). And the particular unity that is actualized by an act of perception is a receptive, rational capacity for knowledge (Kern 2006, pp. 149 f.). The unity 'knowledge' is logically prior to all acts that actualize the unity, i.e. the acts of perceiving something.

Since I have also introduced significant parts of Kern's theory, let me just briefly cite two of her arguments for saying that the receptive rational capacity for knowledge is rational and receptive. Kern gives two related arguments. First, she argues that we can only make sense of the idea of empirical knowledge, i.e. of knowledge of the world, if we conceive of knowledge as a receptive, rational capacity (cf. Kern 2006, p. 184). Second, she notes that if we conceive of knowledge as a receptive, rational capacity we can deal with the skeptic's objections that all conceptions of knowledge face: Agrippa's Trilemma (Kern 2006, pp. 55 ff.) and the Aporia of Knowledge (Kern 2006, pp. 99 ff.). The capacity conception of knowledge manages to reconcile the facticity of knowledge and the fallibility of knowledge that the Aporia of Knowledge seems to leave irreconcilable. Phrased in Kern's terminology, Burge's theory cannot deal with the Aporia of Knowledge because it is a single state view of knowledge, i.e. a view according to which knowledge consists in the description of a single act (Kern 2007, p. 245). Only capacity theories can deal with the Aporia (Kern 2007).

Kern gives what we may call an Argument from the Special Nature of Rational Capacities in order to show that perceptual knowledge is necessarily true and that perceptual knowledge is coeval with knowledge that knowledge is acquired

---

179 On the way it will also help understand how McDowell dismisses Burge's hyper-intellectualization objection concerning perceptual knowledge.

180 Most of Kern's texts are written in German. I have translated the quotations because that allows for more fluent reading of the text. For the first appearance of the expression in my text I give Kern's German original in footnotes. For this quotation Kern's formulation in German is: "sinnliche, vernünftige Erkenntnisfähigkeit" (Kern 2013, p. 394).

181 In Kern's German formulation: Erkenntnis (Kern 2006, p. 16).

by perception. This argument is crucial in the present discussion of the Argument from Fallibility, because it would be an argument against this Argument as well as against Burge's criticism and it could help understand McDowell's response to Burge. Kern explains that perception is a 'rational, sensory capacity to know' (Kern 2013, p. 378) and not 'the description of a single state'[182] (Kern 2013, p. 378). Kern like McDowell holds that knowledge that is based on the actualization of the capacity 'perception' is self-conscious perceptual knowledge: That means that the subject can explain her knowledge by referring to her perceptual experience as a reason for her knowledge. Remember that Kern has an Aristotelian conception of rational capacities (Section 1.3). The self-conscious, rational capacity 'perception' thus is a general capacity and therefore it fully and immediately explains all cases that fall under it. The particular self-conscious character of the capacity 'perception' can be read off from each exercise of the capacity: the capacity 'perception' is a capacity to know by perceptual experience and since it is a self-conscious capacity, the subject has perceptual knowledge and at the same time knows that she knows by perception (cf. Kern 2013, p. 392).[183] In effect it is thus impossible to access the basis for one's perceptual knowledge independently from the knowledge itself.[184]

But how exactly does this conception allow one to explain that we really perceive the fact on which we base our knowledge, so as to rule out error? How can a subject be sure that she really sees that on which she bases her knowledge? Of course, this is exactly the Cartesian skeptical question that Burge poses. The answer of Kern's capacity approach to perception and knowledge is that in actualizing the capacity it is ensured that the capacity was actualized in the right circumstances. If the circumstances had not been right, then the capacity would not have been actualized correctly (Kern 2006, pp. 274 f.). To put it differently: if a subject has knowledge, then the judgment cannot but be true. Knowledge that one's empirical judgment is true thus is not an element in knowing how things are in the world, rather, it itself is an actualization of a rational capacity for knowledge. Knowledge about how things are in the world cannot be analyzed

---

182 In Kern's German formulation: "Bescheibung eines einzelnen Zustands" (Kern 2013, p. 378).

183 For a similar argumentation in Rödl see e.g. (Rödl 2007, pp. 155, 158).

184 Such conceptions are routinely faced with a circularity objection (cf. also the Argument from Concept-Acquisition, Section 2.4), but note that this objection only comes up on an occurrence-based model of explanation, i.e. if one claims that an occurrence is explained by another occurrence. Kern's capacity approach, however, offers an alternative to the very occurrence-based model: an occurrence is explained by something general, namely a self-conscious capacity. The charge of circularity thus is irrelevant on this conception (cf. Kern 2013, pp. 393 f.).

into a judgment and the assurance that the judgment is true, i.e. that it is knowledge.

Let me remind you that Kern's remarks on rational capacities are strongly influenced by Aristotle: Rational capacities are general and time-less, i.e. they are not particular states or acts at a particular time (Kern 2006, pp. 188f.).[185] And yet they are intrinsically related to acts that actualize the capacity and such acts are particular acts at a particular time. The being that possesses a rational capacity possesses a general capacity that can be actualized at particular moments in time. The acts that actualize the capacity only have their identity because of the very capacity. That is the first central trait of rational capacities: Rational capacities thus are constitutive unities, i.e. they are constituted by acts that actualize the capacity but that have their particular identity only because of the capacity (e.g. Kern 2006, pp. 194ff.). That also means that if we identify an act as being an actualization of a rational capacity, we are at the same time manifesting an understanding of the self-same capacity (Kern 2006, p. 205).

Kern suggests that we can understand this particular relation better if we examine a difference between rational capacities and habits: The acts that belong to a particular habit – like drinking coffee in the morning – are intelligible independently from the habit, the acts that belong to a rational capacity are not (Kern 2006, pp. 199f.). This feature also figures in the second trait of rational capacities. They are normative, i.e. identifying an act as an actualization of a capacity carries with it a measure for the exercise of the capacities (Kern 2006, pp. 213f., 251). If we say that Eliza is swimming, we automatically gain the standards for deciding whether Eliza is exercising the capacity successfully or unsuccessfully. The third feature again is closely connected to the first two features: rational capacities explain the acts that actualize them (Kern 2006, pp. 220f., 252). Eliza making a frog kick with her legs in the water is explained by her actualizing her rational capacity 'swimming'. But note that since rational capacities are general, they always subsume both the successful and the unsuccessful case. Kern refers back to Aristotle who holds that every capacity contains its actualization and its opposite (Kern 2006, pp. 218ff.; Aristoteles 2009, IX.2, 1046b4–7). The difference between the successful and the unsuccessful consists in a decision undertaken by the subject who has the rational capacities (Kern 2006, p. 224). The subject decides about the right thing to do in the given circumstances. A subject that possesses rational capacities also possesses *logos*, i.e. the capacity to think, understand and judge. In actualizing a rational capacity she actualizes

---

185 Rödl, too, builds his theory on Aristotles's conception of capacities, see e.g. (Rödl 2010, p. 142).

her *logos*-capacity – clearly a rational capacity – and does what is the thing to do given the circumstances and given the standards of the capacity; in other words, she makes a decision. A rational capacity thus is characterized by such an act of decision and the content that consists in doing what is appropriate to actualizing the rational capacity. The intimate connection between possession of a rational capacity and possession of *logos* is also central for capacities being explanatory; remember, that was the third feature of rational capacities.

Kern calls an account that wants to analyze knowledge into distinct elements, as does Burge's account, the analytic conception of knowledge: it claims that knowledge consists of elements that are more basic than knowledge itself (Kern 2006, p. 182). Her capacity approach opposes the analytic conception and, though Kern never says so herself, what she thus also opposes is the conception of knowledge as justified true belief (JTB). The JTB-conception is an analytic conception of knowledge. In other words, what Kern in fact proposes in response to the skeptic's challenge is to exchange the JTB-conception for the capacity conception, since we face the skeptical problems only because of analytic conceptions of knowledge, such as the JTB-conception. 'Justified true belief' is just an articulation of a more fundamental conception of knowledge according to which knowledge is an act of a rational capacity for knowledge (*Erkenntnisfähigkeit*) (Kern 2006, p. 182).

This insight is crucial for the Burge-McDowell-debate and the Argument from Fallibility. Just as in the section on Conant's framework of two skepticisms, one can again see more clearly that Burge's objections against McDowell's conception of perception and knowledge are on a different logical level. Burge is aiming for an analytic conception of knowledge, but it is just this conception that McDowell – like Kern and Rödl – has gotten rid off.

So Kern reveals that she does not want to find any independent support for the truth of a judgment that would justify calling it knowledge. It is not just that there is no need for such independent support, rather there cannot be any independent support.[186] If one tries to look for independent support for the truth of a judgment to determine that it is indeed knowledge, one is faced with the skeptic's objections and, in addition, one cannot even make sense of the idea of knowledge. That is why the Argument from Fallibility, i.e. Burge's objections, may be ignored. So to sum up: on Kern's conception what ensures that a judgment indeed is a case of knowledge already presupposes (a) that the capacity

---

186 Cf. Kern's criticism of the 'the dogma of the world-independent basis' (Kern 2006, p. 145) and the 'independence-condition for reasons for belief' (Kern 2013, p. 375).

for knowledge is a rational capacity, (b) that things in the world really are as in the knowledge of the world, and (c) that there is knowledge.

Note that in (a) and (c) Kern's account offers two kinds of support for the correctness of the ascription of knowledge. Kern herself does not explicitly distinguish the two, but I think that there is an important difference. The first argument is the Argument from the Special Nature of Rational Capacities: a subject can only know something based on perceiving the world if things are the way they have to be in order for the capacity for knowledge to be exercised correctly. And so if the epistemic perceptual capacity is exercised correctly, there is no way that the subject could not have perceptual knowledge. In other words, no actual knowledge without the correct actualization of the capacity for knowledge. Kern's Aristotelian notion of a "rational capacity" does most of the work in this argument. The act constitutes the capacity and at the same time the act is identified as the act that it *is* by falling under the capacity.[187] In being an act that is caused in the context of the exercise of the capacity C the act constitutes the correct exercise of the capacity.[188] Or as Kern puts it:

> Someone who in believing something actualizes a rational capacity for knowledge does not just have a belief whose truth is non-accidentally sufficiently justified, but she has it exactly because she has acquired it through exercise a rational capacity for knowledge.[189] (Kern 2006, pp. 274 f.)

This Argument from the Special Nature of Rational Capacities has to be distinguished from another line of argumentation that argues for the indispensability of knowledge in all epistemological theories, including skeptic theories (c). This, as we might call it, *Logico-Transcendental Argument*[190], observes that sensory error can only be conceptually determined through cases of sensory knowledge

---

187 This is also in line with Kern's and Rödl's remarks on the explanatory asymmetry of good cases of perception and bad cases of perception: the good case is immediately and fully explained by the actualization of the capacity, whereas the bad case is only indirectly explained by reference to the successful actualization of the capacity and unfavorable circumstances.

188 Cf. also Rödl: The capacity for knowledge "is the cause of the existence of its acts in such a way as to be, at the same time, the cause of their conforming to a normative measure, which thus is internal to these acts" (Rödl 2007, p. 141).

189 The German original: "Jemand, der, indem er etwas glaubt, eine vernünftige Erkenntnisfähigkeit aktualisiert, hat nicht nur eine Überzeugung, deren Wahrheit nicht zufällig hinreichend begründet ist, sondern genau deswegen, weil er sie dadurch erworben hat, daß er eine vernünftige Erkenntnisfähigkeit ausgeübt hat" (Kern 2006, pp. 274 f.).

190 Note that my Logico-Transcendental Argument is not what Kant means by the term "transcendental logic". Kant's transcendental logic aims to explain "that and how ... concepts are applied, or even are possible merely a priori" (Kant 1998, A56/B80).

(cf. Kern 2013, p. 388).[191] The Logico-Transcendental Argument proceeds as follows: The bad case can only be understood as a failed actualization of the good case: it is explained via the good case and unfavorable circumstances, whereas the good case is immediately explained by the actualization. Thus a theoretical approach to good and bad cases of knowledge cannot fundamentally question the existence of good cases of knowledge. This argument differs from the first argumentation (Argument from the Special Nature of Rational Capacities) since the latter aims to show why the actual successful exercise of the capacity ensures that the exercise was successful.

It is important to mark this distinction and to set Kern in the context of Conant's framework because the first argument faces problems that the second argumentation does not face and those problems are extremely relevant for the Burge-McDowell-exchange. Kern's claim that the actualization of a capacity itself ensures that the actualization was a good case conflicts with a later remark on how people react to a perceptual error: Kern argues that the intrinsic connection between fallibility and capacity also explains why a subject is not flabbergasted (Kern 2013, p. 394) if she has to correct her judgment and not call it knowledge anymore, because she had been misperceiving things. If she only had the Argument from the Special Nature of Rational Capacities, Kern could not say that the latter case is a case of knowledge. The exercise of the capacity was not a good case even though at the moment of exercising the capacity the subject would have said that she successfully actualizes her capacity for knowledge. Such an argumentation gets Kern into Burge's line of fire: the possibility of cases of having to correct one's judgment is just what he has been insisting on. The special power of Aristotelian rational capacities seems to fade. The problems with the first argumentation, however, do not mean that Kern's conception cannot help explain why McDowell rejects Burge's objection argumentation and takes himself not to be standing in Burge's line of fire. There is still the Logico-transcendental Argument that seems to be very strong. Also, I will argue that McDowell, unlike Kern, does not defer to Aristotele's story of capacities and thus does not have the problematic Argument from the Special Nature of Rational Capacities.[192]

---

191 Note that the Logico-Transcendental Argument is not the same as Kern's transcendental argument against the skeptic (Kern 2006, p. 149): Kern's transcendental argument argues that the skeptic cannot formulate his argument against empirical knowledge without assuming that empirical knowledge is possible.

192 Note that in her *Quellen des Wissens* (2006) Kern is also more careful about such claims as in the Argument from the Special Nature of Rational Capacities: she puts more emphasis on the role of a causal connection between the content of the judgment that is the actualization of the rational capacity for knowledge: "if the fact had not obtained, then the rational capacity for

So to sum up this section let me say why, according to Kern, Burge cannot claim nor object that perception cannot guarantee the truth of empirical judgments. The problem is that Burge on his conception cannot talk of empirical knowledge because he cannot even conceive of the acquisition of empirical knowledge going well. This deficit then extends to the unsuccessful cases of knowledge by perception. If the capacity was not ever actualized successfully, we would not be able to understand an unsuccessful actualization. An unsuccessful actualization can only be explained by citing the capacity and citing particular circumstances which influenced the actualization of the capacity (Kern 2006, p. 293). The capacity itself immediately explains the successful cases. Note that failure is always a possibility in exercises of a capacity, but in the first place it is a logical possibility (Kern 2006, p. 293). The realized possibility of the unsuccessful case is only derivative of the successful case.

Even though Kern's theory is more focused on explaining empirical knowledge whilst McDowell is more focused on explaining empirical content and empirical knowledge, they both seem to share the Logico-transcendental Argument against Burge's and Burgean conceptions: Burge cannot make sense of "empirical knowledge" (Kern) nor of "empirical content" (McDowell).

Rödl puts forward a Logico-transcendental Argument and a fraternal twin of the Argument from the Special Nature of Rational Capacities, the Argument from the Nature of Self-Conscious Capacities.[193] Adequately presenting the details of the arguments would require an extended excursus into Rödl's theory that is not necessary for the overall project of developing an appropriate conceptualist theory of perception and so, as I said above, I will have to leave it with some brief remarks about the argument's main idea. Moreover, the argument's basic structure is also clear from Kern's argument from Rational Capacities. Rödl puts more emphasis on the self-conscious nature of the argument. The main idea of Rödl's argument can be summarized as follows: When Eliza says 'I think that is raining because I see the rain.' she actualizes her self-conscious capacity for knowledge. In acquiring knowledge by perception Eliza exercises a self-conscious capacity, and therefore also represents her act as an exercise of

---

knowledge [of the perceiving subject] could not have been actualized in such a way that it gives her a reason to believe this fact –e.g. in the shape of perceptual experience of this fact." ["Wenn die Tatsache nicht bestanden hätte, hätte [die] vernünftige Erkenntnisfähigkeit [des wahrnehmenden Subjekts] nicht in der Weise aktualisiert werden können, daß sie ihm einen Grund – etwa in Gestalt einer Wahrnehmung dieser Tatsache – liefert, diese Tatsache zu glauben."] (Kern 2006, p. 270).

193 For Rödl's Logico-Transcendental Argument, see (Rödl 2007, pp. 70, 151) and (Rödl 2010, pp. 141, 149).

the capacity *knowledge by perception*. It is in the nature of knowing something through exercising the capacity of knowledge by perception that one knows that one knows it that way. Knowing as an exercise of a capacity is by its very nature self-confirming. An exercise of the self-conscious capacity of knowledge by perception is an act that contains the knowledge of itself.

Ignoring the Argument from Fallibility III: McDowell's transcendental argument from disjunctivism

Admittedly, McDowell himself does offer another, more transcendentally-minded explanation of why skeptical questions as those asked by Burge may be rejected. He does so in a response to criticism by Crispin Wright: "The Disjunctive Conception of Experience as Material for a Transcendental Argument" (McDowell 2008b). Interestingly enough, neither McDowell nor Burge explicitly refer to the arguments given in this article, but it is helpful to consider this alternative reaction.[194] This response builds on the disjunctive element in McDowell's theory of perception. In the article McDowell engages with Wright's criticism of disjunctivist dealings with skeptics (Wright 2002a). I will neither introduce nor discuss Wright's objections, but only focus on McDowell's side of the story.

You might ask yourself why I have introduced Kern's arguments if one can also find a response in McDowell's work. As I have said, McDowell does not make the backdrop to his argumentation clear, and this background becomes clearer when one looks at Kern's and also Rödl's work. It is also easier to understand McDowell's transcendental argument from disjunctivism when one has learned of the Logico-Transcendental Argument and the Argument from the Nature of Rational Capacities. So what does McDowell do with his transcendental argument from disjunctivism?

McDowell wants to argue against the skeptic about perceptual knowledge about the external world. For simplicity in the context of this section I will fill out this position by Burge's conception. McDowell starts from an assumption that he takes everyone, whether skeptic or not, to accept: experience is of objective reality or at least it "purports to be of objective reality" (McDowell 2008b, p. 380). We take in objective reality directly in our experience. Of course, there are cases in which it only seems to us as if we see how objective reality is, but these are cases which only appear to belong to the class of experiences in

---

194 In *Perception as a Capacity for Knowledge* (2011b) McDowell only refers to the exchange with Wright because he takes an example from Wright's article (McDowell 2011b, p. 46).

which "how things are makes itself visually available to one" (McDowell 2008b, p. 380). The class of experiences in which really "how things are makes itself visually available to one" (McDowell 2008b, p. 380) however is primary and cannot be denied. The possibility of error in perception, of not perceiving objective reality, gives us the disjunctivist's disjunction:

> [P]erceptual appearances are either objective states of affairs making themselves manifest to subjects, or situations in which it is as if an objective state of affairs is making itself manifest to a subject, although that is not how things are. (McDowell 2008b, pp. 380 f.)

As we know the Argument from Fallibility and the skeptic hold against this that even in the best cases perception cannot be more than an appearance, because the subject cannot distinguish the good cases and the bad cases and the possibility of error is ineliminable. The role of perception for knowledge and belief thus does not exceed the highest common factor that the good cases and the bad cases share, namely that it *seems* to one as if how things are objectively is revealed to one in perception. This position is the target for McDowell's transcendental argument against the skeptic.

McDowell argues that on the highest common factor model, the skeptic cannot make sense of "direct perceptual access to objective facts about the environment" (McDowell 2008b, p. 378). Here we see the Kantian skeptic's move against the Cartesian skeptic. This incapacity is detrimental because the skeptic needs the notion of direct access to objective reality in order to even make sense of the derivative notion of appearances in perceptual experience. Note the clear parallels to the Logico-Transcendental Argument. Now, as I have said many times, on the disjunctivist conception a disjunction blocks the skeptic's move from the indistinguishability of good cases and bad cases to the highest common factor model. McDowell goes on to develop a transcendental argument according to which "the disjunctive conception is required, on pain of our losing our grip on the very idea that in experience we have it appear to us that things are a certain way" (McDowell 2008b, p. 382). McDowell's basic argumentation is concerned with the Kantian skeptic, just like Kern and Rödl, but note that their arguments differ in focus: McDowell wants to show that experience is of reality, whereas Kern and Rödl are concerned with the possibility of perceptual knowledge.

McDowell's disjunctivist conception disarms the Cartesian skeptic,[195] and that includes Burge, in the way that we have encountered before. The skeptic

---

195 McDowell does not talk of the Cartesian skeptic in the article, but it should be clear that it makes sense to say that he is dealing with the Cartesian skeptic.

suggests that the ineliminable possibility of error undermines any use of perception as warrant for belief and knowledge. McDowell's disjunctivism, however, transfers the possibility of error into a different frame: it is part of the disjunction that constitutes the nature of perception. Thus referring to the possibility of error does not present an "epistemic predicament" (McDowell 2008b, p. 385). McDowell rejects Wright's objections to disjunctivism as still caught in the framework of the highest common factor conception – and of course, this rejection extends to Burge's objections, too. McDowell also, albeit implicitly, refers to his own conception of perception as a self-consciously possessed capacity:

> What does entitle one to claim that one is perceiving that things are thus and so, when one is so entitled? The fact that one is perceiving that things are thus and so. That is a kind of fact whose obtaining our self-consciously possessed perceptual capacities enable us to recognize on suitable occasions, just as they enable us to recognize such facts as that there are red cubes in front of us, and all the more complex types of environmental facts that our powers to perceive things put at our disposal. (McDowell 2008b, p. 386)

Both responses can be given to the Argument from Fallibility and to Burge's objections – and to a certain extent they are given by Kern and Rödl, namely in the shape of the Logico-Transcendental Argument and the two fraternal Arguments based on the particular nature of rational, self-conscious capacities. On a disjunctivist conception of perception as a capacity the "epistemic predicament" (McDowell 2008b, p. 385) that Burge tries to conjure up does not exist. If we can make sense of the notion of "environmental facts" (McDowell 2008b, p. 379) being directly available to us, there is no such "epistemic predicament" (McDowell 2008b, p. 385). Such a predicament can only exist on a conception which sets up "tendentious ground rules for satisfying ourselves in given cases that we have knowledge of the environment" (McDowell 2008b, p. 379). McDowell also notes that the skeptic's position is incompatible with the fact that we do have extensive knowledge about the world; such knowledge would have to be non-existent if the skeptic was right.[196] The disjunctivist conception empowers the subject to take the positive cases of perception as primary (McDowell 2008b, p. 379).

But there is also a crucial difference between McDowell's and Kern's strategies. The same difference also applies to Rödl's strategy, because they concern those views that both Rödl and Kern defend.[197] Strictly speaking, McDowell's ar-

---

196 Note that this response does not feature in Conant's taxonomy of responses to the Cartesian skeptic.

197 Apart from the parallels in Kern's and Rödl's theory there is one major difference: their theories focus on two different phenomena. Kern focuses on the possibility of empirical knowledge

gument is not just logico-transcendental, but rather properly transcendental: McDowell explains that his argument is a transcendental argument, because it proceeds as follows:

(1) "Experience purports to be of objective reality" (McDowell 2008b, p. 380).

(2) If (1), then we must be able to make sense of the "idea of environmental facts making themselves available to us in perception" (McDowell 2008b, p. 380), because otherwise (1) is not intelligible.

It is only his argument about the skeptic having to presuppose "appearance" to even express his objection that is logico-transcendental.[198]

Let me briefly go into more detail on how Kern's and Rödl's theories differ from McDowell's theory.[199] These differences are crucial, because they will

---

and Rödl focuses on self-consciousness. According to him, self-consciousness is a form of self-knowledge that is both spontaneous and receptive. Moreover, there are two differences in argumentation: Rödl rejects the fallibilist's idea of making a list of circumstances that have to obtain for a capacity to be properly actualized because it would be endless (Rödl 2007, p. 151). Kern, however, holds that the endlessness of such a list is irrelevant; the very idea of starting such a list is flawed, because a conception of a capacity already contains the fact that the circumstances are favorable (Kern 2013, p. 384). The second difference lies in Kern's and Rödl's treatment of cases in which a subject finds that the experience on which she based her judgment was false. Kern holds that the subject would not be flabbergasted at such a revelation, since fallibility intrinsically belongs to a capacity (Kern 2013, p. 394). There is nothing like an incapacity. Rödl on the other hand dismisses such cases as irrelevant. He takes another question to be more pressing: why do we trust our experience to base our judgments (Rödl 2007, pp. 155 ff.)?

198 Note that full-blown skepticism that even doubts (1) would require an additional transcendental argument that would show experience as purporting to be of objective reality as a "necessary condition for some more basic feature of consciousness, perhaps that its states and episodes are potentially self-conscious" (McDowell 2008b, p. 382). McDowell's response to the full-blown skeptic is rather weak, but any discussion of this response would lead us too far astray from our current project.

199 Alan Millar also develops a theory of how perceptual experiences can be reasons for belief. As Millar himself says, this theory is based on McDowell's theory of perceptual experience (cf. Millar 2011a, p. 347), but there are crucial differences. I cannot fully introduce Millar's theory here, nor discuss the relation between McDowell's and Millar's theory, therefore I will restrict myself to the following remarks. Millar holds that the capacity for perceptual knowledge – the "visual perceptual-recognitional ability" (Millar 2011a, p. 343) – and the capacity for knowing that the particular knowledge is perceptual knowledge "work in tandem" (Millar 2011b, p. 238), but he thinks that the conceptual activity in perceptual experience is a "direct response to the visual experiences" (Millar 2011b, p. 238) the perceiver has, and so ultimately his conception rejects the very foundation of McDowell's theory of perceptual experience. Another crucial difference concerns Millar's understanding of the capacity for perceptual knowledge – he

show which of their arguments are helpful for understanding McDowell's conception and his rejection of Burge. I have emphasized that all three projects can be regarded as dealing with Kantian skepticism, but there is an important respect in which Kern's and Rödl's project is not as fundamental as McDowell's project. They try to explain how there can empirical knowledge, knowledge of the world, and knowledge of oneself. Kern starts her argumentation from investigating skeptical challenges. We have to conceive knowledge as a capacity in order to deal with the aporia of knowledge and the skeptic's challenge. And more generally: we have to conceive knowledge as a capacity in order to understand what knowledge is. McDowell, however, is interested in something more basic: He wants to explain how perception can have empirical content and that just includes explaining knowledge of the world and explaining experience of the world. This has been his project ever since *Mind and World* (1996) and it continues to be an essential aim (see McDowell 2008b, p. 380). His interest in knowledge, one might even speculate, is only a by-product of the fact that the human perceptual capacity that gets us empirical content is a capacity for knowledge. This speculation may be substantiated by the following quotation from McDowell's "Perception as a Capacity for Knowledge" (2011b):

> When all goes well in the operation of a perceptual capacity of a sort that belongs to its possessor's rationality, a perceiver enjoys a perceptual state in which some feature of her environment is *there* for her, perceptually *present* to her rationally self-conscious awareness. This presence is an actualization of a capacity that belongs to the subject's reason. Reason is at work, that is, in the perceptual presence to rational subjects of features of their environment. (McDowell 2011b, p. 30f., emphasis in original)

McDowell's question, as I have said following Conant's taxonomy, is a transcendental question: "How can my senses so much as *present* things as being a certain way?" (Conant 2012, p. 14, emphasis in original) Like the other question that has kept McDowell occupied since *Mind and World*, "How can there be such an act as making up one's mind about how things are in the world?" (McDowell 1998d, p. 410), this is a version of the more general question "How is empirical content possible?" (McDowell 1996, p. xxi). McDowell's conceptualist theory of perceptual experience is an answer to all of these questions, and it is this theory which also includes McDowell claiming that perception is a capacity for knowl-

---

conceives of it as a "success notion", i. e. exercising the capacity for perceptual knowledge is exercising it correctly (Millar 2009, p. 224). On McDowell's conception a flawed exercise of a rational capacity still is an exercise of the capacity. For more about Millar's views on perceptual experience and what role recognitional capacities play in it, see e. g. also (Millar 2007; Millar 2008).

edge. As we have seen in his paper responding to Wright's criticism, McDowell's argumentation for the claim that perception is a capacity for knowledge may really be called *transcendental*. In some respects McDowell's transcendental argument is also a Logico-Transcendental Argument, but at the same time it is more than that, because it is not restricted to knowledge.[200]

That is the second difference which is crucial in the exchange with Burge: McDowell does not explicitly state the Logico-Transcendental Argument in response to critics who insist that the fallibility of knowledge (and perception) rules out the possibility of indefeasible warrant. He only says that the possibility of fallibility does not preclude the successful exercise of the capacity that does provide indefeasible warrant. Fallibility is part and parcel of the notion of a capacity. Kern and Rödl say that we cannot even understand what fallibility is without successful cases of knowledge. In other words, knowledge is primary. McDowell gives a transcendental argument for perception being a capacity for empirical content, but the Logico-transcendental Argument is more finely tailored for dealing with the skeptic about knowledge because it fundamentally dislodges the critic's assumption. This is the crucial move that is missing in McDowell's response to Burge.

As I have suggested above, McDowell's transcendental argument can be read to include the Logico-transcendental Argument, but it is certainly not explicit in McDowell's response to Burge. One might find it – at least partly – in his response to Wright, but there, too, it lacks adequate detail. Given that Kern's conception and Rödl's conception in some parts are developments of McDowell's thoughts (e.g. Rödl 2007, pp. 147–158) and might be regarded as elaborations on a special case of "how is empirical content possible?", we should not accuse McDowell of offering a gappy theory but rather of omitting helpful explanations that are implicit in all his statements.

At this point one cannot but acknowledge that it is not too surprising that people like Burge are not satisfied by McDowell's response (e.g. in McDowell 2010a), since McDowell does not give them the basic theoretical grounding that they need to fully understand the scope of his response. The additions that I have made by introducing Kern's, Rödl's and Conant's thoughts and analyses are thus necessary for understanding McDowell's conception. But again, they are not foreign to McDowell, but rather something like an organ transplant from a parent.

---

200 Note that Kern's starting point allows her to offer a better explanation for why perception must be conceived of as a capacity: only if we conceive of knowledge as a capacity, and not as a single state (Kern 2007, p. 245), can we deal with the skeptic's challenge (cf. Kern 2006, pp. 182 f., 184; Kern 2007, p. 258).

Criticism of the perception as capacity-approach

The answers that I have carved out so far build on the particular nature of knowledge by perception as a general rational capacity and on the transcendental role of the successful rational capacity. But it has to be emphasized that the transcendental arguments are stronger than the arguments building on the special nature on rational and self-conscious capacities. They are more promising responses to Burge's insistence, because they show that Burge cannot frame his objections without presupposing that which he wants to question. Therefore I think that the safest argumentation against the Argument from Fallibility lies in emphasizing the primacy of the good, successful case of exercising the capacity, since this is a logical point.[201]

But at the same time I am sure that people like Burge will also be left unsatisfied by the Logico-transcendental Argument. We need to ask why they keep asking how the subject can be sure that things really are as she perceives them? Kern says that they keep asking this question, because they are looking for independent support for the truth of the judgment, when in fact there is no independent support (Kern 2006, p. 145; Kern 2013, pp. 375 f.). They do not see that the question for independent support for knowledge does not even make sense without presupposing that there is knowledge and therefore they still adduce the same arguments. But really, their questions about independent support cannot unsettle the capacity-view of knowledge, because they can only ask their question if the capacity-view holds. Admittedly, the situation for the critic is slightly paradoxical: the critics cannot fundamentally question the indefeasibility of empirical knowledge without previously assuming that there is indefeasible knowledge.

There is no point at which the circle of perception as a rational capacity for knowledge can be left, even though the exercise of this very rational capacity allows one to imagine cases which seem to suggest that one has to leave the circle. Burge's case is an example for this situation. In his attempt at responding to McDowell's conception of perception and knowledge Burge insists that "referential success depends on the causal connections between the environmental condition and the registration of proximal stimulation being normal" (Burge 2011a, p. 50). The causal connections that he imagines are obviously unlike Kern's causal connections that are irreducibly normative; Burge takes empirical science to

---

201 In Rödl's terminology: arguing that perception is "prior to illusion" (Rödl 2010, p. 148) is a strong observation; arguing that perception is "prior in knowledge" (Rödl 2010, p. 148) does not provide a coherent and convincing set up.

help him understand those connections and determine whether they are intact. Yet by focusing on this type of connection Burge only appears to move to another level, the level of empirical science. Kern, Rödl and McDowell show that – try as he might – Burge cannot escape utilizing the notion of knowledge as a standing in the space of reasons because he has to presuppose it in order to even come up with his questions, counter-examples and alternative proposals.

In the end Burge and fellow critics might however invoke what I suggest to call the Argument from Non-academic Concerns. This argument argues that at the end of the day doubting one's sense experience is not an academic, philosophical, theoretical issue and so McDowell's, Kern's and Rödl's logico-transcendental and transcendental observations are irrelevant to the non-academic. What the non-academic skeptic wants to be assured of is the correctness of her current perception and her knowledge. She is also not interested in the questions of Conant's Kantian skeptic: Eliza is not interested in Kern telling her that she knows that her friends are on the bench because her act of perception has to be conceived as an actualization of the capacity for knowledge in order to make sense of the possibility of empirical knowledge. She does not want logico-transcendental support, but empirical support. In other words, she wants to know that the circumstances are favorable. Kern's transcendental argumentation is irrelevant for Eliza if she sees her friends sitting on the bench and wants to be sure that it is really her friends and not some other group of people that look like her friends from a distance.[202]

So what would Kern, McDowell and Rödl respond to this challenge?[203] First of all McDowell would probably refer back to his comment from *Mind and World* that I have already cited above. He is likely to take this comment as definitive:

> Traditional epistemology cannot be vindicated by the sheer possibility of asking, 'How do you know that what you are enjoying is a genuine glimpse of the world?' ... If someone insists on asking that, on some particular occasion, [as does the above Argument, N.E.] an appropriate response might start like this: 'I know why you think that question is peculiarly

---

202 One can describe the objection as a rejection of what Kvanvig calls "academic skepticism" (Kvanvig 2011, p. 32). The critic wants to discuss "pragmatic concerns about what to do and what to believe" (Kvanvig 2011, p. 32) and academic skepticism is irrelevant for such 'pragmatic' theories.

203 I omit Conant from the list of those criticized by the Argument from Non-academic Concerns because in his text he does not explicitly position himself. The case can surely be made that Conant rather belongs to McDowell's side, but I think that it is better to regard him as giving the framework for understanding the dispute between McDowell and Burge and not include him into the dispute as an active participant.

pressing, but it is not.' If the question still stands, nothing particularly philosophical is called for in answering it." (McDowell 1996, p. 113)

Again, clearly, this response is not enough, but after having introduced Kern's and Rödl's theories and Conant's framework, we can add further arguments from the trio that complement McDowell's view. Rödl, Kern and McDowell would probably see Eliza as another victim of the 'independence-condition for reasons for belief' (Kern 2013, p. 375). She thinks that there can be reasons for knowing that her belief that her friends are on the bench is true which are independent of the belief itself and her perception. Yet, Eliza and Burge might interrupt here and insist that this admission reveals that the independence condition cannot be overcome: it is entrenched in human life and thus cannot be disposed off. But Kern, McDowell and Rödl could respond to this contention in at least three ways. First, they might to highlight a theoretical shortcoming: Eliza and Burge, just like all fallibilists, cannot explain why we are even inclined to believe that we know that p in cases in which we really do not know that p. They can only state the possibility of our belief about our knowledge being wrong, but they cannot explain "how I may falsely think I know" (Rödl 2007, p. 156).[204] On the capacity approach Kern, Rödl and McDowell can do that by simply pointing out that our capacity to know that we know that p is fallible. Second, they could refer to Conant's Wittgensteinian way with Skepticism and describe Eliza's life as a life that simply has not been led to nonsense, i. e. to Cartesian skepticism and then led back to the ordinary by a Wittgensteinian (cf. Conant 2012, p. 65). And finally, they could admit that they do not deny that the independence condition is entrenched in human life, but it can only be entrenched in a human life that is defined by the subject possessing rational capacities such as the receptive self-conscious capacity for knowledge. If Eliza was able to look down to the ground of her being, she would see self-conscious rational capacities that permeate her life. It is those capacities that allow her to think that there is anything like independent support for her belief in the first place. And yet the ability to ask for such support also necessarily entails that there can never actually be such independent support.

The Argument from Non-academic Concerns and Conant's remarks on the two varieties of skepticism reveal an insight that might turn out to be disappointing. The debate seems to be only based on a terminological misunderstanding: the Argument from Fallibility, the Burge-side, does not understand that the McDowell-side is interested in Kantian skepticism and the McDowell-side sees itself

---

204 Cf. (Rödl 2007, pp. 148, 155 f.)

unfit to uncover all their theoretical groundwork and background. But I take it that there is more to the debate about the Argument from Fallibility – that is also why I have contributed a close reading and such a large section to discussing it.

If one looks back at the other non-conceptualist arguments against conceptualism, one sees that the McDowell-Burge debate centers on further fundamental questions that are developments of the questions that I have already found in the debate between conceptualists and non-conceptualists (Sections 2.1, 2.2). E. g. what is my idea of the relation between reasons and beliefs? What is the primary case in the relation between reasons and beliefs? Is the primary case that of reasons fully explaining a belief or is it that of reasons never fully explaining beliefs? Kern, McDowell and Rödl clearly subscribe to the former of the two options, e. g. according to Kern, the role of reasons is to show that it is rational to have a certain belief p. As she puts it: reasons are to be rationally compelling. She does not want to give up on this characteristic of reasons and that seems to be a major reason for developing the notion of knowledge as a capacity.

If one does not have such a strong pull towards reasons as rationally compelling, one does not see the need to go 'all the way' with Kern, McDowell and Rödl. Burge, who continues to rebel against what he sees as hyper-intellectualized theories of perception and knowledge (Burge 2011a, pp. 64 ff.), and who takes human perception to be the object of scientific investigation (Burge 2005, pp. 19 ff.; Burge 2011a, pp. 69 f.), clearly does not see why reasons should have to be rationally compelling and why one should aim for a conception of reasons as being rationally compelling for beliefs. Such purely "conceptual inquiries" (Burge 2011a, p. 70) cannot be settled by philosophy only.

This is another fundamental question that we already encountered in the non-conceptualist-conceptualist debate: what is the role of empirical studies in philosophy of perception? I can already say now that it will continue to come up in this study, too. I will return to this question in more detail in the very last chapter (Chapter 9). Burge and McDowell at least are aware of this basic disagreement about empirical studies and I take it that Burge would explain his utter amazement at McDowell's proposal largely by their open disagreement on this issue and not by issues with the notion of rational capacities. Burge does not discuss Kern's theory nor Rödl's theory, but would certainly react in the same way to their thoughts. They would represent a case of philosophy unduly influenced by German idealism: "In trying to protect philosophy from empirical incursion, and to give it a subject matter of its own, the [German, N.E.] tradition succeeds in isolating philosophy from knowledge" (Burge 2011a, p. 70).

The disagreement is obvious, and yet I think that the more profound reason for Burge's amazement at McDowell's disjunctivist conceptualist conception of perceptual experience lies in Burge failing to see the distinction between Cartesian skepticism and Kantian skepticism and most importantly the primacy of the Kantian question as outlined by Conant.[205]

At the end of this section we have got a fuller picture of the capacity approach of perception and have also achieved a more thorough analysis of the recent exchange between Burge and McDowell. It has also become clear how essential the transcendental question is to the conceptualist project. I will return to Burge's and McDowell's disagreement about empirical studies in philosophy of perception in the last chapter of this book.

---

205 There are further examples for fundamental disagreement in the exchange between Burge and McDowell. McDowell rejects the idea of using empirical science to explain how perception works; one of his arguments is that empirical science does not have the appropriate conceptual framework for explicating the workings of "perceptual states of perceivers" (McDowell 2010a, p. 250), it can only explicate the states of "perceptual systems" (McDowell 2010a, p. 250): "[a] state of a perceptual system cannot have the epistemic significance of a perceptual experience that consists in having an aspect of objective reality perceptually present to one" (McDowell 2010a, p. 250). Another argument in McDowell's rejection is that those scientific studies only *seem* to use the same language as the philosopher's investigations on the nature of perception: their use really is oftentimes metaphorical. McDowell is surprised by Burge's amazed response to his proposal, he writes: "I raise a *conceptual* question about how we should understand the language used in such theories. Burge responds, bizarrely, as if to a case of *empirical ignorance*" (McDowell 2010a, p. 251, emphasis in original).

In his second paper-response Burge replies: "I think it clear that answering conceptual questions about a science's language depends on empirical knowledge – knowledge of what the science says. ... Empirical ignorance of the science does prevent conceptual claims about the science from being correct. Conceptual questions are not, in general, independent of empirical knowledge" (Burge 2011a, p. 70). Once again McDowell and Burge are not clear about what they are discussing nor about the fundamental nature of their disagreement. They talk about the language used in sciences, but one can now see that it is about more. They have a fundamental disagreement about the topic of their investigations: McDowell considers transcendental questions and aims for transcendental answers; Burge considers empirical questions and aims for empirical answers. The issue is not really about languages used in science. When McDowell and Burge discuss their respective arguments they do not leave their own framework, thereby preserving their disagreements and in fact extending them to side shows.

I will not discuss McDowell's and Burge's debate about the role of empirical science in understanding perceptual experience just now. According to McDowell, the main problem with Burge's approach is that empirical science can only offer enabling conditions of perception and knowledge, but we have seen in Kern's work that the explanations of perception and knowledge need to be constitutive, too (McDowell 2010a, p. 250). I will get to this topic at the end of the book (Chapter 9) where I will try to point to ways in which conceptualism can embrace empirical studies.

2.8 First Conclusions: Conceptualism Survives the Non-Conceptualist Arguments, But Where Does It Stand?

For years the arguments that I have reviewed in the previous sections have dominated the debates between conceptualists and non-conceptualists. This examination has revealed that the arguments are bound to be uneffective, because they differ in their construals of the underlying terms and in their respective aims. This is certainly most clear for the transcendental project that only McDowell's conceptualism pursues and none of the non-conceptualists. Another such fundamental difference lies in whether the account of concepts and conceptual capacities is circular or not.

I think that my discussion of the different non-conceptualist arguments has established that and why they do not topple conceptualism in general. There are some qualms about certain conceptualist responses given by McDowell, but quite generally there are good conceptualist replies to all of the above non-conceptualist objections. In effect, these non-conceptualist arguments have been shown to be largely ineffective. The Argument from Animal Perception, the Argument from Hyper-Intellectualization and the Argument from Memory Experience will still be allowed to return in developing relational conceptualism, because they are likely to come to the readers' minds when thinking about relational conceptualism. But as I will show they can be countered by relational conceptualism, too.

At the end of this chapter I need to add an important caveat: even though I have just proudly announced that non-conceptualism is done with, that is only partly true. I take myself to have shown that the above non-conceptualist arguments fail against conceptualism, broadly understood, but there are still more non-conceptualist arguments that I have not introduced nor discussed yet. That is because these arguments come from a very different background, namely relationist theories of perceptual experience, and thus put forward different considerations than the above seven arguments. Relationist theories claim that perceptual experience does not have representational content, but rather consists in a relation between subject and object. Usually no one takes relationists to put forward non-conceptualist arguments because they reject both the above non-conceptualist theories, e. g. Peacocke's or Burge's theories, and McDowell's conceptualism. But actually relationism is a non-conceptualist theory, too, and its arguments are non-conceptualist, because they strongly oppose the idea that perceptual experience includes the actualization of conceptual capacities. They think that conceptual capacities only appear at the level of thought about perceptual experience, but not in perceptual experience itself. The relationist anti-representationalist and anti-conceptualist arguments will be introduced in Part III and so there are still other non-conceptualist arguments that need to be discussed. But those arguments, too, will turn out not to harm conceptualism.

Before I get to introducing this additional set of non-conceptualist considerations, we need to once more turn to conceptualism itself in order to follow up on crucial developments in conceptualism itself. All of the non-conceptualist arguments discussed in the previous sections are levelled against conceptualist theories of perception that build on McDowell's claims in *Mind and World* and texts published in the vicinity of this central book. They thus do not concern McDowell's significantly revised conceptualism that he has outlined in his 2008 article "Avoiding the Myth of the Given". That is also why I have waited until now to introduce this revised conceptualism; it would have been hardly touched upon in the above discussion of the arguments against conceptualism. As you will see, some of the arguments also apply to McDowell's revised conceptualist position, but it also has its own set of objections, partly because the revision is influenced by this other special non-conceptualist theory of perception, the relationist theory. In this section I will first introduce McDowell's revised conceptualism, and then start to discuss some of its problems. The discussion of this revised conceptualism will be interrupted by the presentation of relationist positions and objections, because they are required for fully examining McDowell's revised conceptualism. Understanding the advantages and disadvantages of revised conceptualism takes me further towards introducing relational conceptualism, the variety of conceptualism that I take to be the right one for capturing the nature of epistemically significant perception.

3 Examining McDowell's Revised Conceptualism

3.1 Avoiding the Myth of the Given, Travis's Relationism and the Role of Intuitional Content

McDowell's rigor and insistence in rejecting the above array of objections is infamous and so when he openly admits to changes to his conceptualist position this is widely noted and met with surprise. Such substantial changes can be found in the article "Avoiding the Myth of the Given" (McDowell 2009a). The article announces that two of McDowell's previous "assumptions now strike [him] as wrong" (McDowell 2009a, p. 258). First, perceptions are not anymore taken to have propositional content, and second, the content of perceptual experience is not anymore taken to include everything that the subject can know non-inferentially (McDowell 2009a, p. 258). McDowell acknowledges Charles Travis with having induced him to make the second of those changes. The first change can be primarily traced back to objections by Donald Davidson (McDowell 1999).

McDowell starts "Avoiding the Myth of the Given" with some clarificatory remarks on Sellars's Myth of the Given. As we have seen, McDowell interprets the Sellarsian notion of the Myth of the Given as referring to theories which claim that sense impressions by themselves can be taken up in the activities of rational capacities, e.g. a perceptual judgment can be based on simple sensuous intake. Sellars and McDowell object against such 'mythical' positions that sensibility understood as "a capacity for differential responsiveness to features of the environment, made possible by properly functioning sensory systems" (McDowell 2009a, p. 257) cannot be related to rational capacities, because it is not part of reason. McDowell applauds Kant's theory of perceptual experience because it avoids the Myth of the Given – even though, of course, the label did not exist at Kant's time – by arguing that perceptual experience involves the actualization of conceptual capacities. As we already know from his *Mind and World* McDowell wants to take up this idea of Kant. He holds that "in giving one things to know, experience must draw on conceptual capacities" (McDowell 2009a, p. 260). This central tenet of McDowell's conceptualist theory of perceptual experience still holds, but now in "Avoiding the Myth of the Given" McDowell overrules two sub-claims.

In earlier texts McDowell had supposed that if experiences involve actualizations of conceptual capacities, then the content of experience would have to be propositional content. Now McDowell wants to retract this claim: the content of experience is not propositional content, but intuitional content. He also takes back another, a related, claim, namely the assumption "that the content of an experience has to include everything the experience enables its subject to know non-inferentially" (McDowell 2009a, p. 258). If that was correct, then the content of a particular experience would have to include all concepts that are involved in the non-inferentially available knowledge made accessible by the experience. The new position that McDowell wants to adopt here is this: If I have a bird in view, "my experience [simply, N.E.][206] makes the bird visually present to me" (McDowell 2009a, p. 259, footnote added, N.E.). Based on this experience I can know that this bird is a cardinal even though the concept *cardinal* was not part of the content of my perceptual experience. I know that this is a cardinal through actualizing my recognitional capacities for cardinals.[207] It is important to emphasize that this knowledge is strictly non-inferential knowledge, since I can immediately recognize that the bird is a cardinal by using my recognitional capacities and without any acts of inference (McDowell 2009a, p. 258). According to McDowell, it was Charles Travis who put such cases to him and brought him to the changes announced above.[208]

Of course, not all concepts can be allowed to be excluded from the content of the experience and be said to figure in the subject's non-inferential knowledge based on the particular experience. McDowell notes that concepts of proper and common sensibles might be candidates for concepts that cannot be excluded from the perceptual content. In other words, experience at least has to draw "on conceptual capacities which are related with concepts of proper and common sensibles" (McDowell 2009a, p. 260). The concepts of proper and common sensibles might be "natural stopping point[s]" (McDowell 2009a, p. 260), i.e. they have to be part of the perceptual content and must not be introduced by way of activity of recognitional capacities. Such concepts of proper and common sensibles which must not be excluded from the content of the perceptual experience are, for example, color, number, motion (Aristoteles 1995, pp. 418a – 418b): the color of the object, the number of the objects, the object's shape are elements that have to appear in the original content of a particular perceptual experience.

---

206 This is a substantial addition to the quotation, but it helps make the idea clearer.
207 McDowell writes: "[the] content whose figuring in [perceptual] knowledge is owed to the recognitional capacity need not be part of the content of the experience itself" (McDowell 2009a, p. 259).
208 I think that Travis's story of Uncle Willard's bittern (Travis 2013c, pp. 245 f.) and of Pia whom Travis takes to O-see the pig when she does not possess the relevant concept *pig* (Travis 2013c, p. 239) might be cases that convinced McDowell. Note that this remark is not more than speculation, but the cases will return for my development of relational conceptualism and, of course, in the reconstruction of Travis's relationism.

At this point I have to start talking about the second change in McDowell's conception. On his *Mind and World*-conception McDowell would have held that the concepts of proper and common sensibles appear in the propositional content of perceptual experience. In "Avoiding the Myth of the Given" he holds that the concepts of proper and common sensibles appear in the intuitional content of perceptual experience. McDowell introduces the notion of intuitional content in his first amendment to his conception: the content of experience is not propositional, but intuitional.[209] The notion of intuitional content goes back to the Kantian term *intuition* (*Anschauung*). An intuition in Kant's terminology is an *Anschauung*, "a having in view" (McDowell 2009a, p. 260). In his further development of the notion of intuitional content McDowell relies heavily on the following quotation from Kant:

> The same function which gives unity to the various representations *in a judgment* also gives unity to the mere synthesis of various representations *in an intuition*; and this unity, in its most general expression, we entitle the pure concept of the understanding. (Kant 1998, A79/ B104 f., in: McDowell 2009a, p. 260, McDowell's emphasis)[210]

There are thus two kinds of unity in representations, intuitional unity and propositional unity, and *one* function which brings about these two kinds of unity. Intuitional unity is brought about by the categories and propositional unity is brought about by the activity of the categories and categorial judgments. According to Kant, there is a special relation between intuitional unity and propositional unity: the different forms of intuitional unity correspond to different forms of propositional unity. McDowell wants to retain Kant's idea of the correspondence between forms of intuitional unity and forms of propositional unity, but he does not want to accept Kant's idea of the categories. He thinks that we can separate those two elements and find or introduce other forms of propositional unity and their corresponding intuitional unity without having to resort to the Kantian categories (McDowell 2009a, p. 261).

The one example for such a form of propositional unity that McDowell provides is Michael Thompson's notion of "thought and talk about the living as such" (McDowell 2009a, p. 261). McDowell himself does not mention the expres-

---

209 Actually talk of intuitional content already starts in the *Woodbridge Lectures* (e. g. McDowell 2009g, p. 463), but in "Avoiding the Myth of the Given" McDowell is adamant about the change from propositional content to intuitional content in perceptual experience and so I will focus on this text.

210 "Dieselbe Funktion, welche den verschiedenen Vorstellungen in einem Urteile Einheit gibt, die gibt auch der bloßen Synthesis verschiedener Vorstellungen in einer Anschauung Einheit, welche, allgemein ausgedrückt, der reine Verstandesbegriff heißt." (Kant 1998, A79/B104 f.)

sion, but he seems to be referring to what Thompson calls *life-form*. McDowell is scarce with explanations of what Thompson's special notion includes, so let me pause to include some general remarks on *life-form*.

Thompson proposes an analytic Aristotelian approach to *life*, *action* and *practice* (Thompson 2008). Those three concepts are *a priori* concepts. Those *a priori* concepts are accompanied by what Thompson calls *form concepts*. *Life-form*, *intention*, *social practice* are such form concepts. They are distinctive concepts, because they have a special unity that comes with them. Anything that falls under such a form concept exhibits features that are essential to the particular concept. The unity that such form concepts have is a "unity through which the things united can at the same time be understood" (Thompson 2008, p. 11).

McDowell extends Thompson's idea to the form *animal*. As I have said, McDowell's starting point is Kant's claim that there are propositional unities which correspond to intuitional unities and McDowell's Thompson-inspired claim is that *life-form* and *animal* are such propositional unities which have corresponding intuitional unities. *Animal* is the form concept that captures the "distinctive kind of unity" (McDowell 2009a, p. 261) of my experience of the cardinal. Since *animal* is a form concept, it provides a "unity through which the things united can at the same time be understood" (Thompson 2008, p. 11).[211] That means that we can derive non-inferential knowledge from our particular experience because the cardinal falls under the form concept *animal* and is thereby understood. Among the content of this additional non-inferential knowledge are different modes of space occupancy, like "shape, size, position, movement or its absence" (McDowell 2009a, p. 261). These different modes will also include, e. g. "postures such as perching and modes of locomotion such as hopping or flying" (McDowell 2009a, p. 261).

More generally speaking: the form which unifies the object is such that it brings with it different additional features which originally were not part of the intuition, but which still belong to the perceptual object that is unified by the form because the object is unified by the form. This holds e. g. for *cardinal* or *bird* in the cardinal-case. All this follows from the correspondence between intuitional unity and propositional unity and more generally from the involvement of conceptual capacities in experience. This connection also explains an important observation about the double role of cognitive faculties in perception that McDowell emphasizes: the higher cognitive faculty does not just figure in

---

211 There seems to be a parallel to Kern's and Rödl's argumentation in the case of rational capacities, which as I have said, of course, is also Aristotelian. I will not discuss any consequences of this observation, but just want to point it out.

providing the unity of the intuitional content. It also takes the role of productive imagination, i.e. it adds those elements in the perceptual content that are strictly speaking not directly visible, e.g. the backside of a pillar.[212] The suggestion seems to be that it does the same thing in the cardinal-case: it 'adds' the cardinal-ness of the bird to the perceptual content.

McDowell emphasizes that conceptual capacities figure both in intuitional content and in discursive content. In fact, the paradigm of conceptual activity is judging and not perceiving. According to McDowell, it is helpful to think of judgments as an internal discursive activity, i.e. in judging "one makes what one judges explicit to oneself" (McDowell 2009a, p. 262). Of course, intuiting is not a discursive activity. The crucial point, however, is that it is possible to "carve out" (McDowell 2009a, p. 263) discursive content from intuitional perceptual content. This process of carving out transforms the intuitional content "from the categorially unified but as yet unarticulated content of the intuition" (McDowell 2009a, p. 263) into discursive content. This move can be made via linguistic expression. Again, it is obvious that the carving out cannot be done by intuiting only, rather, it is a combination of intuiting and discursive activity.

Still McDowell anticipates that one will ask whether on the revised conception intuitional content really is conceptual. After all, the paradigm of conceptual activity is judging. McDowell, however, insists that both discursive content and intuitional content are conceptual. Intuitional content is conceptual "[b]ecause every aspect of the content of an intuition is present in a form in which it is already suitable to be the content associated with a discursive capacity, if it is not – at least not yet – actually so associated" (McDowell 2009a, p. 264).

The content of an intuition is formed in such a way that it can be "analyse[d] ... into significances for discursive capacities" (McDowell 2009a, p. 264). In order to understand this intimate connection one simply has to look at the Kantian credo that I quoted from McDowell at the beginning. The unity of the intuitional content is a result brought about by the operation of conceptual capacities, i.e. by the unifying function. The same unifying function is active in the unity of judgment. In the latter case the function is actively exercised, in the former it is actualized. In other words, intuitional content is conceptual, because it involves the actualization of conceptual capacities. Yet, one must not think that

---

212 It is interesting to note that McDowell does not say very much more about the role of productive imagination on his theory. Perhaps he had Sellars's views on the productive imagination in mind (e.g. Sellars 1978), but he certainly does not say so explicitly. For insightful observations about the role of productive imagination in Sellarsian theories of perceptual experience, see (Haag 2012) and (Haag 2014).

these claims mean that the intuitional content of experience is fragmentary or incomplete discursive content: "Having something in view, say a red cube, can be complete in itself" (McDowell 2009a, p. 270). That also means that the actualization of the unifying function is not a prediscursive activity.

The potential for discursive activity that is inherent in the intuition also does not have to be exercised. It is a possibility that can be exercised, i.e. the intuitional content can be turned into discursive content and thus be made to figure in discursive activity. The intuitional content then becomes a part of a "knowledgeable judgment" (McDowell 2009a, p. 266). In the Kantian framework this possibility of becoming knowledgeable is put in terms of the claim that an intuition can always be accompanied by an "I think" (McDowell 2009a, pp. 266 f.). An intuition that is accompanied by an "I think", i.e. an intuition that includes "a reference to the first person" (McDowell 2009a, p. 266), is one way in which an intuition can be made to figure in knowledge, i.e. in "knowledgeable judgments" (McDowell 2009a, p. 266).[213] The second way is the non-inferential way of extending the intuitional content as in the cardinal-case: "The intuition makes something perceptually present to the subject, and the subject recognizes that thing as an instance of a kind" (McDowell 2009a, p. 266).

Travis regards this second non-inferential way of acquiring knowledge as in the cardinal-case as the default case for how experience can make knowledge available. McDowell describes him as holding that "conceptual capacities are in play only in our making what we can of what visual experiences anyway bring into view for us, independently of any operation of our conceptual capacities" (McDowell 2009a, p. 267). In other words, perceptual experience operates independently from conceptual capacities and it is only in our thinking about the perceptual experience that they are exercised. I will say more about Travis's theory of perception in Section 5.5 when his relationism is fully introduced. What matters now is that, according to McDowell, Travis's view is only partly right: the position is right in holding that in experience we directly have things in view, but it is wrong in separating conceptual capacities and perceptual experience. By assuming that experience is independent of the operation of conceptual capacities Travis falls into the trap of the Myth of the Given.[214] McDowell's conception, however, manages to make it possible to accept Travis's insight about perceptual experience directly bringing things into view and at the same avoid falling into the Myth of the Given:

---

213 Here the connection to McDowell's views on perception as a capacity for knowledge is obvious.
214 I will get back to the issue of the Myth of the Given in Section 3.3 and Chapter 7.

> Intuitions as I have explained them directly bring objects into view through bringing their perceptible properties into view. Intuitions do that precisely by having the kind of content they have. (McDowell 2009a, p. 268)

The introduction of intuitional content must also be read as a reaction to an objection by Donald Davidson. As we have seen, in *Mind and World* McDowell had tried to take into account Davidson's insight that "nothing can count as a reason for holding a belief except another belief" (Davidson 2001a, p. 141, in: McDowell 1996a, p. 14; McDowell 2009a, p. 268). McDowell was able to accommodate this insight by saying that experiences are actualizations of conceptual capacities. Conceptual capacities are not just involved in belief formation, but also in rational entitlements which come hand in hand with belief formation and judgments. In *Mind and World* these observations were taken to entail that the content of experience is propositional content. But Davidson has observed about this conception that it looks just like his coherentism: if experience has propositional content, then the content of experience is factive; it is a case of taking things to be thus and so and is "caused by the impact of the environment on our sensory apparatus" (McDowell 2009a, p. 269). It looks like "[n]othing is missing" (McDowell 2009a, p. 271) from Davidson's coherentism and so it looks like there is after all no need for McDowell's theory to solve the problem of what can be a reason for a belief.

When in "Avoiding the Myth of the Given" McDowell takes back the claim that the content of experience is propositional content and instead introduces intuitional content, Davidson's objection is overruled. "[S]o long as we do not question the assumption that conceptual content for experiences would have to be propositional" (McDowell 2009a, p. 271), Davidson's objection is correct. But the introduction of intuitional content also comes with McDowell rejecting Davidson's claim that experiencing is "a case of taking things to be so" (McDowell 2009a, p. 269). In experience we have things in view and we are "entitled to take [things] to be so" (McDowell 2009a, p. 269), but we certainly do not turn all experiential content into beliefs. As we have seen above, not all intuitional content is turned into discursive content and so according to McDowell, we must say that experience only allows for entitlement, and entitlement does not entail belief.

McDowell shares this claim with Travis, but does not share Travis's whole view since the view is flawed by Travis not avoiding the Myth of the Given. As we will see, Travis uncouples experience and belief by supposing that experience, albeit non-conceptual and purely relational, can be epistemically significant. I will say more about this fundamental flaw in Travis's theory in later sections, e.g. in my presentation of Travis's theory of perceptual experience and my discussion of Travis's anti-representationalist arguments. McDowell's conception from *Mind and World* went too far by holding that experience has propositional content and turned into Davidsonian coherentism. The way to avoid these two hazards (Travis's Myth of the Given-infected theory and McDowell's *Mind and World*-theory) is simply to take experience to have intuitional content. Talk of intuitional content thus serves at least the following three purposes.

(i)   Intuitions bring things into view. This element acknowledges Travis's correct insight.

(ii) Conceptual capacities are actualized in intuitions, so they are more than mere sensibility. This move avoids the Myth of the Given.

(iii) Intuitional content is conceptual content, and not propositional content, so experience does not entail belief but only entitles the subject to holding a belief, i.e. to taking things to be so. Actually taking things to be so is another step. This move avoids collapsing into Davidson's coherentism.

Again, on McDowell's model the relation between experience and judgment is not a strictly inferential nor even a quasi-inferential relation: "I did not mean to imply that experience yields premises for inferences whose conclusions are the contents of perceptual beliefs" (McDowell 2009a, p. 270). Moreover, I have just noted that the claims about the relation between experience and judgment are not supposed to be based on the assumption that experiences have the same kind of content as beliefs. These traps can be circumvented on the following conception which is McDowell's conception:

> If an object is present to one through the presence to one of some of its properties, in an intuition in which concepts of those properties exemplify a unity that constitutes the content of a formal concept of an object, one is thereby entitled to judge that one is confronted by an object with those properties. (McDowell 2009a, p. 271)

McDowell adds that one might want to object that this approach and the related approaches of Sellars and Kant manifest an over-intellectualization of human epistemic life. Such an objection would, of course, be along the lines of Tyler Burge's hyper-intellectualization objection (Burge 2003; Section 2.3). But in fact this objection is ill-founded and McDowell offers two replies to Burge: one that we know from the discussion of the argument in the conceptualist-non-conceptualist debate and a new, but related, argument. The new argument notes that the fact that rational capacities are operative in experience only means that the content of experience is accompaniable by the "'I think' of explicit self-consciousness" (McDowell 2009a, p. 271). It does not mean that "all of our epistemic life is actively led by us, in the bright light of reason" (McDowell 2009a, p. 271). Our rational, human perceptual life is permeated by conceptual capacities. There are certain conceptual capacities that we are free to exercise, but that are not exercised in all exercises of perceptual capacities. Second – and that is the argument that we know from the conceptualist-non-conceptualist-debate – it is part of the life of human animals that they possess those conceptual capacities and that they can actualize and exercise them in experience and thought.

3.2 Does "Avoiding the Myth of the Given" Provide a Coherent Conceptualist Theory?

In the following paragraphs I will now review McDowell's revised conceptualism. The main question in this examination is:

(a) Does McDowell manage to develop a coherent new conceptualism based on intuitional content?

This question can be asked both by a conceptualist and by a non-conceptualist. Of course, I will be asking it in a conceptualist spirit, but I will also look at two non-conceptualist analyses of McDowell's new conceptualism. I will show that they both mis-interpret McDowell's new conceptualism, but seeing how they mis-interpret it will prove important for uncovering old tenets of revised conceptualism.

There is another crucial question that must also determine the examination of revised conceptualism:

(b) Does McDowell's theory avoid Travis's criticism, more particularly his anti-representationalist criticism?

This question focuses on the exchange between Travis and McDowell, more particularly, the influence that Travis is said to have had on McDowell's conception. Of course, answering this question will have to wait until the introduction of the relationist theory of perception and Travis's anti-representationalist criticism. And so I will postpone answering it until Chapter 6. Let me just say that the answer to the second question will reveal shortcomings in McDowell's reaction to Travis's criticism and in pointing out how one can improve those shortcomings I will open the door to relational conceptualism.

The idea of basic concepts examined more closely

First one needs to look at the role of conceptual capacities for intuitional and propositional unity. I have established that, according to McDowell, the one – and only – reason for saying that experience has conceptual content, which to him is the same as saying that conceptual capacities are implicated by experience, is that it allows us to explain how experience can rationally justify judgments and belief (McDowell 1996, pp. xxiii, 9 ff.). Any other conception is going to fall prey to the Myth of the Given or is going to lead to a coherentist conception. The content of experience should also be conceived of as conceptual content, since experiential content is intuitional content that can be articulated and can thus become discursive content (McDowell 2009a, p. 264). On McDowell's conception "[e]very aspect of the content of an intuition is present in a form in which it is already suitable to be the content associated with a discursive capacity, if it is not – at least not yet – actually so associated" (McDowell 2009a, p. 264). McDowell follows Kant in saying that intuitional content is unified by the same "function" as discursive content (McDowell 2009a, p. 260). This also means that a being that cannot entertain discursive content and that lacks the capacities for propositional unity of discursive content cannot have intuitions. Capacities for propositional unity are conceptual capacities.

Remember also that McDowell wants to take the Kantian claim that "forms of intuitional unity correspond to forms of propositional unity" (McDowell 2009a, p. 261) seriously. Here the picture starts to become more complicated. Kant says that for each of the categories, for each of the forms of judgment, viz. for each of the forms of propositional unity, there is a corresponding form of intuitional unity. As I have said, McDowell does not want to copy Kant's forms of propositional unity but instead seems to want to develop his own inventory of propositional unity. He refers to Michael Thompson's conception of the *life-form* as one type of propositional unity. In a Kantian vein one could say that there is a form of intuitional unity which corresponds to the propositional unity *life-form*. In a supposedly analogous way the intuitional unity of my seeing a cardinal might be captured by *animal*, "because 'animal' captures the intuition's categorial form, the distinctive kind of unity it has" (McDowell 2009a, p. 261). My experience of the cardinal thus would not have to include the concepts *bird* or *cardinal*, but it would contain common sensibles like "shape, size, position, movement" (McDowell 2009a, p. 261) and presumably also proper sensibles.

The idea seems to be this: *life-form* is a formal concept and so when we say that a particular instance falls under the formal concept *life-form* we can say something about the logical form of thought which represents the instance. In the case of Thompson's *life-form* we can say that the instance is the subject in a natural-historical judgment (Thompson 2008, p. 20). The problem with McDowell's explanations, however, is that it is unclear whether we can extend them. What other formal concepts can we find? Can we construe other categorial forms or formal concepts that work like *life-form* and *animal*, say *bird*, *cube*, or *house*? Is there maybe even a special category for every object (or even a scene) that a subject can perceive? How fine-grained are categorial forms? Can there be formal concepts whose instances are non-living entities? Note that we cannot just resort to Kant's categories, because McDowell does not want to have to include them.

McDowell's exemplar category *animal* fits Thompson's life-form concepts, but it is a considerable burden to connect the categorial form of intuitions with Thompson's *life-form* concepts. Thompson's *life-form* is a special logical category that is even supposed to figure as an addition to Frege's categories and clearly it is just this feature of the *life-form* concepts which makes them supreme candidates for being an instance of a propositional unity corresponding to an intuitional unity. But as I said, it is unclear whether we can find other examples.

McDowell's situation can be framed in terms of a dilemma: either his remarks on the categorial unity provided by the category *animal* are easily applied to other categories, but in that case it would be less clear what the special correspondence of propositional and intuitional unity really amounts to, and in how far the concepts really are formal concepts. Or McDowell insists that the category *animal* is special, but then there would be another explanatory gap, namely, questions revolving around which categories are special and why, etc.

What is intuitional content?

The introduction of intuitional content is a central element in McDowell's "Avoiding the Myth of the Given" and it is thus essential to examine the notion "intuitional content" and its affiliate "discursive content". Perceptual experience is said to have intuitional content, but what exactly is intuitional content?

One could argue that McDowell offers an example for intuitional content, when he talks about the correspondence between propositional and intuitional unity:

> [T]he propositional unity in a judgment expressible by 'This is a cube' corresponds to an intuitional unity expressible by 'this cube'. The *demonstrative* phrase might *partly* capture the content of an intuition in which one is visually presented with a cube. (McDowell 2009a, p. 261, my emphasis, N.E.)

According to McDowell, thus, the primary vehicle for expressing the content of an intuition is a demonstrative phrase, a phrase that unites language and particulars. McDowell says more about the relation between demonstrative phrases and intuitions in the Woodbridge Lectures of 1997. I will introduce and discuss his thoughts from those Lectures in the course of this section. Given the peculiar nature of intuitional content it is clear that demonstrative phrases are first choice for expressing them: demonstrative phrases are closest to allowing us to express something unarticulated since they include the unarticulated element; in the above case they include the cube. But interpreting "this cube" as an example for intuitional content does not really answer the question as to the nature of intuitional content. For one, McDowell resorts to discursive expression, "this cube", to describe intuitional content.

All this leads to an important observation about the status of intuitional content: intuitional content seems to be a theoretical construct, introduced to develop a satisfactory account of perceptual experience that avoids the Myth of the Given. In a similar move Sellars introduces sense impressions to explain perceptual propositional attitudes.[215] Sellars admits that accepting the introduction requires accepting the proto-theory underlying sense-impressions (Sellars 1977, §§41 f.). That might mean for McDowell's modified conception that one has to accept the "proto-theory" (Sellars 1977, §§41 f.) underlying the introduction of intuitional content, i.e. that one has to have the aim of avoiding the Myth of the Given, in order to accept that the content of perceptual experience involves intuitional content. The point of these remarks here is this: if someone does not want to avoid the Myth of the Given, then she does not have to introduce intuitional content and cannot even understand the rationale for introducing it. There is no finding intuitional content, unless one wants to avoid the Myth of the Given. I will get back to this observation later in this chapter.

Another possibility for trying to understand the nature of intuitions and intuitional content is by looking at its connection to discursive content. McDowell explains that intuitional content is such that it can always be transformed into discursive content. Intuitional content is content that is given in perceptual experience. It is conceptual content since it implies the involvement of conceptual capacities. Unlike discursive content intuitional content is unarticulated, but it is already present in the appropriate form to be articulated and to figure in judgments and beliefs (McDowell 2009a, p. 264). It has the appropriate form for ar-

---

215 I do not mean to say that Sellars's introduction of intuitions is identical to McDowell's introduction. I think that it is clear that Sellars conceives of intuitions in a different way than McDowell. For a very helpful discussion of similarities and differences, see (Haag 2012; Haag 2014).

ticulation because the possession of intuitional content always implies conceptual capacities, the same conceptual capacities that are involved in discursive content. McDowell notes:

> an intuition's content is all conceptual, in this sense: it is in the intuition in a form in which one *could* make it, that very content, figure in discursive activity. That would be to exploit a potential for discursive activity that is already there in the capacities actualized in having an intuition with that content. (McDowell 2009a, p. 265)

And yet, intuitional content is not discursive content: it is conceptual content, yes, but it is not discursive content, since it is not articulated. McDowell emphasizes that nothing extraordinary happens to the conceptual content in the move from intuitional to discursive activity. All that happens is that certain aspects of the intuitional content are made explicit, are articulated. Even if the subject might need "new discursive capacities" (McDowell 2009a, p. 264) for the articulation, it is still the very same content in the "discursive performance" as it was in the intuition (cf. McDowell 2009a, p. 264).[216] This list of features of intuitional content leaves me slightly puzzled: can we really conceive of content which has all those features? And most importantly, how are we to envisage the transition from intuitional content to discursive content?

At this point it might be objected that I am not treating McDowell's theory fairly, since I am not considering all that McDowell says on intuitions and intuitional content. I should to go beyond "Avoiding the Myth of the Given" (2009a) and also take in what McDowell says in his *Woodbridge Lectures* from 1997; especially the second and third lecture, "The Logical Form of an Intuition" (McDowell 2009g) and "Intentionality as a Relation" (McDowell 2009e), could help me in putting forward a more charitable interpretation of the notion of intuitional content. If I spell out a more charitable interpretation, I will see the questions answered and the puzzlement disappear. More importantly, I should take McDowell's mention of Kant more seriously. So in what follows, I will take up this suggestion, but we will see that the suggestion is mistaken: ultimately McDowell offers two different explanations in the two texts and we are still unable to develop a more coherent picture of intuitional content.

---

216 "The content of an intuition is such that its subject can analyse it into significances for discursive capacities whether or not this requires introducing new discursive capacities to be associated with those significances. Whether by way of introducing new discursive capacities or not, the subject of an intuition is in a position to put aspects of its content, the very content that is already there in the intuition, together in discursive performances." (McDowell 2009a, p. 264)

In the *Woodbridge Lectures* McDowell follows Sellars's trails and adopts Kant's notion of *intuitions*. He goes on to give two definitions of an intuition, only the first of which Sellars would accept. On the first definition an intuition "represent[s] an individual as a this-such" (McDowell 2009g, p. 24). On the second definition intuitions are "shapings of sensory consciousness by the understanding" (McDowell 2009g, p. 34). Sellars would reject the second definition, since it is but one of two kinds of intuitions: on the one hand, there are intuitions that imply actualization of the understanding, but on the other hand, there also intuitions that do not imply actualizations of the understanding. McDowell, however, rejects the second variety of Sellarsian intuitions: there are no intuitions without the understanding. The content of intuitions is "judgment-shaped" (McDowell 2009g, p. 35), but it is special judgment-shaped content, because it is constituted by the subject's perspective and by the special presentness of the object of perception. The object is "*there*" (McDowell 2009g, p. 34), determinately placed if seen from "the subject's viewpoint" (McDowell 2009g, p. 34). McDowell suggests conceiving of the presentness of the object in terms of Gareth Evans's notion of perceptually demonstrative thought (McDowell 2009e, p. 49) and he concludes that "[f]or a conceptual episode to possess intuitional content just is for it to stand in a certain relation to an object ..." (McDowell 2009e, p. 50).

At first sight it seems as if the above suggestion was right and these remarks might answer the critical questions as to the nature of intuitional content. Furthermore they might be a part of answering the critical query about the relation between intuitional content and discursive content. But there is an important problem: in the *Woodbridge Lectures* McDowell talks of judgmental content and not of discursive content. This terminological difference is not a minor difference nor a minor observation. In the *Woodbridge Lectures* McDowell defines intuitional content as "essentially a fragment of judgmental content" (McDowell 2009g, p. 35) and therefore the actualization of the capacity for having an object in view is an actualization of the capacity to entertain states of consciousness with judgmental content (McDowell 2009g, p. 35). Visual experiences "are to be understood on the model of linguistic performances in which claims are literally made" (McDowell 2009i, p. 10): they contain a claim that could be endorsed. A crucial difference between intuitional content and judgmental content thus is that in intuitional content endorsement of the content is withheld, whereas in judgmental content the content is endorsed.

To say that seeings, or visual experiences, contain claims, albeit un-endorsed ones, is to say that in seeings and judgments the same conceptual capacities are implied. In seeings they are actualized with the same "togetherness" (McDowell 2009i, p. 11) that such conceptual capacities have when they are exercised in judgments, say in the verbal statement "There is a red cube in front of me", i.e. in the intuition the conceptual capacities *red* and *cube* have the same logical togetherness as in the verbal statement. But there is another important difference between the involvement of conceptual capacities in intuitions as opposed to judgments: they are not actively exercised, but rather involuntarily actualized.[217] The involuntariness in intuitions stems from the fact that they consist in sense perception of objects that are perceived, i.e. passively received. Sellars talks of the claims contained in perception as "evoked or wrung from the perceiver by the object perceived" (Sellars 1997, §16, in: McDowell 2009i, p. 12) and McDowell says that "in a visual experience an ostensibly seen object ostensibly impresses itself visually on the subject" (McDowell 2009i, p. 13). The object can impress itself on the subject in an intuition only because the subject possesses conceptual capacities, but the capacities are not actively exercised in a judgment or in endorsing the content of a judgment. And yet, possessing conceptual capacities in turn means being able to make overt linguistic claims (McDowell 2009i, p. 12).[218] If we bring these observations together, we get to the following conclusion: "objects speak to us … only because we have learned a human language … [O]bjects come into view for us only in actualizations of conceptual capacities that are ours" (McDowell 2009g, p. 43).

McDowell emphasizes that in spite of the difference between intuitional content and judgmental content the transition between the two is innocuous:

> [W]e can express the content of a Kantian intuition by a phrase such as 'that red cube'. We might suppose that conceptual occurrences whose content can be given like that, with a phrase that is less than a whole sentence, are essentially potential ingredients in some more extensive conceptual goings-on – say, in the judgment that that red cube is too big to fit in the box. (McDowell 2009g, p. 35)

---

217 One could also put the point in terms of Kenny's notion of two-way powers: the actualization of conceptual capacities in perceptual experience is not the actualization of a two-way power, i.e. it is not actualized at will. If the subject possesses conceptual capacities, it cannot not actualize them in perceptual experience, see e.g. (Kenny 1989, p. 22) and also (Kern 2006, p. 222). See also (Pippin 2013) for more on "conceptual activity" in perceptual experience.
218 Even though, as Glock notes, "[m]ost philosophers influenced by Frege and/or Wittgenstein accept that the possession of concepts requires linguistic capacities" (Glock 2010, pp. 325 f.) the relation between concept possession and language capacities is notoriously contested. I will not go into the details of this debate since, as I have said above, McDowell clearly supposes that language capacities are inextricably connected with conceptual capacities (e.g. McDowell 1996, pp. 125 f.; McDowell 2009i, p. 12). For the standard argumentation in favor of the claim see (Davidson 2001b) and (Davidson 2001c). For criticism and an alternative explication of the relation see, e.g. (Bermúdez 2003).

Conceptual episodes can have such phrasal content, such as intuitions, but they can also be 'equipped' "with judgment-shaped contents" (McDowell 2009g, p. 35). Intuitional content "is essentially a fragment of judgmental content" (McDowell 2009g, p. 35) and so the transition from intuitional content to judgmental content seems to contain nothing more but an endorsement. Judgmental content is just enriched intuitional content, it is enriched by an endorsement.

So far so good, but these remarks do not fit with what McDowell says in "Avoiding the Myth of the Given". Look again at the following passage that was the starting point to my critical query about the relation between intuitional and judgmental content:

> [The intuition's content, N.E.] is in the intuition in a form in which one *could* make it, that very content, figure in discursive activity. That would be to exploit a potential for discursive activity that is already there in the capacities actualized in having an intuition with that content. (McDowell 2009a, p. 265)

There is a crucial difference between the two conceptions: the *Woodbridge Lectures* take intuitional content to be a fragment of judgmental content, but "Avoiding the Myth of the Given" emphasizes that intuitional content is neither discursive content nor "fragmentary discursive content" (McDowell 2009a, p. 270). McDowell gives two reasons for this. First, intuitional content is not propositional content – and here I am assuming that discursive content consists in propositional content – because propositional content is "taking things to be so" (McDowell 2009a, p. 269) whereas intuitional content is simply a case of having "one's surroundings [in] view" (McDowell 2009a, p. 269). "Taking things to be so" is a further step from visual experience, it is not *in* the experience, but if one does take the step, one is licensed to do so by one's visual experience.[219] With intuitional content in the picture one can say that visual experience entitles the subject to certain judgments, but "intuiting itself" is no case of "deal[ing] discursively with content" (McDowell 2009a, p. 269). Second, McDowell argues that intuitional content is "not fragmentary discursive content", because it can be complete as it is. It does not have to be turned into discursive content: "[h]aving something in view can enable a demonstrative expression, or an analogue in judgment, ... but the potential need not be actualized" (McDowell 2009a, p. 270).

This crucial difference also affects the above explanation of the transition from intuitional content to judgmental content. In the *Woodbridge Lectures* intuitional content still is conceived as "a fragment of judgmental content" (McDow-

---

219 Note that in this McDowell agrees with Travis.

ell 2009g, p. 35). That is why the transition from intuitional content to judgmental content is so easy: there is a sense in which they are both judgmental content. One is a fragment of a judgment, the other is a full judgment. This difference between the understanding of judgmental content and discursive content might also explain why in a response to Brewer's criticism McDowell feels that he can "stay with the Sellarsian idea that the content of a perceptual experience is propositional content, the sort of thing that could be the content of a claim" (McDowell 2008c, p. 200). But this explanation does not hold for "Avoiding the Myth of the Given", where McDowell gives a different explication of the relation between intuitional content and discursive content. Intuitional content is unarticulated (McDowell 2009a, pp. 269 f.); discursive content is articulated. Propositional content, thus, cannot be the link between intuitional and judgmental content, and so McDowell falls back on the last thing that intuitional content and judgmental content still share, namely the involvement of conceptual capacities. Intuitional content and judgmental content both involve conceptual capacities and consequently they *share* conceptual content. They differ only in whether their content is articulated or not.

At this point, we are not much closer to a satisfactory explanation of intuitional content, and of the relation between intuitional content and discursive content; in fact the situation has worsened. There is now a further problem with the characterization of intuitional content and judgmental content. Looking at the Woodbridge Lectures has revealed that there is another dimension in which intuitional content and judgmental content differ: the one is un-endorsed content and the other is endorsed content. Now we would have to examine what the relation is between judgmental content and discursive content, what the relation is between endorsement and articulation and what happens to endorsement in "Avoiding the Myth of the Given", but I will not try to answer these questions here, as they will lead us further away from our actual topic and it is enough for us to see that the nature of the transformation does not become any clearer by looking at the Woodbridge Lectures.

Moreover, the solution puts excessive demands on the notion "conceptual content" and we are in danger of losing our grip on this notion. McDowell takes conceptual content to be the shared genus of intuitional content and discursive content (McDowell 2009a, p. 264). He suggests that this simply means that conceptual capacities are implicated in the possession of both intuitional content and discursive content. As I have said, in "Avoiding the Myth of the Given" the difference between intuitional content and discursive content is that the content of the former is not articulated and the content of the latter is articulated. Intuitional content is potentially discursively expressible[220] content, and in discursive content the potential is actualized, so it is discursively expressed. But this construction leaves one puzzled about the genus *conceptual content:* two very different species belong to it, one unarticulated content, *intuitional content*, the other articulated content, *discursive content.* The only commonality of intuitional content and discursive content is that they require conceptual capacities. But what does it mean to say that intuitional content and discursive content are two species of the genus conceptual content? What is the relation between conceptual content and discursive content and conceptual content and intuitional content that is implied by saying that they are in a species-genus-relation?

Let us start by looking again at McDowell's explanation of why discursive content and intuitional content are conceptual. For discursive content the obvious answer that we find in "Avoiding the Myth of the Given" is that it is conceptual content that is articulated. For intuitional content things are less straightforward. McDowell writes:

> Nevertheless an intuition's content is all conceptual, in this sense: it is in the intuition in a form in which one *could* make it, that very content, figure in discursive activity. That would be to exploit a potential for discursive activity that is already there in the capacities actualized in having an intuition with that content. (McDowell 2009a, p. 256, emphasis in original)

This quotation can be understood in two ways. The first interpretation lays emphasis on McDowell's remark that "[the] very content" (McDowell 2009a, p. 256) of the intuition is made "to figure in discursive content" (McDowell 2009a, p. 256). McDowell is thus taken to make an observation about the contents of intuitional and discursive content being the same. Intuitional content can be brought to figure in discursive content *qua* being conceptual content just like discursive content. This interpretation suggests that intuitional content and discursive content both are constituted by the same conceptual content.

But the 'Two species of one genus'-claim cannot be understood as saying that intuitional content and discursive content are made up of the very same content, because that would result in an incoherent notion of conceptual content. In discursive content the conceptual content is *articulated* conceptual content and in intuitional content it is *articulable* conceptual content and so one cannot consistently claim that discursive content and intuitional content are

---

220 I take that to mean verbally expressible.

made up of the very same conceptual content. This claim would amount to saying that conceptual content can be both articulable and articulated.

The mistake of this first interpretation is that it takes McDowell to make a statement about the constitution (the 'content') of intuitional content and discursive content. Instead we need to see that "conceptual content" only refers to the presence of conceptual capacities, of the unifying function.[221] So on this second interpretation McDowell's quotation makes a claim about the conceptual capacities that are 'implied' in intuitional content and discursive content: in intuitional content the capacities are actualized and have the potential to be actively exercised; in discursive content the capacities are exercised. One could say that this interpretation is just an extension of Kant's same-function-claim. McDowell explains that in moving from intuitional content to discursive content intuitional content needs to be made to "figure in discursive activity" (McDowell 2009a, p. 256). One makes the intuitional content "figure in discursive activity" (McDowell 2009a, p. 256) by actively exercising the unifying function, i.e. conceptual capacities, that is previously actualized in the intuitional content (cf. McDowell 2009a, p. 264).

Note that in "Avoiding the Myth of the Given" 'actively exercising the unifying function' means something different than in the *Woodbridge Lectures*. In both texts the same capacities that are merely actualized in intuitional content are actively exercised in non-intuitional content. But as I said above there is a small but striking difference in their notions of non-intuitional content: in "Avoiding the Myth of the Given" non-intuitional content is discursive content; and in the *Woodbridge Lectures* non-intuitional content is judgmental content. This difference also extends to what it means to 'actively exercise the unifying function'. In the *Woodbridge Lectures* the 'active exercise of the unifying function' refers to an endorsement of the intuitional content. Judgmental content contains an endorsement. In "Avoiding the Myth of the Given", however, the active exercise of the unifying function refers to an articulation of the intuitional content.

Yet we can bracket this difference for the question of what the 'Two species of one genus'-claim amounts to: saying that intuitional content and discursive content are two species of the genus *conceptual content* seems to mean that both contents require the 'company' of conceptual capacities. In the one case

---

221 Support for this interpretation can also be found in a different context, namely in McDowell's response to criticism by Hubert Dreyfus. There he explains that saying that perceptual experience implies the actualization of conceptual capacities "does not imply anything about the *matter* of the content that is present in that [conceptual] form" (McDowell 2009 m, p. 321, emphasis in original).

they are merely actualized, in the other case they are "actively exercised" (Mc-Dowell 2009a, p. 264). Note that even though there is the above terminological ambiguity about "active exercise" as endorsement or as articulation it is still easier to understand the role of conceptual capacities in its actively exercised variety than in the merely actualized variety. From what McDowell says it is not clear that intuitional content really belongs with the genus *conceptual content*. On certain interpretations of the claim that intuitional content is articulable, we might even be led to argue that intuitional content really is more like non-conceptual content then like conceptual content. Conceptual content then would really only be content in which conceptual capacities are actively exercised, and so intuitional content is not really conceptual content.

The continuing troubles with understanding the nature of intuitional content and its relation to discursive content (and judgmental content) again makes us aware that aiming to avoid the Myth of the Given is a crucial element in McDowell's theory. E. g. McDowell admits that conceptual capacities have to be included in the conception in order to avoid the Myth of the Given: "on pain of the Myth of the Given, capacities that belong to the higher cognitive faculty must be operative in experience" (McDowell 2009a, p. 260). And so it might turn out that assuming that intuitional content and discursive content have conceptual content, and are distinguished by their (un-)articulatedness, is also a theoretical construct which needs to be considered on the basis of a related "proto-theory" (Sellars 1977, §§41 f.).[222] To those who do not see the necessity of avoiding the Myth of the Given this theoretical construction will not be understandable and it will look like an unnecessary invention A related issue will also come up in the discussion of the explanatory order in McDowell's theory (Section 3.3).

So at the end of this section one has to concede that the attempts at explicating the relation between the two species of the genus *conceptual content* are not really satisfactory, because they keep throwing us back to the initial question of what intuitional content really is. We can understand what the relation between conceptual capacities and discursive content is, but it is not fully clear what that relation is like for intuitional content. This situation is potentially dangerous because a possible answer to the question of how to conceive of intuitional content that is articulable might be to say that intuitional content really is non-conceptual content. The next section is going to review – and reject – such an answer by Tim Crane.

---

222 See the above reference to Sellars's introduction of sensations to explain perceptual propositional attitudes (Sellars 1977, §§41 f.).

Isn't McDowell's revised conceptualism really non-conceptualist?

Tim Crane's criticism of McDowell's conception is a good example for the effects of McDowell's ambiguity about the connection 'conceptual content–intuitional content' and the connection 'conceptual content–discursive content' (Crane 2013). Crane argues that in "Avoiding the Myth of the Given" McDowell in effect develops a non-conceptualist theory of perceptual experience. But clearly McDowell does not want to hold a non-conceptualist theory of perceptual experience and by seeing where Crane goes wrong in his interpretation, one can see what is problematically unclear in McDowell's position.

Crane offers the following summary of McDowell's position on intuitional content:

> McDowell insists that the content of an intuition is conceptual, but this is consistent with not *every* aspect of the content actually being conceptualized, or thought about, or made the content of a judgement. (Crane 2013, p. 241)

He then continues:

> The view that not everything that is presented in an experience is conceptualized is one I find very plausible; but I would prefer to call it the view that experience has *non*-conceptual content. (Crane 2013, p. 241, emphasis in original)

In Crane's presentation the conclusion sounds very obvious, but there is a flaw in the reconstruction of McDowell's claims and that is why the conclusion is wrong. This flaw can also be found in Crane's summary of McDowell's new conception:

> Nonetheless, he [McDowell] still insists that the content of an intuition is conceptual, in the sense that 'every aspect of the content of an intuition is present in a form in which it is already suitable to be the content associated with a discursive capacity'. What it is for content, to be conceptual, then is not for it to be conceptual*ized* – in the sense that one has to be actually exercising a conceptual capacity when in a state with such a content – but for it to be conceptual*izable*. (Crane 2013, p. 231, emphasis in original, footnote omitted, N.E.)

In the first of those three quotations Crane makes it appear as if "being conceptualized" (Crane 2013, p. 241), being "thought about" (Crane 2013, p. 241) and being "made the content of a judgement" (Crane 2013, p. 241) are the same, but that is only true if the process of conceptualization is the same as the process of articulation, i. e. it is only true, if being conceptualized is the same as being articulated, and if being conceptualized is the same as being "the content of a judgement".

Crane himself does indeed think that the identification holds, he regards "conceptualization as the discursive exploitation of the content of an experience" (Crane 2013, p. 241), but it is clear that McDowell would want to resist any such conclusion. McDowell does not use the term "conceptualization", but even if he did, it would be unlikely that he would conceive of conceptualized content as content that presupposes the actual exercise of conceptual capacities, and thus is discursive articulated, as opposed to a mere actualization. As we have seen several times, he wants to say that intuitional content is straightforwardly conceptual. And we have also seen that he talks of "the categorially unified but as yet unarticulated content of the intuition" (McDowell 2009a, p. 263) and insists that "[i]ntuiting is not discursive, ... Discursive content is articulated. Intuitional content is not" (McDowell 2009a, p. 262). These remarks clearly contradict Crane's reconstruction of McDowell's theory.

On Crane's understanding, conceptualization is discursive articulation and conceptualizability is articulability. On this understanding, it is right to say that McDowell wants to say "that not everything that is presented in an experience is conceptualized" (Crane 2013, p. 241). But if we put this sentence in McDowell's original wording, we see where Crane goes wrong: McDowell wants to say that "not everything that is presented in an experience is" discursively articulated. Crane is not warranted in concluding that the un-articulated elements are non-conceptual and that McDowell develops a non-conceptualist theory. Instead McDowell still holds a conceptualist theory: everything that is presented in experience is conceptual, it is just that not all elements, all details, of the perceptual content are carved out and discursively articulated.

McDowell could not accept Crane's reconstruction since it would either make him a non-conceptualist, or it would entail that conceptual content and propositional content are identical and it was just part of the introduction of the notion of intuitional content to make room for a type of content that is conceptual, but not propositional. Crane's conclusion that McDowell's conception includes non-conceptual content thus is illfounded.

But we also see that McDowell could take measures to avoid Crane's and similar interpretations. In fact there are three measures that he could take. First, he could say more about the genus-species relation of conceptual, intuitional, and discursive content. Second, he could say more about the role of conceptual capacities in the genus *conceptual content*. And third, as we have also seen in the discussion of the Argument from Fallibility, he could and should put more emphasis on the transcendental character of his project so that readers understand what the theory is about.

Isn't Intuitional Content Inarticulable?

Mark Eli Kalderon also criticizes McDowell's conception of perceptual experience and develops his own set of objections (Kalderon 2011). Kalderon finds an aporia in McDowell's idea of carving out an aspect of the unarticulated, but articulable given. The act of carving out imposes a form on what is carved out and yet at the same time the object of perception is meant to have the appropriate form for discursive activity. On Kalderon's reading McDowell thus claims that the content of perception is unarticulated and yet at the same time exists in the correct form for figuring in discursive activity (Kalderon 2011, p. 238). In other words, McDowell is taken to hold that "perception [can be, N.E.] both non-discursive and conceptual" (Kalderon 2011, p. 237) when it is not clear how this is possible.

Kalderon's objection comes from two sides. First, Kalderon suggests that McDowell does not distinguish between property exemplification (cf. Kalderon 2011, p. 240) and the content of a possible predication (Kalderon 2011, p. 240). McDowell does not distinguish between the actual color of the house wall in the world, orange, and the representational content of the possible predication "the orange house wall". The former would be material of the unarticulated content of perception and the latter would be material for discursive activity. This fundamental difference is the second starting point for the objection. Kalderon here refers back to the work of C.I. Lewis who regarded the given as ineffable. It is ineffable because in describing the given there is always some selection, categorization, relating, emphasizing involved. The given *per se* lacks a form that could figure in discursive activity. On Kalderon's reconstruction, McDowell would obviously reject this claim, since for him, as Kalderon puts it, "every aspect of the unarticulated given is articulable" (Kalderon 2011, p. 239). But according to Lewis and Kalderon[223], this conception is not coherent: if something has "a form that could figure in the content of discursive activity" (Kalderon 2011, p. 239), then it has a generality that no particular ever has, since the content of discursive activity is inherently general.[224] There is a "categorial distinction" (Kalderon 2011, p. 239) between the content of discursive activity, i.e. representations and thoughts, and particulars. This "categorial distinction" also extends to other differences, e.g. "particulars can exceed what is represented in thought, just as what is represented in thought can exceed what is present in the particular" (Kalderon 2011,

---

223 And actually also H.A. Prichard (Prichard 1909; Kalderon 2011, p. 225).
224 As will be seen in Chapter 5, Travis puts forward the same point, cf. (Travis 2006; Travis 2007; Travis 2009). The consideration will figure crucially in the anti-representationalist argumentation.

p. 239). Kalderon concludes that if what is given in perception are particulars, as he takes McDowell to say, then what is given in perception is not unarticulated, but rather even inarticulable. If Kalderon's analysis of perception is correct, then McDowell's claim that the content of an intuition even though unarticulated is given in the appropriate form for figuring in discursive activity is false.

Kalderon adds two objections against McDowell's conceptualist conception in general: first, it is a mistake to think that conceptual capacities must be actualized in perception and, second, it is a mistake to think that we have to avoid the Myth of the Given. As we have seen McDowell refers back to Kant's credo that "[t]he unity of the various representations in a judgment also gives unity to a mere synthesis of various representations in an intuition" (Kant 1929; Kant 1998, A79/B 104 f.). to support his claim that conceptual capacities must be actualized in perception. But Kalderon dismisses this explanation: there is no need for any synthesizing activity in perceiving if what is perceived are particulars, i.e. objects, events, properties, since they are already 'synthesized'. He refers back to H.A. Prichard's theory of perception (Kalderon 2011, p. 236; Prichard 1909, p. 226) and explains that "[i]n seeing the ripening tomato, the object of my sensory awareness, a particular material substance already enjoys a substantial unity" (Kalderon 2011, p. 236).

The argument for saying that it is a mistake to think that we have to avoid the Myth of the Given is interesting. Kalderon complains that it is not clear what exactly the Myth of the Given *is* and so it is not easy to defend oneself against the charge of having falling prey to the Myth of the Given (Kalderon 2011, p. 219). Since the charges are not clear, there can be no "direct response" (Kalderon 2011, p. 220) to the charge, but only an "indirect response" (Kalderon 2011, p. 220). This indirect response can take two routes. First, one can extend one's alternative conception of perception and collect further support for the claim that on this alternative conception, too, perception is epistemically significant (Kalderon 2011, p. 220). Second, one can try to show that those positions that try to avoid the Myth of the Given are themselves susceptible to well-founded criticism and that the Myth of the Given thus is not really a myth nor, for that matter, a myth that has to be avoided (Kalderon 2011, pp. 220 f.).

Kalderon thinks that he has met the second demand by criticizing McDowell's conception (see above). He wants to meet the first demand by developing a relationist conception of perception that from my perspective seems indebted to Charles Travis's theory of perception. Kalderon argues that visual perception is a mode of taking in spatiotemporal particulars in the mind-independent environment. Perception "makes the [perceiving subject] knowledgeable" (Kalderon 2011, p. 225) of the mind-independent environment, since it enables the subject to know things about the environment, provided the subject has the appropriate recognitional capacities (Kalderon 2011, p. 225). Perception thus provides the subject with epistemic warrant; the subject is entitled to make certain judgments. The object of perception is the truthmaker of the related propositions. Kalderon writes:

> In seeing the yellowish red of the tomato I possess a reason that would, in the given circumstance, warrant my coming to know that the tomato is yellowish red, I am authoritative about the yellowish red of the tomato. (Kalderon 2011, p. 228)

But clearly Kalderon's conception itself is problematic. E. g. his dismissal of the Myth of the Given is not well-founded: he criticizes that it is not clear what the Myth of the Given amounts to, but at the same time suspects that he will be charged for having succumbed to the Myth. Moreover, Kalderon's rejection of the involvement of conceptual capacities in perceptual experience conflicts with his claims on perception implying recognitional capacities. I will get back to these issues in the course of this section and in the next section.

Several elements of Kalderon's portrayal of McDowell are clearly debatable, e. g. it is doubtful whether – as Kalderon suggests – McDowell would really subscribe to a sentence like the following: "[V]ision presents us with visible characteristics that we are not equipped to predicate" (Kalderon 2011, p. 238). But I will not argue in length against these infidelities, because Kalderon's criticism albeit partly based on a flawed interpretation of McDowell's conception allows us to apply some pressure on McDowell's conception and thereby see how it could be strengthened. I will only say this much: Kalderon's primary mistake lies in thinking that McDowell holds that experiential content is given in "a form that could figure in the content of discursive activity" (Kalderon 2011, p. 239). Kalderon unfolds this claim as follows: McDowell thinks that experience has the same content as the content of discursive activity and so he thinks that experiential content consists of generalities or maybe even is propositional. But as we have seen, with Crane's objection, McDowell does not necessarily say this. What intuitional content and discursive content have in common is that they are 'accompanied' by the same unifying function. Kalderon might reject this insight by insisting that we do not need a unifying function in perception, since the perceived particular is unified *qua* being an object in the world (see above). But it is not clear that Kalderon's recognitional capacities do not have a unifying function, too.

Furthermore, Kalderon seems to think that McDowell's talk of the unifying function means that the perceived object is really only unified when the unifying function is actualized or exercised, but this interpretation would misunderstand McDowell's transcendental interests and the role of conceptual capacities in perception. Kalderon like Crane misses an essential element in McDowell's theory and by now one may argue that McDowell has failed to emphasize what is crucial to his theory – the transcendental question – and has led readers astray by calling his paper "Avoiding the Myth of the Given". In the next section I will therefore suggest a different emphasis.

3.3 Is Conceptualism Just a Theory that Avoids the Myth of the Given?

Crane's and Kalderon's problems with understanding McDowell's theory correctly meet in McDowell's concern with the project of avoiding the Myth of the Given. In certain passages from McDowell's text it seems that the conceptualist position is just an assumption that we have to subscribe to if we want to avoid falling prey to the Myth of the Given. See for example these two passages:

> So to follow Kant's way of avoiding the Myth of the Given in this context, we must suppose capacities that belong to that faculty – conceptual capacities – are in play in the way experience makes knowledge available to us. (McDowell 2009a, p. 258)

And

> Nothing in what I have said about recognitional capacities dislodges the argument that *on pain of the Myth of the Given*, capacities that belong to the higher cognitive faculty must be operative in experience. In giving one things to know, experience must draw on conceptual capacities. (McDowell 2009a, p. 258, my emphasis, N.E.)

Such suspicions also become prevalent if one concedes that intuitional content is a theoretical construct postulated to explain the epistemic role of perceptual experience (see above). It seems that one needs to accept the proto-theory – including Sellars's claims on the Myth of Given – if one is to accept all further claims on conceptual content, intuitional content, discursive content etc.

If that is how things are for McDowell, then one might be inclined to argue that McDowell is getting things the wrong way around, he is putting the cart before the horse. His number one aim is to avoid the Myth of the Given and that makes it seem like the only reason for us to assume that experience involves conceptual capacities should be our wish to avoid the Myth of the Given. But that is a strange rationale for a theory, and moreover it does not seem to be the only rationale that McDowell had set up in his *Mind and World* and his work after that. What he wanted to do there was show why experience is epistemologically significant (cf. McDowell 1996, p. xvii) and explain how there can "be such an act as making up one's mind about how things are in the world?" (McDowell 1998d, p. 410). Remember also Conant's interpretation of McDowell's theory as dealing with Kantian skepticism; this project is not straightforwardly identical with the project of avoiding the Myth of the Given. It seems that the questions that McDowell has set for himself amount to more than merely avoiding the Myth of the Given.[225] Maybe avoiding the Myth of the Given in effect figures crucially in explaining epistemic significance of perceptual experience and the possibility of objective thought, but even then it only appears as a problem on the way to showing why experience is epistemologically significant, but it is not an issue by itself. McDowell's project should thus be described positively and not as a rejection of a certain set of claims, e.g. McDowell might emphasize the aim of explaining how there can be thought about the world (cf. Conant 2012).

Against my criticism one might try to argue in favor of McDowell that in *Mind and World* he has already shown how there can be objective thought etc. and that we have seen in these explanations that they require us to avoid the Myth of the Given. Any theory falling prey to this Myth cannot provide an adequate account of how perception and judgment are rationally related – and so in "Avoiding the Myth of the Given" he is focusing on a particular topic, namely how really to avoid the Myth of the Given.

The downside of the set-up that this reply suggests is that it does not get those people on board who do not buy into the existence of the Myth of Given. One might ask why this is a problematic downside? Why should McDowell and other conceptualists worry about it at all? It is important because it means that debates about conceptualism can thus be easily distorted or even ended by a simple rejection of the Myth of the Given. Such rejections are particularly simple since there is apparent disagreement about what the Myth of the Given exactly is (see Kalderon 2011). Critics thus will either defend the position against what they take the Myth of the Given to be (e.g. Brewer 2011) or they simply reject the Myth of the Given – or what they take the Myth of the Given to be – and all of a sudden the debate about conceptualism is a debate about the Myth of the Given (e.g. Kalderon 2011). That is very unfortunate because conceptualism is more than the group of those who accept that there is the Myth of the Given and that one must not fall prey to it. One should embrace conceptualism because it adequately describes how experience works, i.e. because it offers an appropriate explanation of how perception can justify belief, how perception and belief can be rationally related, how knowledge can be of the world, how experience figures in knowledge, etc. In other words, it explains how perceptual

---

225 E.g. they also figure in responses to Agrippa's trilemma (cf. Kern 2006).

experience can be epistemically significant and fulfills a transcendental task (cf. McDowell 1998c, pp. 365 f.). It might be part and parcel of this approach that it also avoids the Myth of the Given, but that is only a by-product and not at the center of the conception. Conceptualists must avoid the 'anything goes if it helps us avoid the Myth of the Given'-attitude that I have marked out in the above statements by McDowell, e.g. "… on pain of the Myth of the Given, capacities that belong to the higher cognitive faculty must be operative in experience" (McDowell 2009a, p. 260).

One way of minding this remark is to make as little controversial theoretical background assumptions as possible and so it is better to try to bracket any explicit reference to the Myth of the Given. The conceptualism that this book develops takes just this stance. I will get back to this issue when I develop relational conceptualism in Chapter 7. Another way is to show that theories which reject the Myth of the Given and still want to explain how perceptual experience is epistemically significant really use the same concepts and tools as do conceptualist theories that avoid the Myth of the Given. This can be done, e.g. for Kalderon's theory of perceptual experience that I have briefly introduced above in order to discuss its criticism of McDowell's revised conceptualism.

Kalderon claims that there is nothing like the Myth of the Given and rejects McDowell's conceptualism for this and other reasons (see Section 3.2). Instead, on Kalderon's conception perceptual experience "makes me aware of what reasons there are" and "is thus a mode of reasonableness" (Kalderon 2011, p. 227). In perceiving an object of perception a subject is made knowledgeable of the object: if the subject possesses the appropriate recognitional capacities required for possessing the knowledge made available by perceiving, she will come to know things about the object of perception. Kalderon's non-conceptualist move[226] is to emphasize that the subject is knowledgeable "even if, in the circumstances of perception, the subject lacked the conceptual capacities for knowing some range of propositions" (Kalderon 2011, p. 225).[227]

---

226 As will become clear when I have introduced Travis's theory, this is another indication that Kalderon's theory is a development of Travis's criticism of representationalism. Kalderon's remarks complement Travis's claims about Pia's perceptual experience of a pig when she does not possess the concept *pig* (Travis 2013c, p. 239).

227 In the background of Kalderon's conception there is what Kalderon calls his "truthmaker necessitarianism" (Kalderon 2011, p. 226) and his "radically externalist conception of reasons" (Kalderon 2011, p. 227). The properties of the object of perception and the object itself are truthmakers of the propositions about the object and its properties. "If a particular, *x*–be it an object, event, or property instance–is a truthmaker for a proposition, *p*, then it is necessary that if *x* exists, then *p* is true." (Kalderon 2011, p. 226) The "radically externalist conception of reasons" (Kalderon 2011, p. 226) is part and parcel of this conception: it holds that reasons are not re-

It is plain to see that the notion of recognitional capacities takes a crucial role in important parts of Kalderon's theory: if the subject possesses the recognitional capacities required for the particular instance of perceiving, then she is entitled to judgments about the perceptual experience and even more than that, she is entitled to knowledge. But in the context of Kalderon's conception these claims are puzzling because they conflict with Kalderon's rejection of McDowell's conceptualism. Remember that Kalderon argues that McDowell is wrong to hold that "perception is the sensory actualization of the subject's conceptual capacities" (Kalderon 2011, p. 234). And so the conceptualist will pose the following question in response to Kalderon's theory: how is Kalderon's description of perception – perception as a "mode of reasonableness" (Kalderon 2011, p. 227) that requires recognitional capacities – different from McDowell's description – perception as a capacity for knowledge that is conceptual? It seems that one cannot coherently speak of a subject possessing recognitional capacities without also assuming that the subject possesses conceptual capacities and so Kalderon cannot maintain the dissociation from McDowell's conceptualism. How could perceptual experience that "makes me aware of what reasons there are" *not* imply an actualization of conceptual capacities? There is even a double role for conceptual capacities: first, they are required for the cognitive uptake of what perception delivers, and second, they are what perception must implicate in order for it to make the subject aware of reasons. Perception that is a "mode of reasonableness" (Kalderon 2011, p. 227) must be conceptual.

Kalderon's case indicates that a non-conceptualist theory that wants to explain the epistemic significance of perceptual experience implicitly assumes the same tools and concepts as a conceptualist theory. Conceptualism does not have build its argumentative justification on rejecting the Myth of the Given, instead it should emphasize the inavoidability of conceptual capacities in explaining the epistemic significance of perceptual experience, and its transcendentalist foundations.[228]

---

stricted to psychological states and that such non-psychological reasons do not have to have a propositional structure (cf. Kalderon 2011, p. 226). The obvious question to ask is this: how can "an aspect of how things are independently of [the perceiving subject, N.E.]" (Kalderon 2011, p. 226) be a reason? Kalderon replies that the aspect is made "cognitively accessible" (Kalderon 2011, p. 226) by perception. I cannot here provide a discussion of Kalderon's conception of reasons and truthmakers, but for a more promising alternative conception that takes into account the social role of reasons, see (Wingert 2012).

228 Furthermore, as we have seen in the previous remarks about Kalderon's criticism of McDowell's conception, he completely ignores McDowell's transcendental argumentation (see Section 3.2). The mistakes in Kalderon's rejection of McDowell's conception also persist in Kalderon's remarks on perception as a capacity (Kalderon 2012).

The next step on the way to relational conceptualism is the introduction of the relationist theory of perception. This term actually refers to a set of theories that all claim that perceptual experience consists in a relation between perceiver and object. In this study I will focus on the theories by Bill Brewer and Charles Travis, because it is with those theories that McDowell most actively engages. To be precise, relationist theories do not just criticize McDowell's theory of perception, but rather all representationalist theories, and that also includes non-conceptualist theories. To some extent these new theories are orthogonal to the previous conceptualism vs. non-conceptualism distinctions, but as will become clear, relationists to some extent are also non-conceptualists – they are standardly also committed to central non-conceptualist tenets.

After having introduced relationism I will also get back to answering the second question concerning McDowell's revised conceptualism: (b) Does McDowell's theory avoid Travis's criticism, more particularly his anti-representationalist criticism? The above examination of the coherence of McDowell's revised conceptualism has revealed that central concepts and tenets, e. g. *intuitional content*, and the carving out-relation between intuitional content and discursive content cannot be made coherent. That, of course, puts revised conceptualism at a disadvantage. Further problems will become apparent in the second analysis of McDowell's revised conceptualism. Relational conceptualism will avoid these disadvantages by emphasizing that being a conceptualist does not require one to say that perceptual experience has conceptual content.

Part II **Relationism**

4 Relationism: Perception as Conscious Acquaintance

4.1 What is Relationism?

In this study *relationism* is understood as a broad term: it is to refer to positions which challenge and reject the claim that perceptual experience has representational content. They claim that perception consists in a relation between the perceiving subject and the perceived object. Philosophers who can be called relationists are John Campbell (Campbell 2002), M.G.F. Martin (Martin 2002), Charles Travis (Travis 2004), and Bill Brewer (Brewer 2011). I will not be able to touch upon the various theories, nor go into detail about the subtle, but crucial differences between them.

Matthew Soteriou provides a helpful summary of the central relationist commitment that all these views share:

> [A]t the heart of [the relationist proposal, N.E.] is a view of the conscious character of successful perception that *denies* that the conscious character of that sort of experience [i.e. successful perception, N.E.] is simply determined by the obtaining of a mental state which has an intentional content with veridicality conditions. (Soteriou 2010, p. 225, my emphasis, N.E.).

So, really, relational views are negative: they are non-representational conceptions of perceptual experience. According to Soteriou, their description of the nature of the psychological relation is also negative. Saying that conscious perceptual experience fundamentally consists in a non-representational psychological relation means that "the obtaining of the relation is not simply determined by the obtaining of a mental state that has an intentional content with veridicality conditions" (Soteriou 2010, p. 225).

I said above that relationist theories may also be grouped with non-conceptualist theories, because they reject the claim that perceptual experience implies the actualization of conceptual capacities.[229] But note that it is not constitutive for all relationist theories that they reject conceptualism. John McDowell and Susanna Schellenberg (Schellenberg 2011; Schellenberg 2014) also say that perceptual experience is a relation, but they conceive of it as a cognitive relation. Their conceptions do not square with a clearly distinguishable group of relation-

---

229 They would, of course, also reject the other possible conceptualist claim according to which the content of perceptual experience is constituted by concepts.

ist theories that take the perceptual relation to be essentially non-conceptual.[230] In order to mark the fundamental difference I will reserve the term "relationism" for those theories that reject conceptualism and take the perceptual relation to be non-conceptual. To some extent this terminological move is stipulative, but as will become clear it is also warranted by the dialectic of the project of developing relational conceptualism.[231]

As I just said, I cannot provide full details of all relationist views. In fact for this project it would not be helpful to look at all theories, since not every theory is relevant to conceptualism and the epistemological project, e. g. I will not discuss M.G.F. Martin's arguments. His phenomenological considerations do have important epistemological consequences, but he does not have a straightforwardly epistemological starting point. The two relationists that I will introduce are Bill Brewer and Charles Travis. Their arguments and criticism engage most directly with McDowell's conceptualist theory of perceptual experience.

Brewer's relationist theory is especially interesting to this project, because his previous conception, as detailed in *Perception and Reason* (Brewer 1999), presented a defense and elaboration of a conceptualist theory of perceptual experience based on McDowell's work. His recent arguments against a representationalist position and for a relationist position are thus particularly interesting for any conceptualist theory of perceptual experience. Apart from that his is only the second book-length examination of a relationist position – John Campbell's being the first (Campbell 2002).

Charles Travis is the second philosopher in focus here. His work has also been engaging strongly with McDowell's work. In addition, McDowell explicitly acknowledges that his exchange with Charles Travis has led him to one of the substantive changes that he has undertaken in "Avoiding the Myth of the Given" (McDowell 2009a). That means that in order to understand these changes to McDowell's conceptualist position properly they must be read in the context of Travis's work. That is also why I will first look at the relationist theories and only then continue examining the changes to McDowell's theory after *Mind and World*. There must be something about Travis's thoughts and arguments if they are strong enough to elicit changes in a position which previously was famous for fending off most, if not all criticism (see e. g. McDowell 2002). In the following sections the long-distance aim of this book will become more precise: the development of a coherent position called *relational conceptualism*. We will see that

---

230 Schellenberg calls this variety of relationism "austere relationism" (Schellenberg 2011, p. 714).
231 Thanks to David Lauer and an anonymous reviewer for asking me to be more precise here.

Travis's arguments and thoughts do indeed lend themselves to a coherent conceptualist approach to perceptual experience. The introduction into the two relationist theories will start with Brewer's relationist Object View. Brewer's arguments are arguments against representationalism *tout court*, or as he calls it, the Content View. Travis's arguments are multifaceted: they are (1) arguments against representational theories in general, (2) arguments against non-conceptualist representational theories, (3) arguments against conceptualist representational theories. In the context of this work the arguments under (2) are particularly interesting, because they attack non-conceptualism, the view that opposes conceptualism. Conceptualism itself is in the target area of arguments from (1) and (3), but before I say anything about McDowell's reaction to the arguments, or about possible conceptualist reactions, let's look at the relationist considerations.

4.2 The Object View's Rejection of Representationalism

The Object View: Perception as conscious acquaintance

Brewer argues in favor of what he calls the *Object View* – as opposed to what he calls the *Content View* that is held by representational theories of perception.[232] Brewer's Object View is a version of relationism and so strictly speaking we could call the Object View "relationism", but for reasons of preciseness I will stick to Brewer's own terminology in the description of his conception.

The central claim of the Object View concerns the nature of perceptual experience. Perceptual experience fundamentally is a

> relation of conscious acquaintance between a subject and certain mind-independent physical objects from a given spatio-temporal point of view, in a particular modality and in certain specific circumstances of perception. (Brewer 2011, p. 97)

This conception opposes the Content View which conceives of perceptual experience as follows:

---

232 Note crucially that Brewer's Content View is not identical with Heck's expression "content view" (Heck 2000, p. 485). On Heck's content view, perceptual states and cognitive states have different *contents:* non-conceptual versus conceptual content. Perceptual experience has "non-conceptually constituted content" (Heck 2000, p. 485) and beliefs have "conceptually constituted content" (Heck 2000, p. 485).

[Perceptual experience] is most fundamentally to be characterized by its representational content, roughly, by the way it represents things as being in the world around the perceiver. … The most fundamental account of our perceptual relation with the physical world is to be given in terms of the complete representational *contents* of perceptual experience rather than in terms of our relation with any kind of *object*. (Brewer 2011, pp. 54f., emphasis in original)

Strictly speaking the Content View is identical with representationalism, but again for reasons of preciseness I will stick to Brewer's label. Elizabeth Anscombe, David Armstrong, Fred Dretske, John Searle, Tyler Burge, Christopher Peacocke, John McDowell, Gilbert Harman, Michael Tye and Alex Byrne belong to Brewer's extensive list of defenders of the Content View (Brewer 2011, p. 55).

Brewer puts the development of the Object View into a historic context: his self-proclaimed aim is to

explain how the early modern insight that perception is most fundamentally to be construed as a matter of the subject's conscious acquaintance with certain direct objects of experience is essential to any adequate defence of empirical realism. (Brewer 2011, p. 63)

Empirical realism holds that in perceptual experience mind-independent physical objects are presented to the perceiving subject. The nature of those mind-independent physical objects, however, is independent of any subject's perceptual experience. Brewer regards empirical realism as a commonsense position. In order to reach his aim Brewer discusses what he calls the "Inconsistent Triad" in which early modern empiricists become caught up:

(I) Physical objects are mind-independent.
(II) Physical objects are the direct objects of perception.
(III) The direct objects of perception are mind-dependent. (Brewer 2011, p. 54)

(I) is an expression of physical realism and figures as a "commonsense starting point" (Brewer 2011, p. 1). (II) captures a natural inclination of us to take perception to be acquaintance with a direct object[233] (Brewer 2011, p. 6). Brewer wants to accept (I) and (II), but wants to reject (III). The early modern empiricists took (I) and (II) to imply (III). (III) leads to views like John Locke's empiricism (Locke

---

233 Direct objects are those objects which "provide the most fundamental characterization of perceptual experience" (Brewer 2011, p. 3). This conception is compatible with conceiving of direct objects as objects which allow the subject to acquire non-inferential knowledge, or views on which direct objects are objects which allow the subject to make demonstrative reference. (Brewer 2011, p. 5) Note also that a direct object can consist in a physical event, in parts of a physical object or a collection of physical objects (Brewer 2011, p. 6)

1975, esp. Book II) and George Berkeley's idealism (Berkeley 1998), and obviously to sense-datum theories (e.g. Moore 1993; Russell 1963) as well. In effect,
Brewer wants to embrace the core insights of early modern empiricism, and
show how they can lead to a consistent theory of perceptual experience that
does not hold that the direct objects of perception are mind-dependent (Brewer
2011, p. 13, 93). One step on this way is the rejection of the constructive arguments that early modern empiricists and sense-datum theorists put forward in
favor of (III), i.e. the Argument from Illusion and the Argument from Hallucination (Brewer 2011, p. 13). That means that in order to avoid (III) and consequences like sense-datum theories Brewer has to offer alternative analyses of the phenomena on which the Argument from Illusion and the Argument from
Hallucination are based. Those phenomena are

(a) "[I]ntrospective indistinguishability" (Brewer 2011, p. 98)

(b) Illusion

(c) Hallucination

Let me quickly review the Argument from Illusion and the Argument from Hallucination as presented by Brewer.[234] Both arguments consist in two phases. In
the first stage they observe something about the object of an illusory or hallucinatory perceptual experience and in the second stage they generalize the observation to all veridical perceptual experience. The Argument from Illusion observes that in cases of an illusion like the Müller-Lyer-illusion there is no
mind-independent object that possesses the features that the subject perceives
(Brewer 2011, p. 8). It concludes that the object of an illusion thus must be a
mind-dependent object (Brewer 2011, p. 8). In the second stage the argument
marks that to the perceiving subject the illusory perceptual experience is "subjectively indistinguishable" (Brewer 2011, p. 8) and therefore whatever holds for
the object of the illusory experience must also hold for the object of veridical experience. The conclusion that objects of illusion are mind-dependent objects is
thus taken to also apply to veridical perception (Brewer 2011, p. 8). The objects
of all types of perception are mind-dependent.

The Argument from Hallucination runs like the Argument from Illusion, only
it makes these observations for hallucinations. In cases of hallucination there is
no mind-independent object that is the object of the subject's perceptual experience and so the hallucinatory experience must be of a mind-dependent object

---

234 Cf. also Section 1.3 on McDowell's disjunctivism and Section 2.7 on the Argument from
Fallibility.

(Brewer 2011, p. 10). Since hallucinatory and veridical perceptual experience are "subjectively indistinguishable" (Brewer 2011, p. 10), the insights about the objects of hallucinatory perceptual experience are extended to veridical perceptual experience in the second stage of the argument. Brewer indicates that there are different versions of spelling out the second phase both in the Argument from Illusion and the Argument from Hallucination, but he notes that since all those versions are subject to several problems and objections, his discussion of the two Arguments will focus on the first stage (Brewer 2011, p. 8).[235]

Brewer starts with a discussion of the "introspective indistinguishability" (Brewer 2011, p. 98) of veridical and illusory (hallucinatory) experience, i.e. phenomenon (a). The Argument from Illusion and the Argument from Hallucination both use introspective indistinguishability of veridical perceptual experience and illusory (hallucinatory) perceptual experience to argue for extending their insights about the objects of illusory (hallucinatory) perceptual experience to perceptual experience in general. The Object View rejects this move by offering an alternative interpretation of introspective indistinguishability. Contrary to common argumentation as in the Argument from Illusion or the Argument from Hallucination introspective indistinguishability of experiences does not entail that the experiences really are identical (Brewer 2011, pp. 98 f.).[236] Instead "numerically and qualitatively distinct objects" (Brewer 2011, p. 99) that are introspectively indistinguishable look the same, because they share enough visually relevant similarities with paradigms of certain physical kinds (Brewer 2011, pp. 102 ff.). In order to explain this idea one needs to look at how things come to look a certain way on the Object View: in all cases of perception the object o looks F because – from the perceiver's standpoint and in the circumstances of the act of perception – o has visually relevant similarities with the paradigm exemplars of F (Brewer 2011, p. 101). Introspectively indistinguishable experiences are of different objects, but in particular perceptual circumstances those different objects simply have visually relevant similarities with the same paradigms. Thus introspective indistinguishability does not warrant any conclusions about the substance or matter of experience (Brewer 2011, p. 98). Of course, Brewer knows that the Object View needs to explain what is meant by "visually relevant similarities" and so he adds:

> Visually relevant similarities are identities in such things as, the way in which light is reflected and transmitted from the objects in question, and the way in which stimuli are han-

---

235 In fact, Brewer does not even outline any different versions of the second stage.
236 Of course, that is the key move in a disjunctivist theory that we have encountered in McDowell's, Kern's and Rödl's theories.

dled by the visual system, given its evolutionary history and our shared training during development. (Brewer 2011, p. 103)

So those similarities are determined by things in the external world, e. g. light reflection, but also by what we might call internal goings-on, e. g. the processing of stimuli by the visual system. The other central term in this alternative conception is the idea of the "paradigms":

> [Paradigms are] instances of the kinds in question, whose association with the terms for those kinds partially constitutes our understanding of those terms, given our training in the acquisition of the relevant concepts. They are paradigm exemplars of the kinds in question relative to our grasp of the concepts for those kinds. (Brewer 2011, p. 104)

Now let us turn to illusions, phenomenon (b). How does the Object View conceive of and explain illusions? We have to keep in mind the account of how an object *o* comes to look *F* on the Object View: the object *o* looks *F* because – from the perceiver's standpoint and in the circumstances of the act of perception – *o* has visually relevant similarities with the paradigm exemplars of *F*. On this conception illusions are cases in which the relation between the perceiver and the object is faulty. The object has visually relevant similarities with paradigm exemplars of *F* although it is not an instance of *F* (Brewer 2011, p. 105). The standpoint and the circumstances of perception play their part in bringing about the similarities with the paradigm which are *wrong* similarities.

For hallucinations, (c), Brewer offers a disjunctivist account. Brewer has this to say:

> Hallucinatory experiences have to be characterized by giving a qualitative description of a more or less specific mind-independent scene, and saying that the subject is having an experience that is not distinguishable by introspection from one in which the constituents of such a scene are the direct objects. *No more positive characterization of the experience may be given.* (Brewer 2011, p. 109, my emphasis, N.E.)

Hallucination and veridical perception share no common element apart from appearing indistinguishable. The usual "apparatus of direct objects of experience is ... not applicable" (Brewer 2011, p. 114) to hallucinations, since a hallucination is not of anything mind-independent. The usual apparatus thus cannot help us understand what hallucinations are (Brewer 2011, p. 114). It is true that hallucinations and veridical perception are introspectively indistinguishable, but as we have seen in (a) on the Object View introspective indistinguishability does not mean that hallucinations and veridical perception have identical objects. Brewer calls this explanation of hallucination the "introspective indistinguishability approach to hallucination" (Brewer 2011, p. 109). The claim is that we cannot give a positive account of hallucinatory experience over and above its introspective indistinguishability from a veridical experience (Brewer 2011, p. 109). To entertain a hallucination is to have an experience as of a veridical perceptual scene.[237]

In dealing with the three phenomena Brewer introduces a crucial terminological distinction: the distinction between *thin looks* and *thick looks* (Brewer 2011, p. 121). The above description of the details of how an object comes to look a certain way is a description of *thin looks*: the object *o* thinly looks *F* because – from the perceiver's standpoint and in the circumstances of the act of perception – "*o* has visually relevant similarities with the paradigm exemplars of *F*" (Brewer 2011, p. 121). Thin looks are the basis for *thick looks*: an object *o* thickly looks *F* if *o* thinly looks *F* and the perceiving subject recognizes it *as an F* and actively applies the concept *F* to *o*, i.e. she actively subsumes *o* under *F* (Brewer 2011, pp. 121f.). The crucial step from thin looks to thick looks thus consists in the subject recognizing the object to fall under the particular concept (Brewer 2011, p. 186). It is important to note that concept application on the Object View is an active exercise and involves subsuming a particular under a concept (Brewer 2011, pp. 122, 145).

Brewer applies and clarifies the thin-thick-looks distinction in spelling out how the Object View conceives of a subject perceiving the duck-rabbit (Brewer 2011, pp. 123ff.). Eliza sees the duck-rabbit: the image has visually relevant similarities with the paradigm <duck>[238] and the paradigm <rabbit>, it thinly looks "ducklike and rabbitlike" (Brewer 2011, p. 123). If Eliza notices the similarities to the paradigm <duck>, the image thickly looks ducklike. At the same time the image still thinly looks "ducklike and rabbitlike" (Brewer 2011, p. 123). The same holds when Eliza notices the similarities to the paradigm <rabbit>. Thick looks are "phenomenological fact[s]" (Brewer 2011, p. 124) that include "conceptual classificatory engagement" (Brewer 2011, p. 124): there is a phenomenological change between Eliza seeing the object as a duck or as a rabbit. Brewer notes that most of the time talk of *looks* is interpreted as meaning *thick looks*, but he argues that *thin looks* are equally important for the full picture of looks (Brewer 2011, p. 125).

Having emphasized the importance of experience for judgment and knowledge in his *Perception and Reason* (Brewer 1999) Brewer is very much aware of the epistemological role experience is widely supposed to play. Experience

---

237 As Brewer himself remarks (Brewer 2011, p. 109) his account is clearly strongly influenced M.G.F. Martin's account of hallucinatory experience (Martin 2004).
238 I will use the notation <...> to refer to a paradigm.

grounds and justifies judgment and knowledge about the world. The Object View also explains how we should conceive of the relation between experience and judgment, as well as the relation between experience and knowledge. In Brewer's terminology of thin and thick looks we can put his point like this: an object *o* thinly looking *F* is the basis for this object thickly looking *F* to Eliza, the perceiving subject who possesses and grasps the concept *F*. On the basis of *o* thickly looking *F* to her, Eliza is in the position to make the judgment *that o is F* (Brewer 2011, p. 145). So Eliza judges that *o* is *F* because she sees *o* and is acquainted with *o* (Brewer 2011, p. 145). As a matter of fact it is the object itself that warrants the application of the concept *F* (Brewer 2011, pp. 147 f.).

Let us apply that model to Eliza perceiving the duck-rabbit. Eliza judges that the duck-rabbit is ducklike, because she sees the duck-rabbit and is acquainted with the duck-rabbit and marks out the visual similarities with the paradigm <duck>. She thickly sees that the duck-rabbit is ducklike and thus comes to judge that the duck-rabbit is a duck. Note that this model holds even in the case of an illusion, when *o* in fact is not *F*, because even in this situation Eliza sees that *o* looks *F*, because she perceives visually relevant similarities between *o* and the paradigm exemplar of *F*. Take the Müller-Lyer-illusion as an example: the lines look to be of unequal length, because they share relevant visual similarities with the paradigm <two lines of unequal length> and Eliza judges that the lines are of unequal length, because she recognizes the similarities to the paradigm. She applies the concept *of unequal length*, since the lines thickly look *of unequal length* to her. It is this set of connections which guarantee that Eliza is warranted in applying the concept *of unequal length* to the Müller-Lyer-lines.

In order to explain how knowledge can be had on the basis of experience that is understood as conscious acquaintance with physical objects Brewer needs to go further than just talk of thin and thick looks. He is faced with a challenge that Quassim Cassam takes from Barry Stroud (Cassam 2009b, p. 571; Stroud 2000). According to this *epistemic priority requirement* (Brewer 2011, p. 150; Cassam 2009b, p. 571), every appropriate explanation of knowledge should explain how knowledge of kind K can be acquired without implying or presupposing knowledge of kind K.[239] It looks as if Brewer cannot meet the requirement, since in order for *o* to thickly look *F* to Eliza, Eliza must have some knowledge of the paradigm exemplars of *F*, because she must recognize the visually relevant similarities with the paradigm exemplars of *F* (Brewer

---

239 Note that Brewer introduces the challenge as a version of Sellars's Myth of the Given (Brewer 2011, pp. 149 f.).

2011, pp. 150 f.). But Brewer marks out that this basic knowledge is different from Eliza's knowledge. Her knowledge starts out as *"testimonial knowledge"* (Brewer 2011, p. 154, 156): Eliza sees objects and is told that those objects are *F*. On the basis of this testimonial knowledge she is equipped to acquire perceptual knowledge, which is independent of the testimonial knowledge that was needed at the first stage. So perceptual knowledge comes out of two constituents, neither of which presupposes perceptual knowledge itself: (1) being perceptually acquainted with *o*, (2) recognizing the visually relevant similarities between *o* and the paradigm exemplars of *F*, applying the concept *F* and then judging that *o* is *F* (Brewer 2011, pp. 155 f.).

Brewer on the advantages of the Object View

The strongest opponent of Brewer's Object View is the Content View. It, too, wants to say that in perception we perceive mind-independent objects, but Brewer claims that the Content View proponents fail to reach their aim of arguing for this claim. Their position either turns out inconsistent or transforms into a form of indirect realism. If their position was a form of indirect realism, then they would lose the idea of perceptual experience being of mind-independent objects (Brewer 2011, p. 100).

Brewer presents a number of challenges and arguments, which are supposed to show why the Content View fails. This section brings together the most important arguments: the first set of arguments works against two claims of superiority that representationalists cite. The second set of arguments presents difficulties with which the representationalists cannot cope.

Let us start with the first group: the Content View claims that their conception is favorable, because it can adequately explain the epistemological role of experience for empirical beliefs and also accommodate the phenomenon of perceptual transparency. Brewer objects that relationism can accommodate those tasks, too. In the above section on Brewer's relationist position, we have seen how the Object View accounts for the epistemological role of perceptual experience.

Representationalists mostly use the Argument from Transparency[240] to argue against indirect realist theories and conceptions which posit the existence of qualia (e. g. Tye 2015). The Argument observes that when a subject introspects her own perceptual experience she finds nothing but the objects of her percep-

---

240 The Argument from Transparency is usually traced back to G.E. Moore (Moore 1903).

tual experience; she does not find the quality of the experience or any intermediate objects. In other words, perceptual experience is transparent or diaphonous. From this the representationalist concludes that perceptual experience is constituted by how the world is represented. How the world is represented in the representational content makes up the particular perceptual experience of the subject. Brewer objects that relationism can (and does) also use the Argument from Transparency: on introspecting one's perceptual experience, one finds nothing but the direct objects of one's perceptual experience (e. g. Campbell 2009; Martin 2002). That means that the Argument from Transparency does not favor representationalism over relationism.

Brewer on the disadvantages of the Content View

The second group of arguments presents an extensive list of problems and difficulties for representationalists: (1) The Content View cannot capture the fact that in perception the objects are presented to the perceiver. (2) The Content View cannot offer a satisfying account of illusion. (3) The Content View cannot accommodate the fact that illusions are non-contingently limited. (4) The generality of predication in representational content is inadequate for capturing perceptual experience.

The first problem for the Content View – representational content cannot capture the fact that in perception physical objects are presented – lies in how it conceives of representational content. Representational content is modelled after thought: the "initial model" (Brewer 2011, p. 56) for how to conceive of representational content is 'a is F.' On such a conception there is a general asymmetry between perceptual presentation and representational content, since perceptual presentation is intrisically more basic than representational content of perceptual experience. This initial model does not claim that perception and thought are identical, rather, there are various ways for spelling out the initial model regarding the differences between perception and thought. Those versions can be split up into two sets of strategies. The first group argues that perception and thought are different attitudes with the same content (Brewer 2011, pp. 56 f.).[241] The perceptual propositional attitude is different from other cognitive attitudes. Brewer rejects this strategy because it cannot offer a coherent picture of the grounding function that perception has for thought about the world. It is unclear what the relation is between the perceptual content 'a is F.' and the

---

241 Of course, McDowell's conceptualism in *Mind and World* would fall into this group.

thought content '*a* is *F*.'. If the perceptual '*a* is *F*.' presupposes grasp of the content '*a* is *F*.', it is unclear what explanatory role perception has for thought about the world. If the perceptual '*a* is *F*.' does not presuppose grasp of the content '*a* is *F*.', it is unclear how perception can have an explanatory role for empirical thought, since they seem unrelated. The first strategy requires further argumentation.

The second strategy encompasses theories which argue that perceptual content and thought content are different, e.g. non-conceptual vs. conceptual, demonstrative; belief-independent and belief-dependent etc. (Brewer 2011, pp. 58 f.). There is no specific argument against either of the positions, but Brewer takes the arguments that he sets up against the Content View to cover all different varieties of determining the difference between perceptual content and thought content.

Brewer also rejects conceptions which try to show that if one holds that perceptual experience is of a mind-independent physical world, it is a natural consequence that perceptual experience has representational content (Brewer 2011, pp. 61 ff.). One philosopher to argue this way is Susanna Schellenberg. She observes that in perceptual experience the world seems a certain way to the subject and goes on to argue that this seeming a certain way is captured in the representational content of the particular experience (Schellenberg 2011). Brewer rejects this proposal by outlining an alternative conception on which things looking a certain way to S does not lead to the introduction of representational content. Schellenberg is not warranted in postulating a direct move from things seeming a certain way to the perceiver to representational content of the subject's perceptual experience.

In order to support this verdict, Brewer introduces the following analogy (Brewer 2011, p. 62). For a mind-independent physical object *o* which has features *F*, *G*, …, there are indefinitely many true sentences which have the form "*o* is *F*". *O*'s *existence* however does not consist in the truth of the sentences which contain the object and the features. Simply listing the true sentences also does not explain the existence of *o*. Rather, *o*'s existence itself is what makes the sentences true and thus *o*'s existence is more basic than the true sentences (Brewer 2011, p. 62). Brewer wants to show that something similar applies for a subject's perceptual experience of a physical object. Subject S sees a mind-independent object *o*. Even though there are indefinitely many true sentences which have the form "*o* looks *F*.", and which fit with S's perceptual experience, S seeing *o* still does not consist in the truth of the sentences and also cannot be explained by a simple list of facts of the form "*o* looks F_1", "*o* looks F_2", … "*o* looks F_n". S's seeing *o* is what makes the sentences true and thus is more basic than the true sentences. The looks-sentences do not capture the actual seeing of the physical object.

The second problem is that the Content View cannot deal with illusions (2): serious problems occur for it when it tries to do so (Brewer 2011, pp. 64 ff.). The Content View would try to explain the Müller-Lyer-illusion as follows: when a subject perceives that one line is longer than the other, the two lines are falsely represented in visual experience as being unequal in length. This explanation raises a number of questions. The initial question trades on a consequence of the representationalist conception. If the two lines are falsely represented as being unequal in length, then there must be a correct representation of the two lines. The Object View now asks what the world would have to look like for the Müller-Lyer experience to be veridical (Brewer 2011, p. 65). The question can be reframed as: 'which line is misrepresented in the illusion? Is it the upper line, the lower line or both lines?' McDowell returns to his disjunctivist view and turns down those questions as illegitimate: he insists that the representational content of the experience is simply 'A is longer than B.' Any questions about details do not arise. Brewer however refutes McDowell's reaction. Seeing is essentially fine-grained and determinate and every perception of the Müller-Lyer-diagram is bound to offer more information than 'A is longer than B.', e. g. about the distribution of the lines in space. At the same time, the lines do look a specific length; that is just one of the points of *seeing* the Müller-Lyer-diagram rather than *saying* that line A is longer than line B (Brewer 2011, pp. 65 f.).

In addition to this problem Brewer finds that the representational content of the Müller-Lyer experience is impossible content (Brewer 2011, p. 66). It will include the content that the endpoints of the lines look to be exactly where they are and it will include the content that line A is longer than line B. But if the endpoints are exactly where they are, then they are equidistant and that does not go together with the content that line A is longer than line B. This representational content is impossible content that will never be veridical. In response, a representationalist might try to separate the two contents, but according to Brewer, that means taking the first step to the Object View (Brewer 2011, p. 68). This Content View-response tries to exclude the observation that the endpoints of the lines look to be exactly where they are from the representational content and such a move is only possible if you introduce talk of a relation between the subject and the object, in that case, between the subject and the Müller-Lyer-diagram.

The Content View might try to further argue against the last objection that the impossible content cannot be had in one single experiential instance, rather, it is only if the subject attends to the endpoints, that they look to be where they are and equidistant, and only if she attends to the length of the lines that they look to be unequal in length (Brewer 2011, p. 69). Brewer also makes a similar move by introducing his distinction between thin looks and thick looks, but the Content View does not succeed in paralleling this move to separate the impossible content, since in both attendings the relative length of the lines remains constant: whether the subject attends to the endpoints or whether she attends to the length of the lines only, the lines always look to be unequal in length (Brewer 2011, p. 69). By employing the notion of thin looks the Object View can account for this phenomenon. The Content View cannot rid itself from the impossibility of the content. Brewer's solution, however, is successful, because on his Object View perception does not consist in content, but in a relation. What would be impossible contents on the Content View are simply several thin looks on the Object View.

The third problem notes that the Content View cannot explain the difference between illusion and hallucination (3) (Brewer 2011, pp. 73 f.). Illusion and hallucination differ in that illusion has certain limits, because it involves actually perceiving an object. In other words, illusion is incompatible with "extreme error" (Brewer 2011, p. 73), since there *is* an object that is simply falsely perceived. The Content View cannot include those non-contingent limits to illusion.²⁴²

Additional problems concern the fact that representational content includes predications and predicational classification (Brewer 2011, pp. 78 ff.) (4). According to Brewer, the Content View regards perception as an "abstract act of predicational classification" (Brewer 2011, pp. 80, 84). Eliza sees a ball, she sees 'The ball is red.'. In seeing this she has identified one of the features of the object 'ball'. This identification requires specifying one of the several generalizations which apply to the object 'ball', e. g. shape, size, color. Perceiving thus includes selecting a feature from general features. Since perception is put in terms of representational content, it includes "determinate general way[s]" (Brewer 2011,

---

242 The Content View says that a presentation of a mind-independent object in experience is explained by the fact that the subject's perceptual content "concerns" (Brewer 2011, p. 71) the object. Representational content can be understood as general perceptual content or as singular perceptual content, but both options do not succeed in including the systematic limits to illusions. General perceptual contents would not be able to put limits on the error, apart from some *ad hoc* regulations. As regards singular perceptual contents one could try to say that singular components are like demonstratives, whose successful reference to the mind-independent objects places limits upon the nature and the extent of the error. In other words, the demonstratives would only refer successfully if there are no random errors. Brewer agrees that this might be a promising direction, but only because demonstratives here are taken to be perceptual demonstratives and because error and illusion are limited by the nature of presentation. Those would again be the first steps into the direction of Brewer's Object View.

p. 79) which the object of perception is represented as having: the ball is represented as having the "determinate general way" (Brewer 2011, p. 79) *red*. Since Eliza's perception involves abstracting from other general ways that the ball might be and is thus fixed, her representational content must also be fixed regarding the question when the ball would still count as red and when not. That means that the truth conditions of the representational content are not just fixed by the particular object of perception, but also by the generality of the ways that are attributed to the object, like the redness. This conception of perception must be wrong (Brewer 2011, pp. 78 ff.).[243]

A related problem for the Content View lies in the generality of predication that representations necessarily include. This generality is incompatible with an adequate account of the presentation of particular mind-independent objects in perception. Mind-independent objects cannot be brought together with generality, because generality involves abstraction and mind-independent objects are in general not abstracted from but essentially particular. The Content View thus cannot include the particularity of perceptual experience (Brewer 2011, pp. 80 f.).[244]

In effect, Brewer's last challenge is this: any attempt at saying that representational content does not necessarily involve generality will fail; either because it is circular or because no specification will succeed in saying which changes in the world do make a relevant difference as to the correctness of the experience. The Content View must have a predicational component in representational content and thus in perception, but it cannot specify the worldly changes that are relevant to truth conditions or changes in truth value. It will always end up not accommodating presentation of mind-independent objects in perceptual experience (Brewer 2011, pp. 90 f.). A related very basic underlying issue for the Content View is that it holds that generality and predication bring classification into perceptual experience, thereby always including the "intrusion of conceptual thought about the world presented in perception" (Brewer 2011, p. 84) into the relation of the subject to the world. But according to Brewer, this set-up is fundamentally mistaken: presentation of the mind-independent object itself is the ground for all classification.

In my opinion Brewer's argumentation in the last two arguments is very sketchy and gappy. He wants to argue that the Content View's problem is that it cannot specify the truth conditions for perceptual content. It cannot show that per-

---

243 This argument has crucial similarities to one of Travis's arguments, the Problem of Selection (Section 5.2).

244 This argument is reminiscent of Travis's *Problem of Attaining Generality* (Section 5.2).

ception really represents the particular object that it purports to represent, because its content can be correct for infinitely many other objects.[245] However, it is not at all clear how he gets to this conclusion. His main conclusion is very reminiscent of an objection by Charles Travis against representationalism (the Problem of Selection), but he does not make this connection explicit.

There is a further problem with Brewer's conception of perceptual experience. Brewer at some point describes his position as follows: perceptual acquaintance is secured by "patterns of explanations that are acquired in developing engagement with the mind-independent physical world around us" (Brewer 2011, p. 141). But at the same time the perceptual engagement is not dependent on "actual categorization of that very thing in any acquired manner whatsoever" (Brewer 2011, p. 142). Now, when I look at this characterization of perceptual acquaintance it is not clear to me how it can be independent from actualizations of conceptual capacities in perceptual experience: how can perceptual acquaintance require "patterns of explanations" (Brewer 2011, p. 141) and yet be strictly non-conceptual? Patterns of explanations can only make sense as actualizations of conceptual capacities and so perceptual acquaintance on Brewer's Object View, too, is found to implicitly imply the actualization of conceptual capacities. Note that these "patterns of explanations" (Brewer 2011, p. 141) would not have to involve actual categorizations in order to be conceptual. Brewer suggests as much, but it is not clear why that should be so, they could also just involve the actualization of recognitional capacities.[246]

Brewer's theory is helpful for introducing the relationist motivation and its considerations, but there are internal problems to the theory which make it weak.[247] I think that those problems are rooted in Brewer wanting to develop a relationist theory of perceptual experience that can also explain the epistemic significance of perceptual experience without being conceptualist, i.e. without saying that perceptual experience implies the actualization of conceptual capacities. I will get back to this issue in developing relational conceptualism. Here I want to suggest that we should supplement Brewer's arguments by Charles Travis's criticism of representationalism: Travis's criticism provides the necessary background for understanding the conflict between the generality of representa-

---

245 Brewer goes through a number of responses that the Content View could give, but I will not detail those responses since I will not defend the Content View's claims. For more see (Brewer 2011, pp. 83 ff.)

246 Note that these problems indicate that Brewer's case is like that of Kalderon: both implicitly use the same tools and concepts for explaining the epistemic role of perceptual experience that conceptualist theories use, but do not acknowledge this fact.

247 For further important objections to Brewer's conception see e.g. (Ginsborg 2011).

tions and the particularity of the objects that are perceived. Moreover, Travis does *not* want to bring together a non-conceptualist theory of perceptual experience and an additional non-conceptualist explanation of how perceptual experience is epistemically significant, thereby avoiding Brewer's mistakes. I will thus move to Travis's critique of representational content and his theory of perceptual experience. Some of Brewer's arguments will also become clearer in this Travisian context. Finally, as I have said, Travis's arguments are also significant for Mc-Dowell's changes to conceptualism and for the relational conceptualism developed here: they will be challenges, inspiration and touchstones.

5 Relationism as Anti-Representationalism

5.1 Travis's Anti-Representationalism: the Bigger Picture

Before I can get to Travis's observations about the generality of representations and, most importantly, his criticism of representationalism, I want to look at the 'bigger picture' of Travis's own philosophical theory.[248] This intermediate step will involve the introduction of Travis's key concept *occasion-sensitivity*. In beginning the section on his theory with this introductory background I hope to counter the typical incomprehension that Travis's criticism of the representationalism usually faces. Note that this more general outline will be rather brief, since it is only meant to serve as a foil against which to approach the discussion about representationalism.

An intuitive starting point lies in Travis's pragmatist conception of the meaning of a word.[249] Travis argues against the view that the meaning of a word is intrinsic and can be traced back to facts that determine the correctness condition for the application of the particular word (cf. Dummett, Davidson, Frege). Instead he follows the later Wittgenstein in holding that the use of language is always set in a particular language game. Thus,

> what an expression named in a particular use of language in saying something is fixed ... by the recognizable conditions on treating [an] instance of saying something as it is to be treated, given the use of language it is to be understood to be – for example, on treating it, correctly, as either tue or false. Beyond what an understander would be prepared to recognize as to the correctness of the whole in which a name occurred ..., there are no further facts on which what an expression 'really' names might depend... (Travis 2006, pp. 20 f.)[250]

The main observation is that all facts that are cited to determine the correctness condition of a word might be different in a different language game and therefore cannot determine a unique standard of correctness for a use. That also means that

---

248 In the process of understanding Travis's theory and the nature of the disagreement between McDowell and Travis I have profited greatly from conversations with Alex Davies.

249 I will focus here on Travis's *Thought's Footing* (Travis 2006). Travis offers an analysis of Ludwig Wittgenstein's *Philosophical Investigations* by setting it in relation to Gottlob Frege's examinations of thought, language and logic. I will not say anything about these interpretative claims of Travis since only the tenets of his own conception matter.

250 Travis calls this Wittgenstein's First Principle (Travis 2006, p. 21).

... [w]hat words speak of (or name) underdetermines when the wholes they form would be correct, or correctly responded to (true, complied with, etc.). Any specifiable thing for them to speak of is compatible with various mutually conflicting answers to that question. (Travis 2006, p. 32)[251]

The same holds for representational forms, which are taken to be constituted by their "representing such-and-such as being a certain way" (Travis 2006, p. 32): "any representational form underdetermines when what has, or had, it would be true (complied with, etc.)." (Travis 2006, p. 32).

Truth and correctness are inseparable from the expectations that we attach to the representations, i.e. from what we expect them to mean. That also entails that representations are always "situated representations" (Travis 2006, p. 34). They are set against a background and it is only against this background that the words that make up the representation would be understood in a certain way and could have standards for success in grasping what it is that the subject represented (Travis 2006, p. 33). In Travis's terminology: representations are occasion-sensitive. Alexander Miller captures the idea of "occasion-sensitivity" aptly:

> thoughts and sentences have no correctness conditions independently of particular occasions of use in which the parochial sensibilities of participants in specific linguistic practices come into play. (Miller 2009, p. 213)

If one talks about occasion-sensitivity in perceptual experience, one finds that occasion-sensitivity basically consists in placing things encountered in experience in different ranges, depending on the occasion. Occasion-sensitivity goes hand in hand with the notion of *parochiality*: occasion-sensitivity entails work for parochial sensibilities. In other words, the correctness of occasion-sensitive phenomena is determined by the parochial – by what is close to the subject *qua* being the subject that it is. Travis calls several things "parochial"; he uses the adjective together with sensibilities, e.g. (Travis 2006, p. 60), capacities (e.g. Travis 2006, p. 82), understandings (e.g. Travis 2006, p. 82), and perceptions (e.g. Travis 2006, p. 112). He explains his usage of the expression as follows:

> I use the term 'parochial' here (and throughout) to refer to a trait of mind, or form of thinking, *possessed by a given sort of thinker*, but not necessarily by all thinkers; to what is not required just for being a thinker at all. (Travis 2006, p. 4, my emphasis, N.E.)

---

251 Travis calls this Wittgenstein's Second Principle (Travis 2006, p. 21).

Now, the obvious question to follow this explanation is what thinkers are on Travis's conception? A thinker is a member of a "community of agreement" (Travis 2010f, p. 10) who possesses the community's capacity for *Erkennung*. This insight also helps see the peculiar relation between being a thinker and the occasion-sensitivity of thought and of other representations.[252] In order to understand that representations are occasion-sensitive and to be susceptible to occasion-sensitivity a being has to be a thinker. Her particular capacities for recognition (*Erkennung* and *Anerkennung*) are part of the *parochial capacities* that she possesses as the thinker that she is.[253]

---

252 We can derive this insight from Travis's remarks on why thought is essentially social (Travis 2010e). The skeleton of his argumentation looks like this:
Step 1:
(1) I have a thought.
(2) If I have a thought, I am a thinker.
(3) I am a thinker, and I think that *p*.
(4) I am a thinker and so I belong to a range of thinkers who can think that *p* or not *p*.
Step 2:
(5) The range of thinkers and I form a community of agreement, i.e. we agree as to what would count as *that p* and what would not count so.
(6) Membership in our community is gained by "ability to think the thing in question" (Travis 2010e, p. 11), i.e. sufficient agreement as to what would count as a case of that thing and what not.
(7) Agreement is extendible, just like the community. So further cases can be found and thus I can think of cases which I actually cannot entertain.
Step 3:
(8) As a member of a community I am capable of two types of recognition: recognition as acknowledgment (*anerkennen*) and recognition as pure cognitive achievement (*erkennen*).
(9) Judging is *anerkennen*.
(10) Thinking presupposes sharing a sense of *Anerkennung* of the relevant community.
(11) Sharing a sense of *Anerkennung* goes hand in hand with possessing a capacity for *Erkennung* that is shared by the community.
(12) Exercises of *anerkennen* und *erkennen* are manifest in exercises of recognizing that something counts as a case and something does not count as a case. Such exercises are part of being in a community of agreement.
(13) A thinker who is a member of a community possesses a shared capacity for *Erkennung*.
(14) A thinker possesses a capacity for *Erkennung* and a sense of *Anerkennung* that are part and parcel of being a member in her community of agreement.
253 Travis extends his insights about the meaning of words being occasion-sensitive to rules: They are occasion-sensitive too, and thus also "admit of understandings" (Travis 2006, p. 80). To be precise: Travis also applies his fundamental insights to logical forms and logical notions (Travis 2006, Chapters 3, 4). He rejects the idea that logical forms have definite meaning, i.e. that they can be ascribed occasion-*insensitively*. *Concept, proposition, singular thought* are all occasion-sensitive terms, just like all representations. Those insights are also applied to

The obvious worry about such a view is that it is idealist: how there can be anything like *true* or *false*, if every interpretation has interpretations?[254] Don't we lose truth and answerability on Travis's Wittgensteinian model? Travis's answer is, 'No', since in the end it is still the world that determines whether a truth-evaluable, answerable stance is indeed true or not. The parochial and the occasion fix the standard, and those standards admit of understandings, but once the standard is fixed the world is the only one to judge whether the stance is true or false. Travis thinks that we should still describe this as answerability and truth-evaluability, since it has "perhaps the most crucial feature of answerability (and of truth)" (Travis 2006, p. 88). Being true is a correctness that a stance may have, and one particular instance of taking a stance to be true is to be correct for anybody taking that particular stance. Travis's example is this: Sid says "I'm cooking" and puts food into the microwave. Now we have to decide whether putting food into the microwave indeed counts as cooking, but "once we have made our decision, its scope will be any taking of the stance Sid did. When we commit ourselves to Sid having spoken truly, we thereby commit ourselves to anyone speaking truly anytime they say what he did" (Travis 2006, p. 88). The logical calculus that we develop will be like a language game, in which there are correct moves and wrong moves.

Adrian Haddock provides a clear and concise summary of Travis's main claim that we can keep in mind in the following sections:

> [T]he issue of whether a thought is true on an occasion, its truth-*value* on that occasion, is settled by the world and the world alone; but the issue of *what* aspect of the world makes the thought turn on an occasion, its truth-*condition* on that occasion, is settled by *our* 'relevant parochial perceptions' as to what in the circumstances '*ought* to count' (p. 145) as doing so. (Haddock 2008, p. 547, emphasis in original; page reference by Haddock for Travis 2006)

Travis's conception of perceptual experience is central for this book, since it will figure in the theory of relational conceptualism developed here: it will be the relational element that I adopt for relational conceptualism. There is however an

---

truth, *answerability, proposition, entailment* and *the laws of logic.* They all "admit of understandings" (e. g. Travis 2006, p. 80) and are thus occasion-sensitive. Whether a stance is answerable or not, that is, whether it is truth-evaluable or not thus depends on our parochial understanding: Is it answerable to us as the thinkers that we are? The people who are subject to a rule are those who know about "ways of getting on" (Travis 2006, p. 123). They are "worldly" (Travis 2006, p. 123), i.e., they know what to expect from a certain word, utterance, or action.

254 In the light of the previous footnote we can add: How can there be anything like *true* or *false* if answerability and even the laws of logic are subject to interpretations?

important difference between relational conceptualism and Travis's conception that will continue to show up and stand out: on his conception perception is independent from the actualization of conceptual capacities; conceptual activity and perceptual awareness are separate (e. g. Travis 2013c, p. 241). That is why one may call Travis a non-conceptualist. But at the same time – as we will see – he rejects average non-conceptualist conceptions of perceptual experience (e. g. Peacocke, Evans) as incoherent.

In Part III I will argue that Travis is wrong to claim that perceptual experience does not involve conceptual capacities. Instead I want to suggest that one should read parochial capacities as Travis's equivalent to 'conceptual capacities possessed by human beings'. The particular conceptual capacities of human beings are what makes them thinkers. In other words, parochial capacities are Travis's equivalent of McDowell's conceptual capacities.[255]

Before we can even start thinking about the relational conceptualist theory, we will first have to understand the relational criticism as brought forward by Travis. In the following sections I will thus present Travis's criticism of representational theories of perceptual experience and his criticism of conceptualist theories of perceptual experience. I will start first with the seminal "The Silences of the Senses"-criticism that offers a general critique of representationalist views. The paper will be supplemented by Travis's criticism as brought forward in the last chapter of *Thought's Footing*. After that I focus on Travis's criticism of non-conceptual representational views. This section (5.3) contains the gist of Travis's rejection of representationalism. I then present Travis's criticism of conceptual representationalism that is aimed in particular at McDowell's theory (Section 5.4). I end this chapter by outlining Travis's own conception of perceptual experience (Section 5.5).

At the end of these sections we will have collected a catalogue of Travis's anti-representationalist criticism which will allow us to do three different things: first, we may ignore non-conceptualist theories such as Peacocke's theory because they are ruled out by Travis's arguments. Second, we have set up the context against which McDowell's revised conceptualism must be examined. Third, we have set up large parts of the context for introducing relational conceptualism.

---

255 Note that this identification does not necessarily extend to parochial sensibilities and parochial understandings and the other expressions involving the adjective "parochial".

5.2 Travis's Arguments against Representationalism: the Problem of Selection, the Problem of Incoherent Content and the Problem of Attaining Generality

The Problem of Selection and the Problem of Incoherent Content

The seminal paper for Travis's representationalist criticism is "The Silence of the Senses" (Travis 2004). Travis has recently written a revised version of the article and I will here focus on the revised version "The Silences of the Senses" only (Travis 2013b).[256] I will not discuss the differences between the versions – the first difference is in the title, 'silence' vs. 'silences' – and only highlight differences when necessary. According to Travis, perception places surroundings in view, it presents things as they are. This goes together with a crucial limitation: perception cannot present things as they are not. It cannot do that because perception is "mere confrontation" (Travis 2013b, p. 31). So perception is non-committal, i.e. it involves no commitment to things being one way or another. Perception simply presents and is thus unmediated awareness. In that it radically differs from representing and representation, which are mediated awareness.[257]

Representations are types of mediated awareness. Travis introduces two types of representation: allorepresentation and autorepresentation. *Allorepresentation* consists in a vehicle representing something as thus and so. "[Something] represents in this way only in, and by, making [its] representing recognizable to *one* suitably *au fait* with its circumstances, and with the sort of project thus undertaken" (Travis 2013b, p. 26, emphasis in original). In its committed form, in which a subject commits to the representation representing things as they are, allorepresentations are truth-evaluable. The representational content of representationalist theories has to consist in committed allorepresentations, because only they "can have a face value" (Travis 2013b, p. 27), i.e. they can be accepted or rejected by the subject. A subject can also possess an *autorepresentation*, "a stance towards things being thus and so" (Travis 2013b, p. 26). Representing here is in the attitude of the subject, e.g. it takes things to be thus and so. It represents to herself that things are thus and so. Such representing is not truth-evaluable. Autorepresentations do not have a face value, they cannot be accepted or rejected. More particularly, since autorepresentation is an attitude by the subject it cannot be accepted or rejected by the subject. That also entails that au-

---

256 My interpretation of the claims in "The Silences of the Senses" has profited from a conversation with Keith Wilson about the text.

257 More on Travis's conception of perceptual experience later, in Section 5.5.

torepresentation is not a "source of information as to how things are in our surroundings" (Travis 2013b, p. 28) and therefore cannot be the representational content that representationalists take perceptual experience to have.

There are also two types of unmediated awareness: *factive meaning* and *indicating*. If A *factively means* B, then "If A, then B." holds. A *indicates* B if it is reasonable to expect that A factively means B. That also entails that A generally co-occurs with B: there is reason to expect B if there is reason to expect A. Look at the following example: a truffle pig snuffling beneath a tree indicates truffles beneath that tree and so if I see a pig snuffling beneath a tree I have reason to expect that there are truffles beneath that tree. The pig's snuffling beneath the tree indicates truffles beneath the tree. But note that 'truffles beneath the tree' can be instanced in a number of different ways: "big truffles, small ones,... etc." (Travis 2006, p. 206). It indicates a general condition that follows "as a rule" (Travis 2013b, p. 9) from what indicates thus. Both factive meaning and indicating are very different from representing. First, representing does not involve something following – "as a rule" (Travis 2006, p. 205) – from the representation. Second, indicating depends on how the world is arranged. Travis writes:

> Whether things being as they are with the oak instances what was indicated in its being indicated that there were truffles there is settled by the way nature is relevantly put together. What *does*, in fact, make pigs snuffle? (Travis 2006, p. 206, emphasis in original)

Indicating and factive meaning are unmediated awareness. They provide the basis for mediated awareness, i.e. representing, but they themselves do not involve any mediation. The most important difference between indicating, factive meaning and representing is that something can be represented as so-and-so even though it is not the case whereas factive meaning and indicating cannot be false. If A is taken to indicate B, but in fact does not, that is no case of mis-indicating, rather there is no indicating at all (Travis 2006, p. 206).

Travis claims that representationalist conceptions of perception are false because they are incoherent and untenable. Representationalist positions are those positions which subscribe to the following claims:

(1) Representation is "representing such-and-such as so" (Travis 2013b, p. 24).

(2) "Perceptual experience has a face value" (Travis 2013b, p. 24). The perceiving subject can accept or reject what is presented to her in her experience.

(3) "Being represented to is not autorepresentation" (Travis 2013b, p. 26), i.e. representing to oneself, or taking things to be so.

(4) The relevant representing must be recognizable to us. If perceptual experience has representational content, then one way in which the representational content can be found in experience is by reading the representational content "off of the way ... things looked" (Travis 2013b, p. 34) in the particular experience. In other words, representational content is "looks-index-[ed]" (Travis 2013b, p. 34).

In a nutshell, Travis puts it as follows: "you are my target if you think experiences have a face value" (Travis 2013b, p. 48).[258]

According to Travis, there are two candidates for looks that are looks-indexing representational content: *visual looks* (Travis 2013b, p. 35) (originally *look-like* in "The Silence of the Senses", 2004) and *thinkable looks* (Travis 2013b, p. 40) (originally *look-as-if* in "The Silence of the Senses", 2004), but as Travis argues neither of the two delivers. Representational content is content in which things are represented *as F* and represented *to be F*. Consequently there is a way things (read: things in the particular scene) should be to be as they are represented to be: representational content has correctness conditions. The idea that representational content is looks-indexed entails that 'the way things should be to be as represented' is identical with 'the way things should be to be the way they look', but neither visual looks nor thinkable looks offer anything like representational content. Visual looks do not offer fixed representational content, and thinkable looks offer fixed content, but the content is not representational content.

Let us start with visual looks: "Pia looks like her sister." (Travis 2013b, p. 35) is Travis's example for this type of looks. The case seems straightforward: the representational content of that experience is correct if Pia looks like her sister. So there is a way Pia should be to look like her sister, namely she should be her sister. But we cannot generalize this correctness condition, since that would mean that we could never take our particular visual experience of Pia or of her sister to be veridical. The correctness condition of a particular visual experience cannot be determined by a general correctness condition (Travis 2013b, p. 35).

A related problem appears because the representationalist wants the representational content to be read off from the particular experience, e.g. from the visual looks in Pia looking like her sister. The problem is that we cannot get any correctness conditions for the particular experience of Pia because there are infinitely many ways for things, i.e. the whole scene, to look like and Pia looking like her sister. Visual looks do not "decide how things must be to be

---

258 Peacocke's theory of perceptual experience obviously falls under this description, see e.g. (Peacocke 2001a, p. 254) and Section 2.2.

the way they look" (Travis 2013b, p. 36). Each instance of visual looks is stuck in the situation, in the context, since there are infinitely many ways for things to be in a perceptual experience whose representational content is supposed to represent, say, 'Pia looks like her sister'. 'Pia looks like her sister' would also be correct if Pia looked like herself.

There are thus two problems for representationalists:

(1) Visual looks do not determine one representational content, because things in a scene look like too many things. "Things just have too many visual looks in looking visually as they do" (Travis 2013b, p. 44).

(2) Visual looks do not determine one representational content, because no one, and nothing decides which elements in the visible scene matter.[259]

Travis continues

> Which facts as to Pia's looking (like) thus and so matter, and how, to how things should be to be the way they look simpliciter? Which looks, if any, matter to what is thus represented as so? And how? And why? (Travis 2013b, p. 37)

Answers to the second question are necessary if there is to be such a thing as misperception and a difference between perception and misperception. There can only be mis-perception if there is a way things ought to be, or a way how things would be if perception was correct. But there is nothing that could provide for such selection if experience consists in visual looks. Let's call that the *Problem of Selection*.

A representationalist who wants to embrace those different ways for things and wants to argue that they all fix the representational content would face another problem. The representational content would come out incoherent, because there would be infinitely many different ways for things to be (Travis 2013b, p. 29). That is what I will call the *Problem of Incoherent Content*. Note again the parallel to Brewer's argumentation. The issue basically remains the same as in the Problem of Selection, only now the focus is on what follows if the representationalist tries to accept the relevance of the Problem of Selection. The general problem is this: visual looks cannot determine a way things look *simpliciter*, a way things are full stop, correctness conditions against which a given representational content can be judged. In other words, representational content needs selection and determining, but perception cannot offer anything like this. These two problems, the Problem of Selection and the Problem of Incoherent Content, are what I take to be the problems and complications that Brew-

---

259 Note that here we see the parallel to Brewer's argumentation that I have alluded to above.

er aims to develop for the Content View but fails to spell out and motivate adequately.

Travis's remarks on the second class of representationalist looks, *thinkable looks*, have undergone substantive changes in the most recent version. As I have said, I will not comment on those changes, but simply stick with the revised text. In the revised "The Silences of the Senses" (Travis 2013b) Travis puts the idea of thinkable looks as follows:

> Looking like, on this notion, is a matter of things, or something, having a certain rational force regarding some given proposition; a certain bearing on the thing to think. Such looks, thinkable looks, are not visual looks in the present sense. (Travis 2013b, p. 41)

Travis's example is "It looks as if Pia will sink the putt" (Travis 2013b, p. 40). If I say that, what I am basically saying is, "It looks *to me* as if Pia will sink the putt." Things look to me that way based on what I take to be the case, based on what I gather from the "facts at hand" (Travis 2004, p. 76; Travis 2013b, p. 42). The "facts at hand" indicate that Pia will sink the putt. Whether I am right or wrong depends on what things factively mean, i.e. on what looks to be the case and on how the world contingently is. Those facts are "observer-independent" (Travis 2004, p. 78; Travis 2013b, p. 43). They can appear in a "sentential object" (Travis 2013b, p. 39), e.g. 'Pia will sink the putt' in "It looks as if Pia will sink the putt". The sentential object, the thinkable look itself, is nothing in the world.

In a strikingly clear statement Travis further describes thinkable looks as follows:

> They are not looks to be achieved simply by assuming the right shape, coloration, etc. They are not possessed by what is shaped and coloured as such; not instanced in the world simply in objects, or scenes, looking as they do, being such as to form the visual images they would. They are rather what is to be made of things by a thinker relevantly *au fait* with the world, and knowing enough of what to make of what he is thus aware of. (Travis 2013b, p. 40)

Thinkable looks are not objects in the world, i.e. they are not visual; they are not objects of perceptual awareness: "*[t]hat such-and-such* is not the sort of thing to have a look" (Travis 2013b, p. 40). Thinkable looks are objects of "judgement, or thought" (Travis 2013b, p. 44).

In a thinkable look a certain proposition is given a certain status, that is, it is taken to be the thing to think. That means that the correctness is fixed for thinkable looks, i.e. there is something that is the thing to think – it was just that which was lacking in visual looks. But the representationalist still is not better off, because the content of a thinkable look is not *visual* representational content. The fixing does not involve any representing or representational content. The correctness is fixed by the world. "It looks as if Pia will sink the putt." is correct if and only if Pia does sink the putt. The correctness condition thus consists in what is *indicated by the facts at hand*. The world indicates how things are, but *things looking as if Pia will sink the putt* is not something that is to be seen in the world. I can only gather this thinkable look from what the world indicates to me and what I make of it. The content that I have gathered from that might be representational content or *representing as so*, but it is not anymore something visual.

The indicating simply is in the world, it is there for me to take up, independently of me really taking it up. If I take up what is indicated, I might get representational content, but the representational content is in what I have taken up from what is indicated and not in things looking as they do. The representational content that the representationalist wants, however, must be visible. We might put it like this: the representational content must be in the perceptual experience and not just in the subject's response to the perceptual experience. The representational content of the perceptual experience, *looks*, must include "vehicles of content – the sort of thing that might make representing recognizable to one" (Travis 2013b, p. 42, emphasis omitted, N.E.), as do visual looks. Thinkable looks, however, are not something that is visible to the subject. Travis does not put it like that, but we might say that in thinkable looks I do not represent something that is in the world, a fact that is visually accessible to me. I see something in the world, e.g. my neighbor's car in the driveway (cf. Travis 2013b, pp. 30 f.), and I take that to factively mean, to indicate, that she is at home: it looks as if my neighbor is at home. But things looking as if my neighbor is at home is not one "particular visual look" (Travis 2013b, p. 42) that I might perceive.[260]

As I said at the beginning of this section, indicating and factive meaning do not get us representations: representational content does not determine whether the object represented in fact does exist as represented (Travis 2013b, pp. 34 f.). It is not something that would simply stop representing what it does when one finds out that it mis-represents, as would be the case with factive meaning (cf. (Travis 2006, pp. 101 f.).[261] The representationalist must therefore avoid explicating representations in terms of factive meaning or indicating.

---

260 An obvious question might be why thinkable looks are still called looks. Travis does not discuss this question and I also do not want to engage in any speculation on my side.

261 Travis in passing also rejects the standard motivation for introducing a representationalist conception of perceptual experience: accounting for illusory perceptual experience. He explains that illusions are simply mistakes made by the subject in taking up what is indicated by the per-

These problems with representational content can be found in McDowell's notion of ostensible seeing: McDowell wants experience to have two features: (1) experience can be misleading, (2) the perceiving subject can decide whether she wants to take things to be so or not[262], and he thinks that experience understood as ostensible seeings or demonstrable looks can fulfill those two functions. But the same problems that Travis has described for visual looks and thinkable looks appear again: visual looks do not fix *one* particular way things should be to be the way things look, and the truth of any statement about the way things look depends on the context of the statement. McDowell, however, needs such a particular way things look if he wants experience to be belief-independent and possibly misleading. If the subject is to be able to doubt or not doubt, judge or not judge her experience, correctness is in the picture. Now if correctness is in the picture, then there must be "a way things look fullstop", a determined, fixed way that things look. In effect this comes down to a combination of visual looks and thinkable looks (Travis 2013b, pp. 46 f.): McDowell wants the openness of judgments that is found in visual looks as well as the judgeability against standards and correctness conditions that is found in thinkable looks (Travis 2013b, pp. 46 f.). But representation cannot have both features.[263] We will see a similar objection in Section 5.5 (cf. Travis 2009).

---

ceptual experience (Travis 2004, p. 68; Travis 2013b, p. 33). One can count this rejection as another argument against representationalism, but I think that Travis's remarks on the Problem of Selection and the Problem of Incoherent Content are more important.

262 Cf. the belief-independence of experience.

263 Another self-imposed hurdle for the representationalist is that she wants to include cases of false representing, of 'seeing' things that are not there into her representationalist conception of perception. (Travis takes *see* to be a success verb, so strictly speaking, seeing is not automatically representing, because representational content can represent something that is not there to be *seen*.) In fact, as we have seen, that is often taken to be the main argument for representationalism. The Problem of Selection here returns in different make-up: if you can see things that are not there, it is unclear what makes a subject's experience a veridical experience with a true representational content.

A first set of questions asks about the details *when* something is represented to be there, even though it is not. (Here we see again the parallel to Brewer.) What is it that makes the representational experience false? Is it something in the content? And conversely: what makes the correct representational content correct? We can rephrase the question like this: what more is there in the case of veridical experience that is not in the representational content of illusory experience? The same obstacles as before reoccur. False representation cannot be a case of the subject falsely taking things to be so, because taking things to be so is a case of auto-representing and representational content is more than autorepresenting. It is also not possible to answer the question by talking about the correct cases and saying that the correct cases are cases in which it is indicated that p or that p is to be expected, because representing is more than indicating. Talk of

Let us bring together the main problems that have been set up so far by Travis. Visual experience consists in visual looks and thinkable looks, but neither of them can provide representational content of visual experience: visual looks do not look one way only and so they cannot help fix one particular representational content that would represent that one way they look. Thinkable looks can provide us with representational content that is gathered from the facts at hand, from what is indicated in the world, but that it means that it cannot contain misrepresenting. Also, the world decides whether the indicating was correct or not, unlike in the case of representation. Thinkable looks also are not visible but only based on factive meaning and indicating and thus cannot be perceptual awareness. Representational content simply cannot be what the representationalist wants it to be: she cannot avoid the Problem of Selection and the Problem of Incoherent Content. Travis diagnoses a third problem for the representationalist that is rooted in a central difference between representations and the objects of perception: representations are general, objects are particular. This problem comes out clearest in the last section of Travis's *Thought's Footing:* it is the Problem of Attaining Generality.

The Problem of Attaining Generality

In the final chapter of *Thought's Footing* (Travis 2006), "Harmony", Travis takes another route to his "anti-representationalist" (Travis 2013a, p. 9) critique than in "The Silences of the Senses". This alternative route leads him to a third problem for representationalists: the *Problem of Attaining Generality.* This section details the way to this problem and Travis's conclusions for perception.

Travis starts with J.L. Austin's and Wittgenstein's criticism of simple correspondence theories of truth. Like Wittgenstein, Austin holds that statements are always situated representings. Thus answers to questions of truth are also determined by the circumstances in which the particular statement was uttered. The Tractarian and Strawsonian conception according to which facts and statements mirror one another does not capture the nature of truth. On this wrong conception "the world (things being as they are) would have to be a *perfect* image of the statement (representation) for the statement to count as representing what was *so* as so at all" (Travis 2006, p. 188, emphasis and brackets in orig-

---

visual looks also does not say what makes the experience a veridical experience, as we have seen with McDowell's ostensible seeing. The problem lies in wanting to conceive falsidical and veridical experience in terms of representational content: neither representational content itself nor perceptual experience can make this conception coherent.

inal). Instead Travis argues that representation should be understood as classifying and sorting; the question that each representation faces is whether it is "meritorious" (Travis 2006, pp. 187, 194, 202) sorting. True descriptions are meritorious descriptions (Travis 2006, p. 187).[264]

> The idea of merit is the idea that there is always room in such a meeting of the general and the particular for questions as to whether so sorting things is a sufficiently good way of doing things (though of course such a question cannot make sense unless enough is fixed as to what the sorting is to be good for). (Travis 2006, p. 187)

Travis again specifies the claims which representationalist theories that he targets subscribe to:

(1) Representation is not auto-representing. It can be accepted or rejected.

(2) Representations are truth-evaluable.

(3) Things are represented as thus-and-so in appearing a way. The environment is not taken to represent, rather experience is taken to conjure up representations.

The fundamental problem for any representation, whether they are representations of things – as in perceptual experience – or representations of thoughts – as in statements and judgments – is the following: how do we get from the particularity of things being as they are to the generality of representation? In questions of truth the gap is between the particularity of "the world as it is" and the generality of our representation of the world as being a certain way: how can the world's particularity "achieve the generality of instancing, or failing to, *that* general way for things to be" (Travis 2006, p. 200)? In experience the gap is between the particularity of "things being as they are" and "representation[s] of things as being such-and-such (general) way there is for things to be" and the challenge is: 'how can things being as they are generate such a representation?' There is nothing in the particular "things being as they are" that identifies which generality is

---

264 Travis notes that J.L. Austin supports such a view of truth as being meritorious. Austin rejects the correspondence theory's idea that there are truth-makers, which literally make statements true "independent of any occasion for considering whether the way things are *ought* to count as things being that way, independent of any purposes and points that might give substance to such an ought" (Travis 2006, p. 194 emphasis in original). Instead the correct question to ask is this: "Was [the] description sufficiently merited, given the expectations there would … be of it, for its giving to count as stating *truth*?" (Travis 2006, p. 197, emphasis in original) Truth is not intrinsic to the given way things are (*pace* Frege), but rather depends on the occasions in which things are assessed as true or false.

to apply to it in the representation, i.e. which generality is instanced by it. "Things being as they are" also does not say which other ways would instance the generality, and which instances would not instance the generality. But for a generality to be generated one needs to get to this level. The generality of representation also includes those cases in which the generality is *not* instanced, and if the generality of representations is to be generated from the particular "things being as they are", then "things being as they are" must be able to provide for this generality of cases that are instances and cases that are not instances (Travis 2006, p. 200).

Such theories think that there is an absolute articulation of things being as they are independent from any circumstances or that particular fixed properties of the things determine whether the generality is instanced. But, according to Travis, there is no articulation independent from circumstances. The property cannot say which generality is instanced and absolute articulation also has no measure for determining the generality. Travis concludes that the question that really needs to be asked here is this: "In particular circumstances, for particular purposes, does [Pia's] lips being as they are *merit* being called their being red" (Travis 2006, p. 202, emphasis in original)?[265] The problem that representations inevitably produce thus appears both for true representations of thoughts and veridical representations of experience. As regards truth, "[t]hings being as they are does not identify any particular range of representations as those which, as such, have just the right generality for representing *truly* things being as they are" (Travis 2006, p. 202). As regards experience, "[t]hings appearing as they are cannot by itself decide which representations, with just what generality, would represent things as being as they appear" (Travis 2006, p. 203).

I will call this the *Problem of Attaining Generality:* the properties of the objects do not fix which generality is instanced, since there is always more than one way of seeing things: it is unclear which generality is instanced.[266] Note that the Problem of Selection is different from the Problem of Attaining Generality as the latter is focused on the move from the particular to the general, while the former is more concerned with problems that follow from the generality of representations. But we might conceive of the Problem of Attaining Generality as the flipside of the Problem of Selection.

Representationalists like McDowell and Evans can accept that the "environment itself does not *per se* represent anything as so" (Travis 2006, p. 203), but they still hold that in an act of experiencing things representational material

---

265 In this conclusion Travis follows Austin.
266 For a related observation see (Travis 2013c).

can be generated. Experience conjures up representations (cf. Travis 2006, p. 199). Travis focuses on McDowell's theory of perceptual experience in the chapter and so he discusses McDowell's solution for the Problem of Attaining Generality. McDowell claims that his conception does provide for a way things would have to be to be as they appeared. First, it is only represented as so that the object is a pig, if the world's "being as it is bears suitable responsibility for there appearing to be a pig" (Travis 2006, p. 204).[267] Second, the actualization of conceptual capacities provides for a selection, since the subject must possess the appropriate concepts to perceive the object as *T*. The subject must possess the concept *tapir* for the object to appear to her as a *tapir*. The generality of concepts is taken to correspond to the generality of representation and that means that the selection provided by the concepts that the subject has to possess in order to see the object is the selection that seemed to be lacking in the representational content of the perceptual experience. There is a particular way for things to be, namely "the way things would be [if] they were as they appeared" (Travis 2006, p. 204) to the subject who possesses the concepts that "enable" the particular perceptual experience in the first place (Travis 2006, p. 204).

But Travis objects that "the way things would be [if] they were as they appeared" does not provide correctness conditions for representational content. The supposed solution is based on a confusion about representations, factive meaning and indicating. As I have already said, indicating is based on factive meaning, e. g. '*A* factively means *B*.', and that in turn means that *A* indicates *B*. Factive meaning only looks like a case of representing, in fact it is not. First, indicating does not contain the generality of representation. Admittedly, *A* and *B* are general conditions, which can be instanced in different ways, but their generality is different from the generality of representing. The generality is in the two conditions, *A* and *B*, and not in the indicating. The generality of representations, however, is in the representing itself and not just in the object that is represented and the representing entity. Second, the relation between appearances and representations cannot be determined by what appearances indicate. Indicating is not representing: if things appear a certain way, they are represented as being that way. But things can be other than they appear and, unlike the relation between appearances and factive meaning, the relation between appearances and representations cannot be determined by what appearances indicate.[268]

---

267 We can see McDowell's disjunctivism in this claim (see also Section 1.3).
268 The representationalist wants to say that the representational content of the perceptual experience is determined by how things appear to the perceiver: The object *O* appears to S a certain way, let's say, it appears red. If the object is as it appears, it must be *red*. Otherwise it would not

This crucial difference can also be captured in terms of mis-representing: indicating cannot mis-represent, representations can mis-represent. Another difference between indicating and representing becomes clear if one looks at cases of false representing. This Flamish saying is Travis's example for factive meaning: "If the pigs are walking with straws in their mouths, it will rain" (Travis 2006, p. 101). If it turns out that it does not rain, then pigs walking with straws in their mouths simply does not factively mean that it will rain. But if Pia represents, e. g. says, that it will rain, then, even if does not rain, her utterance will still represent that it will rain (Travis 2006, p. 101). I take it that this idea can be rephrased by saying that there can be falsidical representing, but there cannot be falsidical factive meaning.[269]

---

be represented as red. "If the lips appearing to him as they do is (*inter alia*) their appearing red, then their being as they appear will be (*inter alia*) their being red. Then (and only then) will they be *represented* to be red." (Travis 2006, p. 207, my emphasis, N.E.) But this is no more than a grammatical observation. The account thus fails to capture the nature of representations: Eliza represents to Tom that there are truffles under the oak by saying so. We can suitably ask here, what follows from what Eliza said? How ought her statement to be taken? Her saying that there are truffles under the oak does not indicate a general condition – as the representationalist account suggests – rather, it represents a state as thus-and-so and thus is essentially occasion-sensitive. Note again the difference between *indicating* and *representing*: in the case of indicating different questions would be asked. Take for example the pig snuffling beneath the oak indicating truffles. The question that would be asked here is what it is that follows from the snuffling? It is the presence of truffles. The snuffling indicates the presence of a general condition that admits of instances, i.e. big, small, edible, inedible truffles under the oak or no truffles. So indicating *does* have a fixed content, but it is not representational content, since the content is fixed by the make-up of the world: "Whether things being as they are with the oak instances what was indicated in its being indicated that there were truffles there is settled by the way nature is relevantly put together. What *does*, in fact, make pigs snuffle?" (Travis 2006, p. 206) Representations, however, are not determined by the way the world is built.

269 It is slightly surprising to see Travis add that factive meaning is also occasion-sensitive (Travis 2006, p. 102). He explains that factive meanings are organized in a network. This network of factive meaning comprises the properties of objects of the outer world: each property has a location in the network. Whether a particular object really has the property on a particular understanding depends on the location in the network as well as on the occasion in which something is said about the meaning. But even though both representations and factive meaning are occasion-sensitive, there continue to be fundamental differences between them: the facts of factive meaning are formed by discoveries in the course of investigating what makes a *p* a *p* and what is distinctive about the property that is located in the network. A pig snuffling beneath an oak indicates truffles beneath the oak. What generality is thus instanced is discovered by biologists, e. g. in investigating the mechanisms of pigs' snuffling and more particularly pigs' snuffling truffles. Those things again are open to investigations, and so the following questions can be asked and investigated: "[Does the snuffling] mean there are truffles beneath the oak? In the sense in which it does mean there are truffles, if there are, might there be old rotten ones, or

If the representationalist wanted to insist that experience can be veridical and non-veridical, then there would have to be a fixed generality that determines the truth value. If appearances and experiences had a fixed generality, then a number of questions would have to be answered:

> Suppose it is represented as so, in Sid's experience, that Pia's lips are F. Now let C be circumstances in which Pia's lips would not be as thus represented, but would still be such as to appear as they in fact do. Why were her lips not represented as a way C would instance? Why is that not things being as they appear? Why, for that matter, is it not their being F, on some admissible understanding of being F? (Travis 2006, p. 208)

What Sid perceptually experiences cannot help in answering those questions; nothing in Sid's awareness of the surroundings is helpful here. The representation does not determine the instancing and so the truth-value of the representation cannot be fixed (the Problem of Selection). In addition, the case does not determine the reach of the representation (again: the Problem of Attaining Generality). Just as in "The Silence of the Senses" (Travis 2004; Travis 2013b) Travis concludes that there are no representations in perceivings.[270] The only place in which a variety of representations can be found is the perceiver's response to the perception, but such representations are auto-representations, cases of the subject taking things to be thus and so. Travis observes:

> The harmony of thought and reality, working as it does through what is to be called what, puts no thoughts into the world as such, either as images of our thought about it, or as images of it appearing as it does. (Travis 2006, p. 208)

Note that the above Problem of Attaining Generality and the Problem of Selection also bring with it Travis's rejection of the question of how the reach of the conceptual is determined. It is senseless: there is no rule that determines the relation between the conceptual and reality – because of occasion-sensitivity. The representing is fixed by capacities that we as thinkers possess (Travis 2010b). As I said above, those capacities are a shared sensibility among an extendable community of thinkers. So the reach of the conceptual is fixed by agreement and in mentioning an element from the conceptual the speaker or the thinker fixes the particular reach of the conceptual (Travis 2010b, p. 13). A sub-

---

truffles of some little known poisonous variety?" (Travis 2006, p. 162) In contrast, it is not an object of discovery which generalities are instanced by a representation, because the question does not depend on the make-up of the world.

270 The same conclusion is also in "The Inward Turn" (Travis 2009) and "Is Seeing Intentional?" (Travis 2011).

ject that recognizes the barking and articulating the sound as barking belongs to a community of thinkers that possess the concept *barking*; it is her audience, her community, that determines whether she was right to articulate her experience in that way.

The above sections have presented Travis's more general criticism of representational views. This criticism is supplemented by more specialized arguments against non-conceptual representationalist theories and conceptual representational theories. In the following two sections I will present the arguments in turn and start with the criticism of non-conceptualism. The criticism is helpful for us because it argues against the view that conceptualism has been debating with (see Chapter 2).

5.3 Non-Conceptualist Representationalism as an Incoherent Theory

In the article "The Inward Turn" (Travis 2009) Travis more specifically argues against what he calls the *Stuff Happens Model* ("SH Model", Travis 2009, p. 316) that he finds in representationalist theories, especially in non-conceptual representationalist theories. But first let me interject two remarks. First, a terminological remark: in what follows I will continue to use the hyphenated spelling "non-conceptual" exclusively to refer to non-conceptualist theories. I said in the early chapters of this book that I will refer to non-conceptualist positions by the hyphenated term – the major reason for that was that this spelling more clearly reflects the fact that non-conceptualism rejects conceptualism. But another advantage of this orthographic decision is that it allows me to avoid confusions in the following paragraphs: the unhyphenated "nonconceptual" is reserved for Travis's notion of the nonconceptual that refers to particulars. I will say more about Travis's term shortly; for now I just want to mark out the distinction.

Second, the fact that Travis criticizes and rejects non-conceptual representationalist theories does not mean that he is not anymore or not really a non-conceptualist. He explicitly holds that perceptual experience is independent of all conceptual activity – that makes him a crystal clear non-conceptualist – it is just that he takes the representationalist variety of non-conceptualism to be mistaken. Of course, from my conceptualist perspective he is right to reject representationalist non-conceptualism, but at the same time his own view is not correct, because he does not yet see that his own relationist non-conceptualism is false, too. But more about that later.

The Stuff Happens Model (Travis 2009, p. 316) conceives of perceptual experience as a combination of retina action (affecting the eyes) and "stuff happening", i.e. some inner state. It is the inner state that supplies the answer to the question of what the perceiving subject is aware. In order for the perceiving subject to have perceptual experience "stuff" has to happen. Travis describes its considerations as follows:

> No one, I think, thinks there is any sense of 'see' in which merely to have something 'affect your eyes' – say, form retinal images – is to see it. Why not? A natural, though not inevitable, idea is: before one saw anything, more stuff would have to happen. ... A further natural idea might then be: at a certain point the relevant stuff, or enough of it, has happened. At that point, the perceiver goes into a certain 'internal' state, the upshot of the stuff, where this is one of a specified range of states into which a particular device, 'that which enables vision', might go. In such a state, the idea is, one enjoys visual awareness (or experience). One sees only in enjoying visual awareness. The state decides what visually awareness one thus enjoys; thus, at least, what it is in which one might be seeing something. (Travis 2009, p. 315)

Gareth Evans's conception of perceptual experience is one example for the Stuff Happens Model: perceptual experience is regarded as an informational state, as an "internal state" (Travis 2009, p. 316). Those internal states "float free" (Travis 2009, p. 321) of the world that is in view for the subject, since they can be entertained by the subject even if things are not as presented in the internal state: those internal states are representations. They are not necessarily objects of the subject's perceptual awareness, but they can become an object of her perceptual awareness. Travis summarizes Evans's position as follows:

> ... it seems to me as though that pig is spotted; *ceteris paribus* the relevant state contains the information that that pig is spotted. I thus *can* be aware of the state containing information it does [sic]. *Just* so, for Evans, can perception perform its most central task in a *thinker's* life: allowing how things are to bear, according to their bearing on how to *think* they are; thereby on how to *act*. (Travis 2009, p. 317, emphasis in original)

But this conception of inner states as informational states is problematic: Evans's "internal states" are ambiguous as to which notion of information they contain: internal states are supposed to be (i) conceptualizable and (ii) truth-evaluable. (i) and (ii) relate to two different notions of information: information$_{(i)}$ conceives of information as contained in the scene that the subject encounters and the information can be retrieved by the subject by exercises of her recognitional capacities. "The scene before me may ... contain the information that there is a *bísaro* before me: it makes this recognisable (to one who knows his bísaros)" (Travis 2009, p. 317). There is no room for mis-information on this notion (cf. Travis's notion of auto-representation in Travis 2004; Travis 2013b). Information$_{(ii)}$ conceives of the information as representing something as so. E. g. a road sign "contains the information that Santiago is 48 km [away]. Hence: it says so" (Travis 2009, p. 317). O is represented as *F* and that clearly is truth-evaluable and can be false or correct. That – again – is in the nature of representing. Mis-information is possible on this notion of information. *Travis* argues that the two notions cannot be brought together in an internal state, i. e. an internal state cannot have content that is both conceptualizable and truth-evaluable. But that is just what non-conceptual representationalists are trying to do: Evans, for example, wants to include the possibility of misinformation in experience, but also wants to conceive of experience as something on which conceptual skills can be exercised. As Travis points out, those are two incompatible conceptions of information in perceptual experience. Experience as something on which conceptual skills can be exercised consists in what Travis has been calling *factive meaning* or *indicating*. Experience as possibly mis-informing consists in representations, in representing something *as so*.

Travis defines the central role of perceptual experience as allowing the world to bear on what the subject thinks (e. g. Travis 2009, p. 318).[271] He goes back to Frege in order to establish the role of concepts and particulars in a subject having thoughts about the world. Frege distinguishes between the conceptual and the nonconceptual – here we have Travis's unhyphenated term "nonconceptual": there is "Frege's line" between objects in the world and propositions, concepts and similar entities, between the perceivable and the unperceivable. On the one side[272] there are objects, e. g. the sun, and other "things which, like [the sun, N.E.] reflect or emit light into one's eyes" (Travis 2007, p. 230). They are what Frege and Travis call the *nonconceptual*. Such objects instance generalities, they are particulars that instance generalities – again, that is the unhyphenated nonconceptual. On the other side there are generalities, i. e. entities like *that the sun has set* and concepts. Those entities are not concrete and thus for them questions of truth arise. This side is the conceptual side. The conceptual inherently possesses a special generality: there are always a range of cases which would fit the particular concept or the proposition. *That the sun has set* can be instanced by various scenes, or things being as they are, e. g. by the setting sun in London or over the Pacific Ocean.

Concepts are "satisfied" by things that fall under those concepts. They reach to a range of objects. Grasping a concept presupposes relations between the con-

---

271 Note that here one sees that to some extent Travis, too, is interested in a conception of *epistemically significant* perceptual experience.

272 In "Reason's Reach" Travis calls this the *left side* and the other side the *right side* (Travis 2007 p. 230). Travis's talk of the two sides being the *right* side and the *left* side does not seem to be significant. He only uses it in "Reason's Reach" and I thus omit it.

ceptual and the nonconceptual, i.e. what is instanced and what does the instancing, and between the conceptual elements themselves. Without concepts a subject could not have thoughts about the world, but the possession of those concepts consists in understanding the relation between concepts and their nonconceptual instances. A subject that possesses such concepts in effect has the capacity for acquiring conceptualizable information from its experience (Information$_{(i)}$). Travis's model of perception is as follows:

> Sight affords visual awareness of a scene, and of things, happenings, and conditions obtaining in it: that sloth, the waving of the branches, the blackness of the toast. It thus affords opportunity for exercising certain sorts of capacities: I can recognise, of the scene being visibly as it is, that that is that sloth sleeping, or that toast being burnt. Such is a ... fundamentally important way for perceptual experience to make the world bear, for me, on what to think. (Travis 2009, p. 320)

Now, Travis argues that representationalism cannot allow these insights. The charge that he levels against representationalism is this:

> The SH Model [Stuff Happens Model] cannot allow perception to bring the world to bear on what to think as perception would do. Representation cannot allow it to. So the SH Model of perception is wrong. Representing in or by perceptual experience – notably things as so – requires the SH Model. So there is no room for representation in or by perceptual experience. (Travis 2009, p. 334)

Representationalists provide different ways of spelling out talk of internal states, e.g. introducing a vehicle, like Cartesian *cogitationes* or ideas, or Evans's vehicle-less informational states, but they all encounter the same problem in two different forms: the real, actual objects of experience are left out of the picture.

Internal states, understood e.g. as Cartesian *cogitationes*, are ideas, they are contents of consciousness. Consequently, awareness of Cartesian *cogitationes* can at most show how they are, but not how the world is. Yet, perceptual experience is of the world and the representational content of perceptual experience was supposed to represent the world.[273]

Evans differs from Descartes, because he does not want vehicles, e.g. *cogitationes*, in the picture, but his conception also fails to allow the particular scene's being as it is to bear on what I am to think. Why does it fail? The scene being as it is can only provide factive meaning, it does not include representations of things as thus-and-so. Again: factive meaning is not enough to secure the possibility of mis-information: the scene itself is not truth-evaluable, so

---

273 For related criticism of such positions based on *ideas* see (Travis 2010a).

there must be an additional ingredient, which allows for the mis-information element in the account.

There are two ways for getting the possibility of mis-information in perceptual experience into the picture: according to representationalists, like Evans, mis-information is possible because perceptual experience has representational content. Travis points out again that this move brings the cost of the perceiver not being directly aware of the objects in the world: awareness of an internal state just is not awareness of the scene. Even if one manages to show that one can be aware of the world in one's awareness of an internal state, that does not entail that awareness of the world is the same as awareness of an internal state. In other words, even if representationalists showed that in the representational content of the subject's perceptual experience she is aware of the world, that would not suffice to show that awareness of the world is awareness of the representational content of her perceptual experience. According to Travis, the required additional component is the idea of *commitment*. Only if the subject commits to what she perceives, if she takes it to be true, can issues of correctness, i.e. mis-information, come into play.

Travis also considers the following coherentist-idealist reading of Evans: for experience to have rational bearing on judgment it must have propositional form and that is why experience is *representing as so*. But that, too, is problematic, because *representing as so* brings generalities into play and still does not put us in contact with the world. Experience as *representing as so* only "present[s] our surroundings to us as falling under a certain generality" (Travis 2009, p. 326, emphasis omitted, N.E.): the particular representation will reach to the range of cases of surroundings and the scene being as it is. That would constitute the need for another grasp, namely a grasp of which of those ways are right, and it would open further questions of what would make these ways the right ones. We would end up in what I think we may call a regress. We thus could not think the thoughts we think and it would not be clear why the particular representations are the right representations. At the basis of this lies a further problem: if perceptual experience consists in representations, in inner states, then perceptual experience would only make facts available to the perceiving subject and not the objects in the world (Travis 2009, p. 326).[274]

---

274 Evans might have tried to explicate representation simply as "things appearing a certain way" (Travis 2009, p. 331). "[M]y experience represents things ... as they appear" (Travis 2009, p. 331). Things appearing as they do belongs to the nonconceptual and so representing things appearing as they do gives us nonconceptual representing. But the representationalist still has not rid herself of the range of cases that come with something being represented. She might try to argue that "things appearing as they do", i.e. things being as they are, deter-

It might be surprising to find this problem for representationalism – especially for non-conceptual representationalism – but the problem becomes clear in Travis's additional criticism of the notion of "representational content" as employed on the Stuff Happens Model: Evans and other representationalists assume that there is non-conceptual representational content, but on the conception that Travis has outlined there is nothing like nonconceptual representational content: representational content is essentially conceptual; it always reaches to the general (Travis 2009, p. 321). The nonconceptual that is opposed to the conceptual is not an inner state, rather it is things in the world. Representations can be neither nonconceptual nor non-conceptual and so there cannot be any non-conceptual representational content. The notion simply does not make sense on the Fregean conceptual-nonconceptual-distinction (Travis 2009, p. 321).

The same problem appears for Peacocke's conception of non-conceptual representational content. According to Peacocke, "a perceptual experience represents the world as being a certain way" (Peacocke 1992, p. 61). Experience thus clearly is taken to be representational: there is a way for things to be when they are as represented. On Peacocke's conception such a way for things to be is supposed to be 'non-conceptual', but that is impossible according to Travis, because a way for things to be is general and thus conceptual. It reaches to the nonconceptual, to particulars, as falling under the generality. Travis considers what Peacocke might instead mean by non-conceptual content: Peacocke defines non-conceptual content as content that "cannot be the content of a judgement" (Travis 2009, p. 328), but Travis shows that Peacocke's claims are not coherent. Peacocke also describes the representational nature of perceptual experience as follows: perceptual experience "represents things as thus and so ... the subject then takes experience's word for it – acquiesces in the representing, so judges – or ... resists – declines so to judge" (Travis 2009, p. 329). This clearly is the content of a judgment: what is represented in experience is judged upon by the subject. So actually, on Peacocke's conception of perceptual experience, too, there cannot be non-conceptual representational content.[275]

According to Travis, Peacocke's Argument from Animal Perception (see above, Section 2.1) in favor of non-conceptual representational content also fails: the supposedly non-conceptual content that thinkers and animals are sup-

---

mines the reach of the representation "F is G." But this idea is flawed as well, because 'things being as they are' is a particular case and particular cases do not have a reach, they are particular. They cannot determine the reach of something conceptual. Cf. the Problem of Attaining Generality.

275 That also holds for Peacocke's conception of non-conceptual content as content that does not require concept possession to be entertained.

posed to share is still conceptual, because Peacocke's conception does not get rid of the conceptualization element in the story. The "non-conceptual" content that thinkers and animals are taken to share still reaches to a range of cases, because it is to be judgeable by thinkers. If the content can be judged by a thinker, it must be conceptual content, content that can be in a thought. Thinkers and non-thinking animals could not share this content. Travis also points out that the Argument from Animal Perception does not establish that we need sameness of representational nonconceptual content in order to account for the apparent sameness in experience between animals and humans. There is sameness in the awareness of the same object, not sameness in the representational content.[276] A cat and I might see a bird in a bush, but that is just an instance of the cat and myself being aware of the same object (Travis 2009, pp. 328 f.).

Peacocke wants to argue that an experience is true if the positioned scenario of the particular scenario content is true (see above, Section 2.1). But the problem here again – as in the Problem of Selection – is that there is no way to answer the question as to which scenario would fit Sid's experience if it is as it is. Travis contends that the problems of perceptual experience as representation are insoluble. In order to show this Travis lays down four basic rules which he thinks are generally accepted by representationalists and which will reveal the incoherence of representationalism. The four rules are basically variations of the four tenets that Travis outlines in "The Silences of the Senses"

> Rule 1: "A visual experience should not represent as so what one would need to deduce from other things one had taken in" (Travis 2009, p. 336). The representational content of experience is non-inferred content.

> Rule 2: The representational content of the experience is recognizable to the perceiver.

> Rule 3: Experience can represent falsely.

> Rule 4: Experience cannot misrepresent extremely.

There are two further problems for the idea that experience is representational: the first is that visual experience cannot represent as so, because "things being visually as they are" (Travis 2009, p. 338) contains no hint as to how things must look to be the way they look. E. g. let's say, there are three ways for the sky to look blue; let's call them sky-blue, dark-blue, grey-blue. "[T]hings being visually

---

276 The claim behind this solution also figures in Travis's conception of perceptual experience (see Section 5.5).

as they are" can only say that *that* is the sky looking blue, but it cannot say that this is the sky looking blue, meaning sky-blue *rather than* dark-blue. It would have to do that if it was to provide representations. This is a further developed version of the Problem of Attaining Generality. The problem is this: visual experience cannot represent as so because it does not give any hint as to what the correct representational content would be, it is just the experience it is. Anything more, any hints as to the correct visual experience would be inferred and would thus violate Rule 1.[277]

The second problem appears because the relation between seeing and knowledge also brings "epistemic status" into the theory. Seeing makes one knowledgeable, so it brings with it an "epistemic status" (Travis 2009, p. 340). The epistemic status brings occasion-sensitivity into play. The non-conceptual representationalist cannot deal with occasion-sensitivity because it conflicts with the first rule: if what one sees, i.e. what one becomes knowledgeable about, is occasion-sensitive, then what one sees depends on the circumstances in which the subject is. Those circumstances clearly transcend the limitation that representationalists set on the representational content of visual experience.

Clearly before one can accept this conclusion one needs to see why epistemic status brings occasion-sensitivity with it. Travis employs various ways to show the link between epistemic status and occasion-sensitivity. The main route makes explicit reference to Thompson Clarke, but does not spell out the full background to Clarkean claims, e.g. as in (Clarke 1965). I will strip down the argument to its skeleton in order to just convey the main argument and avoid looking further into Clarke's work. So, let us assume that an experience makes available to Sid the information that there is a baguette before him. What does Sid see? One answer is: 'the baguette.' According to the first rule, Sid's experience should represent it as so that there is a baguette before him. Sid's experience would also do that in cases in which it only looks to Sid as if there is a baguette in front of him. But – and here I am filling some gaps in Travis's argumentation – it might also be argued that Sid sees only "the front surface of a baguette" (Travis 2009, p. 339) and so what is represented is not that there is a baguette in front of him. That there is a baguette in front of him is only inferred from his perception. "Clarke's point" (Travis 2009, p. 340) explains what this example shows:

---

277 The non-conceptual representationalist might try to respond by offering minimalist conceptions of looks and correctness conditions, but they all fail for the same reason (Travis 2009, pp. 338f.).

> [N]o answer is the right one as such to 'the' question what Sid (actually) saw. Rather differ-
> ent answers would be the right ones on different occasions for *saying* what Sid saw. What
> counted, on some such occasions, as what he saw would not do so on others. *And there is*
> *no further occasion-independent fact as to what he 'really' saw.* Similarly, an undyed cotton
> shirt, coloured blue by lasers, counts as then blue on some understandings of what its
> being blue would be, as not blue on others. Besides those occasional ways of drawing a
> blue-non-blue distinction, there is no other. (Travis 2009, p. 340, emphasis in original)

Deciding what the subject saw is "deciding how the world has been brought to
bear on his thought; what about it has been made available" (Travis 2009,
p. 341). This decision depends on the subject's recognitional capacities, more
plainly speaking, on what the subject makes from the visual experience that is
given or 'delivered' to her, how she puts her recognitional capacities to use
and whether she can put them to use in the particular environment. That
means that the recognitional capacities, like "knowing a pig at sight [are also,
N.E.] inherently dependent on hospitable environments" (Travis 2009, p. 341).
What the subject saw is an occasion-sensitive matter and so we cannot ever determine which perceptual representational content is correct. Travis concludes:

> What one sees, so what one's experience *could*, or should, represent as so, depends on the
> circumstances one is in. *What these are depends on when, and why, you are asking.* Which
> destroys the idea that there could be such a thing as a way things are according to an ex-
> perience of seeing. (Travis 2009, p. 342, emphasis in original)

The representationalist can try to resort to two minimalist positions: she could
argue that "what an experience of seeing represents as so is just the *least* one
would ever count as seeing (if one is)" (Travis 2009, p. 342, emphasis in original).
But this would not allow her to exclude the role of circumstance, i.e. occasion-
sensitivity, since perceptual experience and occasion-sensitivity is "incompatible
... with the demands of rule 1" (Travis 2009, p. 343). The representationalist might
also try to insist that it always seems to Sid that there was a baguette; there is
"something-visually-experienced ... [i.e. the] minimal ingredient in an experience of seeing, present [to Sid, N.E.] independent of the occasion for the asking"
(Travis 2009, p. 344). But this minimal ingredient, too, is occasion-sensitive and
so it does not help deal with the challenge.

Travis ends by saying how seeing should be described: seeing is no hybrid
and thus anything remotely like the Stuff Happens Model is bound to fail. Instead "seeing is dynamic" (Travis 2009, p. 345): seeing is no state, but an episode. It affords the subject awareness of the world and "is occasion for exercise
of our capacities for recognising the reach of various bits of the conceptual to
various cases of the nonconceptual" (Travis 2009, p. 346). The physiological

processes that also make up perceptual experience give awareness of the world on which the capacities are exercised. That is another difference between the Stuff Happens Model of representationalists and Travis's conception: on the representationalist conception the physiological processes feed into further processes that make up the perceptual experience of the particular subject. This perceptual experience floats freely from how "*things* ... are visually, or look, or seem" (Travis 2009, p. 347, emphasis in original). The Stuff Happens Model wants to say that retina action leads to awareness of potential awareness of some inner state, but that is wrong: retina action only leads to visual awareness of one's surrounding.

Travis avoids the representationalist's problem: perceptual experience essentially works based on the subject's responsiveness. The subject is responsive to "the scene before [her] eyes" (Travis 2009, p. 348) and in this responsiveness the subject's perceptual experience moves from being afforded by the world, to being "conferred" (Travis 2009, p. 348) by the subject. It is in the responsiveness that mistakes can occur and and mis-perceptions appear. The subject's responsiveness must not be a form of judging (that also separates McDowell and Travis), for otherwise the conception would encounter the representationalist problems. Travis admits that in this article he does not present a fully developed conception, but emphasizes that his claims are mainly meant (a) to argue against representationalism and (b) outline which pitfalls a conception that really recognizes the claim that perceptual experience is what allows the world to bear on thought has to avoid. I will present further positive tenets of Travis's conception of perceptual experience in Section 5.5. This section has shown that Travis is no non-conceptualist as Peacocke, Burge et al. are, but he is also no conceptualist. One sees that most clearly in the following section that presents his criticism of McDowell's conceptualism.

5.4 Travis's Arguments against McDowell's Conceptualism: Perceptual Experience Does Not Have Conceptual Content

Travis's "Reason's Reach" (Travis 2007) is a detailed and focused discussion of John McDowell's conceptualist theory of perceptual experience. Travis frames the discussion in a special terminology (e. g. Travis 2007, pp. 176 f.), but I think that the arguments themselves can and should be presented independently of Travis's special frame. It does not come as quite a surprise after the previous sections, but it is still important to emphasize it at the beginning: Travis supports the *scheme-content-dualism* (Travis 2007, p. 238), i.e. he holds that concepts can be understood independently from sensory intake, and sensory intake can be understood independently from concepts (cf. Davidson 1991; McDowell 2009h, p. 116). Yet, at the same time Travis argues that there are rational relations between the conceptual and the nonconceptual, i.e. the particular.[278] He rejects McDowell's claim that "the space of reasons does not extend further than the space of concepts" (McDowell 1996, p. 14). Very generally, Travis offers two types of arguments for saying that there is a rational relation between the conceptual and the nonconceptual:

(TA) 'Transcendental'-style arguments

(CA) The identification of confusion between the conceptual and the non-conceptual in the conceptualist theory of perceptual experience

Let us start with the transcendental-style arguments. I have chosen this name because they are similar to transcendental arguments. We find three transcendental-style arguments.

First, the transcendental-style argument for the relation between perceptual experience and thought and judgment. In the case of perceptual experience the transcendental-style argument is this: if perceptual experience is to bear on thought and judgment, then there must be a rational relation between the conceptual and the nonconceptual. Perceptual experience does bear on thought and judgment, so there is a rational relation between the conceptual and the nonconceptual (cf. Travis 2007, p. 229). This transcendental argument is very quick, but also straightforward.

Second, the transcendental-style argument for the relation between the world and thought and judgment. We find two versions of the second transcendental-style argument in "The Inward Turn" (Travis 2009). There Travis does not explicitly include rationality and reason into the argument: if the world is to bear on thought and judgment through perceptual experience, then the subject must grasp "how the conceptual reaches to the nonconceptual" (Travis 2009, p. 319), i.e. the conceptual and the nonconceptual must be connected. The world does bear on thought and judgment and so the subject does grasp "how the conceptual reaches to the nonconceptual" (Travis 2009, p. 319). The same structure also holds for showing that perceptual experience must provide awareness of the objects in the world: if the world is to bear on thought and judgment, then percep-

---

278 The conceptual is inherently general. It is instanced by the nonconceptual, i.e. that which is not general. Travis again uses Frege's distinction and his terminology and talks of the conceptual and the nonconceptual. Remember that Travis's notion of "nonconceptual" is not the same as that of the so-called non-conceptualists. Travis's nonconceptual consists of "things being as they are".

tion must be of objects in the world. The world does bear on thought and judgment, and so on.

Third, the transcendental-style argument for the rational relation between experience and judgment. In "Reason's Reach" the emphasis is on the rational relations between the conceptual and nonconceptual and so the transcendental-style arguments are spelled out in slightly different ways. The first argument argues from experience rationally shaping our thought. If perceptual experience "rationally shape[s] our thought" (Travis 2007, p. 194), then reason has to extend beyond the conceptual, since there must be rational relations, i.e. reason relations, between the conceptual and the nonconceptual, i.e. that which is taken in in perceptual experience.[279] The second transcendental-style argument makes use of occasion-sensitivity: occasion-sensitivity presupposes that there is a reaching relation between the conceptual and the nonconceptual. So if representations are occasion-sensitive, then the nonconceptual must be within reason's reach. Clearly, representations are occasion-sensitive and so the nonconceptual, i.e. the particular, is within reason's reach. Why is that? Occasion-sensitivity is based on rightly placing something nonconceptual within different ranges, i.e. as falling under different concepts. The object itself ensures that the articulations are related. Such correct placing can only be possible if the subject possesses the concepts for such placements, and if the nonconceptual and the conceptual are rationally related (Travis 2007, p. 194).

The second type of argumentative strategy notes confusions between the conceptual and the nonconceptual. Travis marks several cases of this confusion. Generally, we can distinguish two kinds of mix-ups between the conceptual and the nonconceptual:

(CA1) Special marks of the conceptual are wrongly taken to be found in the nonconceptual,

(CA2) Special marks of the nonconceptual are wrongly taken to be found in the conceptual.

The first argument, which argues by identifying features of the conceptual that the nonconceptual does not have, comes in the form of an Argument from Occasion-Sensitivity:

---

279 Note that this argument also looks like a *modus ponens*. For a note on the relation between transcendental arguments and *modus ponens* see (Kuusela 2008, pp. 59, 73 n.8) I think that Kuusela's remarks could also be used to argue why Travis's argument is a transcendental-style argument.

(1) Thought belongs to the conceptual.
(2) The conceptual is inherently general and it is inherently occasion-sensitive.[280]
(3) The conceptual always points to a range of cases, which could instance it (Travis 2007, pp. 232 f.).
(4) Cases themselves, i.e. the instances, are particular and *not* occasion-sensitive.

(5) Cases, i.e. the instances, are not conceptual. They are nonconceptual.

The second class of arguments (CA2) comprises various considerations as to differences between the conceptual and the nonconceptual. The nonconceptual is particular and concrete, the conceptual is only arbitrarily specific. The conceptual does not articulate as neatly as the nonconceptual: the nonconceptual articulates into nonconceptual items and their correctness does not depend on any occasion for asking. The articulation of the conceptual is necessarily occasion-sensitive. It depends on the occasion in which the conceptual appears, e.g. the occasion for asking what the perceiver saw. How the perceptual experience of the subject itself bears on the subject's thought is stable, so perceptual experience cannot consist in something conceptual, e.g. *that p*, because its bearing would always be occasion-sensitive *qua* being conceptual.[281]

Travis's remarks on these considerations are particularly confusing, but the main aim of pointing out these differences seems to be a development of the

---

280 See also (Travis 2008).
281 Johan Gersel has suggested in conversation that occasion-sensitivity cannot speak against conceptualism and representational content in perceptual experience because occasion-sensitivity is a strictly linguistic phenomenon. I think that this limitation is mistaken. As I have said above, Travis explicitly says that occasion-sensitivity extends to logical concepts and rules (see fn. 253). They all "admit of understandings" (Travis 2006, p. 80). Even factive meaning is occasion-sensitive (see fn. 269). In fact the whole argumentation in *Thought's Footing* shows how occasion-sensitivity applies to both linguistic and non-linguistic cases. Gersel also puts the further point that occasion-sensitivity is not widely accepted by linguists, but I do not think that this means that occasion-sensitivity must be inexistent. Note also that, as we will see below, McDowell does not reject the phenomenon, but tries to show that his theory is compatible with it.

Jocelyn Benoist has suggested in conversation that in non-linguistic cases one should talk of "contextualism" rather than of "occasion-sensitivity" to capture the phenomenon that Travis is after. This terminological differentiation would allow one to mark a difference between the linguistic case of occasion-sensitivity and the perceptual case, and it might turn out useful in phrasing the reply to Gersel's objection, but I think that ultimately this terminological differentiation is not necessary, as it would lead to unnecessary confusion.

above transcendental-style argument: the conceptualist who tries to show that perceptual experience conceived as the conceptual *can* bear stably on thought would always have to accept rational relations between the conceptual and the nonconceptual (something that conceptualists clearly reject), since the bearing relation itself depends on rational relations between the nonconceptual and the conceptual.

Another important observation marks out that the conceptual also is not 'present' in the sense that the nonconceptual is (Travis 2007, p. 240). Which conceptual items are part of the scene being as it is varies with the occasion for talking about the scene. So what is 'seen' of the conceptual is instable, or more appropriately: occasion-sensitive. One can put the point in terms of thinkable looks (Travis 2013b): thinkable looks are occasion-sensitive, but seeing the nonconceptual is not occasion-sensitive. This point generalizes: something conceptual is never an object of visual awareness. The above and the following considerations can be put under the label *Argument from the Particular Perceptual Presence of Objects.*

"[S]eeing *that p*" and "seeing an object" are crucially different in several ways. Seeing an object is a suitable sensitivity or responsiveness (Travis 2007, p. 238). Seeing that *p* is registering that the object instances a certain way for things to be (Travis 2007, p. 232).[282] It analyzes into (a) seeing what is in view, i.e. the nonconceptual, and (b) "grasping some of its [i.e. the nonconceptual's, N.E.] bearing on the conceptual" (Travis 2007, p. 244). What does grasp of the bearing of the nonconceptual on the conceptual mean? According to Travis, the key to having this grasp lies in expertise. A subject can learn how something nonconceptual bears on what is *such-and-such.* Travis likens this skill to the ability of being able to tell from the barking whether this barking dog is going to bite someone or not (Travis 2007, p. 234).

These insights into the constitution of *seeing that* lead us to further insights as to the different natures of *seeing that* and *seeing an object.* Travis has said how grasping the relation between something conceptual and something nonconceptual is a matter of expertise. This feature presupposes another reason for holding that perceptual experience is not a case of *seeing that:* if *seeing an object* was *seeing that,* then we could not understand how a subject can see an object without knowing what the object is. "[I]f seeing that were seeing an item visible as meat is, one could say: 'Sid saw *that there was meat on the rug,* though clueless

---

282 "To see that the meat is on the rug I must register something else: the instancing by things being as they are of a certain way for things to be, meat being on a rug." (Travis 2007, p. 232)

as to what it was he saw'" (Travis 2007, p. 232, emphasis in original) and to Travis this must be wrong.

These differences regarding the visibility of the object in *seeing that* and the object in *seeing an object* extend to the following additional divergences:

(a) The object exists in the surrounding, whereas *p* is not in the surrounding in the same way.[283]

(b) The object is an object of visual awareness, but *that p* cannot be an object of visual awareness. It is not visible.

(c) *Seeing that* is only an articulation of visual awareness (Travis 2007, p. 244).

These observations are also part of the Argument from the Particular Perceptual Presence of Objects. Travis continues to make related points in the course of explaining why the nonconceptual must be within "the reach of reason" (Travis 2007, p. 244). In a more phenomenologically minded argument against the idea that perceptual experience is conceptual he notes that our experience of the world is simply not experience of "a structuring of concepts" (Travis 2007, p. 243). We do not "visually confront some given battery of conceptual structures" (Travis 2007, p. 243). Travis extends this argument further to make a point that we know from "The Silence[s] of the Senses" (Travis 2004; Travis 2013b): what a subject sees does not articulate neatly according to concepts.[284] Given the apparent occasion-sensitivity of articulation of one's perceptual experience we might make what is just a small step (which Travis himself does not take) to the Problem of Selection: since the perceptual experience does not by itself articulate into the concepts that are instantiated by the objects, perceptual experience cannot tell us which of the concepts that the things could instantiate are in fact instantiated.

Finally, I want to add another argument against conceptual perceptual content that fits neither the transcendental-style arguments nor the confusion arguments, but is still important for Travis. Travis brings it forward in his "Unlocking

---

283 Travis briefly considers a position on which we are able to perceive that a case fits under a generality and in that way perceive the general, but he rejects it as "patent nonsense" (Travis 2007, p. 239): "That the sky is blue" (Travis 2007, p. 239) would be in the world and would be a feature of the sky being blue: features of the conceptual and the nonconceptual would be united. Travis does not say why the position is "patent nonsense" and that is unfortunate.
284 This argument resembles the Argument from Fineness of Grain, but it is also importantly different because as we have seen above the Argument from Fineness of Grain is not about congruence or accordance of the conceptual and the nonconceptual.

the Outer World" that can be read as a continuation of the debate with McDowell (Travis 2013c). McDowell and conceptualists in general seem unable to cover the following case: a subject has acquired a new concept which she can retrospectively apply to a past perceptual experience that she remembers (Travis 2013c, pp. 19 f.). The application of the new concept to the past perceptual experience would be impossible on McDowell's conception, since conceptual capacities are supposed to unify the object of the perceptual experience. There is no room for the new concept to be applied to the past experience, because the object was unified by the conceptual capacities that the subject possessed at the time of the perceptual experience. Travis holds that we need to allow for such situations of applying new concepts to past experience and so we have to detach our access to the particular from our ability to move in the realm of the conceptual: perception cannot involve conceptual activity. I will label this argument the *Argument from New Concepts for Past Experience*. This argument will return in the development of relational conceptualism and also in the explication of Travis's own theory of perception.[285]

Let me end this section with a summary of Travis's criticism of McDowell's position. First, perceptual experience is not *seeing that* and not seeing something conceptual; two important reasons for that are that the conceptual is not visible, and that perceptual experience is awareness of the visible world. Second, the conceptual and the nonconceptual, i.e. the conceptual and the world, must be rationally related if thought and judgment are to be of the world. This also means that the Myth of the Given is no myth (Travis 2007, p. 244): rational relations are not restricted to the conceptual. Positions that restrict rational relations to the conceptual are not coherent. Finally, Travis holds that experience and conceptual activity must be separated: perceptual experience is pure visual awareness, unpolluted by the conceptual. The conceptual only enters at the level of the subject's response. Otherwise we would not be able to explain how a subject can have perceptual experience of things of which it is not knowledgeable (Travis 2007, p. 232).

---

285 This argument is similar to Martin's Argument from Memory Experience (Martin 1992); Section 2.5). Both arguments ask how the conceptualist deals with the possibility of applying newly acquired concepts to past experiences. But there are also important differences since Martin's argument proceeds in a different way than Travis's argument Martin argues from the nature of memory. The content of the subject's memory experience "can be determined independently of which concepts the subject had at the time of perceiving" (Martin 1992, pp. 753 f.). Travis on the other hand argues from the role of concepts in the actual perceptual experience that is then remembered later.

5.5 Perception as Mere Visual Awareness: Travis's Conception of Perceptual Experience

In order to put together an overview of Travis's own conception of perceptual experience I will broaden the textual basis and also include other texts by Travis, including his "Is seeing intentional?" (Travis 2011). In these and the other texts that I have included to present his criticism of representationalism Travis emphasizes that perception is pure "visual awareness" (Travis 2013c, p. 234) or visual "confrontation" (Travis 2013b, p. 31) with objects in the world, with the nonconceptual.[286] Perception thus is non-intentional, not directed at the world. It is a "mental phenomenon", which consists in a "factive, [pure relation] to the way things *are*" (Travis 2011, p. 309). Travis therefore explicitly rejects the possibility of seeing something non-existent: seeing something is seeing what is before one's eyes (Travis 2011, pp. 297, 311).

Providing visual awareness of the world is what Travis identifies as the *task* of perception: perception's task is to allow the world to bear on a thinker's thoughts (cf. Travis 2009, p. 323 and Travis 2013c, p. 241). Perception itself does not involve any conceptual activity (e.g. Travis 2009, p. 320; Travis 2011, p. 288). Any such activity is a response to what the subject is perceptually aware of. Travis explains:

> Seeing the lion before me makes the lion's presence bear on what I am to think as to there being a lion before me: I may, properly, judge that there is on grounds of the lion's presence. The lion's presence may thereby bear, for me, on what else to think–e.g., that I am glad I made my will–according to what it means (as a lion's presence before you means that it would be good to have made a will). (Travis 2011, p. 305)

Perception thus provides opportunities for exercising one's conceptual skills. As we have seen above, these skills consist in being able to link the conceptual and the nonconceptual, i.e. to grasp which concept is instanced by the instance and which concepts could be instanced by the instance.

The following quotation provides a clear summary of the conception and lays open where McDowell and Travis disagree, namely on the question whether conceptual capacities are actualized in perception itself or only in responses to perception:

> Perception's role is to provide awareness of the nonconceptual, or the particular case. Without such awareness there is no seeing, or even taking, the instancing relation to hold between anything and anything (just as there is no taking it to hold without having the con-

---

286 Note that in Travis's remarks perception is mostly restricted to visual perception.

ceptual in view). If perception is to perform this role, it must confine itself to it. Conceptual capacities come into the picture only with our operations in thought on what perception has anyway provided; only with our ability to see when what we have O-seen (heard, felt, tasted) of how things are reveals it as what counts as things being thus and so. (Travis 2013c, p. 241)

The quotation is also noteworthy because it makes use of new terminology that Travis introduces in "Unlocking the Outer World" to further clarify his conception: *O-seeing* and *T-seeing*. "O-seeing" refers to the seeing of an object; it is a "perceptual accomplishment" (Travis 2013c, p. 238). It is the most fundamental form of seeing. It is the seeing that provides opportunities for exercising one's conceptual skills. T-seeing on the other hand is not perceptual, but rather a "function of thought" (Travis 2013c, p. 248). It is not a relation to an object, to something visible, but a relation to a thought. T-seeing involves recognition and that in turn requires conceptual capacities, i.e. "familiarity with what belongs to the conceptual, with that whose instancing one takes in" (Travis 2013c, p. 239). A creature that possesses conceptual capacities grasps where something conceptual reaches and what a particular case instances: "the capacity to recognize a pig as a pig ... [is] one applicable to what was anyway, recognized or not, a pig, and to appreciate how *just that* relates to that certain bit of the conceptual, *for something to be a pig*" (Travis 2013c, p. 239, emphasis in original). The possessor of such capacities will grasp relations within the conceptual realm and relations between the conceptual and the nonconceptual. Recognizing an object, e.g. recognizing a pig, thus refers to two capacities: first, the "capacity to tell a pig at sight; and[, second, the] capacity to recognise what counts as something being a pig as so counting" (Travis 2013c, p. 239). Those recognitional capacities and conceptual capacities are "parochial capacit[ies]" (Travis 2013c, p. 225), capacities that belong to the special psychological design of the thinker and his community of thinkers. Conceptual capacities are parochial capacities. As we have already mentioned above those capacities are a shared sensibility among an extendable community of thinkers. The conceptual is ineliminably "stamped with our shared sensibilities" (Travis 2010b, p. 14), e.g. of recognition.[287]

---

287 Remember that I have suggested that we should read parochial capacities as Travis's equivalent to 'conceptual capacities possessed by human beings'. The particular conceptual capacities of human beings are what makes them thinkers. Travis's "parochial capacities" are the equivalent of McDowell's "conceptual capacities". Note that this does not extend to parochial sensibilities and parochial understandings and the other expressions involving the adjective "parochial".

Travis wants to insist that O-seeing is the basis for T-seeing: there is no T-seeing without O-seeing. We can also see this in a subject that perceives an object, but does not possess the relevant conceptual capacities required for the object. In such a case the subject simply O-sees the object.[288] See for example the case of Uncle Willard's bittern (Travis 2013c, pp. 245 f.). Travis's description of this case helps picture his conception of perceptual experience and is also a good example of Travis's extraordinary choice of examples and deserves to be quoted fully:

> Consider Uncle Willard. Returning from the fens, he presents me with a stuffed bittern. He has thus made a raft of things available for (my) cognition, most of which I am, as things stand, in no position to get. He offers opportunities which I cannot yet exploit. Suppose I am asked whether there are greater bitterns in the fens. I haven't a clue. Staring at the stuffed bittern is no help. But now I study bitterns. In time I acquire the ability to tell the lesser from the greater at sight. Now I look at Uncle Willard's bittern and find in it a message for me. It is, plainly, a greater bittern. So there must be greater bitterns in the fens. In one perfectly good sense, I was given something to get when Uncle Willard gave me the stuffed bird. That bird was full of information about the fens (in the only way our mute friends could be). But it takes sophistication to extract these riches from the bird's *Gestalt*. One must know that there is such a thing as a greater bittern, so know of a certain way for things to be: being one. One thus needs some grasp of what it would be for a thing to be one; then, quite a different matter, of how to tell one (here at sight), in particular, from a lesser bittern. Such things came to me only with time. But as soon as they had come, the bittern stood there, as it long had, ready to serve.
>
> Might perception fit this model? Hasn't it already? Unfortunately, before I could acquire the needed ornithological expertise, Uncle Willard's trophy disappeared–an overly enthusiastic char. I was still to learn that there are both greater and lesser bitterns, much less how to tell the one from the other. Such knowledge was to come, though. When it did, all was revealed to me. I could remember what the stuffed bird looked like–what perceptual experience had then given me to know. Now I could, at last, recognise what I saw, before that char's work, as a case of the instancing, by a certain object's being as it was, of a certain generality, something being a greater bittern. My powers of deduction, and memory of the stuffed bird's provenance, now allow me to conclude that there are greater bitterns in the fens. (Travis 2013c, pp. 245 f.)[289]

---

288 "What Pia O-sees is precisely what does instance a pig being beneath the oak–nothing short of the pig, as it is, beneath the oak, as it is. Such is what is there to be seen. Suppose she lacked, or failed to draw on, the conceptual capacities just mentioned. She would still O-see what was there to be seen, what in fact instances the generality in question. She would just fail to recognise its doing so." (Travis 2013c, p. 239)

289 Of course, this is also Travis's example for the Argument from New Concepts for Past Experience.

The final obvious question that we have to ask of Travis's conception is this: why is the relation between the conceptual and the nonconceptual rational? The answer of this question starts with pointing out that for Travis grasp of the bearing of the nonconceptual on the conceptual is a skill and "admits of expertise" (Travis 2007, p. 234). Travis also notes that perceptual experience can also be "competent experiencing" (Travis 2006, p. 208): in seeing and recognizing a pig Eliza exercises a competence; she demonstrates that she knows a pig when she sees one. There are two types of recognizing: Travis describes the first as a purely cognitive achievement (recognizing$_1$). Frege's term for this is the German *erkennen*. The second type of recognizing is what Frege calls *anerkennen*: "accepting, granting, certifying, conceding, conferring some status for something" (Travis 2006, p. 208). We recognize$_2$ the truth of thoughts and thus, recognizing here is an attitude. Recognizing$_1$ is a competence, it is a case of getting something right, namely getting it right when something's being an *F* is instanced. The competence needs a "hospitable environment" (Travis 2006, p. 208) in which things really are the way we think they are, e. g. no clandestine change of objects in the world has occurred. We need to distinguish "knowing a [p] when one sees one" (Travis 2006, p. 209) from "knowing when to say that [O] is a [p]" (Travis 2006, p. 209), since the latter involves grasp of what it is to be a *p* and grasp of occasions for saying *p, q* etc. of a thing. Recognizing as a cognitive achievement only includes reference to things being as they are and thus it cannot answer questions as to the veridicality of the particular representation: What ought to be called a pig? When ought an object to be called a pig? It is fully in line with the above remarks on occasion-sensitivity of representations, logical forms and rules that such questions can only be settled by the ascriber's perspective, i. e. her particular understanding and the particular environment. The same holds for questions of what is to be. Mere competence cannot settle those questions. In addition, cognitive achievement itself does not even indicate the different considerations that need to be settled for the content to have a fixed content and fixed veridicality conditions.

Now, if a subject possesses the required skills for recognizing the particular nonconceptual-conceptual relation, she can but think the related thought. The rationality here is a *Lutheran rationality* (Travis 2007, p. 235): the particular subject "can think no other" (Travis 2007, p. 235).

> Barking, to one who can tell when it is threatening, ... does bear, when he hears ... it, on what he is to think. Where one so skilled takes it to be the bark of a dog about to bite, that the dog will bite just is what it is rational for him to think. He can think no other; nor should he. Such is one thing rationality is like. (Travis 2007, p. 234)

Eliza sees the book in front of her and she can think no other than 'This is a book', because she has the right expertise. So Eliza takes the object *o* in front of her to be a book, in grasping how the object being as it is bears on what it is. This is exercised expertise. Eliza is an expert "as to the bearing of the [non-conceptual, N.E.] on the conceptual in given matters" (Travis 2007, p. 235). This expertise is not reducible to a relation between two conceptual elements, because the bearing relation could not consist in a relation between two generalities.

In the previous sections I have introduced two important relationist theories and their criticism of conceptualist and non-conceptualist representationalist theories. In what follows we will have to see how McDowell deals with this criticism. For now we can already say so much: he rejects Brewer's criticism (McDowell 2008c, pp. 200–205), and partly accepts and partly rejects Travis's criticism (McDowell 2008c, pp. 258–267). This attitude towards Travis becomes particularly clear in "Avoiding the Myth of the Given" (McDowell 2009a) and "Perceptual Experience: both Relational and Contentful" (McDowell 2013a). I have introduced the revised conceptualism that McDowell develops in "Avoiding the Myth of the Given" and also discussed the coherence of the new theory in Section 3.2, but I had postponed examining whether McDowell's revised conceptualism avoids the relationist objections as he claims it does. This examination is thus up in the next chapter.

6 Why McDowell's Revised Conceptualism Does Not Avoid Travis's Anti-Representationalist Criticism

In the first part of the examination of McDowell's revised conceptualism as presented in "Avoiding the Myth of the Given" the position did not come off looking to well: there were problems with understanding what exactly the newly introduced intuitional content is, and what "conceptual content" refers to in perceptual experience. But this revised conceptualism also needs to be checked for the appropriateness of its reaction to Travis's relationist objections. In "Avoiding the Myth of the Given" Travis is credited with inducing one of the two significant changes and McDowell suggests that "in abandoning my old assumption I am partly coming around to a view [Travis] has urged on me" (McDowell 2009a, p. 259). But that does not mean that McDowell goes all the way with Travis: he takes himself to be invulnerable to Travis's relationist arguments and in "Perceptual Experience: Both Relational and Contentful" (McDowell 2013a) he explains how and why perceptual experience is a relation and has content. I will call this proposal an integrative theory. Of course, such claims as these need to be examined. The question that needs to be asked is whether McDowell's revised conceptualism and his integrative view with perceptual experience being relational and contentful do indeed avoid Travis's non-representationalist objections.

As we have seen, a Travisian position is both anti-representationalist and non-conceptualist, since it also claims that conceptual capacities are not in play in visual awareness itself, but only at a second level of thinking about and judging one's perceptual experience. Clearly, McDowell would not want to incorporate this view (cf. McDowell 2008c), and since I, too, take non-conceptualism to be the wrong approach to perceptual experience, I will only say how McDowell responds to these non-conceptualist objections, but will not thoroughly examine whether the response is appropriate. McDowell does not want to accommodate these objections and I do not think he should accommodate them.

McDowell's rejection of Travis's objections and why it does not succeed

Let me briefly repeat Travis's central objections against representationalist views and against conceptualism. Representational content is content with correctness conditions and so the representationalist faces three problems regarding the relation between correctness and representational content of perceptual experience:

(1) Since representations are inherently general, they do not determine one way for things to be in order for them to be correct. There is no way things are *full stop*, which would provide the correctness conditions for a particular representation. A representation can be instanced by a number of ways for things to be. The representation does not reach to just one instantiation by which it is instanced and therefore cannot have determinate conceptual content (Travis 2013b, pp. 36 ff.). I have called that the Problem of Selection.

(2) It is unclear how one can get from the particulars, from the way things are (in the world), to the representation which it instances. The way things are does not 'point' towards a representation (Travis 2006, p. 200). I have called that the Problem of Attaining Generality.

(3) If the representational content of a perceptual experience contained all the possible ranges that the particular case can instance, the representational content would turn out incoherent (Travis 2013b, p. 37). I have called that the Problem of Incoherent Content.

Conceptualism faces its own share of problems including the following:

(1) If perceptual experience is to bear on thought and judgment, then there must be a rational relation between the conceptual and the nonconceptual. If the world is to bear on thought and judgment, then there must be rational relations between the conceptual and the nonconceptual. I have called those Transcendental-style Arguments. Another version of these arguments points out that there must be rational relations between the conceptual and the nonconceptual if articulations of perceptual experience are to be occasion-sensitive.

(2) If perceptual experience is taken to have propositional content, then it cannot at the same time consist in visual awareness of an object, because *seeing that* is not the same as *seeing an object*. I have called that the Argument from the Particular Perceptual Presence of Objects.

(3) We can apply newly acquired concepts to past perceptual experience, so clearly at the time of experiencing the perceptual experience cannot have been fully conceptual. This consideration includes what I have called the Argument from New Concepts for Past Experience.

McDowell responds to some of Travis's arguments *re* problems of conceptualism, but he does not discuss the objections against representationalism. He simply holds that his talk of "content" is not inflicted by the issues that Travis raises for representationalism. His paper "Perceptual Experience: Both relational and contentful" (2013a) explains what an alternative theory of perceptual experience that brings two strands together, i.e. contentful-and-relational, looks like, but it, too, does not discuss any of Travis's objections in particular.

Before discussing McDowell's proposal, I want to lay out which of Travis's objections the changes in "Avoiding the Myth of the Given" are meant to deal with. At first sight only the change regarding experiential content not containing "*everything* the experience enables its subject to know inferentially" (McDowell 2009a, p. 258, emphasis in original) seems to be due to Travis. The change from propositional content of perceptual experience to intuitional content of perceptual experience traces more clearly to an objection by Davidson. Yet, at second sight one sees that intuitional content is also used to allow for a certain sense in which perception does not represent things as thus and so, but only presents them. In this section I will discuss the relation between the introduction of intuitional content and Travis's criticism and move to the changes about non-inferential knowledge contained in perception at the end of the section. But first, let us look at McDowell's response to Travis's objections. I have already said that he does not discuss the objections which regard his position as a representationalist position, but which objections does he respond to and how?

I will base the examination on three published responses of McDowell to Travis's criticism. One is a direct response to Travis's "Reason's Reach" (McDowell 2008c); the second, "Avoiding the Myth of the Given", must certainly be regarded as a response to some Travisian lines as well, and as I said "Perceptual Experience: Both relational and contentful" responds to Travis and relationists more generally by outlining an alternative conception of perception as contentful-and-relational.

In his "Response to Travis" McDowell puts foward at least four observations against Travis, in addition to his above insistence that the anti-representationalist arguments simply do not concern his conceptualism. The first observation concerns Travis's argument that McDowell wrongly assumes that the conceptual is visible (Argument from the Particular Perceptual Presence of Objects). McDowell points out that Travis identifies *being conceptual* and *being within the sphere of the conceptual*. McDowell's claim that the conceptual is unbounded does not entail that the conceptual is a visible character trait of objects. An object, something that for Travis belongs to the nonconceptual, is within the conceptual sphere when it is perceived, because in perceiving it, conceptual capacities are actualized. But the object itself is not something conceptual (McDowell 2008c,

p. 259). According to McDowell, the impingement of "nonconceptual", particular, objects on thoughts requires the involvement of conceptual capacities in the relation between perceiver and object for otherwise we fall prey to the Myth of the Given. In effect, McDowell's reply comes to this: real world object are not contents of thoughts themselves, but they can be thought about and that involves conceptual capacities.[290] Let me note that here, yet again[291], McDowell does not mention the transcendental framework of his theory, thereby blurring the motivational background and, in my opinion, mis-representing his own theory to his critics.

McDowell also rejects Travis's idea that his conceptualist conception is not compatible with occasion-sensitivity. Any articulation of the perceptual content of a subject's perception is occasion-sensitive:

> If I use words to specify something someone sees to be so, and the words I use admit of different understandings, and the occasion on which I speak determines my words to one of the understandings they might admit, then what I am saying the person sees to be so is that things are as my words would say they are *on that understanding*. (McDowell 2008c, p. 263, emphasis in original)

Also, the "specification of a conceptual capacity admits of different understandings" (McDowell 2008c, p. 263). But note that this reply does not solve the problem. The occasion-sensitivity that McDowell admits to lies in the response to the already conceptual perception. In order to show that his conception is compatible with occasion-sensitivity he would have to show that the conceptual content of the perceptual experience is occasion-sensitive. And if McDowell wanted to show that and at the same time maintain that conceptual content is representational content, he would certainly face the Problem of Selection and the Problem of Incoherent Content.[292]

The third reply by McDowell offers some speculation on the reasons for Travis's rejection of representational content in perception: he suggests that the "hostility" is based in the worry that representational content cannot accommodate the fact that objects are directly presented in experience and not in-directly experienced. The fourth observation then has McDowell insist that he does not reject the idea of an object "imping[ing]" (McDowell 2008c, p. 259) (or "bearing" (Travis 2007, p. 225) in Travis's terminology) on thought via perception.

---

290 Note the parallel to McDowell's argumentation about the objects of perception being thinkables in *Mind and World* (McDowell 1996, pp. 28 f.).

291 As in his direct responses to Burge's criticism (Section 2.7).

292 Relational conceptualism will be able to deal with occasion-sensitivity because it does away with talk of representational content. The solution will be developed in Chapters 7 and 8.

Both replies are disappointingly superficial: first, Travis's rejection of representational content certainly is more than a worry about losing the direct presentation of objects in experience. Travis does mention a worry about the position being idealistic (Travis 2013c, p. 257), but that is just one element in the argumentation. Second, Travis does not say that McDowell wants to abandon the idea of an object impinging on thought via perception. All that Travis does argue is that McDowell cannot make sense of the connection if he takes perceptual experience to have representational content, more particularly if perceptual experience has conceptual representational content. If we bracket the question of whether this argument by Travis is correct, we could picture Travis as a purer version of McDowell in *Mind and World*. There, McDowell wanted to bring mind and world into direct contact. Travis can be read as wanting to continue that project and doing away even with the representational content element in the mediator *perception*.

David Lauer would reject this reconstruction of McDowell's conceptualist theory (Lauer 2014). Lauer argues that McDowell's claim that perceptual experience has conceptual content is not an additional thesis, but just explains how the thesis that perceptual experience implies the actualization of conceptual capacities is manifested in human perception (Lauer 2014, p. 52). There would thus be no problem with Travis's anti-representationalist arguments. But, of course, that is just what I think is disputable and needs to be examined. Most of this section will thus be devoted to the question of whether McDowell avoids the anti-representationalist arguments. That also includes the question of whether McDowell is a representationalist or not. Answering this question is far from simple, since McDowell's explanations can be misleading. Remarks such as the following quotation perhaps led Travis to assume that McDowell renounces the idea of perception having representational content (Travis 2007, p. 227): "Anything that represents things as so has propositional content, and I have been spelling out a conception of intuitions on which they do not have propositional content" (McDowell 2009a, pp. 266f.).

But as we have seen in McDowell's response to Travis's "Reason's Reach" he does not want to give up talk of representational content of perceptual experience:

> What I meant to be indicating to [Travis] was just that I had no particular need for the *word* 'represent' or its cognates. I did not mean to be renouncing the idea that experiences have the sort of content judgments have. (McDowell 2008c, p. 260, emphasis in original).

We know that "the sort of content judgments have" must not refer to propositional content, but to conceptual content. That, however, cannot secure McDowell's conception against Travis's objections against representational content in perception. McDowell's talk of conceptual content could still mean that there is representational content on his conception, namely, if conceptual content turned out to be representational content, e.g. if the concepts that figure in conceptual content together form representations. This textual evidence suggests that McDowell's theory of perceptual experience is a representationalist theory.

Note also the following contradictions that are particularly surprising since McDowell's choice of words is usually very minute. He writes, "I did not mean to be renouncing the idea that experiences have the sort of content judgments have" (McDowell 2008c, p. 260). But five lines after that he adds, "[a]nd though I have stopped thinking experiences have the kind of content that judgments have ... The content of an experience is, as it were, all but propositional" (McDowell 2008c, p. 260).

And see also this surprising statement from his response to Brewer's criticism:

> Talk of content as possibly false fits most easily with taking content to be propositional. I now think it is better to think of the content of experience as intuitional rather than propositional. (See 'Avoiding the Myth of the Given'.) But intuitional content is still content. And it is, we can say, all but propositional. One arrives at propositional content by simply articulating what are already elements of intuitional content. So in commenting on Brewer's paper I am going to stay with the Sellarsian idea that the content of a perceptual experience is propositional content, the sort of thing that could be the content of a claim. (McDowell 2008c, p. 200)

McDowell first notes that experiential content is "intuitional rather than propositional" and then he still wants to think of experiential content as propositional content. Again, these statements suggest that McDowell's theory is representationalist and is thus vulnerable to Travis's objections.

One could try to save McDowell's response to Travis by referring to the interpretation of the relation between intuitional content and discursive content that I have developed in the first critical section on "Avoiding the Myth of the Given" (Section 3.2): intuitional content and discursive content are two species of one genus. When McDowell talks of perceptual content not being "the kind of content that judgments have" (McDowell 2008c, p. 260) he talks about such content as a species of the genus *conceptual content.* When he talks of perceptual content being "the sort of thing that could be the content of a claim" (McDowell 2008c, p. 200) he talks about perceptual content belonging to the same genus as "the content of a claim", i.e. propositional content. However, it is not clear that the contradiction within McDowell's response to Brewer can be solved in the same way. It seems more likely that here he is contradicting himself. Either way, the observations point us to a problem in McDowell's use of the term *content*.

Whether McDowell avoids Travis's objections against representational content of perception by introducing "intuitional content" also depends on what content means. In his texts McDowell uses "content" on its own without qualification (e. g. McDowell 2008c, p. 265), but also as "representational content", as "intuitional content", as "propositional content" and as "conceptual content". I think that he should not use the term without an attributive adjective, since the respective adjective determines what sort of content it is and also, more importantly, whether the conception avoids Travis's objections. If conceptual content consists in concepts – just like representational content on Travis's conception (cf. e. g. Travis 2009) – then conceptual content is general. This also entails that perceptual experience that has conceptual content is mediated awareness of the world and all the problems for the representationalist conception are back in the game. So just deferring to "conceptual content" would not be enough to stir away from Travis's objections.

In order to be clear of Travis's objections McDowell would have to avoid the idea that perceptual experience has representational content, i. e. the newly introduced intuitional content would have to be non-representational. He might try to avoid defining content in terms of correctness conditions, but it is not clear whether the conception could achieve that. McDowell's explications of intuitional content suggest that intuitional content is representational after all. Intuitional content is not propositional content, but it is conceptual content and so still a form of mediated awareness.

At this point, there are three more ways to deal with the issues in finding out whether McDowell avoids Travis's criticism.[293] First, one could try to accept that McDowell's conception contains representational content and say why that is unproblematic. Second, one could criticize Travis's conception and ask how it manages to avoid the problems that he himself sets up. And finally, one can try once more to provide a charitable reading of McDowell's theory to show that it is not representationalist and therefore is not vulnerable to Travis's objections. This third interpretation extends the textual basis and combines the claims in "Avoiding the Myth of the Given" with more recent arguments in McDowell's "Perceptual Experience: Both Relational and Contentful" (McDowell 2013a). On such a reading one could argue on McDowell's behalf that conceptual content is not representational content, because perception is not representation of the

---

293 I am indebted to Logi Gunnarsson for suggesting that the situation may be framed in this way.

world, but presentation of the world to the perceiving subject.[294] The obvious problem with this reading is that it cannot explain why McDowell wants to hold on to talk of 'representational content' and 'content'.[295] In the remainder of this section I will examine these three possible reactions thereby pointing to problematic gaps as well as productive potentials in McDowell's theory.

Let's start with the first reaction, which embraces and defends representational content in McDowell's conception. Such a conceptualist representationalist might admit that whether the representational content of a perceptual experience is correct or not depends on the context of the perceptual experience and the content. In some situations McDowell's cardinal indeed is a bird and in others it is not. And there is a difference between the cases. To be more precise, the different occasions in which the representational content of a particular perceptual experience is correct naturally divide into two types of cases. In type 1-cases it is correct to call the animal a bird, in type 2-cases it is not. Why does this not count as successfully determining correctness conditions of representational content? To this Travis would probably reply that the representationalist again illegitimately presupposes that there is a way for things to be fullstop. She might try to sort the cases according to types, but in doing that she would not be determining the correctness conditions of the particular representation. The parameters would be too vague and so 'correct if bird' would not identify the different cases subsumed in type 1. In addition, it is possible that one case can belong to both types, depending on the exact details of the situation. The representationalist might try to avoid the latter problem by adding as much detail as possible to individuate the particular case, but in doing that she would be leaving the level of representational content and would include what Travis calls factive meaning, i.e. what the facts at hand suggest. What the facts at hand suggest is determined by how the world is built up and does not yield any representational content. She might also try to construct a case which is so determinate that it only belongs to one generality, but such a thought would not be a representation, "because it would not really bring anything under a generality at all" (Travis 2010f, p. 6). Travis takes it that Leibniz has shown that it would also not help if one tried to construct a conjunction of cases in order to close in on that one particular case: such a conjunction requires the subject to grasp all there is to the sum of all cases, but that is impossible for a finite thinker (cf. Travis 2010f, pp. 6f.).

---

294 Cf. McDowell's talk of the world revealing itself to the perceiver (McDowell 1996, p. 54).
295 In developing relational conceptualism I suggest that one should do away with talk of representational content, but, of course, in taking this direction I will reject some of McDowell's claims in his revised conceptualism.

As a last resort the representationalist might suggest that we should understand representationalist content in terms of a disjunction, but again this would not contribute to a successful response to the Problem of Selection. First, perceptual experience is unambiguous, univocal, and so its character could not be properly captured by a disjunction. Second, a disjunction would not identify the different cases and that means that it could not figure in explanations of the transition from perceptual experience to beliefs.

McDowell might put forward a different reply – the second of the three suggested reactions. He might criticize Travis and ask how Travis's conception avoids the intricacies of representations. He might further ask why this path is not open to his own conception, too. McDowell would be right in saying that strictly speaking the Problem of Selection also exists for representations on Travis's theory. But since for Travis representations are only in thoughts and utterances, he only deals with those issues as concerning representational content in utterances and thoughts. The understanding of the representation in thoughts and utterances is fixed by the parochial sensibilities of the subjects; they agree in judgment and their shared expectations of what is to be expected by the speaker saying an utterance fixes how this representation is to be understood at a particular occasion. Agreement in judgment also "*decides* what is to be expected of the world if [the speaker is] right" (Travis 2010f, p. 14, emphasis in original). A community of agreement is "non-geographical, non-ethnic, non-historical" (Travis 2010f, p. 15). The community simply consists of those beings who agree about what counts as a case that instances a particular generality and what does not. Any being who can think the generality in question and takes such-and-such cases as instancing the generality and such-and-such cases as not instancing the generality is a member of the community of agreement. The members of the community might also share "a capacity for *Erkennung* – a capacity to tell what *is* (*does* count as) a case of things being [a particular, N.E.] way" (Travis 2010f, p. 11, emphasis in original).[296]

The representationalist does not have anything like the agreement in judgment which might help her fix the content for the particular representational content of the perceptual experience. Perceptual experience is not based on agreement in judgment. Nothing in appearances, in things appearing as they do, has the capacity to fix which understanding of the representation we want in this situation. There are just too many appearances in the perceptual experience to determine the correctness condition of the representational content, i.e.

---

296 Remember also that Travis follows Austin in holding that true representation is meritorious representation (cf. Travis 2006, p. 187).

when things would be as represented in the subject's experience. Either the conceptualist representationalist and McDowell end up with representational content being impossible content, or the content is so general that it cannot identify the particular perceptual experience.

In this analysis of the different ways of responding to Travis's objections one sees that there is a fundamental disagreement about the nature of perceptual experience between relationists like Travis and people who talk about perceptual experience as representing like McDowell. That also means that saying that in the case of veridical perception the subject directly perceives an object, viz. that there is relation between the subject and the world, and that at the same time there is a correspondence between the world and a representation will never satisfy a Travisian relationist and silence her objections, the Problem of Selection and the Problem of Attaining Generality. It seems unlikely that "Avoiding the Myth of the Given" in its current interpretation can help help overcome the disagreement. The only hope lies in an alternative interpretation of McDowell's claims, a more charitable reading. Maybe there is another interpretation of McDowell's position on which it is non-representationalist after all. That is the third possible way of trying to find out whether McDowell's conception avoids Travis's criticism.

McDowell's attempt at a non-representationalist interpretation of his conceptualism

In his "Perceptual Experience: Both Relational and Contentful" McDowell aims to show that we can say and in fact have to say that perceptual experience is relational *and* contentful, namely by playing an epistemic role. According to McDowell, a "relational conception" holds that "experience enables us to know things about the environment by placing us in cognitively significant relations to environmental realities" (McDowell 2013a, p. 145). To him, cognitive activity and perceptual experience cannot be separated since perceptual experience has "epistemic significance" (McDowell 2013a, p. 147): it is a warrant for perceptual knowledge. Perceptual experience that can play this epistemic role must be conceived as an exercise of a rational "capacity to know by looking" (McDowell 2013a, p. 154). Eliza sees a tower on the hill and her perceiving the tower on the hill warrants her knowledge-claim 'I know that there is a tower on the hill.' But her perceptual experience only has such a "warrant-constituting status" McDowell 2013a, pp. 148f.) because veridical perceptual experience is relational. Veridical perceptual experience brings "environmental reality into view for the subject" (McDowell 2013a, p. 147), and having one's "environmental reality [in] view" (McDowell 2013a, p. 144) amounts to a relation between the subject and the environment that is now in her view. So in effect McDowell argues that the particular epistemic role of perceptual experience depends on the relational nature of veridical perceptual experience. At the same time its particular epistemic role also requires that perceptual experience is contentful, since its epistemic significance consists in making available to the subject knowledge about her environment and knowledge clearly is contentful.

But what does McDowell mean in this context when he says that perceptual experience has content? In this paper on relational-contentful perceptual experience McDowell is very tentative and non-committal about the issue. He only offers two vague possibilities and holds that his theory is compatible with both, not deciding for any of the two (McDowell 2013a, p. 145). On the first interpretation "experiential content is propositional" (McDowell 2013a, p. 144). The second interpretation is difficult to understand from the text only as McDowell does not say much more than that on this interpretation experiential content is "partial" (McDowell 2013a, p. 145), and "less than propositional" (McDowell 2013a, p. 145). Here the attempt at a charitable reading of these remarks brings us back to "Avoiding the Myth of the Given": we could understand this second conception of experiential content as alluding to experiential content as "intuitional content". In a perceptual experience the object is made present to the subject and she becomes knowledgeable by perceiving the object, but the experiential content is not propositional, it is intuitional. This might sound promising, but remember that the first discussion of "Avoiding the Myth of the Given" has revealed severe problems with coherently spelling out the notion of intuitional content. Those problems are likely to persist. And on the first interpretation – experiential content is propositional content – Travis's objections concerning occasion-sensitive representational content, viz. the Problem of Selection and the Problem of Incoherent Content, certainly re-occur. This also becomes clear in the following quotation: "Experiential representing, the representing by experiences that consists in their having content in the way they do, comes in two kinds: bringing environmental realities into view and merelgy seeming to do that" (McDowell 2013a, p. 147). It is not clear how this conception differs from positions which say that perceptual experience has representational content (e. g. Evans 1982; Peacocke 2001). McDowell might be able to get out of the fireline if he said more about the correctness conditions of perceptual experience; if he said why his representational content was not "sworn to veracity" (McDowell 2008, p. 260), as he puts it in his initial response to Travis from 2008, but McDowell does not say how that is.

Another fundamental problem for the integrative proposal occurs because McDowell's conception of relationism is tendentious and thus cannot figure in an unbiased integrative theory. He claims that it is a "shared intuition" (McDowell 2013a, p. 144) that perception enables us to have knowledge about the world by placing us in a relation to the world (McDowell 2013a, p. 144), and the disagreement is only as to whether content is to play a role in perception.

Now, he is certainly right in holding that there is agreement about perception enabling one to have knowledge about the world, but he is wrong in taking relationists to mean this to be the most basic task of perception. In fact, McDowell presupposes the very point at issue by saying that in "plac[ing] our surroundings in view" perceptual experience puts us in "relations to things that perception enables one to know about them" (McDowell 2013a, p. 144). As we have seen, Travis, Brewer and other relationists hold that the task of perceptual experience is to provide awareness, e. g. "visual awareness" (Travis 2013c, p. 238) or visual "confrontation" (Travis 2004, p. 65; Travis 2013b, p. 31) with objects in the world.[297] Perception is thus a "mental phenomenon", which consists in a "factive, [pure relation] to the way things *are*" (Travis 2011, p. 309, emphasis in original). Thoughts, judgments and knowledge only come later, when conceptual capacities are made to operate on what perception has delivered anyway. So Travis would say that by "plac[ing] our surroundings in view" perception does not do more than that. It simply places our surroundings in view *full stop*. Anything like belief or knowledge only comes after that. We can also see this crucial difference if we look at McDowell's definition of relationism: "On a relational conception, experience enables us to know things about the environment by placing us in *cognitively significant relations* to environmental realities" (McDowell 2013a, p. 145, my emphasis, N.E.). Travis's relational conception of perception does not include saying that there is a *cognitively significant relation* to the world (e. g. Travis 2013c, p. 241). In a term taken from Susanna Schellenberg I will call this relationism *austere relationism* (Schellenberg 2011); and McDowell's relationism could be called *epistemic relationism* (my term). McDowell's theory falls under his own conception of epistemic relationism, but Travis's theory does not, since it belongs with austere relationism. So here we have strong indication that in saying that perceptual experience is relational McDowell is not really a relationist like Travis.

McDowell's paper does include Travis's version of relationism, but it is not explicitly argued against in his main discussion. It is only in the very last section that McDowell says that he needs to explain why his conception is "better than … a conception according to which content figures in the epistemology of perception only in connection with our bringing under concepts things perception any-

---

297 Cf. e. g. (Brewer 2011, p. 97).

way places in view for us" (McDowell 2013a, p. 156). This conception would fit the label "austere relationism". In the rest of the article it hardly matters at all: the majority of McDowell's article is instead a rejection of the epistemic version of the Argument from Illusion (McDowell 2013a, pp. 146 ff.). I have introduced and discussed the Argument from Illusion as a version of the Argument from Fallibility, and it is certainly no argument brought forward by austere relationists like Travis and Brewer. So the second problem with McDowell's argumentation in favor of contentful and relational perceptual experience, i.e. in favor of epistemic relationism, is that McDowell introduces the issue of the possibility of perceptual knowledge into his defense of relationism, but this issue is not obviously related to the alternative anti-representationalist, relationist position.

McDowell rejects the relationism that fits Travis's view primarily because it falls prey to "a form of the Myth of the Given" (McDowell 2013a, p. 157). But this argumentation on the grounds of the possibility of perceptual knowledge does not obviously speak against austere relationism. McDowell closes the article with the following words:

> Let me end with this remark. Proponents of the competitor conception [i.e.austere relationism, N.E.] may be confident that there cannot be anything in the accusation of falling into the Myth of the Given, because they think seeing things their way is compulsory if we are to accommodate the intuition that perceptual experience puts us in relation to things in our surroundings. But in this lecture I have undermined that supposed ground for confidence in brushing the accusation aside. (McDowell 2013a, p. 157)

Here the problem is crystal clear: McDowell does not clearly distinguish austere relationism and his (epistemic) relationism. The paper argues for relationism, but those arguments in favor of McDowell's relationism do not address nor rule out austere relationism. Austere relationism rather is rejected for being non-conceptualist, i.e. for saying that conceptual capacities are not actualized in perceptual experience itself.

At this point one might object that I simply have not understood the relevance of McDowell's remarks on perceptual knowledge. The remarks on perceptual knowledge are an important rejection of the skeptic, i.e. her Argument from Fallibility. Remember, she holds that veridical experience of the world that is thought to consist in a relation to the world is indistinguishable from a mere seeming and so we cannot be sure that perceptual experience indeed ever consists in a relation to the world ["environmental reality", McDowell 2013a, p. 146]. From this the skeptic concludes that we cannot ever know that things are a certain way, because it is always possible "that things are not as one believes them to be" (McDowell 2013a, p. 148).[298] As we have seen in previous sections McDowell counters the skeptical observations by his well-known disjunctive maneuver: the mere fact that perceptual experience can be wrong and thus not of the world does not mean that perceptual experience is never of the world. There are simply cases of veridical and non-veridical perception, the former consist in a relation to the world, the latter do not (McDowell 2013a, p. 152; cf. also McDowell 2011b, pp. 42 ff. and Rödl 2010, p. 148).

The issue of knowledge then becomes pressing because McDowell argues that veridical cases of perceptual experience enable a subject to acquire knowledge about the world: the veridical perceptual experience is a "warrant for knowledge" (McDowell 2013a, p. 148) and the perceptual experience is warrant-constituting because of its content. Here the austere relationist comes into the picture again: she rejects this interpretation and holds that knowledge is acquired in an exercise of conceptual capacities that comes second. It is not the perceptual experience itself that warrants the knowledge, but rather only second-order warrant can guarantee that the capacities are appropriately exercised. McDowell wants to introduce an alternative according to which perceptual experience does the warranting all by itself *qua* being self-conscious: "If someone has a bit of knowledge of the kind that is an act of her rationality, she must be in a position to know, just in being in the state that constitutes her knowing, how her rationality is operative in it" (McDowell 2013a, p. 150). Remember that this is so because we are concerned with the knowledge of rational beings that possess conceptual capacities and are self-conscious; their knowledge is a "standing in the space of reasons" (McDowell 2013a, p. 148; cf. also McDowell 2011b). Knowing that one's knowledge really is knowledge is an act of the very same capacity as the act of knowing through perception.

This conception is an alternative to the austere relationist conception of the relation between perceptual experience and knowledge, but McDowell is not explicit on how the austere relationist view is wrong. He does say that two presuppositions force us to take the alternative that he has outlined: (a) If we want perceptual experience to provide conclusive warrant, we need to take this position (McDowell 2013a, p. 151); (b) if the perceptual knowledge is "an act of the knower's rationality" (McDowell 2013a, p. 150), then the warrant is to be something that the knower can know just from her perceptual experience (McDowell 2013a, p. 150). From the perspective of austere relationists these presuppositions certainly appear like mere stipulations and so it is not clear that these remarks and explanations help "[undermine] that supposed ground for confidence" (Mc-

---

298 Note also the parallel structure to the Argument from Illusion (e.g. Ayer 1969).

Dowell 2013a, p. 157) that austere relationists have in the correctness of their own view. McDowell's integrative view thus fails. But one can develop another charitable reconstruction of McDowell's revised conceptualism that is not involved in the meddle that McDowell creates by introducing his biased interpretation of relations.

Another attempt at a non-representationalist interpretation of McDowell's conceptualism

There is still another possible way for explicating a non-representationalist, relationist understanding of McDowell's conception. This charitable reconstruction is more independent from McDowell's own attempts. One step in such a charitable reconstruction of McDowell's conception would be to consider what it is that distinguishes McDowell's talk of representational content from other representationalists' talk of representational content. Maybe one can find an important difference between McDowell's representational theory and other philosophers' representational theory that can help substantiate McDowell's confidence about avoiding Travis's objections. And, indeed, if one compares the motivations of McDowell and the others, one discovers an important contrast that might explain why McDowell takes himself to be less affected by the objections. Usually, representational content is introduced to cope with illusions and hallucinations. Both illusion and hallucination are cases of misperception, in which the world is not as perceptual experience presents it to be (e. g. Tye 2015). In the case of an illusion the object is perceived wrongly and in the case of a hallucination there is no object in the world that corresponds to the object as it appears in the subject's perceptual experience. But the subject does perceive something, something appears to the subject. It cannot be an object in the mind-independent world, because the subject is misperceiving, so it must be representational content, namely how the world is represented to be in the perceptual experience. Perceptual experience can represent that there is an object O even though the object is not there to be perceived by the subject. It can also represent that an object O has the feature r even though the object does not really have this feature. The representational content simply represents an object that has those features which the subject perceives in her misperception.[299] But as we know, McDowell

---

[299] See (Martin 2002) for a reconstruction on these lines; though Martin does not endorse the conception.

rejects such 'conjunctivist' theories of misperception and defends a disjunctivist account (e. g. McDowell 2011b).

In McDowell's theory representational content enters into perceptual experience via another route. As I have emphasized before, McDowell wants to explain how perceptual experience can be of the world and how it can justify judgments and beliefs, i. e. be epistemically significant and this explanation just includes perceptual experience having representational content. In his *Mind and World* McDowell explains that perceptual experience can justify judgments, because perceptual experiences and judgments have the same content, namely propositional content, and involve the actualization and exercise of the same conceptual capacities. Propositional content is a form of representational content, namely, content with veridicality conditions and correctness conditions, and that is why on McDowell's conception perceptual experience has representational content. Sellars's introduction of intentional content can be read as building on similar considerations: Sellars holds that experiences make claims, they have "assertional character" (McDowell 2008c, p. 248), and so

> [t]he content of an experience is the content of a claim the experience makes ... An experience makes its claim in such a way as to represent endorsing it as incumbent on the subject of the experience. That is a way of saying the experience purports to reveal to its subject that things are the way she would be saying they are if she made that claim. (McDowell 2008c, p. 249)

One could also try to make more from McDowell's theory being disjunctivist and give the notion of "intuitional content" another shot at showing its role in McDowell's conceptualism. According to McDowell, experiential content is intuitional content from which discursive content can be carved out. Intuitional content can be construed as content with correctness conditions, but the special quality of McDowell's experiential content is that its correctness conditions are not determined by the subject. In his response to criticism by Brewer (Brewer 2008) McDowell explains that what is present to one in one's experience determines the truth-conditions of the experience simply in being present (McDowell 2008c, p. 203). In effect McDowell offers a disjunctivist theory of truth-conditions of perceptual experience.[300] This disjunctivist move separates McDowell's case from the case of other representationalist, i. e. the feature that ensures that his conception is not subject to Travis's objections. McDowell writes:

---

[300] For interesting remarks on such an interpretation of McDowell's conception see (Bain 2009).

The colour that is visually present to the subject already determines truth-conditions for the experience. The experience is veridical just in case the colour that figures in the subject's visual consciousness is the colour the object has. (McDowell 2008c, p. 204)

It is a feature of experience that in being the experience that it is it makes the experienced object "visually present" (McDowell 2008c, p. 204). McDowell takes this feature of experience to be a key property that explains why the truth-conditions of the experience are given in the experience itself and do not require any additional steps for being determined. On McDowell's conception determining the truth-conditions of one's perceptual experience does not involve any "intellectual step from what one's experience presents to one" (McDowell 2008c, p. 203) The truth-conditions are simple: "The thing has to be the way one seems to see it to be" (McDowell 2008c, p. 204). See for example perceiving a color: "The colour that is visually present to the subject already determines truth-conditions for the experience" (McDowell 2008c, p. 204). One can formulate the following disjunction for the truth-conditions of a perceptual experience: if the object is the way that it is appears, the truth-conditions are fulfilled; if the object is not the way that it appears, the truth-conditions are not fulfilled. One cannot say more about the relation between experience and truth-conditions, because on McDowell's conception experience is not, as he says in his response to an article by Michael Williams, something "sworn to veracity" (McDowell 2008c, p. 254): "... in experience the fact that things are that way is directly available, visually, to the subject of the experience. This is not an idea of something that is sworn to veracity" (McDowell 2008c, p. 254).

This disjunctivist conception certainly is not intuitively satisfying since it seems to amount to not much more than saying 'If the perceived object is present, the perceptual experience is correct, if it is not present, it is not.' Of course, it is reminiscent of the capacity approach to perception and its reaction to the Argument from Fallibility. If the capacity for knowledge is exercised correctly, then we perceive things as they are, because of the particular nature of the capacity for knowledge and for transcendental reasons. But this connection certainly is by no means explicit, and if McDowell wanted to go in this direction, he has certainly not indicated that clear enough. Moreover, I have noted problems with the guaranteeing character of perceptual experience that the capacity approach to perception assumes (Section 2.7).

Another problem also remains: it might still seem that on the disjunctivist conception, too, the 'visual availability' of "the fact that things are that way" seems to be just what Travis calls the looks-indexing claim of representationalist theories – the representational content can be read off from the way things look in the particular experience – and so Travis's analyses seem to still hold for Mc-

Dowell's conception as well. I think that one can now say that it is apt to call McDowell's position representationalist. The alternative interpetations of content did not turn out convincing. Moreover, McDowell uses the expression "representational content" for describing his claims. And if all that perceptual experience did was presenting, then he would not need to talk of representational content in perceptual experience. If he wants to continue using the expression, and use it in the sense outlined, then he will be a representationalist. Remember also the passages that I have quoted above that put him in the representationalist group.[301]

A final attempt to secure the disjunctivist interpretation of McDowell's conception might consist in saying more about the particular connection between intuitional content and the objects of perception. Conceptual content that is intuitional content is non-representational; it is content that can include particulars. Demonstratives and indexicals are such types of conceptual content. On this interpretation the content of perceptual experience contains the object of the perceptual experience. Such an interpretation is supported by McDowell's approving nod to Sellars's claims concerning the connection between intuitional unity and propositional unity:

> Sellars gives a helpful illustration: the propositional unity in a judgment expressible by 'This is a cube' corresponds to an intuitional unity expressible by 'this cube'. The demonstrative phrase might partly capture the content of an intuition in which one is visually presented with a cube. (McDowell 2009a, p. 260, footnote omitted, N.E.)

In the passage to which McDowell refers Sellars writes:

> the idea [is] that we move from representations of the form 'this-cube' which is a representation of a *this-such* nexus, specifically of *this as a cube,* though it is not a judgment and does not involve 'cube' in a predicative position, to representations in which the same nexus and the same content occur in explicitly propositional form 'This is a cube'. (Sellars 1968, p. 5)

Note, however, that the demonstrative expression is an expression of the intuitional content. The intuitional content is expressed as the fragmentary discursive content 'this cube', but it also exists independently of this expression. Being intuitional content, it is complete in itself and not fragmentary discursive content.

What would an alternative interpretation of the "content" in intuitional content thus amount to? "Content" should not be understood as representational

---

301 I am indebted to David Lauer for asking me to be more precise with regard to my claims about McDowell's theory being representationalist.

content, but rather as referring to the object of perception, i.e. as content that contains the object of perception. What we call *content* really is a relation between the perceiving subject and the perceived object. This interpretation could spell out a notion of intuitional content as "unmediated awareness" (cf. Travis 2013b).

It is unclear whether McDowell himself aims at such a conception; the following passage can be read as suggesting as much: "The demonstrative phrase might partly capture the content of an intuition in which one is visually presented with a cube" (McDowell 2009a, p. 260). But at the same time, this reading conflicts with the passages from his responses to Travis and Brewer that I have quoted above. Remember for example McDowell's insistence that "[i]ntuitional content is still content. And it is, we can say, all but propositional" (McDowell 2008c, p. 200). Moreover, there is the above evidence for the claim that McDowell's conception is representationalist.

And, of course, I cannot know whether McDowell would want to follow the route that I have started to sketch out. But that is also not decisive. All that matters is that there is space for a conceptualist conception of perceptual experience that takes up this path: such a *relational conceptualist position* could be developed when one starts from a conception of intuitional content as object-involving, relational, unmediated awareness. In what follows I will take up just this path. In this I will go beyond McDowell's arguments, e.g. I will shed talk of intuitional content. Instead I will argue in accordance with conceptualist conceptions of perceptual experience more generally. Of course, these conceptualist claims will overlap with many of McDowell's arguments and claims, but they are not strictly identical with them. The central tenet of conceptualist conceptions of perceptual experience that will guide the constructive project is that conceptualism amounts to the claim that perceptual experience of rational beings is necessarily infused with the actualization of conceptual capacities. The possession of conceptual capacities is a necessary prerequisite for the perceptual experience of rational beings, since their perceptual experience are epistemically significant, i.e. they can justify judgments and beliefs.[302]

Before I move to developing and spelling out relational conceptualism I need to add the following brief remarks to round up the discussion of the revised

---

302 Conceptualism thus amounts to what Lauer calls "B-F: In actualizations of the human perceptual capacity conceptual capacities are actualized." ["In Aktualisierungen des menschlichen Wahrnehmungsvermögens werden begriffliche Fähigkeiten aktualisiert."] (Lauer 2014, p. 50) But note an important difference: Unlike Lauer I do not think that B-F entails "B-G: Actualizations of the human perceptual capacity have conceptual content" ["Aktualisierungen des menschlichen Wahrnehmungsvermögens sind begrifflich gehaltvoll."] (Lauer 2014, p. 52).

conceptualist position in "Avoiding the Myth of the Given". In the above considerations I have been focusing exclusively on the relation between the introduction of intuitional content and Travis's objections against representational content in perception. But the second change is more explicitly induced by Travis: the content of perceptual experience does not have to include all the concepts that would figure in non-inferential knowledge that can be gained from the particular perceptual experience. The most basic concepts that will always be included in the content of a perceptual experience are concepts of common and proper sensibles. Further non-inferential knowledge is gained by the application of recognitional capacities on the already conceptual content of the perceptual experience. The amendment is strongly reminiscent of one of the problems that Travis raised for conceptualism: the Uncle Willard case and the Argument from New Concepts for Past Experience. The idea in the Uncle Willard case and the related argument was that a subject can acquire new concepts and apply those concepts to past experiences (Travis 2013c, pp. 245 f.). This suggests *inter alia* that the content of perceptual experience cannot include all the concepts which figure in the non-inferential knowledge gained from the perceptual experience. This problem is avoided on McDowell's amended position since it does not anymore claim that all concepts have to be included in the content of the perceptual experience. Recognitional capacities and the "intuition's categorial form" (McDowell 2009a, p. 261) provide enough space to accommodate the Uncle Willard case and also allow for new concepts to be applied to past experiences. The content of perceptual experience is still fully conceptual, but does not have to include all possibly applicable concepts. There are several reasons why this amendment is very important, and one of those is that it deals successfully with Travis's objections in the vicinity of the Argument from New Concepts for Past Experiences.[303]

But note that this is not to say that the amendment is flawless and settles all questions regarding the Uncle Willard case and nor raises new questions. In fact, the amendment seems to leave one with more questions than before, since McDowell does not supplement the prominent role of recognitional capacities with an adequate theory of recognitional capacities. It is not clear what recognitional capacities are; whether they are a kind of conceptual capacities; how they latch on to the perceptual experience, etc. As we have seen previously, the same holds for the "categorial form" of an intuition. McDowell does not spell out the details of the two arguments and leaves the dedicated conceptualist with more ques-

---

[303] For another reason why this amendment is important, namely as a response to a richness-objection, see (Lauer 2014, pp. 56–59).

tions to consider. These questions will be touched upon and answered in developing relational conceptualism in the next part of this book, but the main focus will be on developing a conceptualism that simply takes in the relationist insights and still stays true to the conceptualist project of explaining epistemically significant perceptual experience.

One central terminological move that is already implicit in McDowell's conceptualism, but which I want to emphasize even more concerns the significance of conceptual capacities. In Crowther's terminology that I have introduced in Section 2.2 one could say: I want to read conceptualism as answering the Possession Question (cf. Crowther 2006, p. 251). Conceptualism holds that perceptual experience necessarily implicates the actualization of conceptual capacities in the subject. It does not make any claims about the content of perceptual experience being conceptual, i. e. it does not make any content claims.

Part III **Relational Conceptualism**

7 Relational Conceptualism: a Theory of Epistemically Significant Perception

7.1 Preliminaries

The discussion of McDowell's revised conceptualism has revealed a discrepancy between McDowell's self-evaluation and my assessment: McDowell holds that Travis's non-representationalist arguments do not concern him and that he can thus continue to speak of *content* and *representational content* in perceptual experience. At the same time I claim to have shown that it is not at all clear that McDowell can really avoid the relationist arguments if, indeed, he wants to hold on to saying that perceptual experience has content, whether it be representational content or conceptual content, and if he regards this claim about perceptual experience having representational content as more than a way of speaking.

In what follows I will leave behind the question of whether McDowell's version of representational content is unproblematic; instead I will go beyond McDowell's theory and spell out a conceptualist theory of perceptual experience that does avoid relationist arguments. The easiest and best way of really avoiding non-representationalist criticism and bracketing the problems with McDowell's use of "representational content" is to make do with the term and the notion *representational content*. So I will develop and formulate a conceptualist theory of perceptual experience without resorting to representational content. Talk of *(representational) content* will be reserved for those theories to which the non-representationalist charges apply. The theory that will be developed argues that perceptual experience is not representational, but only a relation between the perceiving subject and the perceived object. Of course, all of this also fits nicely with the above qualification that conceptualism is a theory that claims that perceptual experience in human beings requires the actualization of conceptual capacities, without that implying any claims about concepts figuring in the content of perceptual experience.

The aim of this chapter is two-fold: first, I demonstrate that one can formulate a relational conceptualist theory of perceptual experience and second, I argue that such a relational conceptualist theory is the right theory for explaining the epistemic significance of perceptual experience. It is a theory that fulfills the adequacy condition that I have presented in the Introduction: it is both a theory of perceptual experience and a theory of epistemic significance.

Note that McDowell's published work to some extent leaves some room for a relational conceptualism that drops talk of representational perceptual content, and holds on to perceptual experience being a relation and implying conceptual capacities. See, for example, what McDowell says in his response to Travis's "Reason's Reach" (Travis 2007):

> What my condition disallows is the idea that something, for instance a piece of meat, can impinge on a subject's rationality without conceptual capacities, capacities that belong to reason, being drawn on in the subject's being thus related to it. The idea of such impingement is a myth, a version of the Myth of the Given. ... *But that leaves it open that a piece of meat can impinge on a subject's rationality,* provided that capacities that belong to reason are drawn on in the subject's being thus related to it. (McDowell 2008c, p. 259, my emphasis, N.E.)

This quotation does not refer to any content; the impingement of the piece of meat on rationality is direct, mediated only by conceptual capacities. The space that McDowell leaves open here is the space from which the new position, relational conceptualism, will be developed. Relational conceptualism makes the following claim about perceptual experiences:

> Perceptual experience is a perceptual relation between the perceiving subject and the object of perception, say, a tree. This perceptual relation is the product of the subject drawing upon her conceptual capacities in perceiving the object of perception.

Yet at the same time, given his insistence in wanting to talk of representational content, it is highly likely that McDowell is not willing to go this way with me and that is why this chapter develops a conceptualist theory of perceptual experience that is not committed to being faithful to all claims of McDowell's conceptualism. My new conceptualism frees itself from McDowell in order to save and sustain conceptualism in the face of non-conceptualist relationist criticism.

The new position is relational, but it differs crucially from Travis's theory and other relationist theories that we have encountered so far. The disagreement is about the role of conceptual capacities in perceptual experience. As I have emphasized, standard relationist theories are non-conceptualists. They propound what one can call a 'response view' of the connection between conceptual capacities and perceptual experience. McDowell's response to Travis also makes it clear that this is still the major difference between their theories:

> [I]n my picture we stand in those cognitively significant relations to [particulars][304] by having experiences in which conceptual capacities of ours are actualized. In Travis's picture,

---

304 McDowell actually uses the terminology of the left side and the right side (the non-conceptual and the conceptual) that Travis uses in "Reason's Reach" (Travis 2007, p. 230). As I

by contrast, conceptual capacities are in play, in connection with experience, only in rational responses on our part to [particulars] that experience anyway makes available to us for such responses: for instance in recognizing something we see as a piece of meat. In Travis's picture, the presence to us of [particulars] in experience, available to be recognized or not, as what they are, does not itself draw on capacities that belong to our reason. (McDowell 2008c, p. 261, footnote added, N.E.)

In the sections on Travis's argumentation I have presented some of Travis's arguments for denying that conceptual capacities are actualized in perceptual experience itself, but I still have to examine whether those arguments are appropriate and correct. This examination in Chapter 7 will show that Travis's non-conceptualist arguments fail and that his non-conceptualist theory of perceptual experience gives a wrong account of perceptual experience. For now we can note that Travis's main worry – though sometimes implicit – is that in a conceptualist theory of perceptual experience the perceiving subject loses direct touch with the world (e. g. Travis 2010a, p. 60; Travis 2013c, p. 257). First, if conceptual capacities are actualized in perceptual experience itself, then perceptual experience seems to be of something conceptual and not of objects in the world. Second, rational relations must span the conceptual as well as the nonconceptual on pains of losing rational capacities altogether.[305] The task of perceptual experience is to provide the subject with simple acquaintance of the world. (cf. Travis 2013c, p. 248).

Behind these motives lies another central reason for not thinking that conceptual capacities are actualized in perceptual experience: Travis does not think that there is anything like the Myth of the Given. He does not explicitly deny its existence, but his wording in relating McDowell's claims about a theory of perceptual experience that wants to avoid the Myth of the Given, e. g. scare quotes in using the term *myth,* make it highly likely that he does not think that there is anything like the Myth of the Given (Travis 2013c, pp. 245 ff.).

Travis shares this critical attitude and even denial of the Myth of the Given with Brewer (Brewer 2011) and Kalderon (Kalderon 2011). In fact, as I have noted, it seems to become a common move against McDowell's conceptualism to simply reject that there is anything like the Myth of the Given and to thereby reject conceptualism.[306] I have argued above that conceptualism can and should be re-

---

said, I do not use this terminology because it does not seem to carry any meaning and Travis only uses it in this one article.

305 Remember that this is *nonconceptual* on Travis's terminology; the *nonconceptual* refers to worldly particulars, and is not identical with *non-conceptual.*

306 This argument – 'There is no Myth of the Given, *ergo* there is no need for conceptualism.' – is to be distinguished from an argument that suggests that the Myth of the Given can be avoided

garded as more than a theory avoiding the Myth of the Given, instead it is a theory that explains the nature of perceptual experience and explains what perceptual experience has to be like in order to play an epistemic role. If conceptualists themselves reduce conceptualism to the question of the Myth of the Given, they unduly limit their theory and invite critics to change the subject and discuss the Myth of the Given rather than conceptualism as a theory of the epistemic significance of perception. Not arguing by reference to the Myth of the Given has two simple advantages: one does not unnerve critics who are skeptical about the Myth of the Given, and one does not have to engage in a Myth of the Given-exegesis. So if there is another way to show that conceptual capacities are necessarily actualized in perceptual experience, one should use this path, and I think that showing that conceptualism is the right theory for explaining the epistemic significance of perceptual experience might be just that path.

In the light of the exchange between McDowell and Travis, and the relationist critique of conceptualism it might be surprising to meet a theory that claims to juxtapose McDowell's and Travis's theories. But the two theories are amenable to being brought together. First, as we have seen, McDowell integrates some of Travis's thoughts (McDowell 2009a). Second, and more importantly, McDowell and Travis share central claims and structural similarities. E. g. Travis says that for a being for whom the world is unlocked (I will explain the expression in Section 7.3) the world is revealed in the perceptual experience (Travis 2013c, p. 235). McDowell, too, holds that the world is revealed in experience (e. g. McDowell 1996, pp. 111 f.). Here they even have the same diction. I have also argued that Travis's talk of parochial capacities fits with McDowell's notion of conceptual capacities. The difference lies in the place that conceptual or parochial capacities occupy in the respective theory of perceptual experience (implied in perception view vs. response view) and in the claims about content (representational content vs. relational). This is where *relational conceptualism* comes onto the scene. These intricacies are also why the position is a relational conceptualist position and not a conceptualist relationist position. The core of the position is the conceptualist conception of perceptual experience, and the relationist component is added to this core. The following table summarizes the position of relational conceptualism in relation to McDowell's conceptualism and Travis's relationism.

---

by a non-conceptualist position, e. g. beliefs and judgments can be rationally related to perceptual experience that does not have conceptual content (e. g. Peacocke 2001a).

	McDowell's conceptualism	Relational conceptualism	Travis's relationism
Perceptual content	Perceptual experience has content.	Perceptual experience does not have content.	Perceptual experience does not have content.
Conceptual capacities in perceptual experience	Conceptual capacities are actualized in epistemically significant perceptual experience.	Conceptual capacities are actualized in epistemically significant perceptual experience.	Conceptual capacities are actualized in response to perceptual awareness.

Table 1

One might ask why I have chosen Travis's theory rather than Brewer's or Kalderon's theory to embody the relationist side. I will just give a few related explanations. First, I regard Travis's theory as the most direct and elaborate critique of representationalism and conceptualism. Second, as we have seen, both Brewer's and Kalderon's theories build on Travis's theory. In other words, Travis's theory contains some of the most important arguments against representationalism. Third, there is too much disagreement between Brewer and McDowell for Brewer's arguments to be effective in a McDowell inspired response. McDowell's response to Brewer's relationist arguments does not note one single point of agreement (McDowell 2008c). I have already established above that this is different in the case of Travis.[307] Finally, Travis's distinction between O-seeing and T-seeing that manifests his idea of conceptual capacities as responses will prove useful as a background for introducing and detailing perceptual experience as understood by relational conceptualism.

Put bluntly, on the level of the question of whether perceptual experience has content, I follow Travis's argumentation, i.e. I accept the following arguments against representational content of perceptual experience:

(i)   The Problem of Selection

(ii) The Problem of Attaining Generality

(iii) The Problem of Incoherent Content

---

307 Similar considerations explain why I have not chosen Campbell's or Martin's relationist theories: their respective theories of perceptual experience are too different in focus from McDowell's theory. Campbell focuses on the psychology of perceptual experience, and Martin is more concerned with the phenomenology of perception.

I do not accept or endorse Travis's objections against conceptualism[308], but as I will show they are not really objections against conceptualism itself and especially the newly developed relational conceptualism can very well accommodate the considerations that are behind objections. And on the level of the question of conceptual capacities I follow McDowell, i.e. I accept that perceptual experience that is epistemically significant implicates the actualization of conceptual capacities in perceptual experience.

The argumentation in the following sections proceeds as follows: I first offer a positive description of how perceptual experience should be conceived on the relational conceptualist conception. Then I go back to Travis's theory of perceptual experience in order to further develop the appropriate conception of perceptual experience of rational beings against the background of this mistaken non-conceptualist set-up. Pointing out the shortcomings of Travis's non-conceptualist and relationist theory also helps highlighting how relational conceptualism avoids these mistakes and why it is the appropriate conception of perceptual experience of rational beings. By discussing possible objections against the position in Chapter 8 I further develop relational conceptualism.

7.2 The Nature of Perceptual Experience on the Relational Conceptualist Account

When I look outside the window of this room, I see houses, rooftops, churches, windows, trees, mountains etc. What I see is particular and concrete: it is houses, rooftops, churches, windows etc. It is that particular terrace on the roof of the house opposite our building, it is that particular rooftop – without a terrace – next to it. I see those things. When you look outside your window, or when look around your room, or you move out and about on the streets, you also see particular and concrete things: books, laptops, coffee cups, people, shops, trains, traffic lights, bikes etc. You and I see those things as they appear to us and seeing them we identify them as books, coffee cups, rooftops etc. Perceiving something and identifying something are not separate acts, but go together in beings with conceptual capacities. When I perceive the terrace on top of the house opposite my room I do not do more than that: I see the terrace. But I also do not do less: I am not in an inchoate state of perceptual awareness of

---

308 Travis's objections against conceptualism are: (iv) Transcendental-style Arguments, (v) The Argument from Occasion-Sensitivity, (vi) The Argument from Particular Perceptual Presence of Objects, (vii) The Argument from New Concepts for Past Experience.

nothing particular. I see the terrace opposite my room. If I did not possess the concept *terrace*, I would see a plane roof with lights and chairs on it. Or if I did not possess the concept *roof*, I would see the top of the building. These are all just phenomenal considerations meant to describe what perceptual experience is like for a rational being that possesses conceptual capacities. These considerations are, of course, influenced by conceptualist claims about perceptual experience, but I take it that this is what perception is like for each and every one of us beings that possess conceptual capacities. We always perceive the things that we perceive, and we perceive them as *something*.

This description contains claims about the nature of perceptual experience that are more hidden. Such perceptual experience is irreducible, it cannot be reduced to some mental state or to some pure non-conceptual state. It is not that I perceive the terrace and then later apply the concept *terrace* to it, only then seeing the terrace. I just see the terrace. But such perceptual experience also does not contain any reflection nor any explicit identification. When I see the terrace, this perceptual experience is not captured by my saying "I see the terrace". My seeing the terrace really just is me seeing the terrace.[309] When I say "I see the terrace" I have, to some extent, stopped just perceiving the terrace and have taken a step away from my perceptual experience into my thinking about what I am perceiving or what I was perceiving. That extrastep does not belong to perception nor to my perceptual experience. It might have an influence on it, but that is another issue. In seeing the terrace I only see the terrace.

My seeing the terrace also includes my standing in a relation to the terrace. This relation is a conceptually informed relation that is the product of the actualization of my conceptual capacities in my perceptual experience. My conceptual capacities are actualized in seeing the terrace, but since my conceptual capacities belong to me, my seeing the terrace itself is just a relation between me and the terrace. When you ask me why I have a dreamy look on my face when looking at the other house, I can say that it is because I see the terrace on its roof. Or if you ask me how I know that there is a terrace on the roof of the other house, I will say that I know because I see it. But all of this is one or more steps away from my particular perceptual experience of the terrace. My perceptual experience in itself is nothing more than my perceptual experience.

---

309 Remember that Brewer makes a similar observation: even though there are indefinitely many true sentences which have the form "*o* looks *F.*", and which fit with S's perceptual experience, S seeing *o* still does not consist in the truth of the sentences and also cannot be explained by a simple list of facts of the form "*o* looks F_1", "*o* looks F_2", ... "*o* looks F_n". S's seeing *o* is what makes the sentences true and thus is more basic than the true sentences. The looks-sentences do not capture the actual seeing of the physical object.

These remarks about the nature of perceptual experience in rational beings with conceptual capacities form the core of the relational conceptualist theory of epistemically significant perception. That is what perceptual experience is on this theory account and I will keep coming back to these central claims in developing relational conceptualism.

This conception of perceptual experience allows relational conceptualism to meet the adequacy condition for theories of epistemically significant perception that I have submitted in the Introduction. Remember, there I said that the adequacy condition for a theory of epistemically significant perception is that it must be a unified theory that respects both the perceptual element and the epistemic element in epistemically significant perceptual experience. As will become clear in the following section, presupposing the above conception of perceptual experience provides a suitable basis for a theory of epistemically significant perceptual experience.

7.3 Developing Relational Conceptualism

Developing relational conceptualism against a contrastive background

I have already introduced Travis's theory of perceptual experience at the end of Chapter 5 and this section will repeat some of those tenets, but it will have a different focus as Travis's theory will serve a different function. It will home in on Travis's taxonomy of perceptual experience: O-seeing and T-seeing. This taxonomy will serve as an example of a non-conceptualist theory of perceptual experience, strictly separating perceptual experience and conceptual capacities. As I have said, Travis's theory is a non-conceptualist theory of perceptual experience. You might ask why I have not chosen a properly non-conceptualist theory as that of Peacocke, for example. But Travis's theory is particularly fitting because it is a relationist theory, and since I have argued that a theory of perceptual experience should respect central relationist insights, rather than representationalist insights, it is best to start from a non-conceptualist relationist theory to develop a contrastive relational conceptualist theory. That way I can focus on the conceptual component only. With a non-conceptualist representationalist theory I would have to argue both against non-conceptualism and representationalism. Of course, to some extent non-representationalist considerations are relevant in the exposition of relational conceptualism, but the focus will be on the conceptualist component. Travis's conception will provide a contrastive foil that allows me to highlight the place for relational conceptualism. Examining his theory and its shortcomings thus provides indirect arguments for relational conceptualism.

Travis's taxonomy is built on a fundamental distinction that Travis takes from Frege: it is the distinction between *Vorstellungen* and thoughts. A *Vorstellung* is private to its bearer, it cannot be shared, and each *Vorstellung* requires a bearer (Travis 2013c, p. 226). A being which only has *Vorstellungen* is locked in its inner world (Travis 2013c, p. 234). There are no questions of truth for a being that is locked in, since *Vorstellungen* cannot be shared (Travis 2013c, p. 226). Questions of truth only become relevant if the being can entertain thoughts (Travis 2013c, p. 236).

A being that is "locked in" (Travis 2013c, p. 234) cannot separate her experience, her *Vorstellungen*, from herself as the bearer of *Vorstellungen* (Travis 2013c, p. 226). A being that is not "locked in" is aware that someone else might have the thought that she has, too (Travis 2013c, pp. 226 f.). The crucial change in the experience of the being for whom the outer world is unlocked does not concern the object of her perceptual awareness; she sees the same object as the being for whom the world is not unlocked (Travis 2013c, pp. 236 f.). Rather, the change in her perceptual experience consists in an addition: as Frege says, something non-sensory is added and through that addition the creature goes beyond the possession of *Vorstellungen*, and (non-sensory) thoughts come into the picture (Travis 2013c, p. 236).[310]

As we know, for Travis a thought is that which is intrinsically general. Remember, he approvingly quotes Frege's remark on thoughts: "A thought always contains something which reaches beyond the particular case, by means of which it presents this to consciousness as falling under some given generality" (Travis 2013c, p. 236; Frege 1882, p. 189). A thought is a generality, a way for things to be. Each generality reaches to an "indefinitely extendible range of cases" (Travis 2013c, p. 236, emphasis deleted, N.E.), each of which instances the generality. The being for whom the world is unlocked grasps what it is for an object *o* to be *F*: it grasps how the particular instance participates in the instancing relation; it grasps where it reaches (Travis 2013c, pp. 247 f.).[311] The dif-

---

310 Note that Travis remarks that the common element – the same *Vorstellung* that figures in the perceptual experience of the being for whom the world is locked and of the being for whom the world is unlocked – does not have to play a "substantial role" in the perceptual experience of a being for whom the world is unlocked (Travis 2013c, p. 235).

311 Remember that in Travis's terminology the realm of generality is the realm of the conceptual. The realm of the particular instances which instantiate the generality is the realm of the nonconceptual. The conceptual is identified by the nonconceptual via the instancing-reaching-relation (Travis 2013c, p. 237).

ference between the perceptual experience of beings for whom the world is not unlocked and beings for whom the world is unlocked thus can also be captured in terms of the role of perceptual experience for accessing the world: for a being for whom the world is unlocked, the world is "revealed" by experience (Travis 2013c, p. 235). She has the added capacity for recognition (Travis 2013c, p. 240). If the world is not unlocked, no such 'revelation' in perceptual experience is possible.

This capacity of recognition in beings for whom the world is unlocked also figures in Travis's distinction between two types of seeing: O-seeing and T-seeing. "O-seeing" refers to the seeing of an object, it is a "perceptual accomplishment" (Travis 2013c, p. 238). "T-seeing" on the other hand is not perceptual, but rather a "function of thought" (Travis 2013c, p. 248). It is not a relation to an object, to something visible, but a relation to a thought. T-seeing involves recognition and that in turn requires conceptual capacities, i.e. "familiarity with what belongs to the conceptual, with that whose instancing one takes in" (Travis 2013c, p. 239). A being that possesses conceptual capacities grasps where something conceptual reaches and what a particular case instances: "[t]he capacity to recognise a pig as a pig ... [is] one applicable to what was anyway, recognised or not, a pig, and to appreciate how *just that* relates to that certain bit of the conceptual, *for something to be a pig*" (Travis 2013c, p. 239, emphasis in original). The possessor of such capacities will grasp relations within the conceptual realm and relations between the conceptual and the nonconceptual, i.e. the general and the particular. Recognizing an object, e.g. recognizing a pig, thus refers to *two* capacities: first, the "capacity to tell a pig at sight; and[, second, the] capacity to recognise what counts as something being a pig as so counting" (Travis 2013c, p. 239). But remember that for Travis recognizing an object, i.e. the exercise of conceptual capacities, is a response to one's perception; this is also clear in the remark about "the capacity to recognise a pig as a pig" (Travis 2013c, p. 239) that I have quoted above. The difference between O-seeing and T-seeing mirrors this distinction: it is only in a cognitive response (T-seeing) to a visual accomplishment (O-seeing) that conceptual capacities appear. I will get back to this central difference between Travis's and McDowell's theories of perceptual experience. In fact, dealing with the difference, and avoiding Travis's mistakes will be the major touchstone for my relational conceptualist conception.

A being that is locked in, that does not possess the crucial non-sensory component cannot recognize an object as instancing a certain generality. It cannot see that the object of its perceptual awareness instances a generality. Its perception only provides for awareness of the nonconceptual, i.e. in Travis's terminology the particular object in the world. The additional claim that is crucial for relational conceptualism is that on Travis's conception this also holds for beings that are *not* locked in (Travis 2013c, p. 236): For them perception also only provides for awareness of the nonconceptual. In fact, the very role of perception is to provide any perceiving creature with awareness of that which does the instancing, i.e. the nonconceptual (Travis 2013c, p. 247). It does not or, rather, cannot provide for awareness of the conceptual, since the conceptual is not visible.

According to Travis, this perceptual awareness is

> acquaintance with that which is fit to operate on our sensory transducers (e.g., to form images on retinas). It is awareness of such things as the pig, an episode of snuffling, the pig snuffling, the pig standing just *there* beneath the oak. (Travis 2013c, p. 248, emphasis in original)

Note that it is not entirely clear whether Travis wants to suggest that perceptual awareness is the operation of an object "on our sensory transducers" (Travis 2013c, p. 248) or whether it is just awareness of the object that figures in this (additional) operation "on our sensory transducers". I will come back to this ambiguity, as it will be important in the discussion of the relation between Travis's relationism and McDowell's conceptualism as well as the relation between Travis's and my own conception.

Travis wants to insist that O-seeing is the basis for T-seeing. O-seeing consists in the relation to an object; it is proper perceptual awareness (Travis 2013c, p. 238). T-seeing consists in a relation to a thought and thus involves non-sensory components, namely recognitional capacities and conceptual capacities. Yet it also involves a sensory component: there is no T-seeing without O-seeing. O-seeing, however, is not constituted by those two components: it does not contain a non-sensory component (Travis 2013c, p. 240). If a subject perceives an object, but does not possess the relevant conceptual capacities required for recognizing the object, she simply O-sees the object. O-seeing is a purely perceptual achievement (Travis 2013c, p. 238) and so, according to Travis, we have to say that all perceiving is minimally a case of O-seeing.

I think that this distinction is not exhaustive and for that matter not correct: for a rational being, a thinker with conceptual capacities, perception is never only characterized as O-seeing.[312] The acquisition and possession of conceptual capacities is a life-changing step. It is a point of no return for a being who has taken this step. A being that has taken this step has turned into a thinker. And,

---

[312] The formulation is carefully termed: It does not rule out O-seeing for beings with conceptual capacities. I will explain later why the formulation is hedged. Suffice it to say for now that if O-seeing is the physiological process of seeing – as our above remark suggested – then it would be wrong to rule out O-seeing for conceptually endowed beings.

most importantly for this discussion, this step also means that perception is changed. Of course, my remarks here are not original, but are very much in line with McDowell's conceptualist theory.[313] The following explanation of the special nature of human perception which McDowell puts forward in his exchange with Hubert Dreyfus is but one example for his conception:

> Becoming open to the world [i.e. perceiving the world as human beings do, N.E.] not just able to cope with an environment, transforms the character of the disclosing that perception does for us, *including* the disclosing of affordances that, if we had not achieved openness to the world, would have belonged to a merely animal competence at inhabiting an environment. (McDowell 2009m, p. 315, emphasis in original)

In what follows I will apply the observations about the role of conceptual capacities in the lives of human beings to Travis's conception and I will argue that Travis is wrong in not taking these observations to heart. On Travis's conception the life-changing step of acquiring conceptual capacities only means that the subject can also T-see, but I will argue that this is not enough. We can borrow a phrase from Moran's work on self-knowledge and put the point like this: conceptual capacities "*infuse* and *inform* [the perceptual experience, N.E.], making a describable difference in the kind of [perceptual experience, N.E.] it is" (Moran 2001, p. 31, my emphasis, N.E.).[314] A subject endowed with conceptual capacities has more than two varieties of seeing and more importantly, it has a type of perceptual experience that is a properly "perceptual accomplishment" (Travis 2013c, p. 238) and yet also infused with conceptual capacities. On Travis's model of O-seeing and T-seeing there is no space for this insight, so in an intermediate step I will introduce the notion of "C-seeing" to accommodate this insight and to explicate the nature of such perception. I will then show that the

---

313 See also my discussion of the Argument from Concept Acquisition (Section 2.4).

314 Peter Strawson also uses the metaphor "infusion" in his remarks about perception and imagination in order to claim that perception is infused by objective concepts. Building on Wittgenstein's remarks about aspect seeing he explains: "It would be quite wrong to speak of [the case in which the aspect changes happens "under one's eyes"] as if there were merely an external relation, inductively established, between the thought, the interpretation, and the visual experience; to say, for example, that 'I see the x as a y' means 'I have a particular visual experience which I have found that I always have when I interpret the x as a y'" (Strawson 2008, p. 63, my addition, N.E.). Strawson suggests we should say that "the visual experience is *irradiated* by, or *infused* with, the concept; or it becomes *soaked* with the concept" (Strawson 2008, p. 63, emphasis in original). At this point I cannot discuss the relation of my conceptualism to Strawson's theory, even though such a discussion would be very interesting. But it would require introducing Strawson's theory of perceptual experience and would lead us away from the development of relational conceptualism. Such an examination must therefore be saved for another occasion.

taxonomy of O-seeing and T-seeing must be given up and that for rational beings there is only what I have contrastively labelled "C-seeing". As a result of this the "C-seeing"-label can then be given up because the contrastive background has been shown to be incongruous. But before we get to giving up the background, let me start to explain its falseness.

Inevitability and Directness of Perceiving Something: Two principles of relational conceptualism

On Travis's conception non-rational beings are locked in an inner world, because for them no questions of truth become relevant in their contact with the world. They can only O-see. That rational beings, on the other hand, can O-see and T-see is uncontested for Travis. They can T-see because the outer world has been 'unlocked' for them. They possess the conceptual capacities that are required for the world to be unlocked.

Contrary to my above claim, Travis thinks that rational beings can also O-see. See for example the following instance that he puts forward:

> What Pia O-sees is precisely what does instance a pig being beneath the oak – nothing short of the pig, as it is, beneath the oak, as it is. Such is what is there to be seen. Suppose she lacked, or failed to draw on, the conceptual capacities just mentioned. She would still O-see what was there to be seen, what in fact instances the generality in question. She would just fail to recognise its doing so. (Travis 2013c, p. 239)

There are two problems with this description[315]: first, it does not properly distinguish between the perceptual experience of rational beings and non-rational beings, and second, the description of Pia's perceptual experience is simply not apt. I will discuss the second problem first and return to the problem of the distinction between rational and non-rational animals later.

To be precise, my objection is that Travis's description is not apt to Pia's perceptual experience as *epistemically significant* perceptual experience. Now, why is that the case? The idea is this: even if Pia fails to recognize that what is there to be seen "instances the generality in question" (Travis 2013c, p. 239), that does not preclude that she does recognize that what is there to be seen does instance

---

315 Here the parallel between Kalderon's claims in (Kalderon 2011) and Travis's theory is most striking. As I indicated in fn. 226 Kalderon's claim that the subject is knowledgeable "even if, in the circumstances of perception, the subject lacked the conceptual capacities for knowing some range of propositions" (Kalderon 2011, p. 225) is in line with Travis's interpretation of Pia's case.

another generality. Pia possesses conceptual capacities, and so if she does not possess the concept *pig*, she can still recognize an animal beneath the oak. This fits with Willaschek's example of the person who does not possess the concept *fridge* and does not know what a fridge is and now is found to be looking at a fridge (Willaschek 2003, p. 270). According to Willaschek, this person will still see, e.g. a cupboard-like box, even if she is looking at a fridge and does not possess the concept *fridge* (Willaschek 2003, p. 270).[316] He adds, "[a]n adult human being who does not see the fridge as some thing or other, usually does not see it at all"[317] (Willaschek 2003, p. 270). Call this observation the *Inevitability of Perceiving Something.* When a thinker perceives an object, she will always perceive it as *something.*[318] The adult human being that Willaschek envisages does not O-see, nor T-see, but she sees the box.[319]

---

316 Willaschek actually talks of the person seeing that there is a cupboard-like box, but I will allow myself to drop this phrasing and speak of the person seeing a cupboard-like box in order to avoid issues with propositional content in perceptual experience. Willaschek makes this comment when he rejects Dretske's distinction between sense perception and cognitive perception for human perception (Willaschek 2003, pp. 269–272) and since cognitive perception is often understood as *seeing that* his argumentation concerns and talks of seeing that. But all that matters for my argumentation is Willaschek's observation that 'simple' perception involves the actualization of concepts and that observation is separate from any talk of *seeing that.*

317 "Ein erwachsener Mensch, der den Kühlschrank nicht *als* irgend etwas sieht, sieht ihn normalerweise überhaupt nicht." (Willaschek 2003, p. 270)

318 One can also put the point in terms of Kenny's notion of two-way powers as suggested, e.g. by Kern (Kern 2006, p. 222): the actualization of conceptual capacities in perceptual experience is not the actualization of a two-way power, i.e. it is not actualized at will. If the subject possesses conceptual capacities, it cannot *not* actualize them in perceptual experience. "Looking up at the flashing lights of the advertisements in Piccadilly Circus, one cannot prevent oneself from understanding their message. (How much more beautiful they would be, G.K. Chesterton once remarked, if only one could not read!)" (Kenny 1989, p. 22) in: (Glock 2010, p. 322).

319 The Inevitability of Perceiving Something might also be substantiated with the help of Quassim Cassam's "Categorial Thinking Requirement", i.e the claim that categorial thinking is required "in order to perceive that something is the case and thereby to know that it is the case" (Cassam 2009a, p. 88). Cassam argues that object perception and perceiving *that* something is the case require categorical thinking because the very concepts that are actualized in perceiving, e.g. *cup* and *chipped*, presuppose that one can think categorically (Cassam 2009a, pp. 129 ff., 148 f.). Cassam's theory is very rich, building on insightful analyses of the Kantian theory of perceptual experience, and philosophers in the tradition of Kant, like Beatrice Longuenesse, and John McDowell, but this strength is at the same time the reason why I cannot allow his theory to figure more prominently in this book. Including Cassam's arguments and argumentation would have required shifting more focus on Kant's philosophy, but this shift would have made the book substantially longer, and it would have clashed with the contemporary focus that I have mentioned in the Introduction. Bringing Cassam's theory of epistemic perceptual experience and relational conceptualism together thus must remain for another occasion.

Travis holds that the mind-independent object is the object of the subject's visual awareness, and that is certainly right, but he is wrong in thinking that this means that she is O-seeing. O-seeing is only a perceptual relation between a perceiver and a mind-independent object which does not imply the actualization of conceptual capacities, but if we take the insights of the Inevitability of Perceiving Something seriously, conceptual capacities will always be actualized in the perceptual experience of a being that possesses conceptual capacities: if an adult human being does not see the mind-independent object as *a box*, or as *an F*, or maybe even simply as *an object*, then she does not see it at all. The mind-independent object certainly is outside the realm of the conceptual, but for a being with conceptual capacities the mind-independent object is always an instance, a 'case' (in Travis's terminology, e.g. Travis 2007, pp. 232f.) and as such it instances a generality.

This section will further explicate this fundamental insight of beings endowed with conceptual capacities perceiving instances. But first I need to explicitly state the conceptualist claim:

All perceptual experience of a subject with conceptual capacities is seeing *something*.

The following relationist qualification has to be added and emphasized:

Seeing *something* is not a representation, i.e. it does not involve representational content nor conceptual content.

So relational conceptualism holds:

Perceptual experience is a relation between the perceiving subject and an object of perceptual experience, in which the perceiver actualizes her conceptual capacities and sees the object as something, e.g. sees a house as a house.

There is no intermediary, no representation of the mind-independent object as that instance in such perceptual experience. To the perceiving subject the object is the instance. Underlying this claim is another fundamental observation: the *Directness of Perceiving*. This observation refers to perceiving being devoid of intermediaries.[320] Note that with this claim I keep my word and take McDowell's claim that he is not wedded to the problematic notion of representational con-

---

320 One might also try to formulate this point in terms of "experiential immediateness" (Church 2010, p. 639).

tent to the next level by simply disposing of representational content in perceptual experience.

The relation that is the perceptual experience is the product of the actualization of the subject's conceptual capacities in perceiving the particular object. It is thus neither reducible to nor identical with the spatio-temporal relation between the subject and the perceived object. The spatio-temporal relation is a condition for the obtaining of what I will call the *conceptually informed relation*, but the perceptual relation that constitutes the perceptual experience of a subject with conceptual capacities is more than the spatio-temporal relation: it is a relation in which the perceiver actualizes her conceptual capacities.

The following example might be helpful for illustrating the position. When a doctor sees a human being in a hospital bed, she sees a patient. She does not see an indefinite object and then categorizes it as a patient. Rather she simply sees the patient; in this situation the person *is* the patient. This aspect thus concerns the first principle, the Inevitability of Perceiving Something, i.e. the fact that the mind-independent object is always immediately perceived as a case of a generality. This first principle goes hand in hand with the principle of the Directness of Perceiving. Perceiving *something* does not include any objectionable intermediary that is responsible for the status of the perceived object being a case. There are just two players: the subject that perceives the object and the object that is perceived; the doctor who perceives and the patient who is perceived. In the subject's perceptual experience the object and the patient count as one player. The example also helps understand what I mean when I say that the mind-independent object is *always* something, that it is always a 'case', i.e. that the mind-independent object that the subject perceives is always a particular[321] that instances a generality. In the situation that we are envisaging the doctor cannot *not* see the patient.

One might object that the doctor does not always see the object in front of her as a patient. What if the person that she sees is not just a patient, but also her neighbor, or the friendly bus driver that she saw on the way to work? But this objection does not harm my claims, rather it supports them. Of course, the doctor could see the person as her neighbor or as the friendly bus driver, but then she also sees the neighbor, the friendly bus driver, directly. The person *is* the neighbor (Directness of Perceiving). The important point that the Inevitability of Perceiving Something captures is that she cannot *not* see the object as some-

---

321 Just a quick reminder that "particular" and "general" are still used according to Travis's terminology: "the particular" is "the nonconceptual", "the general" is "the conceptual" (Section 5.5).

thing, whether it be as a patient, her neighbor or the friendly bus driver. If she did not see the patient or the neighbor or the friendly bus driver or ..., she would see nothing, no mind-independent object. The thought can also be illustrated by the rabbit-duck-figure. If I see the figure as a rabbit, it is directly present to me as a rabbit. Of course, I can switch and see the figure as a duck, and then, too, it is directly present to me as a duck. If I did not see it as a duck or as a rabbit, I would see it as pencil scribbling or as a drawing. If I did not see it as something, I would not see it at all.

Travis's objection that representationalist content which contains all possible understandings that the representation might be taken to have is incoherent content (the Problem of Incoherent Content) is not relevant here, since there is no truth-evaluable content in the perceptual experience. If I see the figure as a duck, the drawing of the duck is directly present to me. That means that there is no content that could be incoherent; the object can look different things to a perceiver without that causing any contradiction in the particular perceptual experience since she does not ever see it as the different things at the same time. The central point is that seeing a particular instance with different traits and properties is not seeing it as all those things at the same time. Instead, think of my remarks on associated content – or more appropriate now, with the rejection of perceptual content: associated conceptual capacities – at t_1 S sees the fridge as a fridge; she could also see it as a box, as an emittor of comforting humming or as a piece of kitchen equipment, but she does not actually and necessarily see it as all those things at t_1. The different ways she could see the object as are connected since they are part of a network of concepts and conceptual capacities that the perceiver possesses (see Section 2.4 and e.g. (Davidson 1982, pp. 320f.; McDowell 1996). Because generalities are arranged in such a network, different concepts, i.e. different generalities, will always be applicable to the object. In that one particular moment of perceiving, however, only certain generalities are implied in the subject's perceptual experience. It can be more than one generality that is implied in the experience, but it is never all possible generalities. It is only those generalities whose related concepts are actualized.[322]

---

322 Note the similarity and the differences to Brewer's solution to the threat of incoherent experience and incoherent content (Brewer 2011, p. 126). He distinguishes between thin looks and thick looks: Thin looks of an object are the set of similarities that a particular object viewed from a certain position has with certain paradigms. Thick looks only cover those elements of this set of similarities that are conceptually categorized in a particular instance of perceiving. These conceptualizations do not contain impossible contents. Remember the duck-rabbit: it thinly looks like a duck and like a rabbit, but it thickly looks either like a duck, or like a rabbit (Brewer 2011, pp. 123 ff.). It cannot thickly look like both paradigms at the same time, but it can thinly

This argumentation is built on a conception of perceptual experience as essentially diachronic and cross-modal. Perceptual experience is not like taking snapshots, rather it is a fluent process over time without abrupt breaks or bounds. It is diachronic, one might say.[323] In the process of perceptual experience the subject does not just perceive with one particular sense, rather it is a cooperation of the different senses of the subject that can hardly be disentangled. Remember Noë's insight that you do not "open your eyes and ... are given experiences that represent the scene – picture-like – in sharp focus and uniform detail from the center out to the periphery" (Noë 2004, p. 35). One might be inclined to call such a position 'enactive', but I do not think that is necessary, as I do not want to sign up to the views of enactivism that are currently widely held. All that relational conceptualism wants to say is that perceptual experience is not a process in which steps and contributions can be clearly made out. Perceptual experience must be seen in the context of its exercise and that includes also that it is set in the life of a conceptually endowed, rational being. One cannot say anything substantial about perceptual experience if one looks at it outside of its natural surrounding, which is the life of a rational being, and in unnatural segmentations, e. g. by looking at arbitrary time slices. Think of the following phenomenon in a concert hall: you see and hear a pianist play his part, say, in Brahms's second piano trio. If you see the hands of the pianist moving while he is playing his part and hear him play together with his colleagues, you are more likely to hear the different rhythms and nuances than if you do not see his hands.

There is a query or, rather, an objection that will have been looming large during the above explanations: is this more than simply insisting and repeating that a being that has conceptual capacities does actualize those capacities in perceptual experience? And, in addition, all those explanations have been piling up a heavy burden that comes with the claims that I have made in the course of the explanations. The burden is this: I want to say that all perceptual experience of a being who possesses conceptual capacities is conceptual, but at the same

---

look like both paradigms at the same time. Relational conceptualism, too, avoids the problem of incoherent content because it does not say that perceptual experience has content. But at the same time it overthrows Brewer's distinction between thin looks and thick looks, i. e. between possible ways of looking and conceptualized ways of looking, because thin looks really are thick looks. If one uses Brewer's terminology, the claim of relational conceptualism can be formulated like this: There are no un-conceptualized thin looks and thus the distinction cannot be sustained.

323 Note that Travis, too, says that "seeing is dynamic" (Travis 2009, p. 345), but I do not see that in his theory he takes this claim seriously.

time I want to say that perceptual experience does not have representational content or conceptual content. All perceptual experience is seeing-as, but it is no representation, i.e. it is without an intermediary. How can I say this and why should we say this? Here my conceptualism is also in conflict with McDowell's views. In his response to Travis McDowell writes: "[I]f experiences are actualizations of conceptual capacities, they must surely have conceptual content" (McDowell 2008c, p. 260). It seems as if that statement applies to my proposal, too, and so I cannot argue that perceptual experience implicates conceptual capacities and at the same time argue that it does not have conceptual content or representational content. In order to answer these objections I will further analyze the central features of seeing and say more to explicate the relational conceptualist conception.

The cases of seeing-as are not representations because as we have seen above they do not involve any representing. The perceiving subject cannot but see the object *as F* or *G* or *H* (the Inevitability of Perceiving Something) and in her perceptual experience it is the object that is *F*, or *G*, or *H* (the Directness of Perceiving). The doctor sees the patient as a patient and she cannot but see her (as) *being someone* or *something*. This is one act only in which she directly sees the patient. If Pia (from Travis's example) sees a pig and does not possess the concept *pig,* she will still see the pig as something, e.g. as a grunting four-legged animal, or as an animal. She cannot *not* see the pig. The directness of her perceptual experience means that talk of her seeing the pig *as an F* does not introduce a representation nor conceptual content into her perceptual experience. She sees the grunting four-legged animal and not a representation of the pig as a grunting four-legged animal. The pig, we might say, is the grunting four-legged animal. Language makes it seem as if *as F* introduces a representation into the perceptual experience, since it seems impossible to not use the construction *as F* if we speak about the doctor's perception or any perceiver's perception. But this impossibility of leaving out '*as so-and-so*' is purely linguistic and does not warrant any conclusions about the actual presence of a representation in perception itself. In other words, perceptual experience is just a form of presentation. As I said above, one must be careful not to confuse perceptual experience itself and thought or talk about perceptual experience.

One can put the main claim of the relational conceptualist position negatively in the following schema. Of course, as I have shown and will continue to show, there are also positive formulations of relational conceptualism, but I think that in reply to the objections the negative formulation will be helpful to avoid and counter misunderstandings. The relational conceptualist rejects the following argumentation by rejecting the conclusion (3):

(1) I see the pig *as a pig*. (I see *a* as *F*.)
(2) The pig falls under the concept *pig*. (*Fa*)

___

(3) I see the pig as falling under the concept *pig*. (I see *a* as *Fa*).

The relational conceptualist argues as follows. From the fact that I see the pig as a pig and that the pig falls under the concept *pig* it does not follow that I see that the pig falls under the concept *pig* or that I see the pig as falling under the concept *pig*. To some extent one might say that I simply 'identify' or 'categorize' the pig in my perceptual experience where that does not entail any perceptual experience of a concept.[324]

In addition, I want to again emphasize a distinction that I have already introduced in the positive account of perceptual experience at the beginning of this chapter (Section 7.2). One must hold apart perceptual experience itself and what we talk about when saying what we saw. Of course, any sentences or speech acts reporting what we saw will be linguistic and thus include representations, but that does not mean that in the perceptual experience itself there are any linguistic elements or any representations. Note that at the same time perceptual experience is not non-conceptual, because in the perceptual experience itself the perceiver sees the object or the objects in the scene as certain, particular objects, e. g. pigs, or tables, or a roof. This 'categorization' requires conceptual activity.

One might feel inclined to object that these replies are just trivial observations.[325] My response to this objection is this: triviality does not tell against an argument. I do not see any other way how to conceive of epistemically significant perceptual experience, and if that makes the arguments and the related theory trivial, then so be it. Note also that one could present the argument in a shape that makes it more controversial: one could say that the Inevitability of Perceiving Something really is based on McDowell's transcendental argument for empirical content[326] (Section 2.7). The Inevitability of Perceiving Something holds because it is only if perceptual experience implies the actualization of conceptual capacities that perceptual experience can be *of* the world.[327] But

___

324 I am indebted to Lutz Wingert for suggesting that relational conceptualism may be formulated in this way.

325 Hemdat Lerman has suggested this objection in conversation to me. She also suggested that I could embrace the triviality. The decision to actually acknowledge and embrace the triviality is my own, as are any mistakes related to it.

326 Empirical content here is just short for 'perceptual experience being of the world' and the idea is that the argument also works for content-less perceptual experience.

327 Johannes Haag has suggested in a discussion about the relational conceptualist position that its claims might be tantamount to Sellars's claim that perceptual experience has intuitional con-

this controversionalization comes with an unnecessary limitation of conceptualism, i.e. conceptualism only making a transcendental claim. In Chapter 9 I will suggest that conceptualism must not be limited in this way. And so the Inevitability of Perceiving Something is important on its own, without any controversionalization: the principle – trivial as it may appear – can be held for perceptual experience of rational beings independently from the transcendental argument. As I said, further support for these claims will be given in the following sections and also in Chapter 9, which discusses empirical support for relational conceptualism.

Against a Correctness and Completeness Requirement: More about the nature of perceptual experience on the relational conceptualist theory

Let me emphasize that on the conception developed here perceptual experience does not contain any question of perceiving truely or falsely. Questions of truth only become relevant when what is perceived is converted into representational content, meaning something that is communicable, or rather transmittable. In turn that means that the perceptual relation itself is not transmittable. It cannot be conveyed to someone else, another subject, unless it is transformed into a statement with representational content. Talk about Pia's perceptual experience or the doctor's perceptual experience has to be in the form of a representation, for otherwise we could not discuss it. But Pia's perceptual experience itself is not transmittable, it is only present to Pia. Note that this does not mean that Pia's perception does not involve conceptual capacities. In seeing the grunting four-legged animal her conceptual capacities are operative. She sees something and seeing something means that her conceptual capacities are implied (cf. the Inevitability of Perceiving Something). In other words, perception is agent-dependent and it can only be shared if it is converted into content. It is only if it is converted into content that issues about truth-values become relevant. Note that this does not mean that Pia's experience is not objective. It is still objective because it is of the world.

Travis's observation that "perceiving" is a success word (cf. Travis 2013b, p. 51) has two sides on the relational conceptualist theory. First, perceptual experience is not subject to a Correctness Requirement. If Eliza perceives a pigeon,

---

tent. Unfortunately we had this conversation at a late stage of the manuscript, so I could not follow up on this suggestion. But I encourage readers to follow up on it by reading (Haag 2012) and (Haag 2014) and e.g. (Sellars 1978).

that is what she perceives. Even if the object that Eliza perceives is no pigeon, she has perceived something that was present to her as a pigeon. There is important success in perceptual experience even in cases of misperception. Or more generally: misperception is also a case of perception. Second, perceptual experience itself is neither true or false, it just *is*. It only becomes true or false when it is thought about, or set into a context. Such contexts can consist in other perceptual experiences, in the social world, the world of interaction, or the subject's set of beliefs, i.e. her world-views. Perceptual experience that is thus set in a context is articulated and differs crucially from perceptual experience as described above. The paradigmatic form of articulation is in terms of propositional content.[328]

The most obvious difference between unarticulated perceptual experience and articulated perceptual experience lies in the number of constituents involved: there is not only the object of perception and the perceiving subject, but also the representational content that forms and expresses the representation. The latter introduces issues of veridicality into perceptual experience. I would like to appropriate an observation made by Gareth Evans's on the possibility of error:

> The possibility of error, i.e. questions of truth, only becomes relevant if a judgement is issued subject to the control of agreement – when the speaker is prepared to acknowledge that he is wrong by withdrawing his remark in the face of an incapacity to get others to agree with him, to see things his way.[329] (Evans 1982, p. 294)

---

328 One could also try to conceive of articulation in terms of actions.

329 Yet it has to be noted that I disagree with Evans's set-up surrounding the observation. Evans makes those remarks when he talks about the possibility of error for a subject that notices similarities between objects. Evans distinguishes between the verbal expression of one's reaction to a similarity and a judgment about a similarity. Only the judgment is about the world and only the judgment can be wrong or correct: "'How like his father he is!' constitutes a judgement about the world when it is issued subject to the control of human agreement – when the speaker is prepared to acknowledge that he is wrong by withdrawing his remark in the face of an incapacity to get others to agree with him, to see things his way" (Evans 1982, p. 294). I agree with Evans's description of correctness, but I disagree with his distinction between verbal expressions and judgments. I, too, want to say that only those objects that are "issued subject to the control of human agreement" (Evans 1982, p. 294) can be correct or incorrect. Yet it is counterintuitive to suppose that there could be something like mere verbal expressions that are not "issued subject to the control of human agreement". Even for a mere verbal expression of a reaction there is no reason to suppose that the speaker is not "prepared to acknowledge that he is wrong by withdrawing his remark in the face of an incapacity to get others to agree with him, to see things his way" (Evans 1982, p. 294). In other words, verbal expressions must always be interpreted as judgments.

Two assumptions have been underlying the above observations and need to be made explicit now. First, the actualization of concepts and conceptual capacities in perceptual experience is not subject to a Completeness Requirement, i.e. not all concepts that could be actualized and implied in the perceptual experience have to be actualized and implied in that particular perceptual experience. That is also in line with McDowell's second amendment in "Avoiding the Myth of the Given" (McDowell 2009a, p. 258). Second, it is also not subject to what I have called a Correctness Requirement: the concepts that are actualized in a particular perceptual experience do not have to be correct for the particular case. Nor are they fixed once the perceiver has perceived the scene, but instead can be changed at any given occasion. These assumptions are closely connected. In fact, as will become clear, they are interdependent.

The assumptions also link up with the Inevitability Principle and the Directness of Perceiving. Travis's Problem of Attaining Generality and Problem of Selection rightly mark out that there are always other generalities that could be linked to the instance, and other instances that could be linked to the generality. In other words, different concepts could be applied to an object, and different objects could fall under one concept. Travis's observations are correct, but his objections against conceptualist representationalist theories (Travis 2006, p. 203) do not apply to our account. Given the above rejection of the Completeness Requirement and the Correctness Requirement as well as the rejection of representational content, and in the light of my remarks about associated concepts, Travis's observations just mark a mere fact about perception and perceptual experience. The possibility of applying different concepts to the same object is a possibility that is not actualized in the actual perceptual experience. The subject's perception itself is unambiguous, because it is that subject's perception in that particular situation. The possibility can be actualized in a 'second look', but for this second look, too, it holds that perception is direct and that it is inevitably a case of perceiving an instance.[330] Think again of my remarks about perceiving the duck in the duck-rabbit-figure and the possibility of also perceiving the rabbit in the duck-rabbit-fiture.

One can also put the rejection of the Completeness Requirement and the Correctness Requirement in Travisian terms: I want to say that perception and perceptual experience are occasion-sensitive.[331] There is no fixed set of objects that

---

330 Here again I presuppose Noë's rejection of the snapshot conception of perceptual experience process, e.g. (Noë 2004, p. 35).

331 Here one might consider Benoist's suggestion about occasion-sensitivity and contextualism (fn. 281) and instead put the claim by saying that perceptual experience is contextual, rather than occasion-sensitive. I will still stay with the term *occasion-sensitive* to avoid confusions.

belongs to the scene *simpliciter* and is perceived by each perceiver, because perception and perceptual experience are occasion-sensitive.

These claims about the nature of perceptual experience still face an obvious objection: if it is possible to change, or maybe even 'revise' the selection of concepts actualized in one's perceptual experience, then clearly the actualization of conceptual capacities and concepts must be independent from perceptual experience itself. The actualization of conceptual capacities must be secondary and maybe also at will. Travis would certainly be one to put forward this objection. Remember his example of Uncle Willard's great bittern and what I have called the Argument from New Concepts for Past Experience (Travis 2013c, pp. 245f.): Uncle Willard shows this animal to me and I do not know the concept *great bittern*, nor the species *great bittern*, so I cannot recognize the animal as a great bittern. Later, I acquire the concept *great bittern* and then I think back to that animal which Uncle Willard showed to me and I realize that it was a great bittern that I saw. Travis takes this to suggest that conceptual capacities only figure in my response to what I saw. But – and here I go back to my responses to Martin's Argument from Memory Experience (Section 2.5) – this is a *non sequitur*. From the fact that I can apply a newly acquired concept to previously entertained perceptual experience it does not follow that the previously entertained perceptual experience was devoid of conceptual activity. I still saw the great bittern as an animal. I could have also seen it as a thing which is shown to me by Uncle Willard and which I cannot identify. Those two perceptual experiences involve the actualization of conceptual capacities. The concepts do not exhaust the group of concepts that could be actualized in enjoying this particular perceptual experience, but given our rejection of the Completeness Requirement, there is no need for them to fulfill this demand. One sees that Travis, like Martin, does not understand that the conceptualist theory is concerned with the very possibility of perceptual experience of the world. Their Arguments from Memory Experience and from Past Experience do not show that perceptual experience is independent from the actualization of conceptual capacities.

These observations hold for all perceptual experience of beings endowed with conceptual capacities. And human beings are paradigmatically such beings. Travis's dichotomy of O-seeing and T-seeing albeit false can be used to illustrate the nature of perceptual experience on the relational conceptualist theory. For the sake of clearness I will call the particular perceptual experience of conceptually endowed beings "C-perceiving" and "C-seeing" – but not much hangs on these labels. The following paragraphs so to say make visible a distinct type of perceptual experience in opposition to other types of experience, but really this type of perceptual experience is the only type of perceptual experience for conceptually endowed beings. As I have said, speaking methodological-ly one can say that O-seeing and T-seeing form the background against which C-seeing can be made visible for those who think that there is such a distinction between O-seeing and T-seeing and who also think that there is non-conceptual perceptual experience. But as I have argued throughout this study, there is no non-conceptual perceptual experience and the distinction between O-seeing vs. T-seeing is flawed and so it will eventually be given up.

Carving out the appropriate account of perceptual experience of rational beings

As we have seen, Travis wants to insist that a subject's "parochial capacity for thought" (Travis 2013c, p. 225) does not influence or shape the subject's perceptual experience (see Travis 2013c, p. 225). But throughout this chapter I have been offering support for the claim that Travis's taxonomy of O-seeing and T-seeing does not cover all possible cases of seeing in beings who possess conceptual capacities. In fact the taxonomy must be given up as it builds on a false dichotomy and omits the essential type of seeing for human beings. In this section I will call this type of seeing C-seeing. Note that this additional type of seeing is just one variety of a more general type of perceptual experience. I will mainly talk of seeing, but the same considerations apply for perceptual experience in general.

As I said above, on Travis's conception if a subject sees an object, that is a case of O-seeing. It is a "perceptual accomplishment" (Travis 2013c, p. 238) that consists in the relation between subject and perceived object. T-seeing on the other hand consists in a relation between the subject and a thought, e.g. Eliza sees *that the door is open*. According to Travis, a being who lacks the conceptual capacities for the scene that it sees O-sees the world. He illustrates the claim with the following observation that I have already quoted above:

> What Pia O-sees is precisely what does instance a pig being beneath the oak–nothing short of the pig, as it is, beneath the oak, as it is. Such is what is there to be seen. Suppose she lacked, or failed to draw on, the conceptual capacities just mentioned. She would still O-see what was there to be seen, what in fact instances the generality in question. She would just fail to recognise its doing so. (Travis 2013c, p. 239)

In responding and questioning this illustration, we also again get to the discussion of the difference between the perceptual experience of rational and non-rational creatures. On Travis's theory both a non-rational animal without any conceptual capacities at all and a human being who does not possess the required concept for the object that she perceives enjoy the same type of seeing, namely

O-seeing. But this clearly does not do justice to the perceptual experience of the human being who possesses conceptual capacities. Pia does not "draw on" (Travis 2013c, p. 239) the conceptual capacities needed for seeing the pig in the scene, but that does not entail that she has the same perceptual experience as a non-rational animal that does not possess any conceptual capacities. Travis's description is puzzling: how could a human being's experience be of the same type as the experience of an animal that is incapable of higher level deductions, rationalizations, of that which in Sellars's terminology we might call moves in the space of reasons?

Moreover, remember that Travis himself rejects Peacocke's Argument from Animal Perception by showing that it does not establish that human beings and animals have to have perceptual experience with the same content (i.e. non-conceptual representational content).[332] Travis explains the apparent sameness in experience between animals and humans in terms of sameness in the awareness of the same object, not sameness in the representational content. A cat and I might see a bird in a bush, but that is just an instance of the cat and myself being aware of the same object, the bird in the bush, and not of us sharing the same representational content (Travis 2009, pp. 328f.). It is not clear why those considerations do not also apply to Travis's claim: the apparent sameness in experience by beings that lack the appropriate conceptual capacities is explained by sameness in the awareness of the same object, and not by sameness in the type of seeing, i.e. O-seeing.

At this point already one might be inclined to interrupt the argumentation and put forward a version of the Argument from Animal Perception: it is wrong to say that rational animals and non-rational animals do not enjoy the same type of perceptual experience. Even though we have already discussed the shortcomings of the argument, some readers might still insist on claiming that rational and non-rational animals both have perceptual experience of the world. I understand that this objection may appear pressing, but I still want to postpone discussing it to the next chapter.

If Travis's O-seeing is seeing that is independent of conceptual capacities, and if we want to account for a case of perceptual experience in which the subject lacks a certain appropriate concept, but possesses other concepts and conceptual capacities – as in the above case of Pia who sees a pig beneath the oak,

---

332 Remember: Travis's primary objection against Peacocke's Argument from Animal Perception is that the non-conceptual representational content that thinkers and animals are supposed to share really is conceptual: It still reaches to a range of cases, because it is to be judgeable by thinkers. If the content can be judged by a thinker, it must be conceptual content, content that can be in a *thought*. Thinkers and non-thinking animals could not share this content.

but does not possess the concept *pig* –, and if we want to argue that Pia's case is a special case since Pia is a thinker, we need to augment Travis's dichotomy by adding *a third type of seeing* that covers Pia's case. Note that augmenting Travis's dichotomy also means augmenting any non-conceptualist dichotomy that holds that perceptual experience does not involve the actualization of conceptual capacities – as I have noted Travis is a regular non-conceptualist in this respect, just like other relationists. Now, Pia's case is the case of a human being that possesses conceptual capacities, but lacks a specific concept that is applicable and perhaps most fitting in the perceptual experience of a particular situation. Clearly, Pia's case cannot be covered by T-seeing: she does not possess the concept *pig* and so she cannot be related to a proposition and see *that there is a pig*. Moreover, her seeing the pig undoubtedly is a perceptual accomplishment and thus no T-seeing. But those circumstances do not make her seeing the pig a case of O-seeing. Her perceptual experience is fundamentally different and forms its own variety of perceptual experience. As I have said, I will call this perceptual experience C-seeing or C-perceiving, to distinguish it from O-seeing and T-seeing. Later on I will drop this label because, as I will argue, all perceptual experience in rational beings is C-perceiving and so there is no need for this extra name.

Travis does not see that for Pia's case what I have called the Inevitability of Perceiving Something holds: Pia cannot see the object as nothing in particular, not even as an object, in an act of perception that is supposed to be devoid of conceptual capacities, because that would mean that she does not see the object at all (see above). Second, it is clear that what Pia sees, the object of her perceptual experience, does not fail to instance a generality, it might, e.g., instance the generality *thing*. She might see a thing.[333]

Note that Travis talks of Pia not seeing "the generality in question" (Travis 2013c, p. 239) when she sees the pig but does not possess the concept *pig*. But as I have argued above, not seeing it as instancing "the generality in question" (Travis 2013c, p. 239.) does not mean that one does not see it as instancing any generality at all. The pig, i.e. the object of Pia's perceptual experience, does not instance only one generality and so it is not an insuperable problem if Pia encounters a pig, sees it, but does not possess the concept *pig*.

---

333 One could translate the *Inevitability-Principle* into Travis's terminology. The Inevitability of Perceiving Something is also the *Inevitability of Perceiving an Instance*. Remember that Travis distinguishes generalities (the conceptual) and instances (the nonconceptual): in perceiving an object and thus seeing ____, e.g. *a pig*, I perceive an instance of the generality *pig*. I do not see the generality, but I see the instance of the generality. The conceptualist point is to insist that Pia cannot *not* see the object as instancing a generality. Again, do not be misled by the as-terminology that I have to use in expressing the daim.

In the Problem of Attaining Generality Travis points out that the particular cases do not point towards the generalities to which they belong: "things appearing as they are cannot by itself decide which representation, with just what generality, would represent things as being as they appear" (Travis 2006, p. 203). Travis seems to reject what one might call a conception of perception as divine revelation in ideas. Things do not reveal themselves in perception. On Travis's conception rejecting divine revelation seems to mean rejecting the idea that perception itself reveals anything at all.[334] I think that this conclusion throws out the baby with the bath water and so I want to suggest that one must not read these sentences as saying that the particular instance does not point anywhere, but rather as suggesting that it does not point in only one direction which is the 'right' direction. Rather, there are myriads of generalities to which the instance can point and each generality is right.[335] That is what we should conclude if we take Travis at his word and accept his criticism of representationalist conceptions of perceptual experience. The fact that "... nothing in [the] particulars of the instancing *as such* identifies just what it is it instances – to what range of cases of instancing it belongs, or, more pertinently, what range of cases, to which it might belong, would be instancing *that*" (Travis 2006, p. 200, emphasis in original) does not entail that the particular does not belong to any range of cases, to any generality at all.

For the perceiving subject who possesses conceptual capacities there is no way that she would ever only O-see an object. In other words, there is no way that she would ever have non-conceptual perceptual experience of an object. Her particular capacities are central to her life as a rational being, and once they have been acquired there is no life without those capacities.[336] Thought and perceiving are permeated by the activities of those capacities, whether one calls them 'conceptual capacities' or 'parochial capacity for thought' (Travis 2013c, p. 225).[337] This is the first important stronghold of any conceptualist position.

---

334 The world is only revealed in the subject's response to perceptual awareness (see Section 5.5. and Travis 2013c, pp. 235, 241).

335 Note that if perception is understood as a capacity, there will be further support for the idea of myriads of generalities to which a particular instance can point: A capacity can always be exercised in various ways (cf. Kern 2006, p. 189) and to various degrees of excellence. These variations can be read off from the possibility of numerous generalities pointed to by a particular.

336 Cf. the above appropriation from Moran: Conceptual capacities "infuse and inform [the perceptual experience, N.E.], making a describable difference in the kind of [perceptual experience, N.E.] it is" (Moran 2001, p. 31).

337 Cf. the previous remarks on parochial capacities and conceptual capacities, Section 5.1.

Now, if human beings do not O-see, what type of seeing are they capable of then? Travis's only alternative is T-seeing, but we cannot suppose that for a rational being all seeing is T-seeing. The perception that we are after is a visual accomplishment and T-seeing is no visual accomplishment. In addition, a position that held that all seeing is T-seeing would face well-known worries about whether all seeing is believing, whether T-seeing requires the subject to perceive propositions, etc.[338] Here what I suggest we call *C-seeing* comes into the picture. C-seeing, which we can take to be short for *conceptual seeing*, consists in a conceptually informed relation between subject and object.[339] One example for C-seeing is the above case of the doctor seeing the patient and also Pia who sees the pig.[340] Note that C-seeing is a variety of *C-perceiving* since perceptual experience is not limited to visual perception. One can thus also speak of *C-perceiving* and *C-perception:* epistemically significant perceptual experience is C-perceiving. C-perceiving is both relational and conceptual, i.e. perceptual experience consists in a relation between subject and object, and implies the actualization of conceptual capacities. As I said above, the relation is not just spatio-temporal, but the product of the actualization of conceptual capacities and thus a conceptually informed relation. In what follows the focus will be more on the conceptual element of relational conceptualism, but my remarks will still be explications of *relational conceptualism.*

We can now apply the above characteristics of the nature of perceptual experience to C-perceiving. E. g. C-perceiving itself is neither correct nor incorrect, but can only be correct or incorrect, when the subject acts and puts its C-perception into practice, e. g. in physical or verbal interaction. One who thinks that talk of O-seeing and T-seeing is not mistaken, but instead just has to be completed by the notion of C-seeing would have to say that beings with conceptual capacities, with parochial capacities for thought are capable of C-seeing and T-seeing. About the relation between C-seeing and T-seeing she would have to say that C-seeing and T-seeing can co-occur[341], e. g. Eliza T-sees that there is snow on

---

338 The problems would in effect be those of the "belief acquisition theory" (Fish 2010), so see e. g. (Dretske 1969) for criticism.

339 Cf. McDowell: "the rationality of rational animals informs their perceptual capacities" (McDowell 2010a, p. 248).

340 One might say that beings with conceptual capacities, with parochial capacities for thought are capable of C-seeing *and* T-seeing, but since I argue that the O-seeing and T-seeing-dichotomy is flawed, it would be confusing to express the relation between the two kinds of seeings in this way.

341 Note that I will not discuss how exactly C-seeing and T-seeing co-occur, e. g. whether C-seeing is converted into T-seeing. We might also say that they do not really co-occur, e. g. one option might be to say that what is C-perceived is put in the form of a proposition, or one might say that

the roof, because she C-sees snow on the roof. Note that this possibility for co-occurrence and overlap does not mean that C-seeing is a case of seeing representations, nor that it is a case of propositional perception; perceptual experience is still direct: it is still a case of seeing an object, or, in Travis's terminology a case of seeing an instance.[342] We have also seen this in the example of the doctor seeing her patient; she does not see the patient represented as a patient, but she simply sees the patient (Directness of Perceiving).

As I have indicated above, I am inclined to reject the very taxonomy of O-seeing and T-seeing and so to some extent it is confusing to put forward claims about the relation between O-seeing, T-seeing and C-seeing. But it is a well-earned success if people accept that human perceptual experience is C-seeing, since in accepting C-seeing the most important steps towards a conceptualist theory of perceptual experience have been taken.

I will still briefly discuss the relation between O-seeing and C-seeing, because it will allow me to say more about the nature of C-seeing and to explain why the distinction between O-seeing and T-seeing should be given up. The most important question is whether O-seeing and C-seeing coexist or not, but this question depends on what O-seeing really refers to. In Travis's terminology O-seeing is visual awareness, but as we have briefly noted in the section on Travis's conception of perception, this claim is ambiguous. Look again at the explanation given by Travis. According to Travis, visual awareness is "acquaintance with that which is fit to operate on our sensory transducers (e. g., to form images on retinas). It is awareness of such things as the pig, an episode of snuffling, the pig snuffling, the pig standing just *there* beneath the oak" (Travis 2013c, p. 248, emphasis in original). The ambiguity is this: it is not clear whether Travis wants to suggest that perceptual awareness is the operation of an object "on our sensory transducers" (Travis 2013c, p. 248), i.e. if he talks about the physiological

---

there is an interpretational inferential step between C-seeing and T-seeing. Not much hangs on the question which of the options is appropriate, since for our purposes the mere fact that there is perceptual experience that is C-perceiving and that it is the default perception for thinking beings with conceptual capacities is all that matters. Note that perceptual experience conceived as C-perceiving still consists in seeing objects, i.e. in seeing instancings, and not in seeing representations.

342 Again, as above, conceiving of "seeing K" as "seeing O as K" is misleading. If we framed our conceptualist approach in those terms, it would look as if we assume that perceptual experience involves representational content after all. Remember our above remark about how linguistic constraints might make it appear as if perception does contain a representing intermediary. Again: linguistic constraints do not warrant any conclusions about the nature of perception itself. Such formulations suggest a contrast between the object itself and that which the object is recognized as, but there is no such contrast. The object is perceived – fullstop.

act of perceiving, or whether it is just awareness of the object that also figures in this (additional) operation "on our sensory transducers".

If the first, then O-seeing and C-seeing can coexist, they would just refer to different levels of perception. O-seeing would be 'enabling' (cf. McDowell 1994, pp. 201 f.; McDowell 2010a, p. 250) C-seeing. One interpretation of this enabling-claim could be phrased in terms of the differentiation between the conceptually informed relation and a spatio-temporal relation that I have introduced above. If one takes up this distinction, one might conceive of the O-seeing relation as a mere spatio-temporal relation. This distinction would also lead to a co-existence claim for O-seeing and C-seeing: O-seeing and C-seeing can co-exist because the spatio-temporal relation (O-seeing) is a condition for the conceptually informed relation that constitutes C-seeing. I will say more about the relation between conceptual perceptual experience and its enabling conditions in Chapter 9.

If it is the second interpretation that captures what Travis means, i.e. if O-seeing is supposed to be C-seeing without the conceptual capacities required for the particular scene, then they cannot coexist. On the relational conceptualist conception human beings that have acquired conceptual capacities could not O-see. Or if one puts the relational conceptualist claim in Travis's terminology: there could not be anything like O-seeing for a creature with the parochial capacity for thought. O-seeing would be conceivable only for beings without capacities for thought.

There are also problems for the view that T-seeing is a variety of perceptual experience. It is doubtful whether a relation to a thought is properly called a case of perceptual experience. It seems that such perceptual experience is not perceptual in the same way as 'regular' perceptual experience, e.g. when Pia sees the pig. Of course, these and the above considerations do not defeat the taxonomy, but I think they point to weaknesses that speak in favor of eventually dropping the taxonomy.

The conceptually informed perceptual relation as recognition

A possible explication of the perceptual relation that obtains between a perceiving subject that possesses conceptual capacities and mind-independent objects in the world is in terms of the notion 'recognizing'[343]: the perceiving subject rec-

---

343 Note that recognition here does not presuppose that the object that is recognized has been encountered before. It is not a re-cognition. Another expression that might explicate the relation is 'identification' – it is problematic for its own reasons, e.g. since 'identification' seems to be wedded to 'identity' and seems to be a process that is closer to inferential thinking – but it

ognizes the object.[344] The doctor recognizes the patient. Recognitional capacities can be conceived as a form of conceptual capacities. As we have seen, the notion is common in (non-relational) conceptualist treatments of perceptual experience, e. g. according to the conceptualist, the fine-grained content of experience with a conceptual content can be captured by something like "This is shaped R.", where R is a recognitional concept of a way of being shaped (cf. Peacocke 2001a, p. 250). But as we have seen in Kalderon's theory, recognitional capacities are also used by critics of conceptualism.[345] Travis, too, talks about recognition and recognitional capacities. What he describes as recognition fits perfectly to my (conceptualist) description of perception:

> Pia sees the pig before her eyes. She recognizes what she thus sees as a case of – as instancing – a pig snuffling beneath the oak – a certain generality, a way *for* things to be. Such recognition is what draws on what might rightly be called a conceptual capacity: familiarity with what belongs to the conceptual, with that whose instancing one takes in – grasping

---

can help highlight the message about recognition not presupposing a previous encounter: If recognition did presuppose a previous encounter, it would be like re-identification. But it is not. Instead it is like identification. Another alternative notion might be "categorization", see Section 9.2.

344 It is tempting to call the latter relation an acquaintance relation, because the conceptually equipped perceiver is acquainted with the object that she perceives. But it is inconvenient to use this terminology, because it is inextricably connected with Bertrand Russell's distinction between knowledge by acquaintance and knowledge by description (Russell 1910–11; Russell 1999). Knowledge by acquaintance is based on the perceiving subject's direct awareness, her acquaintance, of the object of perception. On Russell's conception the subject can have direct knowledge of things and direct knowledge of truths (read: propositional knowledge). The former is acquaintance with particulars (sense-data and possibly the subject herself) and with universals. On Russell's sense-datum theory she cannot be acquainted with physical objects and other minds. Direct knowledge of truth is what Russell calls "self-evident truths" (Russell 1999, p. 79), they are that which assert what is given by sense impressions, but they are also logical principles and arithmetic principles, and finally ethical propositions (Russell 1999, p. 79). Both types of knowledge by acquaintance form the basis for knowledge that is derived from them. It is thus potentially misleading to speak of standing in an epistemically significant perceptual relation as being acquainted with the object, because Russell wants acquaintance with things to be logically independent of knowledge of truths. In the first place our epistemically significant perceptual relation is meant to cover the relation to mind-independent objects, too, but it cannot be logically independent of knowledge of truths, i. e. propositional knowledge, because it only obtains if the perceiver possesses conceptual capacities. A subject that possesses conceptual capacities surely at least is equipped to have propositional knowledge and so assuming that the relation that obtains between such subjects and a mind-independent object is logically independent of propositional knowledge cannot be correct on the conceptual model.

345 For an overview of why recognitional capacities might be problematic see e. g. (Peacocke 2001a, pp. 251 f.).

what it is, e.g., for a pig to be snuffling; what makes it recognizable that *this* is a case of it. (Travis 2013c, p. 239)

"Recognition" is recognizing that an object falls under or instances a generality (Travis 2013c, p. 239). Travis distinguishes between two kinds of recognizing: one a "pure cognitive achievement" (Travis 2010e, p. 312), the other a form of acknowledgment. Seeing "that the sun has set" (Travis 2010e, p. 312) is a cognitive achievement, in which you recognize₁ a truth. Judging "that the sun has set" (Travis 2010e, p. 312), is recognizing₂, or rather acknowledging the truth of a truth. In such recognizing₂, *Anerkennung*, a status is awarded to something that one sees. A being capable of such *Anerkennung* is "*equipped* for cognitive *achievements*" (Travis 2010d, p. 227, emphasis in original). The German *erkennen* and *anerkennen* correspond to the distinction which Travis wants to make.

Travis's remarks on recognition are reminiscent of our Inevitability of Perceiving Something. But, of course, our conceptualist conception and Travis's conception do not really co-exist as peacefully as it seems so far: Travis would not say that *either* kind of recognizing is actualized in perceptual experience. More generally speaking, Travis's O-T-seeing taxonomy and his conviction that conceptual capacities are not operative on the level of perception are *incompatible* with our conceptualist conception. This gap becomes particularly clear when we look again at how Travis further analyzes the act of recognizing an object. Recognizing, say, a pig, consists of "two different sorts" (Travis 2013c, p. 239) of capacities: first, "a capacity to tell a pig at sight" (Travis 2013c, p. 239). Second, "a capacity to recognize what counts as something being a pig as so counting" (Travis 2013, p. 239).

The capacity to tell something at sight is a "visual capacity" (Travis 2013c, p. 239). Recognizing "what counts" (Travis 2013c, p. 239) as a pig, on the other hand, is an achievement involving the conceptual and thus is not purely visual – according to Travis, at least:

One cannot recognize a pig *to be* a pig without thereby entering into transactions with the conceptual; without exercising mastery of what the instancing relation relates – so without engaging with thoughts, or drawing on conceptual capacities in the present sense. (Travis 2013c, p. 240, emphasis in original)

Travis wants to align recognizing an object with T-seeing[346]; and this obviously fits his conviction that conceptual capacities are only operative in thoughts. As

---

346 See the following quotation: "[S]eeing *that* the pig is snuffling, so seeing it *to be* snuffling, or muddy, etc. ... is not perceptual. One might see that the pig is snuffling either in seeing the pig

the introduction of C-seeing has shown, conceptualists do not have to say that recognizing is a form of T-seeing. There is nothing like the abyss between perception and the conceptual that Travis seems to fear and so recognizing can be an actualization of a properly visual capacity. The "capacity to tell a pig at sight" (Travis 2013c, p. 239) is indeed a visual capacity, but that does not preclude its implying conceptual capacities. "Tell[ing] a pig at sight" is neither O-seeing nor T-seeing; it is a paradigmatic case of C-seeing – of perceptual experience that is typical for all rational beings, and thus obviously for human beings. Travis thinks that recognizing a pig cannot be O-seeing, because the conceptual is not accessible via the senses (Travis 2013c, p. 240). He thinks that it must be a case of T-seeing, because it is "a matter of recognizing generalities as instanced" (Travis 2013c, p. 240). Such recognition presupposes the possession of conceptual capacities, i.e. access to the conceptual. Acknowledging the existence of C-perceiving opens the way to seeing a way between these two options.

If C-perceiving is perceptual experience that consists in a conceptually informed perceptual relation, and if C-perceiving is a form of recognition, then the conceptually informed perceptual relation can be captured by the term "recognition". So one can conclude that the informed perceptual relation may well be called *recognition*.[347] And since the terminology of C-perceiving is only an aid for explicating the nature of perceptual experience in conceptually endowed rational beings, I now want to formulate the conclusion for perceptual experience of such beings without using the C-perceiving terminology: perceptual experience in rational beings is a conceptually informed perceptual relation. It may be captured in terms of recognition: the subject recognizes the roof. Such perceptual experience is epistemically significant as it can figure as a reason, or reasons, for beliefs.

---

snuffling or in seeing (truffle-hunting) Pia's happy little schottische. Different capacities no doubt are drawn on in each sort of case. But in each case the seeing involves *recognition* of something which need not be recognised for O-seeing. To T-see is to relate to (inter alia) something which is not the sort of thing to be visible, tangible, or etc. – not a possible object of sensory awareness." (Travis 2013c, p. 238, emphasis is original)

347 I have to add one important disclaimer: recognition must not be taken to emphasize that the subject has previously encountered the object of perception, in the sense of 're-cognizing'. Recognition is nothing more than another expression for the direct perception of an object of perception being something, being an instance.

8 Possible Objections against Relational Conceptualism

How does relational conceptualism avoid relationalist arguments?

After I have introduced the notion of *C-perceiving*, and thereby have further explicated epistemically significant perception, there will surely be several critical questions and objections. I will devote the next section to these objections, but the present section is still reserved for a particularly important intermediate step. Let me pause to show that relational conceptualism avoids Travis's anti-representationalist, anti-conceptualist objections.

Let us start with the Problem of Selection. Relational conceptualism avoids this problem by arguing that the selection is implied in being in a conceptually informed relation to the particular object that one perceives. This response does not carry with it issues with the Problem of Incoherent Content since there is no content in perception that could be incoherent. Perception is an informed, epistemically significant relation to the perceived object and not a representation of the world.

At the start of the previous section I have introduced the following objection that McDowell, too, might make (Section 7.3; McDowell 2008c, p. 260) One might think that relational conceptualism cannot really avoid saying that perceptual experience has content. Content enters indirectly via conceptual capacities being implied. The thought seems to be this: if conceptual capacities are implied in perceiving, then perceptual experience must be as general as the conceptual capacities that are implied in it. Perceptual experience thus consists of conceptual content. However, this is a *non sequitur*. Even though conceptual capacities are necessarily implied in perceptual experience, there is no generality in the perceptual experience itself and no conceptual content: the conceptual capacities are actualized in perceiving particulars, objects in the world, and thus in being actualized in perception they are not strictly general anymore.[348] Perceptual experience is a relation between the subject and an object, in which a subject

---

[348] Note that this is also why Brewer's challenges against the Content View do not concern relational conceptualism. Brewer claims that the Content View must have a predicational component in representational content and thus in perception, but it cannot specify the worldly changes that are relevant to truth conditions or changes in truth value. It will always end up not accommodating presentation of mind-independent objects in perceptual experience. There is no such problem for relational conceptualism because there is no predicational component in representational content.

sees the object as something. Note that this argumentation is a version of the negative formulation of relational conceptualism in the previous section (Section 7.3).

These considerations also defuse the Argument from Occasion-Sensitivity that was aiming to show that the conceptual and the nonconceptual (i.e. the particular) are crucially different and that perception can thus not be conceived as conceptual. Concepts are general, and perceived objects are particulars, but saying that perception implicates conceptual capacities does not entail that perceptual experience is in any problematic way general since – again – perceptual experience includes conceptual capacities and the particular perceived objects. These considerations also explain why the Argument from the Particular Perceptual Presence of Objects does not hold against relational conceptualism: relational conceptualism does not say that perception is propositional, or that seeing an object really is *seeing that* there is an object.

I have already explained in the previous section why the Argument from New Concepts for Past Experience fails as an argument against relational conceptualism.[349] The cases that Travis describes – e.g. that after having learned what bitterns look like, where they live etc., a subject is able to go back to her past experience and recognize a bird that she saw as a great bittern – do not tell against saying at the moment of perceiving the bird the subject's perceptual experience was conceptual. The subject did actualize conceptual capacities, these capacities just did not include the concept *great bittern*.

The case of the Transcendental-style Arguments is interesting: Travis argues that in order to show that the nonconceptual, the particular, can bear on the conceptual, the conceptualist would have to assume that there are rational relations between the nonconceptual and the conceptual. It might seem that relational conceptualism does not explain how particulars bear on the conceptual, but rather only presupposes that it does, e.g. in the Inevitability of Seeing Something. Yet this impression is mistaken, and here I can bring together previous arguments and foreshadow arguments that I will introduce in response to critical objections. Relational conceptualism has its own transcendental argument. It holds that we can only make sense of perception being epistemically significant, if we hold that perception is conceptual and object-involving, or as one might say 'objectual'. A tendentious way of formulating this argument is the following: the particular can bear on the conceptual, because perceptual experience *is* having

---

349 The argument also fails against McDowell's "Avoiding the Myth of the Given"-position because – as we have said – McDowell does not want to say that all concepts are included in the content of the perceptual experience (McDowell 2009a, pp. 258 f.).

the particular bear on the conceptual. The point might appear trivial, and in the tendentious formulation is certainly seems trivial, but that is only if one does not see how the argument works and what its motivation is. This response meets the adequacy condition for a theory of the epistemic significance of perception that I have established in the Introduction. It does not privilege the conceptual nor the particular unduly, and also does not entail a problematic rational relation between the particular and the conceptual; rather, it shows that the conceptual and the particular cannot be taken apart in understanding perceptual experience. Perceptual experience is always conceptual *cum* object.

Why is C-perceiving epistemically significant?

Someone who is still critical of this project might admit that conceptual capacities are involved in perception, but object that the mere involvement of conceptual capacities in perception does not show that perception is epistemically significant. This request asks us to show why perceptual experience that is a relation and that implies conceptual capacities is *epistemically significant*, and why exercises of perception, i.e. C-perceiving and C-seeing, are epistemically significant. The notion of perception as a capacity will feature centrally in the discussion of this epistemic character of perception.

Before saying why the perceptual relation 'C-perceiving' is indeed epistemically significant we should again point out what exactly it means for something to be epistemically significant. There are at least two ways of being epistemically significant. First, something that is epistemically significant can be a reason for a belief, it can justify a belief. Second, something that is epistemically significant makes the subject to which it is significant knowledgeable. We can borrow a helpful formulation from Kalderon and say that epistemically significant perceiving "make[s] one knowledgeable of a mind-independent subject matter" (Kalderon 2011, p. 220). It is certainly contested what constitutes knowledge, but it is agreed that knowledge requires – in one way or another – rational grounding. An epistemically significant perceptual relation thus is also distinguished by being a ground, a reason, for knowledge. To some extent the first way of being epistemically significant is fundamental to the second way, and so the second way might be reduced to the first way, but I think it is helpful to make the epistemic function of making a subject knowledgeable explicit and to keep it distinct from simply being a reason for or justifying a belief.

Of course, McDowell's work is the most intuitive place to look for arguments in favor of saying that perceptual experience is epistemically significant since relational conceptualism shares the conviction that perception is epistemically significant with him. The epistemic significance of perception is the central topic of his works. Note that looking for argumentative support in his work does not conflict with the distancing that I have undertaken at the beginning of this chapter: McDowell's conceptualism and relational conceptualism are both committed to explaining the epistemic significance, they only differ in how prominent the task of avoiding the Myth of the Given is in this explanatory project (see Section 3.3).[350]

We have seen in the discussion of the debate between non-conceptualists and conceptualists that one central feature of the appropriate relation between justifier and justified consists in their being rationally related. Clearly such a rational relation is secured if conceptual capacities that essentially include rational capacities are involved in both the justifier and the justified. And this is how relational conceptualism explains that C-perceiving is epistemically significant.

I will, however, not adopt McDowell's exact formulation of "perception as a capacity for knowledge" as it is more circumspect to speak of perception making a subject knowledgeable. The first consideration for this terminological decision is that the term "knowledgeable" makes explicit the potentiality that is central to the relationship between perception and knowledge. Knowledge can be acquired from perception, but even though perception always comes with a view to acquir-

---

350 *Mind and World* (McDowell 1996) explains how it is that perceptual experience can be rationally related to judgments; "Avoiding the Myth of the Given" (McDowell 2009a) and *Perception as a Capacity for Knowledge* (McDowell 2011b) explain how it is that we can acquire knowledge from perceptual experience. As we have seen before, McDowell has the same basic strategy in *Mind and World* and in the newer texts (McDowell 2009a; McDowell 2011b): perceptual experience can be rationally related to judgments and we can acquire knowledge from perceptual experience, because conceptual capacities are actualized in our perceptual experience. Those are the same conceptual capacities that we actively exercise in processes of judging. Since the same conceptual capacities infuse both perceptual experience and judgments, it is plain that perceptual experience can rationally ground judgments. The rationale for the strategy is also the same in the old and the newer conception: since experience and judgment share the same kind of content they are appropriately related, e.g. as justifier and as justified. But we have also seen that the old and the newer position differ in letter: *Mind and World* (McDowell 1996) assumes that the content of perceptual experience and judgments is propositional content; "Avoiding the Myth of the Given" (McDowell 2009a) assumes that the content of perceptual experience is intuitional content and that the content of judgments is discursive content, i.e. only judgments have propositional content. There is also a slight difference in emphasis as regards the role of knowledge: over the years McDowell has started to put more emphasis on the notion of "perception as a capacity for knowledge" (McDowell 2011b, p. 9) rather than 'just' empirical content, judgments and beliefs.

ing knowledge, the potential does not have to be exhausted.[351] The second, related consideration that leads me to talk of being "knowledgeable" is the following: McDowell is right in saying that perception is a way of acquiring knowledge, but his talk of "perception as a *capacity* for knowledge" (McDowell 2011b, my emphasis, N.E.) is potentially misleading. A capacity is exercised well or badly, but the crucial aspect of the relation between perception and knowledge is not whether the capacity for knowledge is exercised well or badly. Rather the question is whether the capacity is used to acquire knowledge or not. Perceptual experience of O can make a subject possess knowledge of O, namely if she exhausts the potential for knowledge that comes with her experiencing O. Eliza can know that there is snow on the roofs from her C-perceiving the snow on the roof, but she can also *not* know that there is snow on the roofs, even though she C-perceives the snow on the roof. Note that the whole sentence could also be formulated with 'perceiving' in the place of 'C-perceiving' – I will soon drop the C-perceiving terminology.

Someone might still insist on asking what it is in conceptual capacities that entails that the perceptual experience of a subject endowed with such capacities is an epistemically significant perceptual relation? How is conceptually informed perceptual experience epistemically significant? Above I have subscribed to McDowell's straightforward answer that I will just repeat here. The capacities that are actualized in perception are the very same capacities that are actualized in epistemic states, and that is why perception can so much as be epistemically significant. I have argued above that perceptual experience in rational beings is perceptual experience that necessarily and inadvertently implies actualizations of conceptual capacities and so by its very nature it is epistemically significant (e.g. cf. my remarks on bundles, diffusion chain and associated content in Section 2.6).[352]

---

351 McDowell alludes to this fact about acquiring knowledge from perception in (McDowell 2009m, p. 159).

352 It is also worth pointing out again that relational conceptualism cannot be rejected by simply questioning the Myth of the Given. Kalderon and Brewer reject the Myth of the Given and yet I have indicated that in explaining how perceptual experience makes one knowledgeable they, too, presuppose that the subject possesses conceptual capacities and actualizes them in its perceptual experience. What matters is that one wants to explain how perception, judgments, beliefs and knowledge are related and then avoiding the Myth of the Given is a by-product. In other words, explaining the epistemic significance of perception is a feat that actually can be undertaken independently of the Myth of the Given. It is only after one has achieved this feat that one finds that one rejects theories that succumb to what Sellars, McDowell and other authors call the Myth of the Given.

Yet, to some extent this answer is not enough. It seems that conceptual capacities are only enabling conditions for the epistemic significance of perceptual experience. So citing conceptual capacities in an explanation of the epistemic significance of perceptual experience seems not enough. Relational conceptualism will be also asked to answer the question of how the epistemic role of perceptual experience shapes out. Or, in other words, how does perceptual experience fulfill its epistemic role? This question is entirely valid and very important, but within the frame of this study I will have to leave it with cursory and general remarks, as any more substantial answer would have to enter into the nature of reasons, the details of reason-giving relations, the normativity of perceptual reasons and other related questions. These additions would overstretch the scope of this book. So let me say only this much. As I have said above, the grounds for perceptual experience taking its epistemic role are laid by perceptual experience implicating the actualization of conceptual capacities and the perceiver seeing objects *as* so-and-so-s, or as one might put it: recognizing them. The implication of conceptual capacities allows for the perceptual intake to figure in reason- and justification-relations since they give the perceiver cognitive access to the object perceived so that she can refer to it in giving a reason.[353] Since conceptual capacities are actualized in perceptual experience the subject can refer to the objects that she perceives in thought and judgment.[354] This observation fits with the claim that the epistemic significance of perceptual experience is manifest in its potential for making the subject knowledgeable. Perceptual experience always has the potential to enable the subject to acquire knowledge about the world. It depends on the subject whether she takes this chance or not.

I will leave open the question of whether the perceptual experience itself is a reason or not, since this question requires and deserves its own thorough treatment. On the one hand, one could say that reasons are propositional in form and thus the perceptual experience itself could not be a reason. On the other hand,

---

353 One might also consider complementing these remarks with a version of what Peacocke calls "informational entitlement" (Peacocke 2005, p. 102). Informational entitlement is an additional source of perceptual entitlement; it consists of background information or informational states that make a certain judgment reasonable. Such information can be found in memory, testimony, and knowledge. Of course, one would have to be careful with not creating an impossible combination of elements from an externalist theory of justification (Peacocke) and a non-externalist theory, such as conceptualism. But I think there might be space to develop the role of background information in relational conceptualism from such a notion as "informational entitlement".

354 For similar considerations that put more emphasis on the objectivity of the thing perceived, see (Lauer 2014, p. 60). I do not subscribe to Lauer's reconstruction as I disagree with his separation between different interpretations of the conceptualist thesis. See also fn. 302.

the perceptual experience can well figure as the 'content' of the reason, as what the reason states (cf. Wingert 2012).[355] For reasons of space limitation I cannot even attempt to take a well-argued for position in this study and thus can only assure the reader that there is room to develop relational conceptualism on this issue.[356]

Perceptual experience as an exercise of the capacity for perception

In the following sections I will emphasize and expound an important aspect of perception that has already been discussed in introducing conceptualism: perception is a *capacity*. This fact is crucial for further explicating relational conceptualism. Perception is a capacity whose exercise leads to perceptual states or episodes. More particularly, it is a perceptual capacity that is manifested in visual, aural, tactile, gustatory etc. experience. One might be tempted to introduce a terminological distinction to capture the difference between perception as a capacity and its exercise, e. g. by reserving *perception* for the capacity and *perceptual experience* for the exercise of the capacity. But that would lead to confusion since most authors use the terms *perception* and *perceptual experience* interchangeably; in writing about the different theories of perception it would thus not be clear whether the terms are used in this technical sense or not. I will therefore mark out explicitly if I talk about the capacity *perception* or the exercises of the capacity by adding that the claim is about the capacity or the exercise.

Perception – you may insert *C-perceiving* here – is a capacity for knowledge, i. e. it makes a subject knowledgeable, because it essentially involves the actualization of self-conscious conceptual capacities.[357] Perception is a capacity for

---

355 See (Church 2010) and (Church 2013) for an account of why we should hold that we can perceive "causal reasons, constitutive reasons, and justificatory reasons" (Church 2010, p. 667). The fact that our perceptual experience comes with an "experience of objectivity" (Church 2010, p. 644) figures centrally in her theory.

356 Mark Schroeder's suggestions for a unified account for inferential and non-inferential evidence are one possible direction that one might want to follow up on. On Schroeder's conception a subject having evidence is "a matter of bearing some presentational attitude ... toward a proposition" (Schroeder 2011, p. 221). And on this understanding of evidence both perceptual experience and belief are fit to be evidence.

357 To be precise, "C-perceiving" can refer both to the exercise of a capacity called "C-perceiving" and to the capacity itself. The capacity *C-perceiving* is a subcategory of the capacity *perception:* It is the shape that perceptual awareness, i.e. perceiving, takes in rational beings endowed with conceptual capacities. When we talk about the perceptual experience of beings with con-

knowledge, because its function 'providing perceptual knowledge' is primary in our understanding how it is possible to have perceptual experience and perceptual knowledge of the world (see Section 2.7). These considerations, of course, can be carried over to C-perceiving. We said that C-perceiving implies the actualization of conceptual capacities: it is direct perceiving and inevitably a case of perceiving an instance. In C-perceiving, too, conceptual capacities are inadvertently exercised, and so C-perceiving is an exercise of capacities. I will now stop talking of *C-perceiving*, since it was just an aid for explicating relational conceptualism. From now on, whenever I speak of *perceptual experience* – unless in some way qualified – I refer to perceptual experience as a conceptually informed perceptual relation.

Important conclusions follow from the above observations about perception being a capacity. If perceptual experience is a manifestation of an exercise of a capacity of rational beings, then there are varying degrees of competence in the exercise of the capacity.[358] The competence of each subject depends on her particular level of expertise. A painter will conceptually grasp many more colors than a biologists. If perception is a capacity, then there are degrees of competence and degrees of expertise in exercising that capacity. Someone who has had the opportunity to train and shape her capacity will be better at exercising her capacity than others. What does that mean in the case of perception?

Let us consider one extreme on the scale of competence and expertise, the expert, to see what follows from this claim. First, the expert, say, a painter, will be less likely to misperceive, i.e. to commit a mistake in exercising her capacity. And, second, the concepts that do appear in the expert's perceptual experience are likely to be more sophisticated or more fine-grained than the con-

---

ceptual capacities such as human beings we may thus say that all perceiving is C-perceiving and all C-perceiving is a case of perceiving. In such exercises of the capacity "perception" an epistemically significant perceptual relation obtains between the perceiving subject and the object of perception. When I C-perceive, I exercise my capacity *perception*. In beings that possess conceptual capacities *perception* thus is a capacity for being knowledgeable. Note that T-seeing is not a manifestation of the capacity *perception*. 'Pia sees that the sun has set' is not a perceptual accomplishment that implies the actualization of conceptual capacities. T-seeing can certainly be the justified basis for knowledge (Travis 2013c), but since it consists in a relation to a proposition it is just not an exercise of the capacity for perception.

358 There is an additional route for arguing that there are degrees of competence in the exercise of the capacity *perception*. I have said that perceptual experience can be captured by the term *recognition* and Travis suggests that recognition is a case of "Competent Experiencing" (Travis 2006). We could thus call perceptual experience of a conceptually endowed being a form of "competent experiencing". For forms of competent experiencing there are certainly degrees of competence depending on the level of skill of the subject.

cepts that appear in a non-expert's perceptual experience. The application to the case of a painter seems fairly straightforward and so let us add an example from auditory perception. Someone who has studied music will recognize a given music piece as an orchestral piece by Brahms, or maybe as the Third Symphony by Brahms and she will be less likely to misperceive the piece (e. g. take a Schumann Symphony to be a Brahms Symphony). Someone who has not studied music will recognize the piece as an orchestral piece, but will not be able to actualize these more fine-grained, 'sophisticated' concepts. I will return to cases of auditory perceptual experience in the last part of this book.

It is also helpful to refer to the analogy that Rödl uses in his rejection of fallibilism[359]. He compares perception as a capacity to a "practical power" like the capacity to juggle five balls (Rödl 2007, p. 151). Here we can use the same analogy to illustrate the two claims about competence and degrees of expertise as regards perception. Concerning a practical power like juggling five balls the first claim ('An expert will be less likely to misperceive.') says that an expert juggler is less likely to fail in juggling the five balls. The second claim observes that an expert juggler juggling five balls is more adept at exercising the capacity. His juggling looks skillful, when my juggling would look amateurish. We are both carrying out the same action, putting the same capacity to practice, but our particular actions differ greatly in style. If we go back to the case of perception, the expert's perceptual experience is more 'accomplished'. The difference in degree does not mean that we have to develop different models in order to account for the particular perceptual experiences of the expert and a non-expert. Both the expert's and the non-expert's perceptual experiences are direct, inevitably perceptual experience of an instance, etc.[360]

The Problem of Selection and of Attaining Generality – again?

An intuitive objection that results from the above claims on perception as a capacity is this: if perceiving is the exercise of a capacity, then it can be exercised correctly or incorrectly and so perceiving has correctness conditions. And so it seems that Travis's Problem of Selection and the Problem of Attaining Generality reappear after all, albeit in a different shape: the relationist conceptualist is forced to determine the correctness conditions of perceptual experience, but

---

359 McDowell's analogy to the capacity of a golfer to sink eight-foot putts could also be used (McDowell 2011b, p 39).
360 Again, of course, the point could be formulated in terms of C-perceiving.

there is nothing in the perceptual experience that determines which correctness conditions are to be met, let alone whether they are met. And if perceptual experience is infused by conceptual capacities, then it is inherently general and does not reach to just one particular instantiation of the general. And so this proposal, too, seems to face the following questions: what selects which conditions are relevant in the particular perceiving? And how is it that the conceptual capacities C1 and C2 are actualized in the particular perceptual experience rather than C3 and C4?

But relational conceptualism can easily do away with this objection, since the first premise is mistaken. On the relational conceptualist theory perceptual experience itself is neither wrong nor false, and neither correct nor incorrect. In cases of misperception, e.g. mistaking a hoverfly for a wasp, there is still what I have called 'a partial success' since the object is present to the subject: the subject sees a hoverfly. The cases are cases of misperception because if one puts them to use or into words, the mistake will likely become obvious. But the perceptual experience is not simply wrong or incorrect. Comparing the case of the capacity of perception to the capacity of playing the piano might help. A person sitting down at the piano, claiming to play the piano, i.e. exercising her capacity to play the piano, will exercise this capacity even if her exercise is bad, e.g. because she plays too many wrong notes or just hammers away at the piano. She still plays the piano – to an important extent. The same holds for perceptual experience: the subject does not actualize her perceptual capacity correctly, but she still actualizes it in a crucial way. In a case of misperception, the perceptual experience is still conceptual, informed, and the object is still present to the perceiving subject. In other words, the opposition is not between correctly exercising one's capacity for knowledge that results in perceiving an object as it is, and wrongly exercising one's capacity for knowledge that results in not perceiving the object at all. If Eliza perceives the wasp and mistakes it for a hoverfly, for a start, she is still right in seeing an insect. In perceiving what she does, Eliza exercises her capacity *perception*, i.e. she is made knowledgeable about objects in the world. The mere exercise of that capacity and the actualization of her conceptual capacities do not require that she perceives things as they really are. Any such implications are secondary. If it turns out that Eliza misperceived the world, we will not be forced to renounce the claim that she has exercised her perceptual capacity for knowledge. Again: the exercise of a capacity can vary in competence and skill and so an unsuccessful exercise of a capacity still amounts to a subject exercising the capacity. The notion of a capacity does not imply that any exercise of it has to be to the utmost standard and result in a success, i.e. in perceiving correctly *and* also acquiring knowledge from one's perceptual experience (Section 2.7).

Moreover, even though I think that the first response does away with the objection, I could add another reply, namely by referring back to the above remarks on the invulnerability of relational conceptualism to the anti-representationalist objections. The most crucial point is this: perceptual experience on the relational conceptualist conception does not represent the world and it does not contain representational content, and this fact already makes Travis's Problem of Selection not applicable to the conception. On the relational conceptualist theory the selection occurs *in* perceiving itself. Of course, there are always other instances and scenes that could be instancings of the generality, but the potentiality is only implicit. The subject's perceptual experience itself is unambiguous, because it is that subject's perception in that particular situation. Again: Perceiving is direct and it is inevitably a case of perceiving something, a case of perceiving an instance. The parallel response holds for the Problem of Attaining Generality: there is no representational content in perceptual experience, there is no intermediate level in perceptual experience at which one might find generalities that have been attained from perceptual experience of the world. Conceptual capacities are directly actualized in perceptual experience, namely in the object being present to the perceiving subject as a particular object.[361]

---

361 It might be objected that this response is just a repetition of the response that Travis attributes to McDowell and that it thus fails for the very same reasons as McDowell's response (Travis 2006, pp. 204f.). Remember: Travis holds that McDowell wants to say that the selection in perceiving is provided by the actualization of conceptual capacities, since the subject must possess the appropriate concepts to perceive the object as *T*. The subject must possess the concept *tapir* for the object to appear to her as a *tapir* (Travis 2006, pp. 204f.). The generality of concepts is taken to correspond to the generality of representation and that means that the selection provided by the concepts that the subject has to possess in order to see the object is the selection that seemed to be lacking in the representational content of the perceptual experience. There is a particular way for things to be, namely "the way things would be where they were as they appeared" (Travis 2006, p. 204) to the subject who possesses the concepts that "enable" the particular perceptual experience in the first place (Travis 2006, p. 204). As I said in Section 5.4 Travis objects that "the way things would be where they were as they appeared" (Travis 2006, p. 204) does not provide truth-conditions for representational content. McDowell's supposed solution is based on a confusion about representations and factive meaning and indicating. Indicating is based on factive meaning, e.g. '*A* factively means *B*.' and that means that *A* indicates *B*. Factive meaning only looks like a case of representing, in fact it is not. First, indicating does not contain the generality of representation. And even though *A* and *B* are "general conditions", which can be instanced in different ways, their generality is different from the generality of representing. The generality is in the two conditions, *A* and *B*, and not in the indicating. The generality of representations, however, is in the representing itself and not just in the object that is represented and the representing entity.

My response to this objection is simple: on my conception perceptual experience does not have representational content, and thus there is no worrying about the relation between factive

There is another objection from Travis's theory that I want to consider briefly. "Effect-representing" is a notion that Travis introduces in order to show that we cannot receive representations or messages directly from nature. Effect-representing is a two-place "relation between [two] historical circumstance[s]" (Travis 2013d, p. 315), e. g. "That teetering rock represents aeons of wind erosion" (Travis 2013d, p. 315). The objects in effect-representing are objects in the world, they are "visible" and they have a "location"; in other words, they are in causal interactions with their surroundings. The possible objection is that the relational conceptualist has all the time only talked about effect-representing. Why would that be a problem? The problem is that if the objection is correct, perceptual experience on our conception is after all representational and not non-representational, relational. We need to examine what Travis has to say about two-place-relations in effect-representation, since relational conceptualism describes perceiving as a two-place relation: the doctor perceives the patient. Eliza sees the snow. In view of Travis's remarks on effect-representing I need to say why this two-place relation is different from the two-place-relation in effect-representing.[362]

The obvious answer to this question is that effect-representing is a form of representation whereas perception is no form of representation (see my claims about the Directness of Perceiving). Perceptual experience is direct, without a vehicle, and so Travis's form "A represents B." does not apply to perceptual experience as relational conceptualists conceive it: the doctor sees the patient, but in perceiving she does not engage in any representing. Also, the two-place-relation in direct perception is fundamentally different from the two-place-relation in ef-

---

meaning, indicating and representing. Of course, if McDowell accepts my interpretation of his conception as dispensing with representational content (Chapters 6 – 8), he will also avoid Travis's objections just as the relational conceptualist does. Since it is not clear that the antecedent is true – remember the passages in which McDowell continues talking of representational content (e. g. McDowell 2008c, p. 260) – I will not make further assumptions about other reactions that he might have to this objection.

362 In Travis's text effect-representing is a problem for representationalists and so there the point of the argument is rather different: according to Travis, the representationalist conception of perception tries to respond to his objections by saying that effect-representing is transformed into allorepresentations. *Representation*, more specifically *allorepresentation* is a three-place relation: A represents B as C (Travis 2013d, p. 319). A is the author of the representation, or the vehicle that does the representing, B is "things being as they are" (Travis 2013d, p. 320), C is "a way for things to be", more precisely, it is the way which the representation claims for things to be. But this attempt at countering Travis's criticism fails because the two types of representing are incommensurable. The relational conceptualist conception is not concerned with this objection, since it does not defend a representationalist position, so I will just leave it out.

fect-representing: it does not consist in a relation between "historical circumstances" and it is not based on any causal relations. The two-place relation in direct perception, i.e. an epistemically significant perceptual relation, or also: recognition, is 'S perceives Q.'.

Again one sees that Travis tries to separate perception and the conceptual, because he seems to worry that perception that includes conceptual capacities is a floodgate to representational content and thoughts in perception and to idealism (Travis 2010a, p. 60; Travis 2013c, p. 257). But this worry is unfounded: linking perception and conceptual capacities only acknowledges the special quality of conceptual capacities of the thinker that human beings are. Actually, as I have said above, it is even impossible to separate perception and the conceptual: there is no nonconceptual without the conceptual; no particular without the general. There might be mind-independent objects, but they would not be part of the nonconceptual if there was no conceptual. In other words, the mind-independent objects would not be particulars if there were no generalities, nothing conceptual, which they instanced.

The Argument from Animal Perception – again?

Above I have briefly noted that the relational conceptualist position might be confronted with a form of the Argument from Animal Perception: it is wrong to say that non-rational animals and rational animals do not have the same type of perceptual experience, since that entails that non-rational animals do not experience the world in the same way that rational animals do. But clearly non-rational animals also experience the world. Conceptual capacities and concept possession do not make a difference to perceptual experience that warrants speaking of different types of perceptual experience. The critic might also add an Argument from Infants' Perception: how do children who do not yet possess a full-fledged conceptual apparatus fit into this conception of perceptual experience?

Someone sympathetic to the relational conceptualist position might question why I am even discussing the Argument from Animal Perception when I have already argued above (Section 2.1) that the argument is not conclusive in the debate between non-conceptualists and conceptualists. Is it going to fare better here? This query is correct, but it is still necessary to discuss such a version of the Argument from Animal Perception since philosophers critical of conceptualist theories (e.g. Peacocke and Burge) will raise an argument of this form. It is a persistent worry that theories of perception do not appropriately account for animal perception (and infants' perception) and so I want to take the worry seriously. The structure of the above objection is such that there is no simple counter-argument to defeat it: it rejects the very foundations and terms of the conceptualist claims, since it argues that conceptual capacities and concept possession do not make a difference to perceptual experience and the epistemic roles it can play. Relational conceptualism argues just that the possession of conceptual capacities is life-changing. But attempting an answer and discussing the argument will once more allow me to further clarify the idea of conceptual capacities in perceptual experience and the conceptualist account of perceptual experience as a relation.

The following summary of the relational conceptualist claims brings out what the Argument from Animal Perception criticizes. Perceiving is a relation between a perceiver and a mind-independent object. There are different types of perceptual relation depending on whether the perceiver possesses conceptual capacities or not or which conceptual capacities she possesses. If the perceiver possesses conceptual capacities, the perceptual relation is an epistemically significant perceptual relation; if the perceiver does not possess conceptual capacities, the perceptual relation is a mere perceptual relation.

A mere perceptual relation is one that yields sensations and sense impressions. An epistemically significant perceptual relation, however, is one that allows for perceptual experience to justify judgments and beliefs and for the subject to acquire knowledge. But why – and that is the question of the Argument from Animal Perception – does the epistemically significant perceptual relation only obtain in subjects that possess conceptual capacities? In response to this question one could repeat McDowell's transcendental argument (Section 2.7), but I will not do that here. Instead I will give a response that allows relational conceptualism to do two things at once: I will use Travis's observations concerning the role of conceptual capacities for thought. With these observations I can offer a response to the critical question and at the same time demonstrate again how Travis's theory fits with conceptualism, and where Travis and conceptualism part ways.

As we have seen, Travis has argued that generalities and particulars, i.e. in his terminology the conceptual (generalities) and the nonconceptual (particulars), are inextricably connected via instancing-relations and reaching-relations. This inextricable connection also means that it is impossible for epistemically significant perceptual relations to obtain without the concurrent possession of conceptual capacities. In other words, the instancing-relation and the reaching-relation both are impossible without conceptual capacities: first, moves in the realm of the general, the realm of the conceptual, are only possible for a subject that possesses conceptual capacities (e. g. rational linkages, deductions, inferences), and, second, the instancing-relation and the reaching-relation both presuppose the possession of conceptual capacities. Thus, according to Travis, conceptual capacities (i. e. parochial capacities) are located in a special web. On the one hand, they are required for moves within the realm of the conceptual. On the other hand, the particular instancing and reaching relations between generalities and particularities identify the general, i. e. the conceptual (Travis 2013c, p. 238). Such identification clearly can only occur in subjects who possess conceptual capacities.

We have seen above that it is at this point that the relational conceptualist theory and Travis's conception part ways. The conceptualist emphasizes that the acquisition of conceptual capacities is a turning point in the life of a being equipped with conceptual capacities, a being that is a thinker. Travis's conception overlooks the impact of the acquisition of conceptual capacities on the life of a thinker. As a thinker one is always capable of reasoning about the world and making moves in the space of reasons. These capacities are not dependent on a fixed set of concepts appropriate for the perceived instance in the world. A thinker is flexible and adept at moving in the space of reasons. If the thinker Pia does not possess the concept *pig*, she will apply other concepts. A being without conceptual capacities will not be able to do that. There is an ineliminable asymmetry between their respective perceptual experience of the pig.

But the Argument from Hyper-Intellectualization – again?

The critic who has raised the version of the Argument from Animal Perception is very likely to be unhappy with the reaction to her objection and my explanations of the relational conceptualist conception. For her, worse comes to worst: the explanations have not calmed her worries, instead they have intensified and joined forces with Burge's Argument from Hyper-Intellectualization (Burge 2003). Not only do we still disrespect non-human animals, I also (still) mis-describe human perception since I over-emphasize human beings' capacity for thought. The conception seems to suggest that human beings are in full control of their cognitive lives, when in fact they are not. This worry also chimes in with Hurley's hyper-intellectualization objection. Hurley criticizes the conceptualist's approach for wanting to understand the human mind. Rather than examining the human being as a thinking being, the conceptualist should start by examining the human being as a being that acts (Hurley 2001, p. 424). In addition, in following Travis (and thereby Frege), we seem to take a chauvinist attitude towards animals: describing them as "locked in" (Travis 2013c, p. 234) suggests that their life is inferior to ours.

There are two responses here. Travis's and Frege's terminology of being "locked in" (Travis 2013c, p. 234) certainly does sound tendentious, but the important consideration really is harmless: it only notes that for non-rational animals what they perceive does not instance a generality (Travis 2013c, p. 234). One might take such descriptions to have an ethical and a normative dimension and draw chauvinist ethical conclusions from them, such as justifying the exploitation of non-human animals in uncountable different ways, but such conclusions are not entailed by the conception itself and thus are not warranted by it. The Argument from Hyper-Intellectualization also reads the remarks on human beings being thinkers and on the acquisition of conceptual capacities as a turning point too strongly. The remarks do not imply anything about full control of cognitive lives. Rather they only take seriously the importance of a human being's particular capacity for thought. It is this capacity which allows a human being to take critical stances, to reflect and consider herself and the world. It is this capacity which makes human beings into persons (cf. Raz 2013, pp. 98 ff.).[363] Being capable of thought, being able to think about the world, and not just encounter it, is distinctive of human beings, and such a capacity does not have to be all-encompassing or omnipotent to be distinctive. Hurley is wrong in holding that the human being as a being that acts is primary. What is central to human beings is that they are capable of thought and that they possess the capacities required for this capability. Note again there is no underlying chauvinism in those lines: there is no need to say that human beings are the only thinkers there are in the universe.[364]

---

363 Joseph Raz' claim that "[r]ationality, namely responsiveness to reasons, is thus constitutive of being persons" (Raz 2013, p. 99) resonates very well with McDowell's views. I think that Raz' insightful remarks about the relation between reason, reasons, rationality and normativity provide excellent material for further explicating McDowell's scarce remarks about conceptual capacities as "responsiveness to reasons as such" (McDowell 2009b, p. 129). Consider e. g. the following considerations that Raz develops: "Roughly speaking we are persons so long as we have rational capacities, and by and large our beliefs and actions are governed by them, which is the same as saying so long as we have beliefs. In brief outline: responsiveness to practical reasons is also constitutive of being a person, for without it there is no action with the intention of doing it" (Raz 2013, p. 98). Unfortunately, it is beyond the scope of this book to spell out how exactly Raz' claims would go together with McDowell's remarks, and I must leave it with promissory note for another occasion.

364 Animals might have conceptual capacities and parochial capacities for thought, but it is an ineliminable fact that – even if they in fact do have thoughts – we are not able to understand their thoughts, simply because they have different parochial capacities. Travis explains this gap as follows: the ascription of thought to another being consists in decomposing the attitude of that other being. We cannot decompose the attitude of a being that does not possess the same capacities as we do because thinking "is an essentially parochial phenomenon" (Travis 2010c,

The influence of conceptual capacities also becomes apparent when one understands that conceptual capacities are not restricted to certain times and parts of human life. They permeate the life of the being that possesses those capacities. Thus we see conceptual capacities in our practices: explaining actions, giving reasons for beliefs, engaging in collective activities, like playing sports. And we see that they are actualized in our perceptual experiences, when we look at the practices that involve our perceptual experiences, most clearly in empirical knowledge and empirical beliefs. Conceptual capacities are part of the particular life-form that being a human being covers and so if we examine the life-form 'human being', we find that there is an epistemically significant perceptual relation.

As a last resort the proponent of the union of the Argument from Animal Perception and the Argument from Hyper-Intellectualization might try to modify her argumentation, while still holding on to her basic claims. She might turn to the Argument from Infant Perception and put forward the following objection: children do not fit with your conception of perception, because they do not possess conceptual capacities and concepts in the same way that adult human beings do. You have to consider whether an infant can stand in an epistemically significant perceptual relation to an object. If you want to say that the epistemically significant perceptual relation only obtains for beings that possess conceptual capacities and concepts, you can either try to insist that infants can stand in such relations to mind-independent objects or you can admit that they do not stand in an epistemically significant perceptual relation to an object.[365] I would thus have to give up my strong emphasis on rational conceptual capacities in the perceptual experience of human beings.

The outlook, however, is not as bleak as the critic wants to suggest. We cannot clearly determine infants' and children's conceptual capacities at different stages in their development and so the obvious response to this objection is to embrace both options.[366] Since children are in a continuous development, in

---

p. 16). Moreover, one would have to deduce the content of the thoughts of non-human animals from their behavior and other related clues, but one can never be really sure whether one makes the right deductions and ascriptions.

365 To be precise, there is another possible option: one could say that the infant stands in an epistemically significant perceptual relation, but it is not a relation to a mind-independent object, but another object, e. g. something along the lines of sense-data. Since I am committed to the empiricist conviction that beings do perceive the external, mind-independent world, it is not advisable to start introducing further, possibly mind-dependent objects. I will thus ignore this option.

366 Of course, one could also give a quick response: it is not clear why the theory of the epistemic significance of perceptual experience should have to account for infants and children. The

some stages of their development they will not stand in epistemically significant perceptual relations to objects, and in some stages they will stand in epistemically significant perceptual relations. We might even allow for saying that those stages can co-occur and overlap.[367] In other words, one cannot determine one singular moment in which a child possesses enough conceptual capacities to count as an adult human being. The acquisition of concepts is gradual, e.g. at one point in its development a child might possess the concept *blue*, but not yet the related concept *colored*. Or it might only possess a proto-concept of *colored*. The crucial point is this: the set of concepts and conceptual capacities of a thinking being gradually becomes more and more complex. At one point simply, its perceptual capacity for being knowledgeable is exercised like in an adult human being. Until then the child develops this capacity and related capacities. And so for the conceptualist it is uncontroversial and unproblematic to accept that children might be taken to O-see, and do not have perceptual experience that is epistemically significant.

---

theory is not meant to cover the perception of rational beings in the making. Nor is it required to explain how human beings are initiated into the community of thinkers with the particular parochial capacities, the conceptual capacities of human thinkers. But as I will argue in the next chapter, dismissive replies such as this one are unsatisfactory.

367 McDowell makes these points, too: In a response to an article by Michael Williams he admits that a child that has not yet acquired color concepts might have nonconceptual "differential shapings of sensory consciousness" (McDowell 2008c, p. 257). But he also adds that the mere fact that a human being has such nonconceptual sensations at one point during its development does not extend to any such conclusions about the consciousness of a human being that has successfully acquired color concepts. In having acquired color concepts the "visual sensory consciousness itself comes to have a conceptual form" (McDowell 2008c, p. 257).

Part IV **Relational Conceptualism and Empirical Science**

9 Broadening the Scope of Relational Conceptualism

9.1 Objections against Conceptualism from Empirical Science

In this final chapter I will look back at the thoughts and consideration that have led to the introduction of relational conceptualism and see where they have led and where they might further lead. The analysis of the traditional debate between McDowellian conceptualists and non-conceptualists has revealed that conceptualism can deal with all standard representationalist non-conceptualist arguments. McDowell has had to make some changes to his theory, but the gist of conceptualism is still the view that perceptual experience in human beings necessarily implicates the actualization of conceptual capacities. The relationist objections leveled against McDowell's conceptualism, however, do not leave the position equally unharmed. Conceptualism manages to reject the relationists' anti-conceptualist considerations, but the anti-representationalist considerations leave McDowell's revised conceptualism in an unstable state. I have thus suggested that relational conceptualism, a position that takes in conceptualist insights as well as relationist insights, is the appropriate theory for explaining how perceptual experience can be epistemically significant. But now, in this chapter, rather than just provide a more detailed summary of the arguments and the argumentation I want to go beyond the previous themes by confronting conceptualism with cases of perceptual experience that have so far been left untreated and empirical work on the nature of perceptual experience. What makes these cases particularly relevant and problematic is that they appear to be incompatible with conceptualism. The first group of cases includes "*unnoticed perception*" (Sieroka 2015, p. 72), the second and third group contains "*unnoticeable perception*" (Sieroka 2015, p. 72): *subliminal perception* (Sieroka 2015, p. 88), and *brain responses* (Sieroka 2015, p. 90). Another important feature of the cases is that they concern aural perception and thus will allow me to say more about how conceptualism applies to other sense modalities. And finally, as I said, in discussing those cases I will also approach a topic that has been avoided so far: the relation between conceptualism and empirical, scientific research on perceptual experience.

I have noted briefly that Burge criticizes disjunctivism and conceptualism for being incompatible with and also ignoring scientific research (Burge 2005, pp. 25 ff.; Burge 2011a, pp. 69 f.).[368] And McDowell offers the complementary re-jection of scientific research on perceptual systems as irrelevant for his project. Empirical science cannot explicate the workings of "perceptual states of perceiv-ers" (McDowell 2010a, p. 250); it can only explicate the states of "perceptual sys-tems" (McDowell 2010a, p. 250) and thus do not get us to "the epistemic signifi-cance of a perceptual experience that consists in having an aspect of objective reality perceptually present to one" (McDowell 2010a, p. 250). The three groups of problematic cases mentioned above allow us to specify Burge's criticism and McDowell's insistence. Burge criticizes McDowell (as well as conceptualism and disjunctivism) for being incompatible with findings about unnoticeable percep-tions. McDowell insists that disjunctivism and conceptualism do not make claims about unnoticeable perception and thus empirical studies on perception would be unhelpful.

In his examination of the relation between time and (un)conscious percep-tion, Norman Sieroka introduces a distinction that is extremely helpful in fram-ing the dispute more clearly and specifying McDowell's conceptualism (Sieroka 2015, p. 124).[369] Sieroka focuses on the nature of auditory perception and distin-guishes three "manifestations of a sound ...[:] (i) the physical sound, (ii) the proc-essed physical sound, and (iii) the perceived sound" (Sieroka 2015, p. 124). The third manifestation of sound is what we would call the actual "hearing experi-ence" (Sieroka 2015, p. 124). Sieroka adds, "My hearing experience is an expres-sion not of the unprocessed but of the processed physical sound" (Sieroka 2015, p. 124). This expression-relation between the second and the third level of per-ception will turn out important for conceptualism's perspective on empirical studies. We will return to it later.

Now, if we transfer this threefold distinction to visual experience, the three "manifestations of" (Sieroka 2015, p. 124) a visual stimulus would shape out like this: (i) the physical visual stimulus, (ii) the processed physical visual stimulus, and (iii) the perceived visual stimulus. On this distinction we can clarify that Mc-Dowell's conceptualism makes claims about the perceived visual stimulus, i. e. the third level, only. Or as McDowell calls it, claims about "perception as a self-consciously possessed and exercised capacity for knowledge" (McDowell

---

368 To be precise, Burge actually criticizes disjunctivism – "Disjunctivism ignores science in specifying ordinary psychological kinds and in doing epistemology. It is a doctrinal and methodological aberration. Philosophical progress will continue to pass it by." (Burge 2011a, p. 71) – but as I have explained in Section 1.3 McDowell's conceptualism – and I take it conceptualism in general – is inseparable from a disjunctivist position and so the criticism applies to conceptualism as well.

369 I am indebted to Lutz Wingert for introducing me to Sieroka's considerations.

2011b, p. 56). Burge and empirical scientists, however, want to make claims about the second level, 'processed physical visual stimulus', too. The question for this chapter thus is this: can conceptualism make sensible claims about the level of 'processed physical visual stimuli'? Note that I will focus on conceptualism, and bracket the issue of disjunctivism, because for relational conceptualism the conceptualist element is more important than its disjunctivist nature. Now, in reply to the question "Can conceptualism make sensible claims about the level of 'processed physical visual stimuli'?" obviously two general answers are possible: *No* and *Yes*. The negative answer 'No.' can be combined with two different additions and the two resulting No-answers fit with McDowell's and Burge's separation views as outlined above:

(a)$_{McDowell}$ 'No, it cannot do that, and it does not want to do that.'

(b)$_{Burge}$ 'No, it cannot do that and that is why conceptualism is wrong.'

In this section I will start describing the initial steps of the affirmative answer *Yes*:

(c) 'Yes, conceptualism can make sensible claims about the level of 'processed physical visual stimuli'.

Before I start with the beginnings of the positive answer, let me briefly say something to those who object that there is no need for me to look at empirical research, e. g. (a)$_{McDowell}$. Is there any need for conceptualism to embrace empirical research? I have already given one reason above. Scientific research on perceptual experience might help us specify the claims of conceptualism. And this reason is based on a more fundamental conviction: empirical science produces knowledge that must not be *per se* excluded from the pool of knowledge from which one develops a theory of perceptual experience – as (a)$_{McDowell}$ in effect does. There is no obligation for us to take in, let alone believe empirical findings, but there is also no reason at all to ignore them. Why should we cut ourselves off from this field of knowledge without even examining its findings? As I said, McDowell offers several reasons why one should do so, and these are certainly valid considerations. E. g. he suggests that the language that empirical scientists use is largely metaphorical and so their findings cannot be transferred to philosophical studies without further ado (McDowell 2010, pp. 249 f.). This and his other related claims certainly contain important truths, but it is nevertheless doubtful whether his separation of examinations of perceptual systems and studies on "perception as a capacity for knowledge" (McDowell 2011b, p. 9) is appropriate, i.e. whether it is really true to the picture and can lead to an apt theory of perceptual experience. I think that this approach is too narrow-minded and I think that relational conceptualism should not follow this strategy. Just as I did in the development of relational conceptualism I will thus separate the claims of conceptualism from McDowell's claims. Conceptualism is simply the claim that conceptual capacities are implied in all perception of beings that possess such capacities and it does not reject the possibility of substantive argumentative support by empirical science.

How conceptualism deals with unnoticed and unnoticeable perceptual experience

On the next pages I will take a selection of Sieroka's examples in order to examine and explicate how conceptualism responds to these difficult cases of perception. We will see that some results can be explained by conceptualism and even support conceptualism. Others might turn out not to concern conceptualism because they are not cases of perceptual experience. Note that since Sieroka focuses on auditory perception, his examples allow me to introduce another complication, namely: what does conceptualism say about other sense modalities than vision? Is conceptualism applicable to other sense modalities at all? That means that if I am able to deal with such complicated examples as Sieroka's cases, I will have achieved two feats. First, I will have clarified the position of conceptualism as regards empirical studies. Second, I will have offered support for saying that conceptualism also applies to other sense modalities than vision.

So let us begin looking at the groups of cases. The first group of cases, unnoticed perceptions, do not concern the disagreement about empirical findings, but they still encompass a type of cases that conceptualists will standardly face. Let us thus start with examining them. Sieroka introduces the following example:

> Assume that a dog is barking outside in my garden. The barking may very well be loud enough for me to notice it, but in fact, being absorbed in reading, say, I do not notice it. Next, assume that my wife is stepping into the room saying 'Look, there's a dog in our garden' which makes me look outside the window, so that I will see the dog and also notice its barking. But something more may happen – something which is phenomenologically much more interesting. I may say to my wife: 'Now that you mention it. I actually heard a dog a moment ago.' (Sieroka 2015, p. 71)

His wife's comment made Sieroka aware both of the dog which is in the garden and of the previous barking. The dog's barking was unnoticed, but it is not unnoticeable (Sieroka 2015, p. 72). Why is this case a problem for the conceptualist? Now, according to Sieroka – and other non-conceptualists will certainly also support his interpretation – this example shows that "somehow or other [he] unconsciously perceived the original barking; somehow or other the barking was perceptually processed without [him] being explicitly aware of it" (Sieroka 2015, p. 71). This observation appears to be a problem for the conceptualist because it looks as if Sieroka did perceive the barking even though he did not actualize any conceptual capacities or did not apply any concepts. But in fact such a case is not a problem for the modified conceptualism that I have developed in this study. The most important reply by this conceptualism – and here it is mostly in line with McDowell's conceptualism – is to insist that not every actualization of conceptual capacities has to be a conscious activity (see e.g. McDowell 2009a, p. 271). Such an activistic notion of the actualization of conceptual capacities befits non-conceptualist views that hold that conceptual activities are only responses to non-conceptual intake (e.g. Brewer 2011, pp. 122, 145), but it does not belong with conceptualism.

Moreover, the different varieties of conceptualism also reject the Completeness Requirement. There is not a concept for every detail of a scene (e.g. McDowell 2009m, p. 320), there is not a unique corresponding word for every concept (McDowell 2009m, p. 320) and not all concepts that can figure in one's perceptual experience have to figure in the actual experience (McDowell 2009a, p. 258). But most importantly, in addition, it is not clear whether Sieroka's conclusion against conceptualism really follows from his example. His description of the event basically is this: 'Yes, I heard the dog, but I did not notice it until my wife alerted me to it.' But from this observation it does not follow that his perceptual experience, albeit unnoticed, was not conceptual. All that follows is that it was not conscious: he heard the dog barking – that means that he did actualize conceptual capacities. He did actualize them in hearing the dog barking; that was just the point of the Inevitability of Perceiving Something (Section 7.3). It is not clear that a case of unnoticed perception necessarily tells against conceptualism. I think that one can argue that the same reactions would hold for other cases of unnoticed perception. Think, e.g., of the example that I have discussed in the Argument from Memory Experience (Section 2.5): I go talk to my colleague in her office, but I do not notice the new book on the table. When I go back to my office I happen to realize that the new book was on her table. Again it is not clear why that tells against me actualizing my conceptual capacities, e.g. the concept *book*, or my capacity for recognizing books that are published by that particular publishing house in perceiving the book. I did not notice the book, but if I had seen it, then I would have seen it as *a book* or as *a book published by that very important publisher of philosophy books*.

At the end of this study I can thus again emphasize the following general observation: conceptualism is not identical with claiming that only concepts, i.e. distinct abstract entities, are applied in perceptual experience; we should take McDowell's talk of conceptual capacities seriously. When conceptualists in the tradition of McDowell say that conceptual capacities are actualized in perceptual experience they mean conceptual capacities understood as "responsiveness to reasons as such" (McDowell 2009b, p. 130) and not just the sterile, abstract application of concepts. Sieroka's summary of conceptualism is also helpful for emphasizing this point. He understands conceptualists as holding that "intentional states are composed of concepts as their inferentially relevant constituents" (Sieroka 2015, p. 45). But conceptualism is not appropriately captured by this claim; and this should be especially clear after McDowell's "Avoiding the Myth of the Given" and at the end of this very book. I have introduced relational conceptualism and this conceptualism certainly does not make any claims about concepts being constituents of intentional states, as e.g. perceptual states, it says that conceptual capacities, including concepts, are implied, activated, actualized in perceptual experience.[370] We can always know that conceptual capacities are implicated in perceptual experience. When a subject can give and understand reasons and base those reasons on her perception, she will have actualized conceptual capacities in her perceptual experience. Of course, these remarks about conceptualism and about perceptual experience not being intentional states that are constituted by concepts are also complemented by the relational side of the conceptualism that I have been developing in this book.

This first group of cases of unnoticed perception is still very much concerned with things that we could see if we did focus on them. Let us move to more difficult cases of "subliminal perception" (Sieroka 2015, p. 88), i.e. cases of presentation that "is below the threshold of awareness" (Sieroka 2015, p. 88). One example for such subliminal perception is the presentation of a modified version of the Müller-Lyer-Illusion. The perceiver is presented with two equally long lines; the characteristic angles at the end of each of the two lines, however, are presented below the threshold of awareness. In this set-up, too, the perceiver sees the two lines as different in lengths, just as she does in the normal case, in which the angles are presented "super-threshold" (Sieroka 2015, p. 89). Sieroka concludes that "[t]his suggests that the angular lines are unconsciously per-

---

370 In Crowther's terminology this would be an interpretation of conceptualism as making a claim about the constitution of the content of perceptual experience, or in Heck's terminology a state view of conceptualism. Cf. (Heck 2000, p. 485) and (Crowther 2006, p. 249).

ceived and do influence the perception of the length of the lines" (Sieroka 2015, p. 89).[371]

So what does conceptualism have to say about subliminal perception? The first answer is straightforward. Subliminal perception is concerned with the second level of perception, the level of processed visual stimuli, but conceptualism only makes claims about perceived visual stimuli. It might seem that one can also respond by referring to the conceptualist rejection of the Completeness and Correctness Requirements, but that response would confuse the levels that we have carefully distinguished with the help of Sieroka. The Completeness Requirement, the Correctness Requirement and also the claim that not every detail of perceptual experience must be captured by a corresponding concept (see above) are claims about the third level, the level of perceived visual stimuli.

Yet this first response might leave one unsatisfied because it seems evasive and the question still is whether conceptualism really can say anything substantial about the second level. I will follow a remark by Sieroka in answering this question. As I mentioned above, Sieroka suggests that the second level and the third level are related by an expression-relation (Sieroka 2015, p. 135). Therefore I want to examine whether conceptualism has something to say about this relation and thereby say something substantial about the second level. The third group of cases, brain responses, will be relevant for this attempt. But before we get to this group and the second level, we should discuss an example of subliminal auditory perception, since one aim of this chapter was also to show that conceptualism is applicable to cases of auditory perception.

Sieroka includes a very interesting study by Daniel Levitin. People can "sing ... pop songs at, or at least very near, its actual absolute pitch" (Sieroka 2015, p. 90) even though they are not absolute listeners, i.e. they are not able to give the name of the tone that they hear (Levitin 2008, pp. 149–154). Sieroka takes the study to "strongly suggest that not only 'absolute listeners' process the auditory feature pitch adequately on an absolute scale" (Sieroka 2015, p. 90). "[E]veryone perceives absolute pitch, but most people only do so *unconsciously and non-conceptually*" (Sieroka 2015, p. 90, my emphasis, N.E.). These findings are then extended to hearing mistakes in "a music performance" (Sieroka 2015, p. 90). "[N]early everyone is able to detect certain uncommon features or slips in a music performance, although most of the time he or she may be unable to name them" (Sieroka 2015, p. 90). And Sieroka comes to the following surprising conclusion: "the difference between listeners is not so much that

---

371 Another related phenomenon is, obviously, blindsight.

only some of them have an auditory memory[372] or exhibit a certain fineness in hearing, it is only that most of them lack the appropriate concepts for putting certain acoustic features into words" (Sieroka 2015, p. 90, footnote added, N.E.). On this construal the listeners who are not absolute listeners do not have the same awareness as absolute listeners, but they can still mark out mistakes and express them in their behavior. According to Sieroka, this, too, is a case of subliminal perception that speaks against conceptualism (Sieroka 2015, p. 90).

Yet again, one can justifiably say that these findings do not tell against the conceptualism supported in this book. Sieroka seems to think that conceptualism would have to say that hearing a mistake means that one possesses the concept that corresponds to the very mistake and captures its details, but it is not clear why conceptualism should be committed to such a strict claim. The subject might actualize her capacity for recognizing the simple song "Jingle bells" and then she will hear the mistake; if asked about her experience, she will say that something was wrong, say, in the chorus, e.g. by saying that something was wrong 'in the middle bit'. That is all that the conceptualist wants and claims. Why should she even say that the subject actually needs the concept that applies to the particular acoustic feature to actualize her conceptual capacities in her auditory perception?[373] Yet this answer is again concerned with the third level of perception, and so now we really need to move on to examine the relation between the second level, neural activity, and the third level, perceiving.

One striking example for a brain process at the second level, the level of "processed physical sound" (Sieroka 2015, p. 124) is *mismatch negativity* (MMN). Mismatch negativity is a brain response that only occurs for auditory perception, but not for any other sense (Sieroka 2015, p. 141).[374] More particularly it is "a negative difference in the auditory evoked response" (Sieroka 2015, p. 141).

---

372 Levitin says more about "auditory memory", but I will have to bracket this element here. For more, see (Levitin 1994; Levitin/Rogers 2005).

373 There are other questions that one might ask about this study, e.g. is the ability to sing a pop song at its actual pitch the same as the ability to "accurately name the absolute pitch of a sound" (Sieroka 2015, pp. 89–90) one hears? And more generally: why should 'normal' listeners be judged according to the standard of the absolute listener? This claim would seem to presuppose an underlying continuity between normal listeners and absolute listeners when in fact it is conceivable that their auditory perception differs radically. It might be better to align relative listeners and 'normal listeners'. I will not be able to discuss this and related questions here as they would lead us away from the theme of this final chapter. But an examination of Levitin's studies (Levitin/Rogers 2005) might turn out insightful for conceptualism and thus deserves to be pursued in another context.

374 For the particularities of MMN and its advantages for research see (Näätänen 2000).

One can detect this brain response when a subject perceives a sequence of sounds that is interrupted with a non-matching sound, a "deviant" (Sieroka 2015, p. 141). E.g. the subject hears a string of repeated piano tones which is interrupted by another piano tone, e.g. DDDDDFD. The F "evoke[s] an MMN" (Sieroka 2015, p. 141). MMN consists of two sub-processes: "regularity formation" (Sieroka 2015, p. 144), in which the subject hears a regularity in the tones, and "deviance detection" (Sieroka 2015, p. 144), in which the subject hears the tone that deviates from the regularity. Note that MMN is not conscious and is not noticeable. Sieroka suggests that the deviance detection is "the physiological analog of an unnoticeable perception" (Sieroka 2015, p. 148). He explains that the

> findings [on MMN] suggest that auditory cortical functions can process sensory and categorical information in a kind of single manner and that the abstracted auditory features are not necessarily conceptually accessible and sometimes not even behaviourally discriminable. (Sieroka 2015, p. 143)

MMN is a candidate for a "pre-conceptual state" (Sieroka 2015, p. 148). It also occurs in sleep (Sieroka 2015, p. 143) and in coma, more specifically, a few days before the patient regains consciousness (Näätänen/Tervaniemi/et al. 2001, p. 284). Yet, it is important to note that the regularity formation-side of MMN is "highly context- and attention-dependent" (Sieroka 2015, p. 144) and so MMN does not really precede *all* attention. Rather, what matters is that "the MMN is elicited without focused attention" (Sieroka 2015, p. 262 fn. 22). Note also that the amplitude of an MMN "depends on long-term experiences and cultural background" (Sieroka 2015, p. 142). For example, in one study in which Finnish speakers were presented with a string of Finnish vowels of one phoneme that was either interspersed with Finnish vowels from another phoneme or with Estonian vowels from another phoneme their MMN for the Finnish vowels was significantly higher than for the Estonian vowels (Näätänen/Lehtokoski/et al. 1997; Näätänen/ Tervaniemi/et al. 2001; Sieroka 2015, pp. 142f.).[375]

But even though MMN is a candidate for a "pre-conceptual state" (Sieroka 2015, p. 148), really, it is not a problem for the conceptualist. In fact, if interpreted correctly, it rather seems to speak in favor of conceptualism. Brain responses "are physical states or entities which are statistically correlated with [certain] perceptual states" (Sieroka 2015, p. 95) and as we have seen they are dependent "on long-term experiences and cultural background" (Sieroka 2015, p. 142); they

---

375 The Finnish vowels that made up the primary row are also Estonian vowels and so for Estonian speakers the enhancement of the MMN was equal for both kinds of interspersed vowels (cf. Näätänen/Lehtokoski/et al. 1997, p. 433; Näätänen/Tervaniemi/et al. 2001, p. 286).

are thus connected to conceptual capacities of the perceiving subject. That seems to count in favor of conceptualism. The brain response MMN was supposed to show that perception is independent from conceptual capacities, but if MMN is also dependent on context, "long-term experiences" (Sieroka 2015, p. 142) and the subject's background, MMN is not independent from conceptual capacities. As we saw, context etc. are even said to influence the amplitude of the MMN. That is an invitation for conceptualism to say how MMN is compatible with talk of conceptual capacities being actualized in perceptual experience.

As I said, Sieroka holds it against conceptualism that apparently "auditory cortical functions can process sensory and categorical information in a kind of single manner and that the abstracted auditory features are not necessarily conceptually accessible, and sometimes not even behaviourally discriminable" (Sieroka 2015, p. 143). But when one looks at the flipside of this objection one sees that it is not clear that it really impedes conceptualism. The positive claim behind the objection is that the "abstracted auditory features" (Sieroka 2015, p. 143) are conceptually inaccessible. This claim can be understood in two ways. On the first understanding it is easy for conceptualism to respond to it by raising the following question: how could we even understand these "abstracted auditory features" (Sieroka 2015, p. 143), let alone, detect and examine them if they were conceptually inaccessible? Note that this response presupposes that the second and third level of perception are interlocked (without saying more about the exact nature of this connection).

The second interpretation allows more detailed responses. On this interpretation the conceptualist is faced with abstracted auditory features that the subject cannot hear *even* if she does pay attention to them (Sieroka 2015, p. 143). In response the conceptualist can choose one of the following two options or even offer both. She might point out that she does not argue that every brain process is expressed on the level of perception and so not every brain process needs to be captured by conceptual capacities. Partial conceptual inaccessibility would thus be no problem. Or, second, she might suggest that there are ways of indirect conceptual accessibility, e. g. via the EEG; and so the abstracted auditory features might be indirectly recognizable.[376] In addition, the conceptualist can give another more general response by confronting the critic with an important question: are abstracted auditory features that the subject cannot hear even if she does pay attention to them cases of perceptual experience at all? Can they even speak against conceptualism as a theory of perceptual experience?

---

376 Cf. Sieroka on Husserl's remarks on the existence of retention and protention (Sieroka 2015, pp. 178 ff.).

It is clearly worth pursuing all three answers. They all require conceptualism and the critic to further examine and specify the relation between the level of perceived sense impressions and processed sense impressions, e.g. neural activity. There is, for example, some promising indication that the position of conceptualism can make substantial claims – even concerning MMN. When "the deviation is above the perceptual threshold, the amplitude of the MMN is often found to be correlated with discrimination accuracy" (Sieroka 2015, p. 143, and cf. Kujala/Kallio/et al. 2001; Näätänen 2000). This correlation might point towards an expression-relation between neural activity and perception in cases in which perception is above the threshold of awareness.

This is also why the following possible objection against the above considerations does not stick. One might object that I have just explained how conceptualism can deal with empirical challenges, but that this is not relevant to neuropsychological work itself. There is no pay-off for such empirical experimental work from my replies, let alone from the conceptualist theory itself. But my above remarks about possible connections between MMN and conceptual capacities suggest that this objection is mistaken. These remarks indicate ways how there can be valuable interactions between conceptualism and empirical neuropsychological works. Taking into account the perspective of a theory that is not based on neuropychological methods and findings can help neuropsychologists see which conclusions are warranted and which are too quick. Of course, my conclusions about the influence of conceptual capacities on MMN might also be too quick, but I think they are on the right track and considering them seriously will certainly allow conceptualism and neuropsychological research to take important steps. They might, e.g. be the starting point for understanding the expression-relation between the different levels of perceptual experience.[377]

9.2 Support for Conceptualism from Empirical Science

Promising support for conceptualism comes from research conducted by Nancy Kanwisher and Kalanit Grill-Spector. In a paper from 2005, Grill-Spector and Kanwisher claim to show that object detection and object categorization are consistently linked: "as soon as you know that [the object] is there, you know what it is" (Grill-Spector/Kanwisher 2005, p. 152).[378] They thus reject the traditional

---

377 For more focused analyses of auditory perception in particular, see e.g. (O'Callaghan 2007; O'Callaghan 2014; Leddington 2014).
378 I am grateful to Robyn Repko Waller for making me aware of this paper.

model of visual object recognition (Grill-Spector/Kanwisher 2005, p. 152) that we will call the two-step model. According to the two-step model, object detection and object categorization are separated, i.e. the subject first singles out the object ("object detection", Grill-Spector/Kanwisher 2005, p. 152) and then perceptually categorizes the object ("object categorization", Grill-Spector/Kanwisher 2005, p. 152). In terms of the debate about conceptual capacities in perceptual experience we can say that Kanwisher and Grill-Spector reject the non-conceptualist 'response view' of concepts as a response to input that Brewer, Travis, Kalderon, Peacocke, and many others defend. The two-step model of object recognition thus can also be regarded as a psychologist's version of non-conceptualism.

I think that Grill-Spector and Kanwisher's studies may be taken to reveal that object detection and object categorization are consistently linked: if detection fails, categorization success is only at chance level and vice versa (Grill-Spector/Kanwisher 2005, p. 157). Also, detection and categorization are consistently equal in "processing time" (Grill-Spector/Kanwisher 2005, p. 156). If we put their findings in terms of the debate about conceptualism, we can say that they show that visual perception involves the actualization of conceptual capacities; it is immediately conceptual. Their research thus speaks in favor of the Inevitability of Perceiving Something.

Let us see how Grill-Spector and Kanwisher get to their conclusions. In their studies they examined three processes: object detection, object categorization and object identification. In object detection tasks the participants were asked to report whether a gray-scale photo contains an object or not (Grill-Spector/Kanwisher 2005, p. 153). In object categorization-tasks the participants were asked to categorize the objects in the pictures at a basic level, e.g. *car, house, flower* (Grill-Spector/Kanwisher 2005, p. 153). Object identification tasks were "within-category identification-tasks" (Grill-Spector/Kanwisher 2005, p. 153): The participants had to discriminate exemplars from a particular subordinate level category (e.g. *Jeep*) from other members of the category (Grill-Spector/Kanwisher 2005, p. 153). In all experiments the participants' detection performance and their categorization performance consistently had same accuracy, and identification performance was always lower (Grill-Spector/Kanwisher 2005, p. 154). In addition, subjects did not need more processing time for object categorization than for object detection. Identification, however, took significantly longer than either detection or categorization (Grill-Spector/Kanwisher 2005, p. 154). These results give evidence against the two-step model of visual object recognition since they suggest that object detection and object categorization are consistently linked. If the two-step model was correct, then accuracy would have to be independent for detection and categorization.

The most important experiment to support the claim that there is a direct linkage[379] between detection and categorization was this: the participants were shown two images, each followed by a masking stimulus. For the detection-categorization-relation they were first asked in which interval the object appeared and then whether the object was a car or a face. For the detection-identification-relation they were first asked in which interval the face appeared and then whether the face was Harrison Ford or someone else. For the detection-categorization-relation the participants' performance in categorizing was significantly better in successful detection cases, and correspondingly their detection performance was significantly better in successful categorization (Grill-Spector/Kanwisher 2005, p. 157). "[S]uccess on each task predicted success on the other task" (Grill-Spector/Kanwisher 2005, p. 157). In other words, for a significant number of participants it held that when the participants were right in saying that there was an object, they were also right in categorizing the object; and conversely, when they were right in categorizing the object, they were right in detecting that there was an object.

For the detection-identification relation there was no such result. Generally, the participants' detection performance was significantly higher than their identification performance and, more importantly, identification performance depended on detection performance, whereas detection performance did not depend on identification performance (Grill-Spector/Kanwisher 2005, p. 157). These results suggest that detection and categorization are consistently linked; detection and identification however are not (Grill-Spector/Kanwisher 2005, p. 157). As Grill-Spector and Kanwisher put it: detection is prior to identification and "identification occurs after the category has been determined" (Grill-Spector/Kanwisher 2005, p. 158).

Now, how do these findings support a conceptualist theory of perceptual experience? Remember, I said that conceptualism is a position that claims that perceptual experience of human beings that is epistemically significant – as is all perceptual experience of human beings – presupposes possession of conceptual capacities and directly implies the actualization of those conceptual capacities in perceptual experience. Of course, Grill-Spector and Kanwisher's findings do not say anything about epistemically significant perceptual experience, but they can be taken to support the claim that conceptual capacities are directly actualized in perceptual experience. We can conceive of the conceptual capacities that we have been talking about as the expressions of the categories that are ap-

---

379 I will not be able to say more about the 'linkage' at this point since that would be part of the project of further spelling out the details of the expression-relation (Sieroka 2015, p. 177).

plied in the (process of) categorization. Remember also again Sieroka's remarks on the expression-relation (Sieroka 2015, p. 135). And then what these results show is that detecting an object is concurrent with knowing what kind of object it is – at least on a very basic level – and thus with the actualization of conceptual capacities.

Finally, Grill-Spector and Kanwisher also tentatively suggest that object detection and object categorization involve the same mechanism. That, too, would be welcomed by the conceptualism developed here. One could try to say that what Grill-Spector and Kanwisher call "the same mechanism" being involved in object detection and object categorization are actualizations of conceptual capacities. And so in effect both object detection and object categorization involve the actualization of the same conceptual capacities. As it stands Grill-Spector and Kanwisher's research does not offer more than initial support for the claim that visual perceptual experience is immediately conceptual, but there is also no denying that there *is* such initial support.

Conceptualism and developmental psychological theories on conceptual development

Even though I have just suggested that one should read Grill-Spector and Kanwisher's findings as favorable for conceptualism, at the same time it has to be admitted that there are objections against Grill-Spector and Kanwisher's methodology that one must not ignore. Susan Carey puts forward such an objection. She holds that categorization behavior should not be used to build a theory of concepts, because categorization behavior does not allow one to distinguish between the concepts themselves and one's knowledge about entities that is used in the categorizations. As Carey puts it: there is a mix up between *concepts* and *conceptions*. Conceptions are the "beliefs that we hold about the entites that fall under a concept" (Carey 2011a, p. 123; see also Carey 2009, pp. 497 f.).[380] And if one examines categorization behavior in order to understand concepts, one is unable to distinguish the beliefs about entities that fall under concepts from the concepts under which the entities fall.

This seems to pose a problem for Grill-Spector and Kanwisher because they clearly base their conclusions on the categorization behavior which they exam-

---

380 For a prominent application of the distinction between *concept* and *conception* in political philosophy see Rawls's distinction between the concept *justice* and a conception of justice (Rawls 2009, p. 9).

ined in the experiments. But a conceptualist might reply by accepting the mix up between concepts and conceptions. This is exactly how it should be, since concepts and conceptions cannot be clearly separated. Moreover, she might add that this objection against the method of Grill-Spector and Kanwisher does not speak against its helpfulness for substantiating conceptualism. Carey's point only concerns theories that want to develop a psychological theory of concepts, and conceptualism is not after a theory of concepts. It is a theory of epistemically significant perceptual experience, and that includes claims about the role that concepts play in perceptual experience, but does not require a theory of the psychology of concepts. I have to leave it at these brief and evasive remarks on this important issue, since saying anything more substantial about it would require saying significantly more about psychological methodology, and I cannot provide this in the present context.

But I still want to stay with Carey for a moment and give more details of her theory of concepts. There are several reasons for that: first of all, Carey proposes a psychological theory that is aware of the different functions of the term *concept* in psychology and philosophy and other areas, and her aim is not just to explain concepts, but also their function in thought (Carey 2009, p. 487). I will soon say what she means by "concepts". Second, Carey is not just aware of the different functions of the term, but also brings them together. Her focus is on psychological studies, but that does not mean that she is blind to philosophical considerations (Carey 2009, pp. 489 ff.). Most importantly for this book, her theory can be read as containing support for central conceptualist claims. Her aim certainly is not to defend a conceptualist theory of perceptual experience – but rather to explain the acquisition and development of concepts – and yet several of her claims and considerations speak in favor of conceptualism. Her theory thus may be taken to speak against McDowell's outright rejection of psychological findings. And, finally, her theory is also fitting for this final part as her understanding of representations is one of *mental representations*. Remember, I have included this interpretation of the term "representation" in the Introduction, but have hardly touched upon it since then. So now is the time to talk about concepts as mental representations. Carey's book is extremely rich and includes an impressive number of studies on the details of concepts, concept acquisition, conceptual development, etc., but since we are at the end of this book my overview and the considerations following it will have to be cursory. I can thus only start to indicate how conceptualism might be compatible with and profit from engaging with psychological work on concepts.[381]

---

381 Of course, I cannot even attempt to actually discuss Carey's theory in this context. For a set

Carey's aim is to explain the "human capacity for conceptual representation" (Carey 2009, p. 3) that is amazingly complex and spans from such concepts as *red, object, number* to complex concepts like "*evolution, electron, cancer, infinity,* or *galaxy*" (Carey 2009, p. 3). As I said, on her theory concepts are "mental representations" (Carey 2009, p. 4), "units of thought, the constituents of beliefs and theories" (Carey 2009, p. 5). Her theory of conceptual development is thus set within the context of a "dual theory of conceptual content" (Carey 2009, p. 5; Block 1986, Block 1987): conceptual content is determined by reference – the causal connections between the concepts, i.e. mental representations, and the entities they refer to – and its internal conceptual role, i.e. "how the representation functions in thought" (Carey 2009, p. 5). That also means that she argues against prototype theories of concepts, internalist theories of concepts, radical concept nativism, pure information theory, and empiricist theories (Carey 2011a, pp. 122f.). It is unfortunate that I have to be swift here, but the details would be for another book, and so I will just say that empiricist theories are her particular target. They claim that all concepts are built from sensory representations (e.g. Locke 1975), but clearly this cannot be right, as it does not work for most concepts, e.g. such as *cause* or *good* (Carey 2011a, p. 114). Her alternative suggestion is that concept development is not just based on perceptual primitives, but also significantly based on conceptual primitives, so-called "core cognition". Those primitives are conceptual and yet innate (e.g. Carey 2009, p. 67). Carey identifies three domains for core cognition: causal and spatial representation of "middle-size, middle-distant objects" (Carey 2009, p. 449), the representation of agents, their goals, communicative interactions, etc. (Carey 2011a, p. 114), and representations of numbers (Carey 2011a, p. 114). Core cognition in general has representations that "cannot be reduced to perceptual or sensorimotor-primitives" (Carey 2009, p. 67) and plays a conceptual role. It thus has conceptual content. Note that core cognition is not exclusively conceptual, e.g. it is not the conceptual content from which scientific theories are created (Carey 2009, p. 22), but as Carey argues, there are important continuities, as well as discontinuities, between the different levels of cognition (Carey 2009, p. 24). The representations of core cognition are created by "innate perceptual input analyzers" (Carey 2009, p. 67) that "compute perceptual representations" (Carey

---

of objections from psychologists and philosophers, as well as Carey's replies, see Issue 3 of *Behavioral and Brain Sciences* (2011, Vol. 34). Burge also provides a short comment (Burge 2011b, p. 125), but I think that he misunderstands Carey's theory, as Carey, too, makes clear in her reply (Carey 2011b, pp. 154f.).

2009, p. 448).[382] Again, for details I will have to refer you to Carey's texts, but before I give you quick examples let me briefly note why a relational conceptualist does not have to be uncomfortable with integrating such a theory that talks of representations. The representations that Carey talks about are mental representations, we are not anymore at the level of any linguistic representations that are too general. She talks about brain states. Let me just give some quick examples: perceptual input analyzers can analyze, e.g. "color, pitch, or bumber" (Carey 2009, p. 451). And young chicks have "an innate perceptual analyzer that specifies what a conspecific looks like" (Carey 2009, p. 17). And finally, another important explication: when Carey says that core cognition is innate, what she means is that the capacities are not the result of any learning process.[383] More particularly, the "input analyzers that identify [the] referents [of the representation] are not the product of learning" (Carey 2009, p. 115).[384]

You might already start to see, why Carey's work is indeed interesting to the conceptualist. She basically provides material for undermining the Argument from Animal Perception and the Argument from Infant Perception because she breaks down the sharp distinction between conceptual and non-conceptual. For the Argument from Infant Perception the central insight is that innate core cognition is conceptual and this core cognition is part of the very perceptual process in all human beings, no matter what their age, so the conceptualist theory of perceptual experience is on to something right. Of course, the core cognition of an infant is not identical to the core cognition of an adult, so its conceptual-ness will not be recognizable in the same way as the conceptual-ness of adults' core cognition, but it is still conceptual. For the Argument from Animal Perception her findings are equally interesting. I have cited the example of an innate input analyzer in young chicks, and indeed, Carey holds that non-human animals and human beings both have core cognition. Overlap and paral-

---

382 The representations that are thus created are iconic, i.e. "the parts of the representation represent parts of the entities that are represented by the whole representation" (Carey 2011a, p. 116).

383 Carey cites interesting considerations for why she may say that the input analyzers are innate even though she only refers to studies with infants of two months or older. For the details see (Carey 2009, pp. 453–456; Carey 2011a, p. 115).

384 I cannot here say anything about several central features of Carey's theory, e.g. she argues that conceptual development in infants shares essential features with conceptual development of theories (Carey 2009, Chapter 11). Or she makes insightful observations about discontinuities in conceptual development (Carey 2009, Chapters 8–9; Carey 2011a, pp. 117–120) and theories of concepts in general (Carey 2009, Chapters 12–13). They are crucial for her goal of explaining the human capacity for creating complex, abstract concepts, but they are not essential to the book – at least not at this stage – and so I have to leave them out.

lels between the core cognition of non-human animals and human beings, especially infants, certainly exist and this overlap might be what in their responses to the Argument from Animal Perception McDowell (and Brewer) called "substantial continuity" (McDowell 2009b, p. 133) between non-human animals and humans. This response might thus appear to be less hand-waving. At this point you might wonder whether Carey's findings are really all that helpful, more particularly whether they provide evidence for conceptualist claims based on transcendental arguments. This is an important question, but I would like to postpone it.

Let me instead first say more about why Carey can be taken to support a conceptualist theory of perceptual experience. She explains that object representations of infants are conceptual because their representations of objects ("object-files", Carey 2009, p. 70) are not reducible to perceptual primitives and are "inferentially interrelated with other representations that themselves cannot be reduced to sensory primitives" (Carey 2009, p. 103). Remember, these two features, i.e. they "cannot be reduced to spatiotemporal or sensory vocabulary" (Carey 2011a, p. 114) and they play a "rich, central, conceptual role" (Carey 2011a, p. 114)[385], are what makes the representations have conceptual content.

Carey bases all of the above claims on interpretations of a vast amount of studies and findings, and I cannot possibly do justice to this rich background. But let me point to one experiment that is, again, very interesting for conceptualism. Actually Carey introduces the experiment in the context of discussing whether the representational system of 12-month-old infants bases object-individuation on object properties or object kind-sortals, but for us another point is relevant here. In the experiment adults see "an unfamiliar irregularly shaped black plastic object [emerge] from behind a screen and [return], followed by an unfamiliar, spherical, green fuzzy object" (Carey 2009, p. 268) and Carey reports that "adults would represent this event in terms of different objects even if they had not encoded them as a telephone and a tennis ball – indeed, even if they had never seen telephones and tennis balls before" (Carey 2009, p. 268). Ten-months olds fail to distinguish these objects (Carey 2009, pp. 267f.), but as I said, I am not interested in this developmental observation. Instead, I hope, the description of the adults' perceptual experience in the experiment has rung a bell: the description of adults' perceptual experience, of course, fits perfectly to the conceptualist principle that I have called the Inevitability of Perceiving Something. Even if the adult does not assign a certain kind concept to the object, she perceives the objects as distinct and individuates it. Carey does not

---

385 Such a "rich, central, conceptual role" (Carey 2011a, p. 114) also manifests itself in their role in "working memory models", decisions leading to actions, etc. (Carey 2011a, p. 114).

say more about this particular element of the experiment, but such findings are certainly interesting to follow up on.

Finally, Carey's work also supports the close link that McDowell's conceptualism and conceptualism in general find between concepts, conceptual capacities and language. She explains that language acquisition and conceptual development are intimately related: "the representations in core cognition support language learning, providing some of the meanings that languages express" (Carey 2011a, p. 117). And, in turn, language learning makes "representations more salient or efficiently deployed" (Carey 2011a, p. 117). E.g. in experiments verbal labels facilitated object individuation by infants – they were able to individuate objects three months earlier than infants for whom the objects were not verbally labeled (Carey 2009, p. 270 f.; Xu 2002).[386]

I am well aware that these observations will not wow non-conceptualists nor critics of conceptualism and they will certainly not make them change sides. But if one looks at the main issue and the starting point of this chapter, one sees that these observations are not too bad. Remember that I started with two negative answers to the question "Can conceptualism make sensible claims about the level of 'processed physical visual stimuli'?" Both Burge and McDowell, a non-conceptualist and a conceptualist, thought that conceptualism is incompatible with empirical work on perceptual experience – McDowell saying that it should not have anything to do with it, and Burge suggesting that it (or rather disjunctivism) is defeated by empirical findings. I had set out to show that there are good grounds for saying that the affirmative Yes-answer is the right one – "Yes, conceptualism can make sensible claims about the level of 'processed physical visual stimuli'." And I think that my discussion of Sieroka's work on auditory perceptual experience, Grill-Spector and Kanwisher's study and the brief visit to Carey's theory of concept development do support that this affirmative answer can be worked out. That is why these considerations should not be regarded as unimportant or even scoffed at.

There is however one important proviso. Above I have postponed the question of whether Carey's findings can support a conceptualist theory that is based on transcendental considerations such as McDowell's, Kern's and Rödl's. The same question, of course, also appears for Grill-Spector and Kanwisher's findings and my dealings with MMN etc. But now I have to fess up to it, and I will do that by biting the bullet. I think that it is true that the empirical findings cannot support a conceptualist theory that feeds itself from transcendental con-

---

386 For consequences of this, see (Carey 2009, pp. 277 ff.) and also more generally, Chapter 7 "Language and Core Cognition" in (Carey 2009).

siderations, but I think that this is not all there is to conceptualism. It should have become clear throughout this book that I do not think that McDowell's strictly transcendental conceptualism is the right way to go for a theory of epistemically significant perception. I have argued that he is on the right track for explaining epistemic significance of perceptual experience, but in order to do justice to the perceptual component one needs to embrace central relationist insights. Moreover, conceptualism must be formulated in terms of conceptual *capacities* being actualized in perceptual experience and this formulation also leads to the introduction of conceptualist principles, such as the Inevitability of Perceiving Something. A conceptualist theory thus defined can also accept empirical support for the claim that concepts, conceptual capacities, rational capacities and logical capacities are integrated into perceptual processes. It will be able to put forward the following two theses:

(1) Conceptual capacities must be implicated in perceptual experiences in order for perceptual experience to be epistemically significant.

(2) Empirical psychological work suggests that conceptual capacities play central roles in the perceptual experience of human beings.

Of course, if one thinks that philosophical claims cannot be substantiated, supported or defeated by scientific, empirical findings, one will not be interested in the studies that I have cited as supporting conceptualism and one will also reject the second claim of conceptualism. One will argue that scientific studies can never account for perception as a self-conscious capacity – that would be the McDowellian line.[387] But I think that such a restrictive view about which evidence can provide arguments for philosophical theories – in this case the view that scientific findings are unfit as arguments for philosophical theories – is misled. As I said at the beginning of this chapter one would be ill-advised to ignore this vast field of research. Philosophers should not blindly accept all empirical work that is conducted, but they also should not reject all empirical work as inherently irrelevant. Rejecting all empirical work means impeding one's own considerations and excluding oneself from scientific discourse about how things are in the world, in our case about human perceptual experience. I hope that this chapter has started to show how philosophical theories and empirical findings can be brought together for mututal support. And I hope to have presented compelling support for the claim that there are two central conceptualist theses of relational conceptualism, of a theory of epistemically significant perceptual experience.

---

387 Thanks to Sebastian Rödl for asking me to be more precise here.

9.3 Roots and Routes for Relational Conceptualism to Trace

Relational conceptualism will have to further spell out and determine its relation to at least two other theories that are evidenced by empirical studies. Michael Tomasello's developmental psychological work on human thinking and John Campbell's relationist theory. Tomasello's work might provide conceptualism with detailed findings and claims about the acquisition of conceptual capacities in human beings. The starting point for this elaboration lies in the following claim: human capacity for collective intentionality is the basis for particularly human thinking, communication and cooperative action, i.e. the capacity for collective intentionality distinguishes human beings as beings that can communicate and act together from other non-human animals (Rakoczy/Tomasello 2008, pp. 403 ff.; Tomasello 2008, pp. 2 ff.; Tomasello 2014, pp. 3 ff.). The basis for this capacity lies in the biological set-up of humans, it is in their nature. But in order for a human being to actually develop this capacity she has to be brought up in a human community (Tomasello 2002, pp. 68 ff.; Tomasello 2014, p. 6). Tomasello's observations concerning human thinking promise to be fruitful for explicating and substantiating the thesis that conceptual capacities are necessarily actualized in human perceptual experience.[388]

The case with Campbell is more tricky, but also very important for the relational element in relational conceptualism. Campbell develops a relationist, non-representational conception of perception that wants to explain the fact that "[i]t is experience of the world that puts us in a position to think about it" (Campbell 2002, p. 1) and yet at the same time his argumentation is *non-conceptualist* (e.g. Campbell 2002, pp. 120 – 124). Campbell's work would thus have to complement the previous discussions of Travis's and Brewer's rejection of conceptualism. Campbell argues that perceptual experience understood as "conscious attention" (Campbell 2002, p. 10) explains how we can so much as identify objects and refer to them in demonstratives. Conscious attention makes conceptual thought and action in the world possible (Campbell 2002, p. 114). Campbell's remarks on "underlying information-processing systems" (Campbell 2002, p. 5) in the subject's brain are particularly relevant to relational conceptualism. A relational conceptualist would have to examine Campbell's explanations of "high-level visual processing of the visuomotor system" (Campbell 2002, p. 5) as the basis for conscious attention and also his explanations on visual selection processes (Campbell 2002, pp. 28 ff.), because he takes those processes to explain how "experi-

---

388 For considerations about how McDowellian conceptualism and Tomasello's theory can be brought together see (El Kassar 2008).

ence of [one's] surroundings provides [one] with knowledge of what is there" (Campbell 2009, p. 648). His project – if successful – thus explains how "experience of the world is a way of grasping thoughts about the world" (Campbell 2002, p. 121) by looking at underlying processes of the visual system. The details of this approach will be relevant for any attempts at further developing relational conceptualism, be it as a supporter or as an opponent.

Finally, for another route that relational conceptualism should take up, I would like to go back to the Introduction. There, I have indicated that one problem in the field of theories of perceptual experience is the term *representation* itself, or more particularly the fact that its particular meaning in the different contexts and theories is not clear. I have referred to Hannah Fenichel Pitkin's study on *representation* in the realm of political philosophy as a possible role-model (Pitkin 1967). A study of "representation" in the philosophy of perception would have to look at recent developments involving representationalism, intentionalism, relationism etc. It would have to extend the topic, e. g. by discussing aesthetic experience, and it would have to examine related terms like *representational content, content, sensation*. Another central focus should be on subject matter and the motivation of the different theories of perceptual experience. I have limited the scope of my study to epistemically significant perceptual experience, claiming that all perceptual experience of rational beings such as humans is epistemically significant. This limitation has also determined my adequacy condition for a theory of perceptual experience – it was supposed to do justice to perceptual experience and to its epistemic role. Other theories limit their approaches by taking cases of epistemic crisis as test cases: how does the theory deal with the everpresent possibility of epistemic crisis? Can it offer one account that explains both epistemic crisis and normal perceptual experience? Yet other theories aim at unified accounts that explain both human and non-human perceptual experience. Each approach has its advantages, but I continue to find it most interesting to start from a practice, in this case, from the fact that our perceptual experiences work as reasons for beliefs and judgments, and to see what philosophy has to say about it. At the end of this book it is certainly clear that it has a great deal to say about it. And I hope that this book, as every good book, is really only the beginning; it is an invitation to go back and rethink our concepts, conceptions, and how we think about the world.

References

Aristoteles (1995): *Über die Seele (De Anima)*. Hamburg: Felix Meiner Verlag.

Aristoteles (2009): *Metaphysik*. Hamburg: Felix Meiner Verlag.

Ayer, Alfred J. (1969): *The Foundations of Empirical Knowledge*. London: Macmillan.

Ayers, Michael (2002): "Is Perceptual Content Ever Conceptual?". *Philosophical Books* 43. No. 1, pp. 5–17.

Ayers, Michael (2004): "Sense Experience, Concepts and Content. Objections to Davidson and McDowell". In: Ralf Schumacher (Ed.): *Perception and Reality. From Descartes to the Present*. Paderborn: mentis, pp. 239–262.

Bain, David (2009): "McDowell and the Presentation of Pains". *Philosophical Topics* 37. No. 1, pp. 1–24.

Berkeley, George (1998): *A Treatise Concerning the Principles of Human Knowledge*. Oxford: Oxford University Press.

Bermúdez, José L. (2003): *Thinking Without Words*. Oxford: Oxford University Press.

Bermúdez, José L. (2009): "The Distinction between Conceptual and Nonconceptual Content". In: Brian McLaughlin/Ansgar Beckermann (Eds.): *The Oxford Handbook of Philosophy of Mind*. Oxford: Oxford University Press, pp. 457–473.

Bermúdez, José L./Arnon Cahen (2015). "Nonconceptual Mental Content". In: Edward N. Zalta (Ed.): *Stanford Encyclopedia of Philosophy (Spring 2015 Edition)*. URL = <http://plato.stanford.edu/archives/spr2015/entries/content-nonconceptual/>.

Bernstein, Richard J. (2002): "McDowell's Domesticated Hegelianism". In: Nicholas H. Smith (Ed.): *Reading McDowell*. London: Routledge, pp. 9–24.

Bertram, Georg W./David Lauer/Jasper Liptow/Martin Seel (2008): *In der Welt der Sprache. Konsequenzen des semantischen Holismus*. Frankfurt am Main: Suhrkamp.

Block, Ned (1986): "Advertisement for a semantics for psychology". In: Peter A. French (Ed.): *Midwest Studies in Philosophy*. Minneapolis: University of Minnesota, pp. 615–678.

Block, Ned (1987): "Functional role and truth conditions". In: *Proceedings of the Aristotelian Society* 61. pp. 157–181.

BonJour, Laurence (2013): "Epistemological Problems of Perception". In: Edward N. Zalta (Ed.): *Stanford Encyclopedia of Philosophy (Spring 2013 Edition)*. URL = <http://plato.stanford.edu/archives/spr2013/entries/perception-episprob>.

Brandom, Robert B. (1994): *Making It Explicit: Reasoning, Representing, and Discursive Commitment*. Cambridge, Mass.: Harvard University Press.

Brewer, Bill (1999): *Perception and Reason*. Oxford: Oxford University Press.

Brewer, Bill (2001): "Replies". *Philosophy and Phenomenological Research* 63. No. 2, pp. 449–464.

Brewer, Bill (2005): "Perceptual Experience Has Conceptual Content". In: Matthias Steup/Ernest Sosa (Eds.): *Contemporary Debates in Epistemology*. Oxford: Blackwell Publishing, pp. 217–230.

Brewer, Bill (2008): "Perception and Content". In: Jakob Lindgaard (Ed.): *John McDowell: Experience, Norm, and Nature*. Oxford: Blackwell Publishing, pp. 15–31.

Brewer, Bill (2011): *Perception and Its Objects*. Oxford: Oxford University Press.

Burge, Tyler (2003): "Perceptual Entitlement". *Philosophy and Phenomenological Research* 67. No. 3, pp. 503–548.

Burge, Tyler (2005): "Disjunctivism and perceptual psychology". *Philosophical Topics* 33. No. 1, pp. 1–78.

Burge, Tyler (2011a): "Disjunctivism again". *Philosophical Explorations* 14. No. 1, pp. 43–80.

Burge, Tyler (2011b): "Border crossings: Perceptual and postperceptual object representation". *Behavioral and Brain Sciences* 34, p. 125.

Byrne, Alex (2001): "Intentionalism Defended". *The Philosophical Review* 110. No. 2, pp. 199–240.

Byrne, Alex (2003): "Consciousness and Nonconceptual Content". *Philosophical Studies* 113, pp. 261–274.

Byrne, Alex (2005): "Perception and Conceptual Content". In: Matthias Steup/Ernest Sosa (Eds.): *Contemporary Debates in Epistemology*. Oxford: Blackwell Publishing, pp. 231–250.

Byrne, Alex (2009): "Experience and Content". *The Philosophical Quarterly* 59. No. 236, pp. 429–451.

Byrne, Alex/Heather Logue (2008): "Either/or". In: Adrian Haddock/Fiona Macpherson (Eds.): *Disjunctivism: Perception, Action, Knowledge*. Oxford: Oxford University Press, pp. 57–94.

Byrne, Alex/Heather Logue (Eds.) (2009): *Disjunctivism : Contemporary Readings*. Cambridge, Mass.: MIT Press.

Campbell, John (2002): *Reference and Consciousness*. Oxford: Oxford University Press.

Campbell, John (2008): "Sensorimotor Knowledge and Naïve Realism". *Philosophy and Phenomenological Research* 76. No. 3, pp. 666–673.

Campbell, John (2009): "Consciousness and Reference". In: Brian McLaughlin/Ansgar Beckermann (Eds.): *The Oxford Handbook of Philosophy of Mind*. Oxford: Oxford University Press, pp. 648–662.

Carey, Susan (2009): *The Origin of Concepts*. Oxford: Oxford University Press.

Carey, Susan (2011a): "Précis of *The Origin of Concepts*". *Behavioral and Brain Sciences* 34, pp. 113–124.

Carey, Susan (2011b): "Author's Response". *Behavioral and Brain Sciences* 34, pp. 152–167.

Cassam, Qassim (2009a): *The Possibility of Knowledge*. Clarendon: Oxford University Press.

Cassam, Qassim (2009b): "Knowing and Seeing: Responding to Stroud's Dilemma". *European Journal of Philosophy* 17. No. 4, pp. 571–589.

Church, Jennifer (2010): "Seeing Reasons". *Philosophy and Phenomenological Research* 80. No. 3, pp. 638–670.

Church, Jennifer (2013): *Possibilities of Perception*. Oxford: Oxford University Press.

Clarke, Thompson (1965): "Seeing Surfaces and Physical Objects". In: Max Black (Ed.): *Philosophy in America*. London: George Allen and Unwin, pp. 98–114.

Collins, Arthur W. (1998): "Beastly Experience". *Philosophy and Phenomenological Research* 58. No. 2, pp. 375–380.

Conant, James (2012): "Two Varieties of Skepticism". In: Günter Abel/James Conant (Eds.): *Rethinking Epistemology 2*. Berlin, New York: Walter de Gruyter, pp. 1–73.

Crane, Tim (1988): "The Waterfall Illusion". *Analysis* 48. No. 3, pp. 142–147.

Crane, Tim (1992): "The Nonconceptual Content of Experience". In: Tim Crane (Ed.): *The Contents of Experience*. Cambridge: Cambridge University Press, pp. 136–157.

Crane, Tim (2013): "The Given". In: Joseph K. Schear (Ed.): *Mind, Reason, and Being-in-the-World: The McDowell-Dreyfus Debate*. London: Routledge, pp. 229–249.

Crane, Tim (2014). "The Problem of Perception". In: Edward N. Zalta (Ed.): *The Stanford Encyclopedia of Philosophy* (Winter 2014 Edition). URL = <http://plato.stanford.edu/archives/win2014/entries/perception-problem/>

Crowther, Thomas (2006): "Two Conceptions of Conceptualism and Nonconceptualism". *Erkenntnis* 65. pp. 245 – 276.

Davidson, Donald (1982): "Rational Animals". *Dialectica* 36, pp. 317 – 328.

Davidson, Donald (1991): "On the Very Idea of a Conceptual Scheme". In: Donald Davidson: *Inquiries into Truth and Interpretation*. Oxford: Clarendon, pp. 183 – 198.

Davidson, Donald (1992): "A Coherence Theory of Truth and Knowledge". In: Ernest LePore (Ed.): *Truth and Interpretation*. Oxford: Blackwell, pp. 307 – 319.

Davidson, Donald (2001a): "A Coherence Theory of Truth and Knowledge". In: Donald Davidson: *Subjective, Intersubjective, Objective*. Oxford: Clarendon Press, pp. 137 – 153.

Davidson, Donald (2001b): "Rational Animals". In: Donald Davidson: *Subjective, Intersubjective, Objective*. Oxford: Clarendon Press, pp. 95 – 105.

Davidson, Donald (2001c): "Thought and Talk". In: Donald Davidson: *Inquiries into Truth and Interpretation*. Oxford: Clarendon, pp. 155 – 170.

Davis, Wayne (2005): "Concepts and Epistemic Individuation". *Philosophy and Phenomenological Research* 70. No. 2, pp. 290 – 325.

deVries, Willem (2011). "Wilfrid Sellars ". In: Edward N. Zalta (Ed.): *The Stanford Encyclopedia of Philosophy (Fall 2011 Edition)*. URL: <http://plato.stanford.edu/archives/fall2011/entries/sellars/>.

deVries, Willem/Timm Triplett (2000): *Knowledge, Mind, and the Given*. Indianapolis/ Cambridge: Hackett Publishing Company.

Dorsch, Fabian (2011): "The Diversity of Disjunctivism". *European Journal of Philosophy* 19. No. 2, pp. 304 – 314.

Dretske, Fred (1969): *Seeing And Knowing*. Chicago: University of Chicago Press.

El Kassar, Nadja (2008): "Erste und zweite Natur – Zu John McDowells Begriff der Bildung". In *Lebenswelt und Wissenschaft. XXI. Deutscher Kongress für Philosophie – Sektionsbeiträge*. URL: <http://www.dgphil2008.de/fileadmin/download/Sektionsbei traege/05 – 1_El_Kassar.pdf>

El Kassar, Nadja (2011): "Das Argument der Tierwahrnehmung als Schlüssel in der Debatte um begriffliche Wahrnehmung". *XII. Deutscher Kongress für Philosophie*. Ludwig-Maximilians-Universität München. URL: <http://epub.ub.uni-muenchen.de/12616/>.

El Kassar, Nadja (2013): "Primitive Normativität als Antwort auf Saul Kripkes Regelfolgen-Skeptiker?". In: Miguel Hoeltje/Thomas Spitzley/Wolfram Spohn (Eds.): *Was dürfen wir glauben? Was sollen wir tun? – Sektionsbeiträge des achten internationalen Kongresses der Gesellschaft für Analytische Philosophie e.V.* Online-Veröffentlichung der Universität Duisburg-Essen (DuEPublico). URL: <http://duepublico.uni-duisburg-essen.de/ servlets/DocumentServlet?id=31200>, pp. 39 – 46.

Evans, Gareth (1982): *The Varieties of Reference*. Oxford: Clarendon Press.

Fish, William (2010): *Philosophy of Perception. A Contemporary Introduction*. London: Routledge.

Fodor, J. (1998): *Concepts. Where Cognitive Science Went Wrong*. Oxford: Oxford University Press.

Forman, David (2008): "Autonomy as Second Nature: On McDowell's Aristotelian Naturalism". *Inquiry* 51. No. 6, pp. 563 – 580.

Frege, Gottlob (1971): "17 Kernsätze zur Logik". In: Gottfried Gabriel (Ed.): *Schriften zur Logik und Sprachphilosophie aus dem Nachlass*. Hamburg: Felix Meine Verlag, pp. 23 f.

Frege, Gottlob (1918–1919): "Der Gedanke". *Beiträge zur Philosophie des deutschen Idealismus* 2. pp. 58–77.

Gadamer, Hans-Georg (1990): *Hermeneutik I. Wahrheit und Methode*. Tübingen: Mohr.

Gadamer, Hans-Georg (2004): *Truth and Method*. London: Continuum.

Gaskin, Richard (2006): *Experience and the World's Own Language: A Critique of John McDowell's Empiricism*. Oxford: Oxford University Press.

De Gaynesford, Maximilian (2004): *John McDowell*. Cambridge: Polity Press.

Genone, James (2006): "Concepts and Imagery in Episodic Memory". *Anthropology and Philosophy* 7. No. 1/2, pp. 95–107.

Ginsborg, Hannah (2006a): "Aesthetic Judgment and Perceptual Normativity". *Inquiry* 49. No. 5, pp. 403–437.

Ginsborg, Hannah (2006b): "Empirical Concepts and the Content of Experience". *European Journal of Philosophy* 14. Vol. 3, pp. 349–372.

Ginsborg, Hannah (2006c): "Kant and the Problem of Experience". *Philosophical Topics* 34. No. 1–2, pp. 59–106.

Ginsborg, Hannah (2011): "Perception, Generality and Reasons". In: Andrew Reisner/Asbjørn Steglich-Petersen (Eds.): *Reasons for Belief*. Cambridge: Cambridge University Press, pp. 131–157.

Glock, Hans-Johann (2010): "Concepts: Between the Subjective and the Objective". In: John Cottingham/Peter Hacker (Eds.): *Mind, Method and Morality: Essays in Honour of Anthony Kenny*. Oxford: Oxford University Press, pp. 306–329.

Grill-Spector, Kalanit/Nancy Kanwisher (2005): "Visual Recognition. As Soon as You Know It Is There, You Know What It Is", *Psychological Science* 16. No. 2, pp. 152–160.

Gubeljic, Mischa/Simone Link/Patrick Müller/Gunter Osburg (2000): "Nature and Second Nature in McDowell's Mind and World". In: Marcus Willaschek (Ed.): *John McDowell: Reason and Nature*. Münster: Lit Verlag, pp. 41–50.

Gunnarsson, Logi (2010): *Philosophy of Personal Identity and Multiple Personality*. London: Routledge.

Gunther, York H. (Ed.) (2003): *Essays on Nonconceptual Content*. Cambridge, Mass.: MIT Press.

Haag, Johannes (2012): "Some Kantian Themes in Wilfrid Sellars's Philosophy". In: B. Centi (ed.): *Kant in the 20th Century. Sonderband von: Paradigmi. Rivista di critica filosofica* 30, pp. 111–126.

Haag, Johannes (2014): "McDowells Kant". In: Christian Barth/David Lauer (Eds.): *Die Philosophie John McDowells*. Münster: mentis, pp. 179–202.

Haddock, Adrian 2008: "Thought's footing: A theme in Wittgenstein's 'Philosophical Investigations' By Charles Travis". *Philosophical Quarterly* 58. No. 232, pp. 546–550.

Haddock, Adrian/Fiona Macpherson (Eds.) (2008a): *Disjunctivism: Perception, Action, Knowledge*. Oxford: Oxford University Press.

Haddock, Adrian/Fiona Macpherson (2008b): "Introduction: Varieties of Disjunctivism". In: Haddock, Adrian/Fiona Macpherson (Eds.): *Disjunctivism: Perception, Action, Knowledge*. Oxford: Oxford University Press, pp. 1–24.

Harman, Gilbert (2006): "Christopher Peacocke. The Realm of Reason". *Philosophical Review* 115, No. 2, pp. 243–246.

Heck, Richard G. J. (2000): "Nonconceptual Content and the 'Space of Reasons'". *The Philosophical Review* 109. No. 4, pp. 483–523.

Heck, Richard G. J. (2007): "Are There Different Kinds of Content?" In: Brian McLaughlin/Jonathan Cohen (Eds.): *Contemporary Debates in Philosophy of Mind.* Oxford: Blackwell Publishing, pp. 117–138.

Hinton, John M. (1967): "Visual Experiences". *Mind* 76. No. 302, pp. 217–227.

Hunter, David (2008): "Self-Consciousness – By Sebastian Rödl". *Philosophical Books* 49. No. 3, pp. 272–274.

Hurley, Susan L. (2001): "Overintellectualizing the Mind". *Philosophy and Phenomenological Research* 63. No. 2, pp. 423–431.

Husserl, Edmund (1992): *Logische Untersuchungen.* Hamburg: Felix Meiner Verlag.

Kalderon, Mark Eli (2011): "Before the Law". *Philosophical Issues: The Epistemology of Perception* 21. pp. 219–244.

Kalderon, Mark Eli (2012): "Experiential Pluralism and the Power of Perception". Manuscript available online. Retrieved 02.08.2012. <http://philpapers.org/archive/KALEPA-2>.

Kant, Immanuel (1929): *Critique of Pure Reason (transl. Norman Kemp Smith).* London: Macmillan.

Kant, Immanuel (1998): *Kritik der reinen Vernunft.* Hamburg: Felix Meiner Verlag.

Kelly, Sean D. (2001a): "Demonstrative Concepts and Experience". *The Philosophical Review* 110. No. 3, pp. 397–420.

Kelly, Sean D. (2001b): "The Non-conceptual Content of Perceptual Experience: Situation Dependence and Fineness of Grain". *Philosophy and Phenomenological Research* 62. No. 3, pp. 601–608.

Kenny, Anthony (1989): *The Metaphysics of Mind:* Oxford University Press.

Kern, Andrea (2006): *Quellen des Wissens.* Frankfurt am Main: Suhrkamp.

Kern, Andrea (2007): "Lebensformen und epistemische Fähigkeiten". *Deutsche Zeitschrift für Philosophie* 55. No. 2, pp. 245–260.

Kern, Andrea (2012): "Knowledge as a Fallible Capacity". In: Stefan Tolksdorf (Ed.): *Conceptions of Knowledge.* Berlin; Boston, Mass.: De Gruyter, pp. 215–241.

Kern, Andrea (2013): "Wahrnehmung als Erkenntnisvermögen". In: Sebastian Rödl/Henning Tegtmeyer (Eds.): *Sinnkritisches Philosophieren.* Berlin: de Gruyter, pp. 369–396.

Kriegel, Uriah (2002): "Phenomenal content". *Erkenntnis* 57. No. 2, pp. 175–198.

Kujala, Teija/J. Kallio/et al. (2001): "The mismatch negativity as an index of temporal processing in audition". *Clinical Neurophysiology* 112. No. 9, pp. 1712–1719.

Kuorikoski, Jaakko (2008): *Varieties of modularity for causal and constitutive explanations.* Paper presented at the Philosophy of Science Assoc. 21st Biennial Mtg (Pittsburgh, PA) > PSA 2008 Contributed Papers.

Kuusela, Oskari (2008): "Transcendental arguments and the problem of dogmatism". *International Journal of Philosophical Studies* 16. No. 1, pp. 57–75.

Kvanvig, Jonathan (2011): "Epistemic Justification". In: Sven Bernecker/Duncan Pritchard (Eds.): *The Routledge Companion to Epistemology.* London: Routledge, pp. 25–36.

Lauer, David (2014): "Offenheit zur Welt: Die Auflösung des Dualismus von Begriff und Anschauung". In: Christian Barth/David Lauer (Eds.): *Die Philosophie John McDowells.* Münster: mentis, pp. 37–62.

Leddington, Jason (2014): "What we hear". In: Richard Brown (Ed.): *Consciousness Inside and Out: Phenomenology, Neuroscience, and the Nature of Experience.* Dordrecht, Heidelberg, London, New York: Springer, pp. 321–334.

Lerman, Hemdat (2010): "Non-conceptual Experiential Content and Reason-giving".
  Philosophy and Phenomenological Research 81. No. 1, pp. 1–23.
Levitin, Daniel J. (1994): "Absolute memory for musical pitch: Evidence from the production of
  learned melodies". *Perception and Psychophysics* 56, pp. 414–423.
Levitin, Daniel J. (2008): *This Is Your Brain On Music: Understanding a Human Obsession.*
  London: Grove/Atlantic.
Levitin, Daniel J./Susan E. Rogers (2005): "Absolute pitch: perception, coding, and
  controversies". *Trends in Neurosciences* 9, No. 1, pp. 26–33.
Lewis, Clarence Irving (1929): *Mind and the World-Order. Outline of a Theory of Knowledge.*
  New York: Dover.
Lindgaard, Jakob (Ed.) (2008): *John McDowell: Experience, Norm, and Nature.* Oxford:
  Blackwell Publishing.
Locke, John (1975): *An Essay Concerning Human Understanding.* Oxford: Clarendon Press.
Logue, Heather (2013): "Visual Experience of Natural Kind Properties: Is There Any Fact of the
  Matter?" *Philosophical Studies* 162: pp. 1–12.
Logue, Heather (2014): "Experiential Content and Naive Realism: A Reconciliation". In: Berit
  Brogaard (Ed.) *Does Perception Have Content?* Oxford: Oxford University Press,
  pp. 220–241.
MacIntyre, Alasdair (1977): "Epistemological Crisis, Dramatic Narrative, and the Philosophy of
  Science". *Monist* 60. No. 4, pp. 453–472.
Madison, Brent (2011): "Peacocke's a priori arguments against skepticism". *Grazer
  Philosophische Studien* 83. pp. 1–8.
Margolis, Eric/Stephen Laurence (Eds.) (1999): *Concepts: Core Readings.* Bradford Books/MIT
  Press.
Margolis, Eric/Stephen Laurence (2014): "Concepts". In: Edward N. Zalta (Ed.): *The Stanford
  Encyclopedia of Philosophy* (Spring 2014 Edition). URL =
  <http://plato.stanford.edu/archives/spr2014/entries/concepts/>.
Martin, Michael G. F. (1992): "Perception, Concepts, and Memory". *The Philosophical Review*
  101. No. 4, pp. 745–763.
Martin, Michael G. F. (2002): "The Transparency of Experience". *Mind & Language* 17. No. 4,
  pp. 376–425.
Martin, Michael G. F. (2004): "The Limits of Self-Awareness". *Philosophical Studies* 120,
  pp. 37–89.
McDowell, John (1994): "The Content of Perceptual Experience". *The Philosophical Quarterly*
  44. No. 175, pp. 190–205.
McDowell, John (1996): *Mind and World: With a New Introduction.* Cambridge, Mass.: Harvard
  University Press.
McDowell, John (1998a): "Criteria, Defeasibility, and Knowledge". In: John McDowell:
  Meaning, Knowledge, and Reality. Cambridge, Mass.: Harvard University Press,
  pp. 369–394.
McDowell, John (1998b): "Knowledge by Hearsay", In: John McDowell: *Meaning, Knowledge,
  and Reality.* Cambridge, Mass.: Harvard University Press, pp. 414–443.
McDowell, John (1998c): "Précis of 'Mind and World'". *Philosophy and Phenomenological
  Research* 58. No. 2, pp. 365–368.
McDowell, John (1998d): "Reply to Commentators". *Philosophy and Phenomenological
  Research* 58. No. 2, pp. 403–430.

McDowell, John (1999): "Scheme-Content Dualism and Empiricism". In: Lewis Edwin Hahn (Ed.): *The Philosophy of Donald Davidson*. Chicago u. a.: Open Court, pp. 87–104.

McDowell, John (2000): "Responses". In: Marcus Willaschek (Ed.): *John McDowell: Reason and Nature*. Münster: Lit Verlag, pp. 91–114.

McDowell, John (2002): "Responses". In: Nicholas H. Smith (Ed.): *Reading McDowell*. London: Routledge, pp. 269–305.

McDowell, John (2003): "Hegel and the Myth of the Given". In: Wolfgang Welsch/Klaus Vieweg (Eds.): *Das Interesse des Denkens Hegel aus heutiger Sicht*. München: Wilhelm Fink Verlag, pp. 75–88.

McDowell, John (2007a): "What Myth?" *Inquiry* 50. No. 4, pp. 338–351.

McDowell, John (2007b): "Response to Dreyfus". *Inquiry* 50. No. 4, pp. 366–370.

McDowell, John (2008a): "Avoiding the Myth of the Given". In: Jakob Lindgaard (Ed.): *John McDowell: Experience, Norm, and Nature*. Oxford: Blackwell Publishing, pp. 1–14.

McDowell, John (2008b): "The Disjunctive Conception of Experience as Material for a Transcendental Argument". In: Haddock, Adrian/Fiona Macpherson (Eds.): *Disjunctivism: Perception, Action, Knowledge*. Oxford: Oxford University Press, pp. 376–389.

McDowell, John (2008c): "Responses". In: Jakob Lindgaard (Ed.): *John McDowell: Experience, Norm, and Nature*. Oxford: Blackwell Publishing, pp. 200–267.

McDowell, John (2009a): "Avoiding the Myth of the Given". In: John McDowell: *Having the World in View. Essays on Kant, Hegel, and Sellars*. Cambridge, Mass.: Harvard University Press, pp. 256–272.

McDowell, John (2009b): "Conceptual Capacities in Perception". In: John McDowell: *Having the World in View. Essays on Kant, Hegel, and Sellars*. Cambridge, Mass.: Harvard University Press, pp. 127–144.

McDowell, John (2009c): "The Disjunctive Conception of Experience as Material for a Transcendental Argument". In: John McDowell: *The Engaged Intellect: Philosophical Essays*. Cambridge, Mass.: Harvard University Press, pp. 225–240.

McDowell, John (2009d): "Hegel's Idealism as Radicalization of Kant. In: John McDowell: *Having the World in View. Essays on Kant, Hegel, and Sellars*. Cambridge, Mass.: Harvard University Press, pp. 69–89.

McDowell, John (2009e): "Intentionality as a Relation". In: John McDowell: *Having the World in View. Essays on Kant, Hegel, and Sellars*. Cambridge, Mass.: Harvard University Press, pp. 44–65.

McDowell, John (2009f): "Knowledge and the Internal Revisited". In: John McDowell: *The Engaged Intellect: Philosophical Essays*. Cambridge, Mass.: Harvard University Press, pp. 279–287.

McDowell, John (2009g): "The Logical Form of an Intuition". In: John McDowell: *Having the World in View. Essays on Kant, Hegel, and Sellars*. Cambridge, Mass.: Harvard University Press, pp. 23–43.

McDowell, John (2009h): "Scheme-Content Dualism and Empiricism". In: McDowell, John: *The Engaged Intellect: Philosophical Essays*. Cambridge, Mass.: Harvard University Press, pp. 115–133.

McDowell, John (2009i): "Sellars on Perceptual Experience". In: John McDowell: *Having the World in View. Essays on Kant, Hegel, and Sellars*. Cambridge, Mass.: Harvard University Press, pp. 3–22.

McDowell, John (2009j): "Sensory Consciousness in Kant and Sellars". In: John McDowell: *Having the World in View. Essays on Kant, Hegel, and Sellars*. Cambridge, Mass.: Harvard University Press, pp. 108–126.

McDowell, John (2009k): "Towards a Reading of Hegel on Action in the 'Reason' Chapter of the *Phenomenology*". In: John McDowell: *Having the World in View. Essays on Kant, Hegel, and Sellars*. Cambridge, Mass.: Harvard University Press, pp. 166–184.

McDowell, John (2009l): "Subjective, Intersubjective, Objective". In: John McDowell: *The Engaged Intellect: Philosophical Essays*. Cambridge, Mass.: Harvard University Press, pp. 152–159.

McDowell, John (2009m): "What Myth?". In: John McDowell: *The Engaged Intellect: Philosophical Essays*. Cambridge, Mass.: Harvard University Press, pp. 308–323.

McDowell, John (2010a): "Tyler Burge on Disjunctivism". *Philosophical Explorations* 13. No. 3, pp. 243–255.

McDowell, John (2010b): "What is the Content of an Intention In Action?" *Ratio* 23. No. 4, pp. 415–432.

McDowell, John (2011a): "Anscombe on Bodily Self-knowledge". In: Anton Ford/Jennifer Hornsby/Frederick Stoutland (Eds.): *Essays on Anscombe's Intention*. Cambridge, Mass.: Harvard University Press, pp. 128–146.

McDowell, John (2011b): *Perception as a Capacity for Knowledge*. Milwaukee, Wisconsin: Marquette University Press.

McDowell, John (2013a): "Perceptual Experience: Both Relational and Contentful". *European Journal of Philosophy* 21. No. 1, pp. 144–57.

McDowell, John (2013b): "Tyler Burge on Disjunctivism (II)". *Philosophical Explorations: An International Journal for the Philosophy of Mind and Action* 16. No. 3, pp. 259–279.

McGurk, Harry/John MacDonald (1976): "Hearing Lips and Seeing Voices". *Nature 264*, pp. 746–748.

McLaughlin, Brian/Jonathan Cohen (Eds.) (2007): *Contemporary Debates in Philosophy of Mind*. Oxford: Blackwell Publishing.

Millar, Alan (2007): "The State of Knowing". *Philosophical Issues* 17. No. 1, pp. 179–196.

Millar, Alan (2008): "Perceptual-recognitional Abilities and Perceptual Knowledge". In: Haddock, Adrian/Fiona Macpherson (Eds.): *Disjunctivism: Perception, Action, Knowledge*. Oxford: Oxford University Press, pp. 330–347.

Millar, Alan (2009): "What Is It That Cognitive Abilities Are Abilities To Do?". *Acta Analytica* 24. No. 4, pp. 223–236.

Millar, Alan (2011a): "How visual perception yields reasons for belief". *Philosophical Issues* 21. No. 1, pp. 332–351.

Millar, Alan (2011b): "Knowledge and Reasons for Belief" In: Andrew Reisner/Asbjørn Steglich-Petersen (Eds.): *Reasons for Belief*. Cambridge: Cambridge University Press, pp. 223–243.

Miller, Alexander (2009): "Review: Charles Travis: Thought's Footing: A Theme in Wittgenstein's Philosophical Investigations". *Mind* 118. No. 469, pp. 211–215.

Moore, George E. (1903): "The Refutation of Idealism". *Mind* 12. No. 48, pp. 433–453.

Moore, George E. (1993): "Sense-Data". In: George E. Moor/Thomas Baldwin (Eds.): *Selected Writings*. London, New York: Routledge, pp. 45–58.

Moran, Richard (2001): *Authority and Estrangement: An Essay on Self-Knowledge*. Princeton, New Jersey: Princeton University Press.

Näätänen, Risto (2000): "Mismatch Negativity (MMN): Perspectives for Application". *International Journal of Psychophysiology* 37. No. 1, pp. 3–10.

Näätänen, Risto/Anne Lehtokoski/et al. (1997): "Language-specific Phoneme Representations Revealed By Electric and Magnetic Brain Responses". *Nature* 385. No. 6615, pp. 432–434.

Näätänen, Risto/Mari Tervaniemi/et al. (2001): "'Primitive Intelligence' in the Auditory Cortex". *Trends in Neurosciences* 24. No. 5, pp. 283–288.

Nagel, Thomas (1974): "What is it like to be a bat?". *Philosophical Review* 83, No. 4, pp. 435–450.

Neurath, Otto (1932/33): "Über Protokollsätze". *Erkenntnis* 3, pp. 204–214.

Nida-Rümelin, Martine (2010): "Wissen von innen. Buchkritik: Sebastian Rödl *Self-Consciousness*". *Deutsche Zeitschrift für Philosophie* 58. No. 6, pp. 1001–1005.

Noë, Alva (2004): *Action in Perception*. Cambridge, Mass.: MIT Press.

Noë, Alva (2008): "Reply to Campbell, Martin, and Kelly". *Philosophy and Phenomenological Research* 76. No. 3, pp. 691–706.

Noë, Alva (2010): "Vision Without Representation". In: Nivedita Gangopadhyay/Michael Madary/Finn Spicer (Eds.): *Perception, Action, and Consciousness: Sensorimotor Dynamics and Two Visual Systems*. Oxford: Oxford University Press, pp. 245–256.

O'Callaghan, Casey (2007): *Sound: A Philosophical Theory*. Oxford: Oxford University Press.

O'Callaghan, Casey (2008): "Seeing what you hear: Cross-modal illusions and perception". *Philosophical Issues* 18. No. 1, pp. 316–338.

O'Callaghan, Casey (2014): "Auditory Perception". In Edward N. Zalta (Ed.): *The Stanford Encyclopedia of Philosophy* (Summer 2014 Edition). URL = <http://plato.stanford.edu/archives/sum2014/entries/perception-auditory/>.

Pappas, George (2014): "Internalist vs. Externalist Conceptions of Epistemic Justification". In: Edward N. Zelta (ed.): *The Stanford Encyclopedia of Philosophy* (Fall 2014 Edition). URL = <http://plato.stanford.edu/archives/fall2014/entries/justep-intext/>.

Peacocke, Christopher (1983): *Sense and Content*. Oxford: Oxford University Press.

Peacocke, Christopher (1992): *A Study of Concepts*. Cambridge, Mass.: MIT Press.

Peacocke, Christopher (1994a): "Rationality, Norms and the Primitively Compelling: A Reply to Kirk Ludwig". *Mind & Language* 9. No. 4, pp. 492–498.

Peacocke, Christopher (1994b): "Reply: Non-conceptual Content: Kinds, Rationales and Relations". *Mind & Language* 9. No. 4, pp. 419–430.

Peacocke, Christopher (1998): "Nonconceptual Content Defended: Comment on McDowell's 'Mind and World'". *Philosophy and Phenomenological Research* 58. No. 2, pp. 381–388.

Peacocke, Christopher (2001a): "Does Perception have Nonconceptual Content?". *The Journal of Philosophy* 98. No. 5, pp. 239–264.

Peacocke, Christopher (2001b): "Phenomenology and Nonconceptual Content". *Philosophy and Phenomenological Research* 62. No. 3, pp. 609–615.

Peacocke, Christopher (2004): "Explaining Perceptual Entitlement". In: Richard Schantz (Ed.): *The Externalist Challenge*. Berlin: de Gruyter, pp. 441–481.

Peacocke, Christopher (2005): *The Realm of Reason*. Oxford: Clarendon Press.

Peacocke, Christopher (2009): "Concepts and Possession Conditions". In: Brian McLaughlin/Ansgar Beckermann (Eds.): *The Oxford Handbook of Philosophy of Mind*. Oxford: Oxford University Press, pp. 437–456.

Pippin, Robert (2002): "Leaving nature behind: or two cheers for 'subjectivism'". In: Nicholas H. Smith (Ed.): *Reading McDowell*. London: Routledge, pp. 58–75.

Pippin, Robert (2013): "What is 'Conceptual Activity'?" In: Joseph K. Schear (Ed.): *Mind, Reason, and Being-in-the-World: The McDowell-Dreyfus Debate*. London: Routledge, pp. 91–109.

Pitkin, Hannah F. (1967): *The Concept of Representation*. Berkeley, Los Angeles: University of California Press.

Prichard, Harold A. (1909): *Kant's Theory of Knowledge*. Oxford: Oxford University Press.

Putnam, Hilary (1994): "Sense, Nonsense, and the Senses: An Inquiry into the Powers of the Human Mind". *The Journal of Philosophy* 91. Vol. 9, pp. 445–517.

Quante, Michael (2000): "Zurück zur verzauberten Natur – ohne konstruktive Philosophie?: McDowells Naturbegriff in 'Mind and World'". *Deutsche Zeitschrift für Philosophie* 48. No. 6, pp. 953–965.

Rakoczy, Hannes/Michael Tomasello (2008): "Kollektive Intentionalität und kulturelle Entwicklung". *Deutsche Zeitschrift für Philosophie* 56. No. 3, pp. 401–410.

Rawls, John (2009): *A Theory of Justice*. Cambridge, Mass.: Harvard University Press.

Raz, Joseph (2013): "Reason, Rationality, and Normativity". In: Joseph Raz: *From Normativity to Responsibility*. Oxford: Oxford University Press, pp. 85–101.

Rödl, Sebastian (2007): *Self-Consciousness*. Cambridge, Mass.: Harvard University Press.

Rödl, Sebastian (2010): "The Self-Conscious Power of Sensory Knowledge". *Grazer Philosophische Studien* 81. No. 1, pp. 135–151.

Roskies, Adina L. (2008): "A New Argument for Nonconceptual Content". *Philosophy and Phenomenological Research* 76. No. 3, pp. 633–659.

Roskies, Adina L. (2010): "'That' Response doesn't Work: Against a Demonstrative Defense of Conceptualism". *Noûs* 44. No. 1, pp. 112–134.

Russell, Bertrand (1910–11): "Knowledge by Acquaintance and Knowledge by Description". *Proceedings of the Aristotelian Society, New Series* Vol. 11, pp. 108–128.

Russell, Bertrand (1963): "The Relation of Sense-data to Physics". In: Bertrand Russell: *Mysticism and Logic and other Essays*. London: Unwin Books, pp. 108–131.

Russell, Bertrand (1999): *The Problems of Philosophy*. London: Dover Publications.

Schear, Joseph K. (Ed.) (2013): *Mind, Reason, and Being-in-the-World: The McDowell-Dreyfus Debate*. London: Routledge

Schellenberg, Susanna (2006): "Sellarsian Perspectives on Perception and Non-conceptual content". In: Michael P. Wolf/Mark N. Lance (Eds.): *The Self-Correcting Enterprise: Essays on Wilfrid Sellars* (*Poznań Studies in the Philosophy of the Sciences and the Humanities, vol. 92*). Amsterdam; New York: Rodopi, pp. 173–196.

Schellenberg, Susanna (2011): "Perceptual Content Defended". *Noûs* 45. No. 4, pp. 714–750.

Schellenberg, Susanna (2014): "The Relational and Representational Character of Perceptual Experience". In: Berit Brogaard (Ed.) *Does Perception Have Content?* Oxford: Oxford University Press, pp. 199–219.

Schroeder, Mark (2011): "What Does It Take to Have a Reason?" In: Andrew Reisner/Asbjørn Steglich-Petersen (Eds.): *Reasons for Belief*. Cambridge: Cambridge University Press, pp. 201–222.

Schwitzgebel, Eric (2014): "Belief". In: Edward N. Zalta (Ed.): *The Stanford Encyclopedia of Philosophy* (Spring 2014 Edition). URL = <http://plato.stanford.edu/archives/spr2014/entries/belief/>.

Sellars, Wilfrid (1968): *Science and Metaphysics: Variations on Kantian Themes*. New York, Humanities.

Sellars, Wilfrid (1969): "Language as Thought and as Communication". *Philosophy and Phenomenological Research* 29. No. 4, pp. 506–527.

Sellars, Wilfrid (1977): "Some Reflections on Perceptual Consciousness". In: Ronald Bruzina/Bruce Wilshire (Eds.): *Crosscurrents in Phenomenology.* The Hague: Martinus Nijhoff, pp. 169–185.

Sellars, Wilfrid (1978): "The Role of Imagination in Kant's Theory of Experience". In: Henry W. Johnstone, Jr. (Ed.): *Categories: A Colloquium.* University Park: Pennsylvania State University Press, pp. 231–245.

Sellars, Wilfrid (1997): *Empiricism and the Philosophy of Mind. With an Introduction by Richard Rorty and a Study Guide by Robert Brandom.* Cambridge, Mass.: Harvard University Press.

Shams, Ladan/Robyn Kim (2010): "Crossmodal influences on visual perception". *Physics of Life Reviews* 7. No. 3, pp. 269–84.

Siegel, Susanna (2010): *The Contents of Visual Experience.* Oxford: Oxford University Press.

Sieroka, Norman (2015): *Leibniz, Husserl and the Brain.* Palgrave macmillan.

Soteriou, Matthew (2010): "Perceiving Events". *Philosophical Explorations* 13. No. 3, pp. 223–241.

Soteriou, Matthew (2014): "The Disjunctive Theory of Perception". In: Edward N. Zalta (Ed.): *The Stanford Encyclopedia of Philosophy* (Summer 2014 Edition). URL = <http://plato.stanford.edu/archives/sum2014/entries/perception-disjunctive/>.

Steup, Matthias/Ernest Sosa (Eds.) (2005): *Contemporary Debates in Epistemology* Oxford: Blackwell Publishing.

Strawson, Peter (2008): "Imagination and Perception". In: Peter Strawson: *Freedom and Resentment.* London: Routledge, pp. 50–72.

Stroud, Barry (2000): "Understanding Human Knowledge in General". In: Barry Stroud: *Understanding Human Knowledge: Philosophical Essays.* Oxford: Oxford University Press, pp. 99–121.

Thompson, Michael (2008): *Life and Action: Elementary Structures of Practice and Practical Thought.* Cambridge, Mass.: Harvard University Press.

Thornton, Tim (2006): "John McDowell's *Mind and World*". In: John Shand (Ed.): *Central Works in Philosophy.* Chesham: Acumen, pp. 291–315.

Tomasello, Michael (2002): *Die kulturelle Entwicklung des menschlichen Denkens.* Frankfurt am Main: Suhrkamp.

Tomasello, Michael (2008): *Origins of Human Communication.* Cambridge, Mass.: MIT Press.

Tomasello, Michael (2014): *A Natural History of Human Thinking.* Cambridge, Mass.: Harvard University Press

Toribio, Josefa (2007): "Nonconceptual Content". *Philosophy Compass 2/3.* pp. 445–460.

Travis, Charles (2004): "The Silences of the Senses". *Mind* 113. No. 449, pp. 57–94.

Travis, Charles (2005): "Frege, Father of Disjunctivism". *Philosophical Topics* 33. No. 1, pp. 307–334.

Travis, Charles (2006): *Thought's Footing. Themes in Wittgenstein's Philosophical Investigations.* Oxford: Oxford University Press.

Travis, Charles (2007): "Reason's Reach", *European Journal of Philosophy* 15. No. 2, pp. 225–248.

Travis, Charles (2008): "On Constraints of Generality". In: Charles Travis: *Occasion-Sensitivity. Selected Essays.* Oxford: Oxford University Press, pp. 271–290.

Travis, Charles (2009): "The Inward Turn". *Royal Institute of Philosophy Supplement* 65, pp. 313–349.

Travis, Charles (2010a): "Frege's Target". In: Charles Travis: *Objectivity and the Parochial*. Oxford: Oxford University Press, pp. 55–88.

Travis, Charles (2010b): "Introduction". In: Charles Travis: *Objectivity and the Parochial*. Oxford: Oxford University Press, pp. 1–30.

Travis, Charles (2010c): *Objectivity and the Parochial*. Oxford: Oxford University Press.

Travis, Charles (2010d): "The Proposition's Progress" In: Charles Travis: *Objectivity and the Parochial*. Oxford: Oxford University Press, pp. 193–228.

Travis, Charles (2010e): "Thought's Social Nature" In: Charles Travis: *Objectivity and the Parochial*. Oxford: Oxford University Press, pp. 301–324.

Travis, Charles (2011): "Is Seeing Intentional?". In: Sandra Laugier & Christophe Al-Saleh (eds.) *John L. Austin et la philosophie du langage ordinaire*. Hildesheim, Zürich, New York: Georg Olms, pp. 287–311.

Travis, Charles (2013a): "Introduction". In: Charles Travis: *Perception. Essays After Frege*. Oxford: Oxford University Press, pp. 1–22.

Travis, Charles (2013b): "The Silences of the Senses". In: Charles Travis: *Perception. Essays After Frege*. Oxford: Oxford University Press, pp. 23–58.

Travis, Charles (2013c): "Unlocking the Outer World". In: Charles Travis: *Perception. Essays After Frege*. Oxford: Oxford University Press, pp. 223–258.

Travis, Charles (2013d): "The Preserve of Thinkers". In: Charles Travis: *Perception. Essays After Frege*. Oxford: Oxford University Press, pp. 313–351.

Tye, Michael (1995): *Ten Problems of Consciousness*. Cambridge, Mass: The MIT Press, Bradford Books.

Tye, Michael (2000): *Consciousness, Color, and Content*. Cambridge, Mass: The MIT Press, Bradford Books.

Tye, Michael (2015): "The Puzzle of Transparency". In: Alex Byrne/Jason Cohen/Gideon Rosen/Seana Shiffrin (Eds.): *The Norton Introduction to Philosophy*. New York: Norton.

Wedgwood, Ralph (2007): "Christopher Peacocke's *The Realm of Reasons*". *Philosophy and Phenomenological Research* 74. No. 3, pp. 776–791.

Willaschek, Marcus (2003): *Der mentale Zugang zur Welt. Realismus, Skeptizismus und Intentionalität*. Frankfurt am Main: Vittorio Klostermann.

Williams, Michael (2001): *Problems of Knowledge: A Critical Introduction to Epistemology*. Oxford: Oxford University Press.

Williamson, Timothy (2000): *Knowledge and Its Limits*. Oxford: Oxford University Press.

Wingert, Lutz (2012): "Was geschieht eigentlich im Raum der Gründe?". In: Dieter Sturma (Ed.): *Vernunft und Freiheit. Zur praktischen Philosophie von Julian Nida-Rümelin*. Berlin, Boston: de Gruyter, pp. 179–198.

Wittgenstein, Ludwig (1953): *Philosophical Investigations*. New York: Macmillan.

Wright, Crispin (2002a): "(Anti-)sceptics Simple and Subtle: G. E. Moore and John McDowell". *Philosophy and Phenomenological Research* 65. No. 2, pp. 330–348.

Wright, Crispin (2002b): "Human Nature?". In: Nicholas H. Smith (Ed.): *Reading McDowell*. London: Routledge, pp. 140–159.

Xu, Fei (2002): "The role of language in acquiring object kind concepts in infancy". *Cognition* 85. No. 3, pp. 223–250.

Author Index

Subject Index